The Low Countries

Cover:

Koen van den Broek, *Blue Border (detail)*, 2001.

Oil on canvas, 180 cm x 120 cm.

Private collection. Courtesy White Cube, London

© Sabam Belgium 2013

TLC

2013 The Low Countries

ARTS AND SOCIETY IN FLANDERS AND THE NETHERLANDS

21

**Published by
the Flemish-Netherlands
Association**
Ons Erfdeel vzw

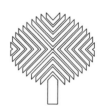

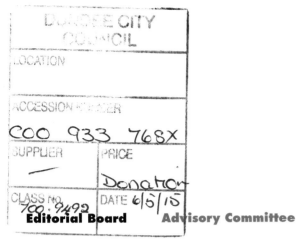
Editorial Board

Chief Editor:
Luc Devoldere

Deputy Editors:
Dirk Van Assche
Frits Niessen
Reinier Salverda

Members:
Saskia Bak
Derek Blyth
Tom Christiaens
Pieter Coupé
Anton Korteweg
Filip Matthijs
Hans Vanacker
Tomas Vanheste

Advisory Committee

André Brink, Cape Town, South Africa
Christopher Brown, Oxford, United Kingdom
Bram Buijze, The Hague, The Netherlands
Ian Buruma, New York, USA
Patricia Carson, Ghent, Belgium
Jan Deloof, Zwevegem, Belgium
Jeroen Dewulf, Berkeley, CA, USA
Theo D'haen, Leuven, Belgium
Bruce C. Donaldson, Melbourne, Australia
Jane Fenoulhet, London, United Kingdom
Charles Ford, London, United Kingdom
Amy Golahny, Williamsport, PA, USA
Jaap Harskamp, London, United Kingdom
Adrian van den Hoven, Windsor, Ontario, Canada
Jonathan Israel, Princeton, NJ, USA
Frank Ligtvoet, New York, NY, USA
Gitta Luiten, Amsterdam, The Netherlands
Martin Mooij, Capelle a / d IJssel, The Netherlands
Gary Schwartz, Maarssen, The Netherlands
Paul R. Sellin, Los Angeles, CA, USA
William Z. Shetter, Bloomington, IN, USA
Johan P. Snapper, Berkeley, CA, USA
Kees Snoek, Rotterdam, The Netherlands
Paul Vincent, London, United Kingdom
Leo Vroman, Fort Worth, TX, USA
Rudi Wester, Amsterdam, The Netherlands
John Willemse, Pretoria, South Africa
Michael J. Wintle, Amsterdam, The Netherlands
Manfred Wolf, San Francisco, CA, USA
Joanna Woodall, London, United Kingdom

Contents

The Unbearable Lightness of Borders

Chronicle

———

Next page:

Francis Alÿs, *The Green Line*

(Sometimes doing something poetic can become political and sometimes doing something political can become poetic)

In collaboration with Julien Devaux, Rachel Leah Jones and Philippe Bellaiche, Jerusalem, 2004

Video documentation of an action

Photo: Rachel Leah Jones

Francis Alÿs (Antwerp, 1959) is an artist and compulsive walker. In 2004 he walked along the Green Line through Jerusalem with a tin trailing green paint. The Israeli General Moshe Dayan drew the border on a map with a green pen after the Arab-Israeli war in 1948. The motto of Alÿs' filmed performance was: 'Sometimes doing something poetic can become political and sometimes doing something political can become poetic'.

'Borders' are the theme of this edition. The inspiration for it is the commemoration of the Treaty of Utrecht in 1713, which was proclaimed exactly three hundred years ago. This European peace treaty put an end to a century of unremitting war on the old continent. It also laid the foundations for a new distribution of power. Spain lost its global power, to the benefit of England. France consolidated its victories on its northern border. While the Republic of the Netherlands stood by and watched. The de facto border between the Kingdom of France and the Southern Netherlands - to become the Austrian Netherlands in 1713 - was established. A border that has barely changed since then. Today it is still the border between Belgium and France, between Flanders and France, and here in Flanders, where I am writing this, between the Dutch and French languages.

Borders shut off, shut up and shut out. They limit and keep dull. According to the mantra of false cosmopolitanism, that is. But suppose all borders were contingent: they are where they are, but could have been drawn differently. Those who constantly want to discuss them and tinker with them open up a Pandora's box. Borders do indeed limit, but only in the sense that they determine what we are and are not. They make the 'other' possible. And isn't the paradox of borders that you must accept them if you want to transcend them? Recognised borders are the best conceivable vaccine against the epidemic of walls, said Régis Debray in *Éloge des frontières* (Gallimard, Paris, 2010).

Our subject then is borders: historic borders such as the Roman *limes* once was. We follow the northern border of the Imperium Romanum from Katwijk at the Dutch coast to Xanten in Germany. We examine the language border in this book, too: a line that was drawn across Belgium fifty years ago, in 1963. It has ensured pacification and stability. We wonder whether there is a border in the Netherlands between the Randstad and the rest of the country, and between the Netherlands above and below the Great Rivers. We also investigate the border in Ostend that people seeking asylum and happiness in the United Kingdom come up against. Who are these people? What drives them? We examine the new mental border, too, the fault line in Western democracies between the well and less well-educated. And, finally, we look at the border between the Latin ('Romanitas') and Germanic ('Germania') world in this book. Is it all in the mind, or not? Do the Southern Netherlands – or Belgium – constitute a transition between the two?

As we work right on the border between Flanders, Belgium and France, we have decided to cherish borders, to allow ourselves to be honed by them. Let us, above all, learn to live with them. In Europe, after all, we have no other choice.

In the rest of the yearbook, as usual, we present writers and artists. The renovation of the Rijksmuseum and the Stedelijk Museum in Amsterdam are covered; the Gruuthuse manuscript is there, too, alongside the Majorana particle and the election results. We take a look at the cities of Oudenaarde and Sheffield, the establishment of the Dutch monarchy in 1813, the development of the stock exchanges in Bruges, Antwerp and Amsterdam, and the complexities of the name of the language spoken in the Low Countries. *Tolle et lege,* again.

11

LUC DEVOLDERE | *Chief Editor*

Shifting Frontiers

The Treaty of Utrecht (1713) and its Consequences

[LUDO MILIS]

Frontiers are fascinating. They fascinate us because their very existence, their permanence or transience, and their impact are so all-embracing, so fundamental to our lives. They are one of the most important factors in creating social order and regulating social interaction. Within them, forms of solidarity are forged, and beyond them the image of the 'other', the 'foreigner', is created. 'We' as opposed to 'them'. From a national perspective, the route of a frontier is seen as something sacred, rooted in the nature of things. But war is always lurking around the corner. And after war comes the peace which, depending on the balance of power, moves frontiers this way or that in a perpetual merry-go-round of boundaries that are supposed to be perpetual. Wars and treaties therefore have a two-fold impact. On the one hand, they separate territories that once enjoyed a joint existence and, on the other, they bind together regions that once lived apart as strangers. A boundary that is drawn in this way works in two directions: it embraces and binds; it rejects and alienates.

Resolved at last to put an end to the war

The Treaty of Utrecht was one of the pivotal events in the territorial organisation of Europe. By virtue of the frontiers that it dismantled and imposed, it restored order to an international community that had lost its way.

The peace treaty put an end to a long conflict that had been fought out between the leading European states, or rather between their absolute rulers, during the years around 1700. By attaching themselves first to one ally, then another, each attempted to strengthen their international position. The interests of their own families always took precedence and were usually justified as a synonym for the political interests of their territories. France, Portugal, Prussia, and Savoy were the leading actors who, on 11 April 1713, after lengthy negotiations reached a Peace that, significantly, they signed bilaterally, not collectively. Also involved were the United Provinces, the Northern Netherlands, which had wrested sovereignty from their Spanish overlord in 1648. On that same day they signed a treaty with France which not only agreed peace terms, but also dealt with trade and shipping.[1] Another member of this international

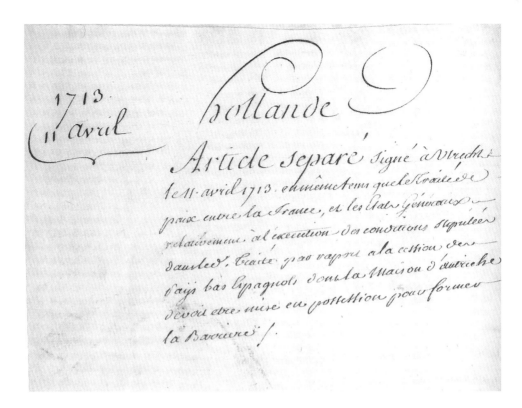

orchestra, in fact emerging as the overall winner, was Great Britain.[2] In high politics it is not usually admitted that self-interest forms the basis of agreement. So it was claimed that everything had been done for the well-being of their subjects, of those who had suffered fiscal extortion and sacrificed their persons and their property to appease their rulers' thirst for power. The treaty between France and Great Britain expressed it, unconvincingly, as 'consulting as well the advantage of their subjects, as providing (as far as mortals are able to do) for the perpetual tranquillity of the whole Christian world, have resolved at last to put an end to the war, which was unhappily kindled, and has been obstinately carried on above these ten years, being both cruel and destructive, by reason of the frequency of battles, and the effusion of Christian blood. And for promoting this their royal purpose, of their own proper motion, and from that paternal care which they delight to use towards their own subjects, and the public weal of Christendom...'[3]

Usually the victors in peace negotiations try to capitalize on their victory and force the losers to foot the bill, and the Peace of Utrecht was no exception. Even so it has gone down in history as the first negotiated treaty, because in the closing years of the seventeenth and the early eighteenth century exhaustion and war-weariness were so universal that nobody, except perhaps Great Britain, was able to sound the triumphal trumpet. But peace did not come easily. The ambassadors negotiated for months in Utrecht before reaching agreement. Incidentally, the United Provinces themselves, which in the seventeenth century, their Golden Age, had played such a dominant role on the European and colonial stage, lost that position during this period.

Treaty of Utrecht, 11 April 1713, pen and ink on paper. This addendum concerns the handing over of the Spanish Netherlands to the Austrian dynasty. © Archives du Ministère des Affaires Étrangères, Paris

Gerardus Mercator, *Vlaen-deren - Exactissima Flandriae Descriptio* (1540). Detail. Canon pointing to France near Cassel (today in France, Département du Nord)

The cause of all those years of uncertainty had been the drawn-out dynastic situation in Spain. When Charles II became King of Spain in 1665 he was a sickly child of four, which was enough to arouse the predatory interest of other princes. Dynasties had always used political marriage as the preferred strategy to control the future. They therefore hunted through their genealogies for family connections which might legitimise a claim to the Spanish inheritance, an inheritance which, apart from Spain itself, also included the Southern Netherlands, parts of northern Italy and an enormous colonial empire as well. Power and prestige, gold and silver beckoned the potential victor. The most imposing ruler of the time was, of course, Louis XIV. France's Sun King had been on the throne for almost 45 years and had developed an unrivalled 'grandeur' that even today is still reflected in the Hall of Mirrors in Versailles. A people on its knees was a price that did not unduly concern the Bourbons, either Louis or his successors. Louis dreamed of an empire that would unite France and Spain, but it was a dream that could never be shared or accepted by the other members of the club, in particular the Austrian Habsburgs.

Nevertheless, in his will Charles II had named Philip of Anjou, the grandson of Louis XIV, as his successor. So it was inevitable that when Charles died in 1700 the so-called War of Spanish Succession broke out. It turned into a World War 'avant la lettre', fought out across Europe and, of course, on the high seas. Fighting continued for many years, mercenary armies were recruited, talented army engineers were hired and populations were squeezed dry.

Prelude in the Low Countries

In the Netherlands disaster had struck much earlier. The Eighty Years War had broken out in the mid-sixteenth century when the territory rose in revolt against its ruler, the King of Spain. There were various reasons for the conflict. First and foremost, the tradition of extensive provincial autonomy, even at the level of the individual cities, had been systematically undermined by the growing absolutism of the rulers, Charles V and Philip II. Furthermore, the Reformation had successfully taken root in the Low Countries and its autonomy of religious thinking meshed perfectly with the critical self-awareness of a territory that had become rich through trade and industry. But ultimately it was political and, especially, military circumstances that decided the outcome: a disastrous partition. In 1648, when the Peace of Munster was signed and the Eighty Years War, the 'Dutch Revolt', came to an end, the Netherlands were indeed carved up. The North – the United Provinces – became sovereign and independent, while the South remained under Spanish rule. The North became a world power; the South hardly had room to move within Spain's worldwide empire. In the North, the Reformation dominated through a primarily Calvinist Reformed structure. In the South, a strict Catholicism was imposed that reflected the absolutist models of Spain and Rome.

It was a sad time for the Southern Netherlands. Economically it was hard hit by the closing of the Scheldt. Antwerp was no longer 'emporium mundi', the centre of world trade, a position which Amsterdam took over. Furthermore,

France lurked greedily in the wings, as she had done before 1648 under Louis XIII. Absolutism was blossoming and Louis XIV's territorial strategy of 'natural frontiers' was proving successful. Wars and truces succeeded each other but uncertainty remained France's trump card. The Bourbons gnawed away at bits of the Netherlands. The Peace of the Pyrenees (1659), of Aix-la-Chapelle (1668), of Nijmegen (1678) and Rijswijk (1697) recorded these somewhat capricious territorial changes in international treaties. But the last treaty already hinted that some areas might have to be returned to the Southern Netherlands and, although much remained French, Louis XIV was compelled in his final years (he died in 1715) to restore many of his gains. Incidentally, the boundary that was then drawn still corresponds roughly to the present frontier between France and Belgium. So for many decades the Spanish Netherlands was squeezed between France and the United Provinces. Both had their own plans to use the territory as a buffer zone. The administration of the Southern Netherlands combined a weak, incompetent mixture of royal dirigisme from Spain and a modest pursuit of greater autonomy by the royal governors and councils in Brussels. The United Provinces worked closely with Great Britain against French expansion into the Low Countries, even though their other interests on the high seas and in the colonies were often in direct conflict.

Left: The Victories of Philippe V, King of Spain, under the command of Duke of Vendôme. Almanach Royal, 1712.
© Bibliothèque nationale de France, Paris

Right: The Fall of Douai, taken by Duke of Villars (1713). Almanach Royal, 1713.
© Bibliothèque nationale de France, Paris

European politics during that period were a confused tangle. So we shall confine ourselves to summarising the events that were important for the Netherlands. In 1691 Maximilian of Bavaria, a pawn of the Austrian dynasty, was appointed Governor General of the Spanish Netherlands. In 1700, as already mentioned, Philip of Anjou, the twelve year old grandson of Louis XIV, became King of Spain. From then on, Louis XIV was effectively in charge of the Spanish Netherlands until Maximilian reappeared in 1704. An Anglo-Batavian coalition subsequently conquered large areas of Flanders and Brabant. Maximilian became 'Sovereign of the Netherlands', which by now was limited to Namur and Luxemburg. All this simply meant that Spain's hold on the Southern Netherlands had been irretrievably lost.

With the Peace of Utrecht, the Spanish, or by now ex-Spanish, territory passed initially and briefly to the United Provinces which, once suitable guarantees had been negotiated, handed it over to the Archduke of Austria. Since 1703, the Archduke had been calling himself King Charles III of Spain, based on the Spanish claims of his father the Emperor Leopold I. From 1711 he would also bear the title of Holy Roman (that is German) Emperor as Charles VI.

The Spanish Netherlands become Austrian

The Peace of Utrecht thoroughly shuffled the global pack of territorial cards. French possessions in North America, more particularly in Canada, passed into British hands. Also important was that the British took over the Spanish monopoly of the slave trade, the *asiento*. Furthermore, Gibraltar and Minorca became British, which enabled the seafaring nation to control access to the Mediterranean. In Italy, Spanish possessions were divided between Savoy and Austria. The former gained Sicily and Milan, and the Kingdom of Naples and Sardinia went to Austria.

On 11 April 1713, by virtue of the treaty, Charles VI became the new ruler of the Southern Netherlands, but it was not until 1716 that the formal terms of the transfer to the Austrian dynasty were agreed with the Dutch and the British. The negotiations led to the so-called Barrier Treaty of 1715, a year after the Treaty of Rastatt was supposed to have confirmed the terms of the Peace of Utrecht.

The Barrier Treaty

From now on Dutch troops would be able to garrison a string of forts and fortified towns along the newly established southern frontier with France at the expense of the Austrian Netherlands.[4] It would constitute a fortified line facing a similar

The Catholic Netherlands, known by the name of Flanders, divided up by the treaties of Utrecht, Rastatt and Antwerp, by Louis-Charles Desnos (1766) © Cultuurbibliotheek, Bruges (www.cultuurbibliotheek.be) ex. 2007/2916

line which the French had built earlier in the last quarter of the previous century, the so-called *Pré Carré* designed by the military engineer Vauban. Some of these fortifications have recently been restored.[5]

The Barrier Treaty was not a success for any of the parties involved. The Catholic Austrian Netherlands had to tolerate the celebration of Protestant liturgy in the Dutch garrisons and, even worse, had to foot the bill too. This form of occupation continued for as long as France posed a threat, which it did until 1748. After that the Empress Maria Theresa refused to go on paying for the Dutch garrisons, and, under her successor Joseph II, the Dutch presence came to an end in 1782.

If the importance of historical facts is measured by the length of time their effects are felt, then the Treaty of Utrecht must score highly. The territorial reorganisation and the balance of power which the Great Powers imposed in 1713 remained intact, in spite of many wars, disputes, combinations and alliances, until the outbreak of the French Revolution in 1789. In the years that ensued, the Revolution would spread its Republican and Napoleonic ideologies throughout Europe, and the collapse of the French Empire would in turn lead to a new order at the Congress of Vienna in 1815. Here, the leading role of Great Britain on the world stage became more obvious than ever.

How is a frontier experienced?

The divisions imposed by the Treaty of Utrecht upon the Southern Netherlands in 1713 is a good historical example of the two-way effect that frontiers can have which was touched on earlier. The fact that it is a recurring phenomenon implies that there is some kind of pattern.

We can illustrate this by looking at the state institutions. Once the successive partitions were in place, the central institutions in the Netherlands could not continue to operate across the new boundaries. The areas conquered by France after 1668 ceased to be subject to the Great Council of Mechelen, which functioned as the Supreme Court, but fell under the legal authority of a *conseil souverain* in Tournai, which in 1714 became a parliament, in the sense of a court of appeal, and moved to Douai. Similarly, the Audit Office (Chambre des comptes) in Lille, which kept a check on state finances, lost its coordinating authority and, for the Austrian territories, was moved to Brussels. In the territory now belonging to France, *intendants* were appointed. As executive officials they would exercise a huge influence on the systematic assimilation of the new acquisitions into the French system. Supreme authority was naturally exercised by Vienna and Paris respectively.

The ideologies underlying the two administrations were based on different premises. On the French side, absolutism had triumphed, even though in the 18th century it was less coercive than previously. The Austrian Habsburgs, by linking their name to the concept of 'Enlightened Despotism' took an important step forward towards rationalising government policy.

However the new boundaries did not mean that all the structures were dismantled. In 1559, under Philip II of Spain, the episcopal sees in the Netherlands were redrawn. The medieval organisation was done away with and the new structure was intended to reflect the reality of a united Netherlands under the Habsburgs. But because of the independence of the Northern Netherlands and the

French conquests in the 17th century, some dioceses ended up partly or entirely in different countries. The dioceses of Tournai and Ypres, for example, extended on both sides of the border. Although state institutions encouraged estrangement, this was held in check by the cross-boundary structures of the church. Bishops recruited parish priests without taking account of their geographical origins.

We can also take a closer look at the road network. Apart from the old Roman roads, for centuries towns and villages had been connected by little more than paths and tracks. Only in the 17th century was there any large-scale road building, mainly for military purposes. In this the French took the lead and it enabled them to defend their northern frontier very effectively. The Spanish tried to follow their example, but progress was only really made under the Austrian administration. The frontier changes of 1713 meant that the road which went from Lille to Dunkirk via Ypres ran partly through 'enemy' territory. The French hurriedly rectified this by rerouting it via Cassel.[6]

The Balance of War and Peace, print made by Romeyn de Hooghe (1712). Registration number: 1868,0808.3456 © The Trustees of the British Museum.

A satirical broadside indicating the balance of power between European states during the negotiations leading to the Peace of Utrecht (1712). In the centre a balance, on the left of which are three armed men brandishing swords labelled 'Brit, Batavier en verder Bondgenôté' (British, Batavian and other allies) and "Wighs" (Whigs), the foremost man tramples a torn paper lettered 'Prulliminaria', i.e. the preliminaries of the peace. The balance is held by Justice. In the left-hand, lower pan are emblems of religion and liberty; in the other pan are emblems of war, French monarchy and Roman Catholicism and hypocrisy. Beside Justice are, on the right, true believers and suffering and, on the left, heaven's providence and heaven's wrath, represented by angels wielding a fiery sword, a fulmen and flail.

The traditionally busy communication between the Netherlands and the ceded territories was made more difficult by the mercantilist policies of France. Mercantilism was a centralised system designed to protect the home market and strictly control imports and exports. Not surprisingly it was fiercely resisted by the merchants of Lille and its surroundings who wanted to go on doing business with the Netherlands as they had always done. The corollary to the strict border policy was, of course, a well-developed contraband network with its own tracks, practices and codes. Only when the European frontiers were thrown open twenty years ago did smuggling finally enter the realms of folklore.[7]

The most striking feature of the 1713 frontiers was the impact on language. Gradually but steadily, because of a whole range of factors, Dutch, which had always been the native language of what is now French Flanders, was replaced by French. It is a process that is only now, after three centuries, being completed.[8] The native inhabitants who have clung to their dialect are either dead or at least very old. Education in the mother tongue was banned in the nineteenth century and is rarely, if at all, available. The language, like most minority languages in France, is not passed on to the younger generation. Only in local variants of French do Dutch words and expressions live on, as for instance in the Dunkirk dialect.

The speeding up of communications within national boundaries during the last two centuries has helped to implement the ideal of centralism: compulsory education, military service and the media. Minister Jules Ferry, who during the Third Republic introduced mandatory primary education (in French) in order to raise standards and emphasise and streamline the Frenchness of every citizen, estranged the inhabitants of the French periphery from their traditional native cultures.[9] It not only applied to the Flemings; it also affected the Basques, the Bretons, the Corsicans and others.

The end of the frontier?

Of course not! It is not the case that 'more Europe' will put an end to frontiers, even if they are now increasingly becoming internal boundaries. The nation states, after all, have nurtured many other traditions: differences in language, loyalty to different capital cities. Education systems teach a different past, and indeed a different present, which at times can be unrecognisable to those who live just over the border. Nevertheless, the frontier is always being breached. Demographic research shows that around 1700 marriage partners were always sought locally and it is striking how the 1713 frontier witnessed a growing trend in cross-border choices.[10] Anyone who nowadays looks at the marriage announcements in De Panne, a resort situated on the French border, will notice how love has made the frontier wafer thin. The boundary posts that here and there are a reminder of how dynasties and empires long confronted each other are now no more than nostalgic witnesses to a distant, ever-changing past.[11]

The cross-border worker, the creation of contrasting economic realities who in the past used to commute from Belgian Flanders to France, now travels mainly in the opposite direction. This kind of exchange is not only economically important, but socially and sociologically too. Getting to know each other, sometimes in defiance of long-standing prejudices, also means learning to appreciate each other.[12] ■

1. Traitez de Paix et de Commerce, Navigation et Marine entre La France et Les Etats Generaux Des Provinces Unies des Pays-Bas Conclus à Utrecht le 11 Avril *1713*.

2. Through the Act of Union of *1707* England and Scotland were united to create the kingdom of Great Britain.

3. G. Chalmers, *A Collection of Treaties between Great Britain and other Powers* (London, *1790*), vol. *1*, p. *341* (source gallica.bnf.fr) (www.heraldica.org).

4. Since *1697* the United Provinces had been given the international right to garrison a number of forts in the South. In the Treaty of *1715* (and later one in *1717*) those on the western flank were limited to Namur, Tournai, Menin, Veurne, Waasten, Ypres, Knocke and Dendermonde.

5. They are part of the 'Network of Small Fortified Towns'. This is a touristic and cultural project about the evolution of fortifications and defensive systems. The project is supported by the EU as part of the Efro-Interreg II programme. The best restored and touristically the most attractive are those of Grevelingen, Sint-Winoksbergen and Ypres.

6. F. Lentacker, *La frontière franco-belge. Etude géographique des effets d'une frontière internationale sur la vie des relations* (Villeneuve d'Ascq, *1973*), pp. *65-66*.

7. Dany Boon's film, *Rien à déclarer* [Nothing to declare] of *2010* plays on the differences and similarities along such a frontier, the fictitious French Courquain and the Belgian Koorkin.

8. There is a whole bibliography on French Flemish and the debate about its status and its chances of survival. See H. Ryckeboer, *Frans-Vlaams* (Taal in stad en land, *3*, Tielt, *2004*) and C. Moeyaert, *Woordenboek van het Frans-Vlaams* (Leuven, *2005*), and its supplement: *Nieuw oud Vlaams* (Ypres, *2011*).

9. At his inauguration as French president, François Hollande paid tribute to the memory of Jules Ferry because of the way his legislation helped to emancipate the ordinary citizen.

10. L. Milis, *'State Boundaries and Ethnic Alienation: Perspectives on Research into the Alienation Processes of French Flemings'*, in: L. *Milis, Religion, Culture, and Mentalities in the Medieval Low Countries,* (ed. J. Deploige et al., Turnhout, *2005*), pp. *369-384*.

11. A few examples: a boundary marker from 1779 in Menin, a string of border posts in La Flamengrie near Bavay (*1781*), a border post on the beach between De Panne and Bray-Dunes from the Dutch period (*1819*).

12. We have consulted a number of general histories: L. Trenard, ed., *Histoire des Pays-Bas français* (Toulouse, *1972*); C. Bruneel, *'De Spaanse en Oostenrijkse Nederlanden (1585-1780)'* in: J.C.H. Blom & E. Lamberts, eds., *Geschiedenis van de Nederlanden* (Rijswijk*1993*), pp. *181-218*; L. Bély, *La France moderne 1498-1789*, (Paris, *1994*); A. Lottin & Ph. Guignet, *De Charles Quint à la Révolution française* (*1500-1789*) (Arras, *2006*).

Language Border

[GEERT VAN ISTENDAEL]

On my desk is a picture postcard. I turn it over and read the words: *Frontière linguistique à Riemst/Bassenge*. On the front is a colour photo. To the right is a mobile telephone mast. At least, I think that's what it is. Just to the left of centre is a fluttering Belgian tricolour. The flag is attached to a fence, one of those that you see by the thousand all over the world, made of chicken wire, with iron support posts and topped by a single strand of barbed wire. Between the fence and the mast runs a narrow road. The only other things in the picture are five trees and, in the background, woodland nestled up against a low hill. Take away the flag and you have a landscape that could be almost anywhere: France? Germany? England? Even Poland as far as I'm concerned. But the back of the postcard provides the answer: this is Belgium. And not only that, this is the very essence of Belgium: the language border. In the eyes of quite a number of foreigners, Belgium *is* the language border.

The photographer has not just picked a random spot along this language border that symbolises so much that is Belgium. Riemst is the municipality where the president of the Flemish Parliament lives: Jan Peumans, a convinced Flemish nationalist, even though he himself declares that, if there were such a thing as reincarnation, he would want to be reborn as a French-speaking Belgian, a Walloon. Bassenge was part of the (Flemish) province of Limburg until legislators fixed the language border in 1962 and placed the village in the (Walloon) province of Liège – quite rightly, because almost everyone in the village spoke French. The municipality of Bassenge produced one of the greatest Walloon writers ever, Conrad Detrez – born on a language boundary, later transcending and pushing back all boundaries; a priest in the Bishopric of Liège, revolutionary in Brazil, French citizen and diplomat, homosexual, AIDS victim.

But the photo does not simply depict Belgium. It tries to evoke European history. The mobile telephone mast suggests a watchtower; the fence is a hint at an iron curtain. I reject that reference. The French-language Belgian writer Patrick Roegiers, who lives in Paris, once described the language border as *une honte, un crime et un drame*.[1] He was making a reference to the Berlin Wall. I think that is unworthy of him. I have seen with my own eyes how deadly effective that Wall was. I have seen with my own eyes the boundless joy of the East Germans when they threw themselves into the first breaches. Anyone who

compares the Belgian language border with the Berlin Wall or the Iron Curtain does not know what they are talking about. Throughout the entire Belgian language struggle, just two people have died, and both of them died a very long way from the language border. That border is not a scandal, not a crime and most definitely not a drama. It is not even typically Belgian.

Language border at Riemst/ Bassenge © Michel Castermans

Older than Belgium

The language border is much longer than the line that runs through Belgium. And it is older than Belgium.

My country gained its independence in 1830. But the language border was already there in the time of Charles the Great. That's around a thousand years. And we can go even further back. When Julius Caesar arrived here, he encountered a mix of Germanic people, Celts and heaven knows what else.

The northern part of Gaul did become more or less Romanised over time; it was, after all, a Roman province. But as the empire began to crumble and more and more Frankish tribes began advancing through our lands, a great deal of Gaul changed into a Romano-Germanic patchwork. It took centuries for the linguistic 'islands' to adapt to the foreign language areas surrounding them. The language border is thus the line where Germanisation and Romanisation held each other more or less in balance, not only in terms of the territory that is today called Belgium, but in an entire swath of Europe from Northern France to, say, Northern Italy.

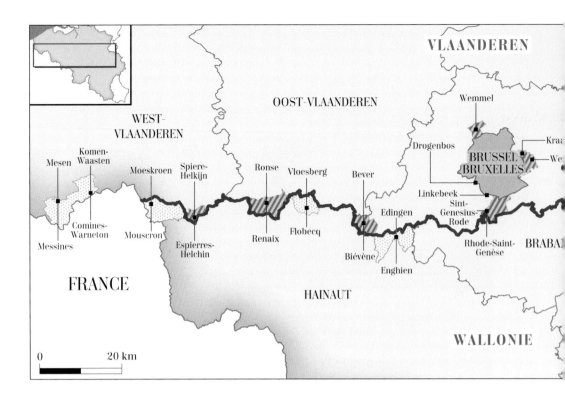

There is another, fascinating hypothesis: the language border follows the line which marked the southern limits of a now extinct pre-Celtic language, a language which was still in use by a number of tribes when the Roman legions arrived. The region above that boundary was barely populated, and effectively presented an open door to the invading Germanic tribes. The language border could therefore be more than two thousand years old. The languages it separates are just different today. The boundary remains, the languages change.

The language border has cut across our territory since time immemorial then. Princes, citizens, farmers: everyone knew that people spoke differently on the other side. No one was troubled by this. If you travelled from Ghent to Tournai, you spoke French. Or, to be more accurate, you spoke Picard. And if you travelled from Liege to Leuven, you tried your hand (or rather your mouth) at Brabant dialect. Occasionally, a village or community switched from one language to the other. For example, the tiny Belgian village known as Sittert-Lummen in Dutch is today French-speaking and bears the appealing name of Zétrud-Lumay. Until the fourteenth century, it was known as Zetrud or Setrut, and in 1386 the name Zittert appeared. And where in 1576 the entire toponomy was in Dutch, in 1681 all official documents were written in French. In 1743 there was a minor dispute about the use of language in a court case; evidently the transition was not yet entirely complete. One or two other similar cases have also been recorded. For centuries, then, the language border has barely moved. For centuries it was recognised as simply a given, in the same way that a stream or a hill would be recognised.

We must not think that people considered language use to be of negligible importance. The above incident from 1743 testifies to the contrary. In the Duchy

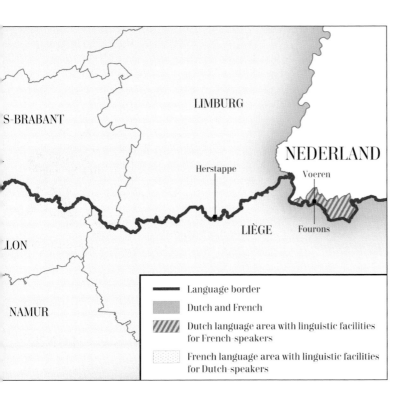

LIMBURG

S-BRABANT

NEDERLAND

Herstappe

Voeren

LIÈGE

Fourons

LLON

NAMUR

——— Language border

Dutch and French

////// Dutch language area with linguistic facilities
for French speakers

French language area with linguistic facilities
for Dutch speakers

of Brabant, for example, it was unthinkable that a resident would appear before a court that did not speak his language. This wise mediaeval arrangement only changed when France annexed our region at the end of the eighteenth century. Henceforth, the language of officialdom, and therefore also the compulsory language for the courts and lawyers, was French. The French occupier shattered the languid neighbourliness of Dutch and Walloon dialects by imposing one language on both – that of the ruling elite in Paris. We should not forget that during the French Revolution the majority of the *citoyens* spoke no French, and that it would take decades before that changed.[2]

Le flamand aux animaux et aux domestiques

In 1830, the homeland of the language border gained its independence. Immediately, the Belgian ruling class decided to ignore the language of the majority for serious administrative affairs and serious education. The only official language was French. It was not that the ruling class was made up of malign Walloons who were eager to suppress the poor Flemings. The elite of *the entire country* – in Flanders, Wallonia and Brussels – spoke French. The fact that they accounted for less than 2 percent of the population was of no importance at all. They alone had the right to vote; they alone had political power.

They drew a different language boundary, one that was not geographical. Few foreigners are aware that there was also a non-territorial language boundary, a *social* language boundary. That boundary was situated exclusively *within* the Dutch-language area. It separated the upper and lower social echelons in

Flanders through language. It has lost much of its significance today, but it still exists, discreetly, in the background, and in my view has been more important in the whole language struggle than the boundary between Flemings and Walloons.

In the Flemish countryside, language separated those who owned the land from those who worked it. In the towns, the better-off middle classes quickly began speaking French, and the less well-off would have been only too pleased to do so. Paradoxically enough, those French-speakers still almost always called themselves Flemings; they were (and are) even proud of it. But they spoke French and considered it perfectly normal that they had the right to use French everywhere in public life. There is a sentence that I always use to illustrate the social language boundary. I heard it years ago from the mouth of a French-speaking inhabitant of Ghent: *On parlait le flamand aux animaux et aux domestiques*. One spoke Flemish to animals and servants. In that order. Almost all the language laws in Belgium were devised to take away the language rights of the upper class in Flanders. And all those laws were consistently approved by French-speakers and Dutch-speakers together, albeit in varying proportions.

In the nineteenth century, one could walk through a Flemish town and believe oneself to be in Northern France. Shops were called things like cordonnerie or bonneterie, the Bruges street Rozenhoedkaai had become the *Quai du Rosaire* and a street in Ghent called Ham was rather cunningly disguised as *rue du Jambon*. Until the 1960s, French was seen everywhere in the streets of Flanders. Those days are gone. Today, there is no doubting that the language of the Flemish region is Dutch. If anything, in the most recent years the biggest invasion has been from English, but on that point Flanders is no different from somewhere like the Netherlands, for example.

Language censuses

The 'Dutchification' of Flemish public life was only really consolidated thanks to the language boundary – not the geographical boundary, because that had existed for centuries, but the *statutory fixing* of that language boundary.

Belgium was the first country in the world to count its languages. The results of the first census (1846) are sometimes surprising. Today, for example, the Brussels Capital Region is officially bilingual, though few would contest the numerical predominance of French-speakers. In 1846, 18 of the 19 municipalities which now form the Region contained a Dutch-speaking majority; in 12 of those municipalities, that majority was between 90 and 100 percent. After 1846, therefore, something happened around Brussels which had not happened in all the centuries previously: the language boundary moved drastically.[3]

Brussels is the great exception. Even after independence in 1830, the language boundary remained amazingly stable. Outside Brussels, changes were a rarity. Sometimes the French-speakers had the advantage, elsewhere it was the Dutch-speakers. Three examples: in 1846, more than 70 percent of the inhabitants of the small town of Edingen (Enghien) were Dutch-speaking; in 1947 55 percent were bilingual and 4 percent spoke only Dutch. The town is now part of Wallonia. Also in 1846, three-quarters of the residents of the village of Rekkem, in the province of West-Vlaanderen, spoke French; in 1947 this had fallen to 10 percent and more than half reported that they were bilingual. Today,

Rekkem forms part of Flanders. The third example is Spiere. 90 percent of the residents of this village spoke French in 1846; in 1947 it was 27 percent, and a large group were bilingual. Spiere is now also part of Flanders, though with minority rights for the French-speakers.

Care was sometimes needed in the Belgian language censuses. Margins of error can never be avoided entirely, but the Belgian language censuses gradually became imbued with a political significance. Flemish politicians were quick to rage about what they described as falsification, manipulation and stealing of territory, especially – though not exclusively – in and around Brussels. They disputed the results (in 54 municipalities following the 1947 census), arguing that they had been used as a means of systematically moving the language boundary to the disadvantage of Dutch-speakers. Flemish public opinion demanded a fixed language boundary. The 1947 language census was the last.

The route laid out for the language border in the laws of 1962 and 1963 was the result of a careful study of the local situation on the one hand and on the other of fiercely divisive debates in Parliament. In 1948, on the initiative of the Walloon Christian Democrat Pierre Harmel, a Centre was founded whose tasks included studying the route of the language border. One Fleming and one Walloon, Jan Verroken and Jean van Crombrugge, acting *independently* of each other, studied the linguistic situation along the entire length of the language border, hamlet by hamlet, street by street, farm by farm. To their own amazement they discovered that the two routes, that of the Walloon and that of the Fleming, were identical but for a few minuscule exceptions. As a result Verroken withdrew his own map and co-signed that of his Walloon colleague. Everyone agreed that they had both done an excellent job, and the course of their border was approved by the Harmel Centre in 1952. But it was another ten years before the Belgian parliament, partly based on the decision by the Harmel Centre, finally – after the long-winded, never-ending debates – fixed the language border by law. From that point on, the language border coincided with the provincial borders wherever that was feasible.

For the first time, the country was divided into four language regions: Dutch-speaking, French-speaking, German-speaking (yes, Belgium also has a German-speaking minority) and the bilingual region comprising the 19 Brussels municipalities. French and Dutch were given equal status in Brussels, but the monolingual areas became genuinely monolingual, with a few exceptions along the language border.

Le droit du sol

Strikingly, French-speakers refused for a long time to accept the language border, even though the law had been approved by the Belgian parliament with a large majority. Many French-speakers voted against, but a substantial proportion also voted in favour.

There were some problems after 1962, starting with the villages in the Voeren region, which had been assigned to Flanders. But the Voeren question was resolved years ago. The language border did not move.

Until very recently, French-speaking politicians refused to accept the demarcation of Brussels. It is true that any number of (French-speaking)

MOESKROEN | MOUSCRON

© Jonas Lampens

Bruxellois have moved into the Dutch-speaking environs of the city; city-dwellers moving out in search of green space – it happens all over Europe. But these city-dwellers spoke a different language from the villagers around them, and they refused to acknowledge the language of their new home. The result is that the Brussels periphery, although officially Dutch-speaking, houses tens of thousands of French-speakers. In six municipalities they have full language rights, the notorious *facilities*.

For Flemings, the spread of Brussels like an oil stain, swallowing up more and more Flemish communities, is a classic horror scenario. They will accordingly defend their monolingual status stubbornly. Being monolingual means only that a citizen speaks Dutch in his relationship with the government. At home, he can use whatever language he chooses, because the Belgian legislator has always kept out of private language use as a matter of principle.

Many French-speakers, however, consider it unacceptable that they cannot use French in every town hall. They defend what they call *le droit de la personne*, in other words, they want to be able to use their language anywhere. They accuse the Flemings of imposing a barbaric, almost Teutonic territorial law, *le droit du sol*. In doing so, they conveniently forget that there is one country in Europe which rigorously applies le droit du sol: France. Anyone who suggests that France is monolingual should free themselves of that illusion by reading the books referred to in note 2. Switzerland is another example of a country where territorial law is applied to maintain linguistic peace.

And what of Belgium?

As long as no one sought to impose their language on anyone else, there was no need for anyone to resist anything. And since 1962, no one *can* impose their language. So there is no focal point for resistance anymore. And it is precisely that which is the strength of our statutory language border. Even in the controversial Brussels periphery, we have succeeded in coming to an arrangement.

Friendly, democratic and decisive

The most recent problem in the environs of Brussels actually has less to do with French-speakers. A third of children in the Flemish territory surrounding Brussels do not speak Dutch at home, and this is a growing trend. Many of them, though by no means all, speak French with their parents – though there is also English, German, Berber, Turkish and a host of other languages.

For most immigrants, Belgian language legislation is impenetrable. They often do not even realise that our country is bilingual. They are irritated beyond measure when a simple civil servant behind the counter in a Dutch-speaking municipality simply applies Belgian law and speaks only Dutch. Rejoinders such as fanatic, narrow-minded and worse are not uncommon. That is unfair. Flemish house-to-house newspapers, folders published by the municipality, crèches and sports clubs are today all making heroic efforts to provide multilingual explanations.

The blissful indifference of centuries past will never return. It is our task to defend the language border, in a friendly, democratic but decisive way. Because in Belgium, the language border is the foundation of the peace that all of us want. ▥

Translated by Julian Ross

NOTES

1. Roegiers, *P., Pauvre Belgique, pauvres c...!*, in: Frontières. Grenzen. Borders, Passa Porta Magazine # 0, *2011*, p. *28*.

2 See e.g. the standard work by the American historian Eugene Weber, Peasants into Frenchmen: *The Modernization of rural France, 1870-1914*, Stanford, *1976* and also Braudel, *F., L'identité de la France*, Part I, Paris, *1986*, pp. *78-83*.

3 For all figures, see: Rillaerts; S., *La frontière linguistique, 1878-1963*, Courrier hebdomadaire du Crisp, nr. *2069-2070*, Brussels, *2010*.

A Country Divided

Of Old and New Boundaries

[CYRILLE OFFERMANS]

The French Revolution is usually considered to be the political outcome of the 18th century Enlightenment. Without the anti-feudal intellectual firepower of the *philosophes* the surge of popular anger that culminated in the storming of the Bastille is hard to imagine. But perhaps of equal importance for European history were the *negotiations* leading up to the Peace of Utrecht, precisely because they were negotiations. It is true that in 1713 the philosophical enlightenment had not yet begun, outside the Netherlands at any rate. However, the diplomats had already set an example, presumably unconsciously following Montaigne, whose relativism marked an early refuge of intellectual non-violence in the bloody wars between Protestants and Catholics that were tearing the continent apart.

But naturally the end of the religious wars did not mean the end of religious differences. Even in the traditionally tolerant Netherlands they continued to give rise to conflict between, roughly speaking, the Protestant North and the Catholic South, even if they were now fought out on the pulpit or in the press instead of in the street. A stray traveller from Brabant who disturbed the Sunday peace in Staphorst might have hell and damnation called down upon his head but it never led to the type of military violence, that continued to take place on the streets of Belfast until the beginning of the 21st century. Instead, for some time the various confessional groupings found themselves sharing the same goal: they wanted to obtain financial equality with the publicly funded, though strongly Christianized, education system. They did not succeed until 1917.

The prolonged controversy over school funding was therefore not a continuation of the wars of religion with different weapons, but the attempt of different Christian communities to secure a place in a secular, liberal society where, with state assistance, they could enjoy an education and training based on the fundamentals of their faith. It led to the extreme fragmentation of society that went under the name of 'pillarisation', which only came to an end after the 1960s – at least *de facto* - when the explosion of prosperity, faster and more radical than in other European countries, gave rise to an irresistible wave of de-Christianization and mass atheism.

Stubborn resistance to these developments was and still is found only in the string of more or less adjacent municipalities that came to be known as the

'Bible Belt', like an echo of the ultra-conservative Christian fundamentalists in the south-eastern states of America. In this belt of land that stretches from the islands of Zeeland to the west of Overijssel, the word of Calvin is declared with greater self-confidence than ever to be the definitive version of Christianity. Not only is the godless theory of evolution rejected but every area of human-directed endeavour is seen as evidence of inadmissible arrogance and the handiwork of the devil. So there is opposition to abortion, euthanasia, voting rights for women and the separation of sex from reproduction. On the other hand, there is support for reintroducing the death penalty and an apparent unawareness of any contradiction.

However, all in all this is an anachronistic ideological curiosity to which less than one percent of the population adhere. Outside the Bible Belt people rapidly discarded the faith of their fathers. Indeed it was disturbingly rapid, because it is questionable whether the universal Christian morality that was rejected, including the qualities of self-control, self-restraint and moral self-improvement, had been sufficiently replaced by adequate non-metaphysical, empirical equivalents. By now, I think, the answer to that question is unambiguous. But no matter what, the churches became deserted and the religious and philosophical adjectives were replaced by the names of associations of sports, music and broadcasting or disappeared inside cryptic acronyms. The Netherlands, like the entire western world after the Second World War, and more intensively after the collapse of communism in 1989, fell under the spell of full-scale de-ideologization.

The only ideology to remain, though it could not be labelled as such because that would have suggested some ineluctable social necessity, was that of the free market. Virtually all the political parties, including the Christian parties and the social democrats, more or less committed themselves to the free market's technocratic view of politics. Politics was no longer the expression of people's passionate, democratically-inspired involvement in public affairs, but a question of 'minding the shop', to use the weary sounding words, spoken by the Catholic Prime Minister Piet de Jong, which he uttered during the heyday of the cultural revolution in the 1960s (between 1967 and 1971), of all times, to characterize his own administration and that of his successors. Under the 'purple' coalitions of Wim Kok between 1994 and 2002, the social democrats ridded themselves of their last 'ideological feathers'. The Christian parties were left on the sidelines for the first time in eighty years. However, instead of using that time to strengthen their original religious roots, they were the ones, who seemed to have discovered a new missionary goal in the universal preaching of the neoliberal faith.

Cut from the same cloth

'The aim of the state is freedom' Spinoza

All these developments have created a situation in which little remains of the old religious contrast between the North and South Netherlands. What remain are vague cultural differences which are hardly if at all coloured by religion. Everybody knows the clichés about the near-brutal bluntness, straightforwardness, frugality and efficiency of the northerner in contrast to the near-hypocritical equivocation, long-windedness, generosity and reserve of the southerner, which are the respective legacies of joyless Calvinism and its ascetic iconoclasm on the one hand, and unprincipled Catholicism with its baroque image culture on the other. But without denying these legacies it is quite clear that they are inextricably mixed up with socio-economic differences and differences in power, wealth and degrees of development. And they are more a reflection of the contrast between town and countryside, or rather between the *Randstad* (the conurbation of western Holland between Amsterdam, Rotterdam, The Hague and Utrecht) and the provinces, even though in the Netherlands also that contrast is now relatively small.

A good indicator of cultural levelling between north and south is the culture of popular festivals which was imbued in earlier times with specific local and religious elements and played an important 'purifying' role in maintaining and strengthening the local community. It was especially true of the Carnival festival in the south. Nowadays there are few who know that carnival was part of the Catholic festival calendar, that it was the last opportunity for excess, particularly of food and drink, before giving oneself over inexorably to a strict regime of fasting for forty days in a form of a collective *Imitatio Christi*. After being baptized, Christ spent forty days fasting in the wilderness before he embarked on his epoch-making preaching mission. According to the Carnival-experts, the true 'carnivalist' has become a solitary figure. And that is the consequence of two developments: an invasion from people from the north to the southern carnival centres, and an exodus of southerners to the winter sport centres. Nothing is left of the authentic, moralizing street carnival. In the cafés one only hears schmaltzy Dutch *schlagers* while the standard carnival outfit comes from the same clothing factory that dresses the supporters of the Dutch football team or followers of the Friesian skating marathon.

Developments like this don't take place without difficulties. Just as earlier stages of modernization provoked a counter-reaction to the levelling process, the same is happening again. We are witnessing numerous attempts to change the image of regional culture. In every province, whether Friesland, Gelderland or Limburg, serious efforts are being made to persuade Brussels to promote their dialects to the status of an official regional language. A curious desire, by the way, as dialects exist in practice at village level and a genuine regional language is an abstraction that nobody actually speaks. Dialect societies are

popular, place-name signs in virtually all the provinces outside the *Randstad* are bilingual. However it is a form of museumization, a greenhouse cultivation of traditions outside the daily context in which they originally functioned. In the wild, dialects are unmistakeably in decline.

Schilderswijk. The Hague

Town and Province

Not only has globalization lessened the importance of the contrast between north and south but it has also affected all bipolar contrasts including that between town and countryside. This has always been relatively small in the Netherlands, thanks in particular to its century-old decentralized political culture, the short distances, and the easy accessibility of even the far corners of the country. And recent revolutionary developments in information and communications technology have made the differences even smaller. At least, in a number of important respects.

For example, the assumption that juvenile delinquency is specifically a problem in the larger cities is less and less true. To be sure, Amsterdam, Rotterdam and The Hague do continue to score high statistically, but not much if at all higher than provincial cities like Vlissingen, Delfzijl or Appingedam. Featuring in the top ten 'child-unfriendly' municipalities measured by child mortality, poverty, school drop-outs, delinquency and youth unemployment one also finds Heerlen and Kerkrade (in the far south) and Leeuwarden and Pekela (in the extreme north). But more striking than a slight overall improvement in these figures is the growing division along ethnic lines: there is a stubborn group of derailed, mainly immigrant youth who are proving difficult to draw into integration programmes. These young people, both in the Randstad and in the provincial towns, live in disadvantaged districts.

Nevertheless, in a number of respects the differences between the big cities in the West and the peripheral areas of the North, South and East Netherlands seem to be increasing in recent years. A shrinking population and lack of work have caused a steady flow, particularly among the better-qualified, from the provinces to the *Randstad* where the opportunities are far greater. And this

Almere

process further strengthens the demographic imbalance and the economic and cultural impoverishment of the provinces, even though the impact has been far less than the dramatic desertion of the countryside in countries like France and Spain. In the end, it is primarily global economic and demographic developments that are redefining the relationship between the *Randstad* and the provinces. This can best be illustrated by the recent history of Amsterdam.

Consumerism as self-expression

Thirty years ago Amsterdam was a city in decline. Housing and living conditions in the older working class districts like the Jordaan and the Pijp were poor, squatters and junkies were a problem and the result was a massive exodus to new housing estates in the suburbs and new commuter towns like Almere and Lelystad. Between 1963 and 1984 the population of the city fell spectacularly from 870,000 to 680,000. Demolition and rebuilding projects took no notice of traditional proportions, the intricate network of pre-automobile streets and the historic architecture.

This lack of historical awareness became painfully obvious in the demolition of the extensive Jewish quarter, which dates back to the sixteenth century. Large nondescript blocks appeared on the Jodenbreestraat and the Weesperstraat. A large part of the development of the Waterlooplein suffered a similar fate. A statue of Spinoza looks out over the now unrecognizably changed district in which he lived before being expelled from the Sephardic community in 1656. In that area the new town hall was built and, adjacent to it, an Opera house, an ugly colossus defying all sense of historical proportion and which has met with a great deal of local opposition - though to no avail.

But the Amsterdammers did not resign themselves to this wilful destruction, which was changing historic places into what the Parisian anthropologist Marc Augé would later call *non-lieux* or 'non-places', lacking any particular identity and creating only loneliness and uniformity. In 1975 their resistance had more success. Although the notorious Nieuwmarkt riots were unable to halt demolition for a metro tunnel, they did prevent the building of a highway straight through the neighbourhood. Slowly but surely, changes came about that made the city once again residentially attractive. Parallel to a renewed historical awareness of *lieux de mémoire* (a term used by the French historian Pierre Nora to indicate places that embody the folk memory), the guiding principles of urban renewal became restoration, renovation and a discrete architectonic focus.

Particularly the young, progressive intelligentsia felt comfortable in this environment. The well-educated no longer automatically moved to the suburbs as soon as their children were born. The disadvantages of often dreadful living conditions were more than compensated for by urban vitality, especially in the artistic and cultural fields. The city became an experimental laboratory for new future-oriented social and ecological life styles. Nowhere was so much creative energy invested in alternative initiatives and projects. No place else was so richly endowed with specialized museums, galleries, theatres, cinemas, concert halls, educational institutions, research and debating centres, editorial offices, exotic shops and restaurants, bookshops, political, philosophical and literary cafés. This informal and ever-evolving environment seemed to be the ideal biotope for a flexible, cosmopolitan, and creative class.

For several decades now, Amsterdam has again been booming, just like London, Berlin, Copenhagen, Hamburg and, on a smaller scale, Utrecht and Maastricht. Its present population is (again) nearly 800,000 and it is expected to continue to grow. It exercises a huge attraction on newcomers who can find few opportunities elsewhere in the country, especially in the declining regions. It also attracts tourists and day-trippers from all over the world who are keen to look or to buy, in spite of the fact that the biggest museums have been in scaffolding for years and the centre of the city, because of the construction of the new metro, is an enormous building site.

The city is also the stage for new forms of leisure activities in which shopping merges with going out and cultural activities. Indeed, particularly for young people who communicate incessantly, consumption itself has become an important form of self-expression and therefore a cultural activity. Similarly, in much contemporary visual art, now largely absorbed by film, photography, design and advertising, people are very ready to pay for names, labels and symbols that create the feeling of belonging to the avant-garde of a cosmopolitan mass culture. Lack of depth has the advantage for both producers and consumers of making it all easily and smoothly interchangeable.

International concerns like Nike, Adidas, Apple, Levi's, Vodafone, Starbucks and Taschen take advantage of it. In prominent places around the city, they open their own shops which focus on creating a total, almost religious, identification with the brand (or 'experience' as the collaborative trend watchers like to call it). Producers of cosmetics, lingerie and accessories colonize the chic department stores like the Bijenkorf, creating shops within shops, comparable in some ways to nineteenth-century arcades, Walter Benjamin's 'dream houses'. The main difference is that parading in front of the show-off branches of Gucci, Vuitton and Versace are grim-looking guards who are supposed to enhance the sense of exclusivity for their *nouveaux riche* clientele, who often come from Russia or China.

A divided country

New differences were inevitable. The make-up of the population in the big cities has changed drastically, while in the provinces it has remained more or less stable. The *Randstad* is home to every conceivable nationality. About fifty percent of the population are immigrants, of whom roughly half come from Surinam, the Antilles, Turkey and Morocco. Although Amsterdam in particular has always been a hospitable, cosmopolitan metropolis - in 1650 it was estimated that between a third and a half of the population had been born outside the Republic - the integration of non-Western, Muslim and partially illiterate immigrants has not been without its problems, although they have been considerably smaller than those faced by Paris, London or Brussels.

The big cities in the Netherlands are multicultural, also in the negative sense of the word. Different population groups tend to live in separate districts, and the children attend different schools. In some districts, such as the Painters' District (*Schilderswijk*) and the Transvaal Quarter (*Transvaalkwartier*) in The Hague, segregation is practically total. But segregation in the Netherlands is mainly a result of socioeconomic circumstances and not a deliberate population policy - for at least the last ten years, it has been more like the opposite. Talk of 'gated communities' is only metaphorical and despite a few serious incidents invariably fanned by anti-Islamist alarmism in the popular press, there is nothing that suggests a revival of the religious or racist warfare of the past.

Nevertheless, for a long time populist parties were not only successful in the cities (Rotterdam and The Hague) but also in the rural areas. The 'Ring of Canals', referring to the wealthy centre of Amsterdam, became a populist term of abuse for the 'left-wing elite' who, while they personally were not involved in the problem of the 'Moroccan street-rabble', were full of understanding for their behaviour. Yet the electoral success of populism was due less to conscious Islamophobia than to a painfully direct experience of the destruction of the original homogeneous social environment of the working-class districts in the *Randstad* and a vague but not unjustified fear of social and economic decline in the mono-cultural provinces.

The future is uncertain. After the parliamentary elections of September 2012 it seems as if political populism, at least temporarily, is in retreat. Whether it also represents a turning point in the long-discredited neoliberal faith in the optimizing effect of treating the world as a market place and consequently in the measures being adopted to combat the economic crisis remains to be seen. The essential thing is to prevent a growing 'bulge' of - mainly - immigrant youth, both poorly educated *and* highly qualified, who have no social prospects. After a fairly hysterical decade, the Netherlands is a divided country, not explosively divided and torn apart, but without a heartfelt concern for the public interest in general, and new, ambitious programmes of integration and pacification in particular, the pressures of the economic crisis could yet make those divisions explosive and deeper. ▧

Translated by Chris Emery

Germania, Romanitas and Belgitude

Borders and Border Issues

The story's been well-known in Germany since the '50s: when the then Federal Chancellor, Konrad Adenaur, had to go to Berlin he took the train from Cologne – of which he had been mayor until the rise of the Third Reich. Over the Hohenzollern Bridge, with its equestrian statues of the Prussian monarchs, the train crossed the Rhine leaving the silhouette of Cologne Cathedral behind it. Soon afterwards Adenauer pulled the curtains and remarked: 'Hier fängt Asien an' – Asia starts here.

A charged anecdote, but telling. The Catholic Rhinelander, Adenauer, who had never had much use for a Germany dominated by the shadow of Prussia, was well aware that Trier and Cologne had been important Roman cities and that Christianity had taken root there right back in the days of the Roman Empire – not much later than in Lyon or Tarragona. For Adenauer – and for others, like Heinrich Böll, the German Rhineland was part of Romanitas, and lay on the 'good' side of the oldest and most important border in Europe, the Roman *limes*, the dividing line between the *pax augusta* and the barbarians. To a certain extent it was a romantic vision, an idealised self-image. But it also explains Adenauer's powerful rejection of Nazism in the years 1933-45, facilitated his easy relationship with De Gaulle, and was eventually an important motive for embedding the Federal Republic in Western Europe, with its capital not in Frankfurt, Hamburg or Munich but in Bonn.

The anecdote also shows that we construct borders in our minds according to conceptual patterns of identification. *Die wahren Grenzen sind im Kopf.* Adenauer's identification of a Romano-Christian westward-looking Rhineland was counter to the dominant view. That view had the demarcation between Germanic and Romanic Europe run not along cultural historical borders but along linguistic lines – the border between the Romance and Germanic language groups. In that view language was the characteristic that had most influence on the character of a person or people; language was, indeed, the whole people. Whether you speak a Germanic or a Romance language is like whether an engine runs on diesel or petrol, or a computer with Windows or Linux. In the course of the nineteenth century this identification between language and 'the whole people' became so loaded that it turned into a quasi-anthropological dogma. On the Romanic side a language with linear syntax, simple grammar

and a way of thinking that was correspondingly aimed at clarity and lucidity (*ce qui n'est pas clair n'est pas français* – if it's not clear, it's not French); on the Germanic side a language with a complex grammar and syntax (*Schachtelsätze* - sentences structured like matryoshka dolls) and, correspondingly, a way of thinking that was aimed at perspicacity and profundity. On the Romanic side concepts such as esprit and civilisation, and on the Germanic side concepts such as *Geist* and *Kultur*.

A stereotype no less simplistic and silly than that of the frugal Scots, un- fathomable Chinese or dumb blondes, but nonetheless one with a widespread, centuries-long grip on European thought.

Left: Oudenaarde. Bridge over the river Schelde. 'Atten- tion. You are now leaving the French Kingdom'. Installation by Johan Van Geluwe

Right: Oudenaarde. Bridge over the river Schelde. 'Atten- tion. You are now leaving the Holy Roman Empire of the German Nation'. Installation by Johan Van Geluwe

Wit and judgement

It is characteristic of stereotypes like this that they are seductive systems in which everything - but everything - can be accommodated and categorised. The magnificence and splendour of Catholicism and the showy protocol of monarchism are referred to as Romanic from that viewpoint, while the sense of political and religious responsibility demonstrated by republicanism and Protestantism are supposedly Germanic – as typified by the Swiss cantons, the Scandinavian countries or the Dutch Republic of William of Orange and Hugo Grotius. They contrast totally with the southern European mentality recognised in the Semana santa of Seville or the veneration of the saints by Neapolitans or Sicilians. Everyone will feel tempted to nod in acknowledgement: 'tiens, indeed'. Lucrative 'intercultural management' courses comprise little more than a string of this sort of 'Ah-ha' effect revelation. Because of it we neglect to ask: what about the formal hierarchy of the Prussian, Protestant monarchy, the fervent shock and awe ceremonial of Hitler's Nuremberg party days? Do they speak German in that citadel of the European Reformation, Geneva? Is Europe not bursting with counterexamples?

The putative, imaginary border between Germanic and Romanic Europe is, like any cultural generalisation, a nice *jeu d'esprit*. In the terminology of John Locke's philosophy of learning it belongs to the faculty of 'wit', that lively ingenuity that allows us to see the similarities between things that are diverse; but what is lacking is Locke's complementary concept of 'judgement', the ability to recognise differences and contradictions and form balanced opinions about them. Such stereotypes are successful because of their wit, but are lacking in any real reliability because of their lack of judgement, and those who base their decisions or actions on them build on sand.

Herzliche Grüsse aus
Deutschland, Holland, Belgien und Neutralgebiet.

Moresnet

However, that is just what a great many people have been doing indefatigably over the last two centuries. Since 1648 the major political conflicts have occurred around the external borders of France and Germany, and where they have clashed with each other the rhetoric raged that the characters of Germanic and Romanic peoples were irreconcilable, indeed that there was even a sort of hereditary enmity between them. It began with Louis XIV's claims to the Duchy of Brabant, Lorraine and the Alsace. Acquiring the Rhine as the eastern border of France originated as one of the megalomaniac Sun King's dynastic delusions that was translated into a pragmatic geopolitical policy by his military right hand, Vauban. Since then it has remained an ideal of French foreign policy despite all the regime changes. In spite of their very diverse political backgrounds and constitutional positions, Danton, Napoleon, Thiers, Clemenceau and de Gaulle all revealed the ambition to obtain a natural border on the north-eastern side of the French hexagon, along the Rhine. That would be an effective solution to the fear of encirclement by the Habsburg realms that had haunted France since the days of Francis I and Charles V.

So it comes down to pragmatic geopolitics, comparable to the Russian drive for ice-free sea ports. Culture had nothing to do with it, and the fact that non-Romance languages were spoken along the Rhine did not worry the French leaders one iota. If Basques and Bretons could share the blessings of French government, why should not Flemings and Alsatians?

After the conquest of Strasbourg by the French, we see that this French expansion was sharply censured on the German side - and with cultural arguments at that, especially as important German intellectuals such as Herder and the young student, Goethe, had lived there for a time on the eve of the Romantic period. Strasbourg Cathedral was seen as a living sign of the genuine German DNA of the city (as if Gothic architecture were not equally at home in Chartres and Rheims!). Against France's geopolitical, pragmatic arguments about power, German romantics brought ideals and cultural and historic arguments into the fray. That happened repeatedly in the course of the nineteenth century: during the Congress of Vienna, during the Rhine crisis in 1840 and with the annexation of Alsace-Lorraine in 1871. Thanks to Talleyrand's subtle diplomacy, France was able to keep its grip on the Alsace and on Strasbourg in 1813-1815, despite being the loser in the Napoleonic wars, which provoked Ernst Moritz Arndt's resounding pamphlet *Der Rhein, Deutschlands Strom, nicht Deutschlands Grenze*. In exchange for the French grip on Strasbourg the Cologne-Trier area, later Adenauer's *Heimat*, was brought under Prussian rule – much against the will of the population.

'Europe's Grand Canyon'

Germany's Rhineland hackles were raised again in 1830, when Belgium became an independent, Paris-oriented state, and in 1840 battle songs were once more being written, like *Die Wacht am Rhein* ('Lieb' Vaterland, magst ruhig sein, treu steht und fest die Wacht am Rhein') and the *Rheinlied* ('Sie werden ihn nicht haben, den freien deutschen Rhein'). After the Franco-German war in 1870-1871

Borderstone (now between Belgium and France) from 1819 with N(etherlands) on one side and F(rance) on the other
© Michiel Hendryckx

Germany was able to restore honour to the German Empire (under Prussian leadership now) and add Alsace-Lorraine to it, in one go, a so-called final restoration of the 'natural' situation that had been disrupted by Louis XIV. Like the people of the Rhineland, when it was annexed by the Prussians in 1815, the population of Alsace-Lorraine endured this change in 1871 with very mixed feelings.

Why go into all this detail? For two reasons. Firstly the tug-of-war between an expansionist France and a no less expansionist Prussian Germany is the real reason why the Germanic-Romanic antithesis was able to develop from an informal cultural *jeu d'esprit* into such a fierce and dominant ideology about a 'Europe's Grand Canyon'. This Germanic-Romanic split came about somewhere between 1805 and 1815. It pretends, it is true, to refer to a much older pattern, but that is deceptive. Nationalism invokes a long memory but actually has a rather short history.

Secondly the Germanic-Romanic divide creates a life-size problem in the fracture area between the two sides' claims. Alsace and the German Rhineland were not the only objects of the Prussian and French craving for annexation; the Low Countries were also claimed by both parties – by Napoleon as 'deposits left by French rivers' and by Arndt and his followers as part of the Rhine basin, which ought to be German from Basle to Rotterdam. Belgium's East Cantons know all about it; Luxembourg, too, and to a lesser extent even the Dutch province of Limburg (Belgian from 1830 to 1839, Dutch-German from 1839 to 1867).

Throughout the whole of the nineteenth and early twentieth centuries the history of the Low Countries was a balancing act on the slack wire of the Germanic-Romanic rhetoric. The language struggle in Belgium was seen as a reflection in miniature of the larger confrontation. The Flemish Movement was saddled with the sympathy of its German brethren as an 'outpost' (fateful concept) in the anti-French struggle. The Belgian communal debates followed the

Borderstone (now between Belgium and France) from the 18th century with the Austrian Eagle
© Michiel Hendryckx

lines of the Germanic-Romanic pattern: Francophones used the smug rhetoric of pragmatic hegemonism, the Flemish on the other hand countered with shrill cultural-historical arguments about descent and tradition. This left the Flemish emancipation movement exposed to the accusation of German-style ethnic essentialism. That accusation was all too often justified (and that should give Flemings pause for thought); but it is also all too often used as a debating trick to obscure real grievances from view caused by overbearing Francophone superciliousness. *Plus ça change...*

Round 1900 Henri Pirenne introduced the notion of *belgitude*, which was characterised by the fact that since time immemorial the Southern Netherlands have formed an interface between *Germania* and the old Roman Empire. In the preface to his *Histoire de la Belgique* Pirenne makes a virtue out of necessity. That Belgium has no natural borders, nor one common language, nor a history of political unity, just happens to be the essence of the country. It is a crossroads, open on all sides, with the old Roman trade route from Cologne to Boulogne as its aorta, later the line along which the language border would crystallize. That way of looking at things is really a matter of convenience and Pirenne's penchant for discerning deep anthropological structures behind the historical events seems outdated nowadays. But it does enable Pirenne to make the present Belgian state the subject of great history, which stretches back well before 1830, and to extract the country from the dilemma of the all-dominant Germanic-Romanic divide. Because that is what Pirenne realized quite clearly: language borders and former Roman borders are not absolute fixities. They crack, overlap, and shift – and they form the areas of cultural exchange and cross-pollination that make Europe worthwhile. In that respect Pirenne is a precursor of Adenauer; both refused to be pinned down to Romanic-Germanic Procrustean beds.

Borderstone (now between Belgium and France) from the 18th century with the French Lilies
© Michiel Hendryckx

The most moving and edifying example of this sort of position can be found on the German border near the outskirts of Aachen. There was a small area there, which, owing to its rich deposits of zinc ore, was kept out of the geopolitical carve-up at the Congress of Vienna. From 1815 to 1914 Moresnet was a neutral condominium, a microcosm of the Low Countries, as the Low Countries are a microcosm of Europe. The residents there decided round 1900 to declare themselves the first Esperanto-speaking community in the world, under the name 'Amikejo', land of friends.

Obviously that was not enough to turn the tide of world history. In August 1914 it was precisely there, near Gemmenich, that the German armies crossed the Belgian border, not far from the Voerstreek, which was to remain an obstacle in Belgian communal politics until well into the twentieth century. But one hundred years later, the touching idealism of the inhabitants of Amikejo, their deconstruction of the Germanic-Romanic dilemma, offers people of the 21st century more inspiration than the muscular language of Jules Destrée or Hugo Verriest.

Those who draw borders create borderline cases. It is characteristic of Europe that, given the multiplicity of languages on this continent, its territory is criss-crossed by a veritable web of linguistic and cultural borders - *un enchevêtrement de frontières*, as Paul Hazard (born in Noordpeene) called it. Most Europeans know what it means to live near a border, and in the proximity of foreigners and/or people who speak a different language. Those who want to tighten up the borders or totalize them (like Louis XIV, or the architects of the Germanic-Romanic divide or their followers, the fantasts who want to split Belgium up between the Netherlands and France) impoverish the seed-bed of Europe's cultural wealth. The best Europeans are those who know how to live with borders and in border areas, and who realise that we should demand intercultural tolerance not only of other people, but especially of ourselves. ∎

Translated by Lindsay Edwards

Stranded on the Border of the Promised Land

Ostend's Transit Migration Problem

[TOM CHRISTIAENS]

Since the 19th century, artists have allowed themselves to be seduced by the charms of the Belgian seaside resort of Ostend. But in recent years, the seaport has also been a magnet for refugees trying to cross the Channel to England illegally, in search of a better life. However, the gate to the promised land is heavily barred and bolted for these transit migrants.

'This evening, I'll risk it again,' Cucy says determinedly. For the third time already he will try to board a lorry that is going to cross the Channel by ferry to Ramsgate, in Great Britain. Will he, as is so often the case, cut open the canvas of a semi-trailer, or cling onto an undercarriage? And how is he hoping to outwit the CO_2 scanners, the heartbeat detectors and the police dogs? Too many questions and not a single answer. Cucy holds his cards close to his chest. 'The police can read my mind.' The 45-year-old Tunisian had worked for the previous five years as a taxi-driver in London, but when his work permit was not renewed, he was deported from the country. 'I want to be with my wife and daughter. Is that so abnormal?'
Cucy is one of the dozens of paperless refugees who try every day to reach England via the port of Ostend. They are called transit migrants, since they are birds of passage. They mainly come from Morocco, Tunisia, Egypt, Algeria, Palestine and Iraq and have fled from their homeland for political or social reasons. One of these is homosexuality, but talking about this with them is taboo. In recent years it has been striking that one out of ten fortune-hunters is a minor. Twelve-year-old children are no longer an exception.
Just how many of these undocumented travellers live in the seaside resort nobody knows for sure. Just under fifty, the town administration asserts – 250 according to the CAW, the only organisation on the Belgian coast that takes care of illegal aliens. The police and welfare organisations are well aware that the number of transit migrants in Ostend has greatly increased in recent years. The Belgian and French coastlines function in this respect as communicating vessels. 'Because of the tough dissuasive policy in Calais, and certainly since the closing of the refugee camp in Sangatte, they more often come to Ostend,' the head of CAW, Tine Syns, states. 'It's like seagulls. If they are chased away from the centre of the town, they move to the suburbs. Transit migrants also move away from places where things get too hot.'

Drop-in centre

Ten o'clock. Now and then people walk into the CAW drop-in centre, in the heart of the town. While five minutes further on the latest fashion is being bought, here an old man is handing out sandwiches, yoghurt and apple juice to some refugees. The expiry dates of some of the products have already passed. Even so, the food is gratefully accepted. The Ostend man comes along every day with food packages. He was nearly nicknamed *Papa Noël* because of it. 'If he wasn't here, we'd all go hungry', says Ramzi in amazingly good English. 'For, forgive me for saying this, the Belgians are a cold lot, they don't care about people worse off than themselves. People spit and glower at us as if we were criminals.'

Ramzi fled from Tunisia and ended up in Ostend via France. You find him every morning at the drop-in centre. To eat, for a cup of coffee, to take a shower, to relax in front of the computer or TV, or simply to wile away his loneliness. Every Tuesday, a legal adviser visits the drop-in centre, and on Thursdays a nurse to provide minor medical assistance. Those seriously ill are referred to local doctors, who often treat them for free. 'The centre is the only place where we feel safe and are not constantly harassed,' says Ramzi, who has his leg in plaster. 'Broke it when I had to run from the police.'

Every morning, the CAW is paid a visit by about 60 undocumented migrants. In the afternoon, the centre is open for deprived Ostenders. This calls for streamlined assistance. Sometimes the demand for help is greater than the welfare workers can cope with. Particularly in spring, when there are the most transit migrants in Ostend – between 300 and 500, according to the CAW – it is all hands on deck at the drop-in centre. Then harsh words may be uttered, and small fires need to be put out. For anyone staying in a foreign country and suffering from hunger can get desperate from time to time and prepared to violate regulations. Even so, no criminal behaviour is tolerated at the centre apparently. Refugees who go too far – stealing a roll can sometimes lead to a brawl – will be dealt with by the group itself.

'We, too, as a welfare organisation, have had to learn how to treat this new group of paperless people,' Tine Wyns says. When the CAW came into contact with transit migrants for the first time, in 2008, there was considerable tension between the migrants, the staff and the local homeless. In 2010 the pressure was off for a while, when, with the aid of subsidies from the Flemish authorities, it was possible to open a separate day centre for the undocumented migrants. But these subsidies were a one-off measure, and the centre had to close again after a year.

Today, the transit migrants form a fixed group within the operations of the Ostend CAW. But apart from a small provincial subsidy, the organisation received no extra money from the authorities because of this. 'You may wonder whether transit migrants really belong to our target group. After all, they are travelling through and do not intend to stay here.' Tine Wyns raises the question purely rhetorically. 'The CAW has the mission to help those most vulnerable in our society. We make no distinction on the basis of statute or land of origin. Which is why we also take in these undocumented people. No matter how much flak we occasionally get for doing so. It is claimed, for example, that the help we give entices more refugees to Ostend. Rubbish, of course. As long as there is a port here, people will want to try to cross the Channel to England via our town.'

'A family, a small house, a job and peace of mind – is that too much to ask?' Hossion repeats this probably three times while hiding his tear-stained face in his hands. The Algerian is only 23, but all hopes of a better future seem lost. He has tuberculosis, a disease that is found in people living in poverty and bad conditions.

Hamid Hisari knows them all – the dramatic account of people stranded in Ostend. As an intercultural intermediary, he is their most important contact person at the CAW. They knock on his door for help with issues related to food, housing, medicine and legal dossiers – or simply to pour out their troubles. 'On the run and in search of a better life. All refugees tell the same story,' Hisari says. 'The story of their life is often so harrowing that it becomes implausible and they have to tone down the facts if anyone is to believe them.'

It all sounds familiar to Hisari, for he himself is a political refugee from Afghanistan. His brother and eleven other family members have all been murdered, and he has not heard anything from his father since he was abducted in 2001. Four years ago he arrived in Belgium with a diploma in political and social sciences and international relations in his pocket. He speaks no less than nine languages, including Russian, Arabic and Dutch. There are only a few migrants in Ostend that the CAW intermediary cannot talk with. And they also confide a great deal to him.

Most of the refugees are still in contact with their family. But what they tell the home front does not always tally with reality. 'When they ring their parents, they often give a rosier picture of the situation than is the case,' Hisari relates. 'Since their parents have often paid a hefty sum of money for their journey – sometimes to human traffickers – they do not want to disappoint them. They are also too ashamed to admit that they have to survive in Belgium under bad conditions. Some of them dare not return, because they have borrowed money from their family for the journey and are no longer able to pay it back.'

The migrants who are able to speak without fear emphasise that they have no greater wish than to remain in their own country. 'Believe it or not,' Tunisian Ramzi says,' I fled because it was dangerous. I won't return until my country is once more a democracy. Then I will pick up my former life once again.'

But before that comes about, these transit migrants have set their sights on only one destination: England. And Ostend is the port to freedom, to their

promised land. Some of them talk about it as if it were a paradise – the new Valhalla. And do not dare readjust that picture. 'Often it is all they have to hold on to, their only hope of survival,' Hisari says. Most of the migrants want to go to England because they have family and friends there, because they believe that there are loads of jobs there, and particularly because they say they will not be constantly 'harassed' by the police.

Dissuasive policy

Police: no word evokes more anger and fear in the Ostend refugees. Police are said to let their dogs loose on them to maul them, to beat up illegal aliens, pee on their clothes, tear up the Koran, throw them naked into cells and leave them

there for days without food or drink.

Philip Caestecker, superintendent of the Ostend police, knows the grim stories that circulate about his units – and they irritate him immensely. 'How many times do we have to defend ourselves against such fabrications? I can understand that the police don't arouse much sympathy among the illegal migrants and certain welfare organisations, but I'm fed up with us being portrayed as monsters and man-hunters.'

An enquiry conducted by Comité P, the external body that controls Belgian policing, exonerated the police almost entirely of all allegations.

'You know, I really do understand the difficult humanitarian situation in which many of these refugees find themselves,' Superintendent Caestecker says. 'They are sometimes poor souls who have paid suspect characters a fortune to get to Belgium. I can even manage to understand a person stealing because he is hungry, though that doesn't mean I approve of it. But the law is the law, and facts do not lie. In recent years, more and more illegal transit migrants have come to Ostend and are increasingly causing trouble and committing petty crimes. They also increase the feeling of insecurity in the town. As a police force, we have the task of dealing with criminal offences and tracking down people who are staying in this country without a valid permit.'

And the officials responsible for order, the port and town authorities, are doing so by means of an increasingly active dissuasive policy. In autumn 2011, Operation Zephyr began. Local police units and the maritime police search specifically for transit migrants several times a week. Anyone unable to produce their papers is rounded up, locked up for a maximum of 24 hours and on release is ordered by the Immigration Service to leave the country. Almost a year after the launching of Operation Zephyr, the police had carried out over a thousand arrests during almost 100 operations, an average of ten refugees per operation.

The harbour area itself has been more heavily secured in order to keep out undesired visitors. Last year, €400,000 was invested in new high fences and hi-tech cameras, so that today the harbour area is a sealed-off island.

Reports appear in the press that cast doubt on the results of the Ostend dissuasive policy. In the summer of 2012 it was said that during the first half of the year 374 illegal migrants were picked up in the port of Ostend. That was 40% lower than during the same period the previous year. The reason for the decrease was not immediately apparent, but the town expressed satisfaction with the results. The police also announced a marked fall in the number of thefts from cars. Many property crimes in Ostend, car break-ins and shoplifting in particular, are blamed on people without papers. As a result of the tightened controls, the police also noted fewer buildings broken into by squatters in the town centre and a reduced feeling of insecurity.

Even so, refugees continue every day to play a cat-and-mouse game with the police, in the hope of being able to climb unseen aboard a ferry for England. 'Since the police have stepped up controls, the number of migrants in Ostend has not fallen; it is just that they are less visible in the street scene because they hide themselves away better and come out less during the daytime,' says CAW employee Hisari. 'They now walk around in smaller groups so as to be less conspicuous. But they still want to get to England, that hasn't changed. Every month probably another thirty may make the crossing.'

The transit migrants also find better ways of getting round the harbour controls. They avoid the CO_2 scanners by breathing out into plastic bags, and put the apparatus that detects heartbeats on the wrong track by wrapping themselves in aluminium foil.

Police Superintendent Philip Caestecker also knows about these techniques. He admits that the dissuasive policy in Ostend offers no structural solution for the transit migration issue in his town. 'You won't hear me saying that as a result of our campaign to tighten things up there are fewer undocumented people in Ostend,'

Caestecker says. 'I can only state that we have got the negative consequences of their being here – the nuisance and petty crime – under control, and have even been able to reduce them. The problem of transit migration, and probably that of the organised networks of human smugglers and traffickers, is one that the politicians will have to resolve at an international level. As long as nothing happens there, we are simply beating our head against a brick wall.'

The welfare workers often use this expression as well when transit migration is the subject of conversation. Hisari doesn't mince matters: 'Transit migration is an insoluble problem, but not a single politician dares touch it with a bargepole, for it doesn't win any votes,' he states firmly. 'An organisation must be set up as soon as possible that provides these transit migrants with better information about their situation, offers them legal advice, discusses their possibilities on the labour market, and gives them a realistic picture of the European countries of which they have such a utopic view. In that way, you prepare them for a return to their own country.'

Rubbish dump

'Not even a dozen scanners and cameras will stop me getting across to England,' Hossion predicts. The former policeman, who claims he fled Iraq after death threats, was stranded in Ostend after peregrinations via Greece and France. He has already been here a year.

Would I like to know what he does during the daytime to kill the time? In the morning he goes to the drop-in centre to freshen up, in the afternoon he looks for a place to sleep. He is prepared to show me his hiding place. Along with his Algerian friend Moustafa they walk through the harbour area, past large cranes and boats, and hundreds of metres of fences spiked with barbed wire. 'This is my five-star hotel,' says Hossion, pointing at a deserted shed. 'This is where I slept last night, along with three others, until the police chased us out this morning.' A dirty mattress amidst rubble, discarded furniture and rats. A rubbish dump - that is the best way of describing his sleeping place. Moustafa asks me to take a photo: 'Otherwise people won't believe us. Everyone thinks we tell lies and lead a life of ease here – but this is the reality.'

Hossion and Moustafa show me some other sleeping places: a rusty sloop, a collapsed warehouse, an empty house. On the run from the police, they have to sleep at a different location every night, in and around the harbour or in the town centre. In the Maria-Hendrikapark – known in Ostend as 't Bosje – dozens of people without papers used to stay. Since the police have been checking it regularly, it has become a no-go zone for the homeless.

We stop for a while on the bridge by the harbour. 'Every day we come here to look at the ferry,' Moustafa says. 'One day, it will take us with it to England.' What follows is an account of the beauty of London. His GSM interrupts his account. News from the other side: the previous night, four Algerians managed to reach Ramsgate. Moustafa's eyes gleam with hope. 'Have you ever seen Big Ben?' Before I can even answer, the two refugees nervously make off, in different directions. A police car comes into view. ∎

Translated by John Irons

Along the *Limes*

The Frontier of the Imperium Romanum in the Netherlands

Imperium Romanum
ca. 200 A.D.

*Here a wretched race is found, inhabiting either the more elevated spots of land,
or else eminences artificially constructed, and of a height to which they know by
experience that the highest tides will never reach. Here they pitch their cabins; and
when the waves cover the surrounding country far and wide, like so many mariners
on board ship are they: when, again, the tide recedes, their condition is that of so
many shipwrecked men, and around their cottages they pursue the fishes as they
make their escape with the receding tide.'*
Pliny the Elder, *Naturalis Historia*, 16, 1, 3 (ca. 47 AD)
(translated by John Bostock and H.T. Riley (1855))

'Did you know that the Netherlands and Egypt were once part of the same
empire?' my companion asks the lad ferrying us across the Old Rhine at Valkenburg, between Leiden and Katwijk. We had cycled here from Leiden. What
must once have been the most northerly branch of a mighty and unpredictable
river was now reduced to a modest and pleasant stream.

'It must have been a very old empire, then,' the boy answers solemnly. We
tell him that with this crossing we are now leaving that empire, but he just
stares at us as though flabbergasted.

Seen from this ferry in the orderly, planned and tamed landscape of the central Netherlands, it takes a while before you become aware of the landscape
from the beginning of our era that the Romans found between Katwijk, Leiden, Utrecht and Arnhem. At that time this branch of the Rhine wound its way
through the country as the northernmost arm of a mighty river that split into
a delta before emptying into the North Sea. The skies above it were cloudy for
most of the year; it rained there and it blew, the land was low-lying marshland
with mounds known as terps rising out of it.

In the sixth decade before Christ Julius Caesar became the first Roman to march as far as the Low Countries with his legions. Twice he crossed the Rhine in Germany. Twice he crossed the Channel to England from a French beach. By about 50 BC he had defeated and subjected the Celtic and Germanic tribes he encountered on his way through France and what is now Belgium. For him it was partly a matter of *Lebensraum*, but his main purpose was to harden his legions and bind them to him. Those legions would make him the most powerful man in Rome. He was murdered in 44 BC and after a civil war his great-nephew and adopted son Octavian achieved absolute power as the Emperor Augustus. During his reign the Romans returned to the Low Countries around 15 BC, this time in a more methodical and organised way. The intention was nothing less than to cross the Rhine, conquer the Germanic tribes and expand the Empire as far as the Elbe. As their base for the assault the generals chose Nijmegen on the Waal, the southern arm of the Rhine. Augustus' stepson Drusus was

Hadrian's Wall
© Michiel Hendryckx

the senior general. He had canals dug and dams constructed which affected water-levels in the Delta - to the dismay of the native population. The Romans were thus the first creators of the Dutch landscape. And they must have made a great impression on the local Germanic tribes: they were shorter of stature, but well-drilled, organised and equipped with technically superior weapons. The brave but undisciplined rabble of Batavians (in the Betuwe) and Cannefatans (in North and South Holland) was no match for them on the field of battle.

Tour of inspection

In the early years of the second century AD a Roman officer who would later become Emperor made a tour of the Rhine forts. He went to learn and to inspect. I have decided to follow in his footsteps. Using the *Tabula Peutingeriana* as my guide and mentor. The *Tabula* is a medieval copy of a late-Roman road map, which you

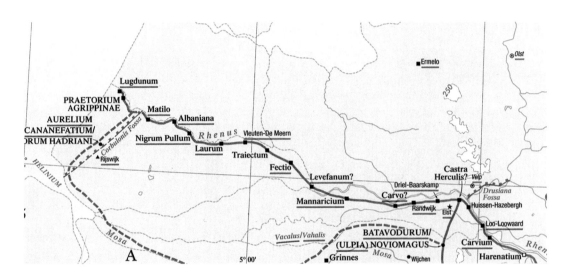

have to read in the same way as a metro map: from one stop to the next. From this map I select Lugdunum (Katwijk); Praetorium Agrippinae (Valkenburg); Matilo (Leiden, Roomburg); Albaniana (Alphen aan de Rijn); Castra Herculis (Arnhem?); Noviomagus (Nijmegen); Colonia Ulpia Traiana and Vetera (Xanten).

Barrington Atlas of the Greek and Roman World, edited by Richard J.A. Talbert. Detail

After Drusus' early death in 9 BC his brother Tiberius took over operations on the Rhine and consolidated the Roman positions. Tiberius was a careful and systematic general. His successor Varus was less so. In the notorious battle of the Teutoburgerwald (which actually took place in Kalkriese near Osnabrück) in 9 AD, the Germans made mincemeat of his three legions. Varus was killed and the legionary standards, the famous Eagles, were captured by the Germans. The disaster almost proved too much for the aged Emperor Augustus. The policy of expansion was abandoned. The Romans pulled back across the Rhine.

I cycled from Leiden to Katwijk, once a solidly orthodox Christian village of fishermen, market gardeners and, in summer, holidaymakers, who took over the whole place. Today there are very few fishermen and the market gardeners have also disappeared. Above the dunes gleams the golden dome of a Sufi temple,

challenging the Bible. Only the holidaymakers remain. The esplanade looked dank and dejected. The river mouth itself is silted up and subdued, trapped in sluices, obliterated by *Waterstaat* (the Water Management Agency). Yet this is *Lugdunum Batavorum*, the furthest guard post on the northern frontier of the Roman province of *Germania inferior*.

Somewhere here, if we are to believe Suetonius, in the late 30s AD Caligula declared war on the sea. He drew up his legions on the beach, had catapults and siege equipment brought up. Did he want to copy Caesar, who had twice travelled to England? He boarded a trireme, put to sea and returned to the beach. Then he sat on a podium, just like King Xerxes, who in 480 BC observed the sea-battle between the Greeks and Persians at Salamis from a position on land. Then he had the trumpets sounded and finally commanded his soldiers ... to collect shells and fill their helmets and the pockets of their clothing with them. 'This is the booty which the ocean owes to Rome and its Emperor.' To commemorate his victory he had a tall lighthouse constructed on which fires would burn at night to guide ships on their way.

A storm in 1520 exposed the ruins of that lighthouse on Katwijk beach. A 1581 woodcut by Ortelius shows an imposing square ground plan: a base 72 meters square on which would have stood a lighthouse sixty meters in height, later (under Charlemagne?) surrounded by an additional wall.

Now it has all been engulfed by the sea, and all we can do is peer at a spot there in the water. Long ago Katwijk folk used to tell how their nets would regularly get caught on stones from what they called 'Kalla's tower'. It sounds too good to be true. Caligula's lighthouse? An imitation of the *Pharos* of Alexandria on this Dutch beach: sixty metres high?

That Caligula probably did visit the mouth of the Rhine is apparent from a wine-cask found in the area which originates from his personal vineyard. But did Caligula do his shadow-boxing here? Didn't he have shells collected in the vicinity of Boulogne? Was that submerged ruin really once a lighthouse? Wasn't it perhaps a granary? And did it later become a customs fort, the 'Brittenburg', the 'fort' at Britten, which was demolished after the Old Rhine silted up around 1000 AD?

Under Caligula's successor, Emperor Claudius (41-54), the north-western frontier of the Empire was further fortified. Twenty-four *castella*, or forts, were built along the Rhine.

Archeon. Alphen aan de Rijn
© Jeroen Wijnands

Twenty-four hours later I am standing on Corbulo Quay in Voorburg (Forum Hadriani) beside the river Vliet. The streets in this tranquil area – a well-heeled middle-class suburb – not far from The Hague are named for Hadrian and Aggripina.

In the late 40s of the first century AD Corbulo had a canal a good thirty kilometres long dug between the Rhine and the Maas so that the Romans would no longer have to travel by sea. Today the canal flows peacefully along, with trees hanging over and boats bobbing on it.

A little later I shall see the canal again in the Roomburg district of Leiden, when I stand on the quayside of Matilo military camp. There is no water, but somewhere here the Corbulo Canal must have joined the Rhine. A replica of a sunken boat has been set up there. Further on some green water is turning into a pool or a fishpond.

Here in Roomburg the fort has been rendered visible within a park. A cautious approach has been employed. Between the apartment blocks, the children's playground and the vegetable gardens lies the ground plan of the Matilo *castellum*. I like this minimalist approach: it shows you only the area the fort occupied, you have to imagine the walls and watchtowers, the water in the canals for yourself. You walk along the straight streets of the camp, which cross each other at perfect right angles. There is almost nobody here, just a woman with a walking frame, a jogger, a carrier tricycle with six children propelled by two women. Ravens settle on the clods of ploughed earth.

In 69 AD the Batavians, led by Julius Civilis, rebelled against the Romans. It so happened that after the death of Nero in 68 several generals were competing for the imperial crown, and the Batavians took advantage of this. All the *castella* along the Rhine were destroyed. But the Romans always come back. Those who submit are spared. Those who resist are destroyed.

After being defeated Julius Civilis negotiated his surrender on a wrecked bridge over a river ('Nabalia') in the land of rivers. Was this a bridge over the Waal, the Rhine or the Maas? We don't know. The surviving text of Tacitus' *Historiae* breaks off in mid-sentence at the start of the negotiations. Civilis expresses his admiration for Emperor Vespasian and describes him as his friend. What else did the defeated resistance fighter/terrorist say to the Roman general Cerialis? What happened to him? Was he pardoned? Banished? Or simply murdered and thrown in the river? Whatever their leader's fate, the Batavians were back under the Roman yoke. Not long afterwards they were again valued allies of Rome, free of taxation and providers of loyal elite troops.

When Hadrian makes his inspection tour of the Low Countries in the summer of 121 he orders soldiers to be recruited from the local population: clear proof of the Romanisation of the area. He also has a road built from Katwijk to Xanten on a dike that runs along the ring of forts. Everything is rebuilt and strengthened. And then it's a matter of waiting for history to catch up with this frontier.

With the first tsunami of barbarian invasions, beginning in 240, the forts on the Empire's northern frontier were abandoned. The rising water-level in the Rhine probably also played a part in this. It is no coincidence that the coins found in the ruins of the Brittenburg near Katwijk date from no later than 270 AD.

Re-enactment

Archeon is the first historical theme-park on the *limes*. It is located in Alphen aan de Rijn where once stood the *castellum Albaniana*. Here for a fee one can see 'slices of life' from Prehistory, Roman times and the Middle Ages. The Roman times turn out to begin very precisely in 12 BC (more or less the moment when the legions first turned up here, though that was mainly to prepare for a crossing of the Rhine). That period ends in 406. We know that on New Year's Eve 405-406 Germanic tribes crossed the frozen Rhine near Mainz and poured into Gaul. The beginning of the end.

In the car park a legionary in full kit is on duty to set the tone: 'Good morning, sir'. Posters ask me: 'How Roman are you?' and 'Have you got Roman blood in your veins?' I don't want to know. In the park I bump into a bunch of middle-aged Englishmen marching themselves somewhat stiffly into a sweat. The orders – yelled in Latin – are supposed to turn this *cohors Britannica* into a smoothly operating unit that will impress tourists with its *esprit de corps*. The attendants in sandals and tunics are getting ready for the day's work. A young woman whose roots clearly lie in the 'warm parts of the kingdom', but who has to look like a Roman matron here and now, tells me that the cohors descends on the park every few years. Complete with wives and children. The latter sell trinkets in the little shops by the bathhouse while their men play at being Romans. The woman herself had studied art history in Utrecht and done her dissertation on Mesopotamia. Yes, this is her full-time job. And she clearly enjoys it. Re-playing history. Re-enactment. In *Archeon* one can also visit a tavern and a temple. And in the afternoon, she tells me, I can watch a genuine gladiatorial combat. But the *limes* calls. And I travel on past Zwammerdam (*Nigropullum*, Black Hen!) and Bodegraven, whose *castellum* has yet to be discovered, to Laurium. Otherwise Woerden, occupied by the French in the disaster year of 1672 despite being part of Holland's waterline. Here I go in search of *Parking Castellum*. In this underground car park the results of the excavations are shown on a handful of boards and display cases. Four Roman river craft have been found here, but the wood was so soggy and rotten that it proved impossible to salvage them. A bit later I am sitting on a terrace in the market next to Sint Petrus Church and studying today's Batavians: tall, friendly, with their eyes wide open. This tribe produces sporting heroes and Olympic medallists in profusion. The girls who

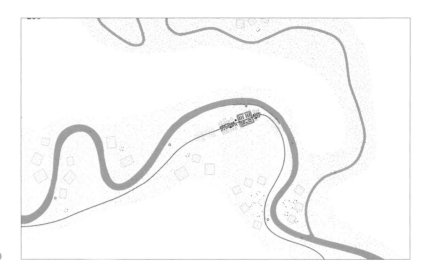

Utrecht A.D. 200

wait on the customers are blonde, efficient and transparent. Their t-shirts label them *(h)eerlijk* (fair), *(bio)logisch* ((bio)logical) and *'natuur(lijk)* (natur(al)), and so they are. Cycling across the church square come some Turkish Dutchmen. Or so I assume, from the dark creases in their faces and their meticulously trimmed moustaches. Woerden is reputed to be the most average town in the Netherlands. This is where people test new products and try to plumb the soul of the people. The town has everything, from a prayer house to a cannabistro (sic!). When I move on, I discover I have been sitting on the wall of the castellum: a line marking its outer wall runs diagonally across the market square.

I leave Vleuten (Fletio) and the Hoge Woerd *castellum* in Leidsche Rijn on my left and head for Utrecht. The town welcomes me with a cloudburst, thunder and lightning. Looming above the Amsterdam-Rhine Canal is the office block of *Waterstaat*. In this part of the world it was the Romans who first tamed the water and safeguarded the land. Two millennia later the Dutch have perfected their work: '... their tireless hands manufactured this land, / drained it and trained it and planed it and planned', to quote the English poet James Brockway who found refuge in this country after the last war.

On Cathedral Square in Utrecht is a milepost which says that Vleuten – De Meern is 7.8 kilometres away and Fectio (Vechten) is 6.22. Within the *castellum* that the Romans built here in a bend of the Rhine, further protected by the Vecht, there now stands the cathedral and its tower. *Traiectum*, a crossing-point. From here the Anglo-Saxon Willibrord converted the Frisians to Christianity in around 700 AD. The Catholic cathedral became a Reformed church in the sixteenth century, though in 1672 the French made it Catholic again for a year. Today it is a fair-trade church and one can hire it. To the Catholic boy I once was that still seems a bit odd. As you walk round the church you stumble on the metal strips in the paving which demarcate the walls of the Roman fort and light up in the dark. The university faculties of humanities and law still lie more or less inside the fort. In the late sixteenth century the *Église wallonne* behind the cathedral, the old Sint Petrus, received the first Protestant refugees from Tournai and, a century later, French Huguenots. Today the third wave consists of Africans who have fled their French-speaking countries. Rome no longer

Utrecht A.D. 2000

has any say in the *castellum*, but the clergy still speak a Latin language there.

Trying to place the *castellum* in the centre of this much-expanded city, I seek the north, where the Rhine was. Perhaps the Oude Gracht, Utrecht's longest dining table, is a small branch of the Rhine which once protected the western side of the *castellum*. Be that as it may, that evening I sit beside it and enjoy pasta provided by an Italian from the Veneto. From time to time he throws some bread in the water to stir the ducks from their lethargy and suddenly rouses swarms of seagulls – the most shameless of all birds, and now everywhere to be found. It turns out that the cathedral tower has a carillon and canoes slip past. The urban idyll of a summer evening in the heart of the Netherlands, one of the most densely populated and most prosperous parts of the world, has long ago supplanted the edge of the world, the endless morass, the desolation of the terp.

Over the dike

Right next to the motorway sits Fort Fectio, hermetically sealed within an orchard belonging to the Province of Utrecht. 'They won't let you stick a spade in the ground', says the lady from the *Werk aan de Linie* (Work on the Line) Foundation in the other fort next to it. Fort Vechten is part of the new Dutch waterline built in the nineteenth century to protect the Randstad against enemies from the east and south. Artillery, and especially aircraft, would have no trouble bypassing this line. The fort itself is the property of *Staatsbosbeheer* (the forestry commission) and is hidden from sight by water and trees, but nowadays *Werk aan de Linie* is permitted to let out the casemates for parties and celebrations.

Levefanum was once a Roman *castellum* at the junction of the (Crooked) Rhine and the Lek. Today Wijk bij Duurstede is a pleasant little town that maintains the high water level in its harbour by means of a metal gate. The castle was the residence of the bishops of Utrecht. Ruysdael painted a mill there.

In the early Middle Ages there was a flourishing trading post here by the River Dorestad on the border between the Franks and the Frisians. The Vikings came and looted it. Towards the end of the ninth century the settlement gradually dwindled away.

It takes me a while to realise that since the time of the *limes* the course of the rivers has changed. The fort stood on the other side of the water, south of the Lek, in the water-meadows near Rijswijk.

I take the car ferry across the river and drive past Rijswijk to Maurik (Manna-ricium). From there I take the Rhine Dike past Kesteren (Carvo) to Randwijk and Driel. Here the once majestic Rhine retains only its waywardness and the expansive water-meadows which hide the river itself from view.

Before Arnhem (Castra Herculis?) I turn south and head for Nijmegen, the key point in the defence of *Germania inferior*. Next morning I am standing on the Kops Plateau outside the town. A woman taking her dog for a walk takes me to the spot where I can see the dead-flat Ooi polder stretching all the way to the Waal. Did Drusus stand here about 12 BC, estimating his chances of conquering the vast lands on the other side of the Rhine?

'We're standing on a lateral moraine,' the woman says. 'In the Ice Age huge quantities of earth and stones were pushed as far as this by the advancing ice. The ice stopped here, and when it melted it left these hills.'

On the Ubber country road – the very same road which ran behind the *limes* from Katwijk to Cologne – I happen upon the Porta Romana, which is now an apartment block. On the street corner a short film tells me that this was the site of one of the gates of the army camp where the Tenth Legion was based in the first century.

I abandon my search for the bridge where Julius Civilis negotiated with the Roman general Cerialis and drive from Nijmeghen to Xanten (Vetera) in Germany. The Thirtieth Legion Ulpia Victrix, founded by Trajan and named for his victories in Romania, was quartered here from 122 and would remain here for about two hundred years. Alongside the camp a town grew up: Colonia Ulpia Traiana.

The decline set in with the silting up of the Rhine around 250 AD and the German incursions. In the fourth century the inhabitants retreated into a part of the town then known as Tricensima.

In the late eighth century people came on pilgrimage ad sanctos, 'to the saints', to Xanten, to the graves of holy martyrs in the town's cathedral. One of these was Victor, a converted legionary.

In Xanten the Germans have opted for reconstructing the Roman town: here one can see walls and towers, a tavern and a port temple, a genuine amphitheatre where the Egyptian props for a performance of Aïda contrast with the cathedral towers behind them. There is a brand new museum. Everything is neat and tidy. Too neat and tidy for my taste.

The shifting *limes*

On New Year's Eve 405-6 the *limes* was overrun once and for all when Vandals, Alans and Suevians crossed the frozen Rhine near Mainz and swarmed into Gaul. Four years later Rome would be sacked for the first time since 390 BC by the Visigoth Alaric. The Romans pulled out of the Rhineland and left the defence of their northern frontier to the Franks. Nominally these remained loyal subjects of Rome. They continued to speak Latin, but in reality they were now sovereign and would extend their authority southwards.

Looking at the historical *limes* in the Netherlands of today, one can only conclude that it never was a hermetically sealed frontier. From Claudius on, the Romans used the Rhine as an artery for the transport of trade goods and troops. The remains of freight-carriers have been found at Zwammerdam, Alphen aan den Rijn, Woerden and Utrecht. Like Hadrian's Wall in Northern England, the *limes* was rather a line where the movement of goods and people could be regulated, a way of demonstrating, here at the edge of the world, that one was a world power.

When I was in Xanten I briefly considered taking a boat to Cologne: *Colonia Agrippina*, the capital of *Germania inferior*, linked to Boulogne by a network of military roads (the most northerly branch of which was the line Cassel, Courtrai, Velzeke, Asse, Tienen and Tongeren). It is said that, some time after the invasions in the mid-third century, the Romans withdrew behind this line and used the area to the north of it as a buffer zone, at most retaining the friendship of the Germanic tribes who lived there. Around this last line of defence, this last *limes*, the language frontier gradually crystallised: to the north of it people

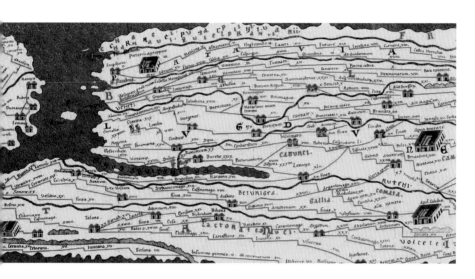

Tabula Peutingeriana (ca. 1200). Codex Vindobonensis 324. Nationalbibliothek, Vienna. Detail

would eventually speak a Germanic language, to the south a Romance language derived from Latin. And today that limes runs diagonally through Belgium. It is often said that that line, and Belgium itself, still marks the transition between Northern and Southern Europe, between the Latin and the Germanic world. But that is another story. ■

Translated by Tanis Guest

FURTHER READING

Philip Parker, *The Empire Stops Here. A Journey along the Frontiers of the Roman World*, Pimlico, London 2010.

Limes Atlas, Redactie Bernard Colenbrander, Uitgeverij 010, Rotterdam 2005.

Jona Lendering and Arjen Bosman, *De rand van het Rijk. De Romeinen en de Lage Landen*, Athenaeum-Polak & Van Gennep, Amsterdam,2010.

www.limes.nl

www.entoen.nu/romeinselimes

Towards a Diploma Democracy?

The Gulf between the Population and the New Regents

[MARC HOOGHE]

The second half of the 20th century will go down in history as the era of the educational revolution. University campuses throughout the Low Countries were expanded, more polytechnics were built, and the average education level rose visibly. Women, in particular, made up their centuries-long educational disadvantage relative to men within the space of a few decades. The benefits to society of this educational revolution have already been described at some length: Belgium and the Netherlands have evolved into knowledge economies, in which the services sector is much more important than industry.

At the same time, however, this increase in the average education level in the Low Countries has led to the drawing of new social boundaries. To simplify somewhat, a century ago a highly educated person was still the exception rather than the rule. In a typical rural village, only the doctor, the notary and the pastor had enjoyed a higher education; the education level of the rest of the population was much lower. The situation today appears actually to be reversed. For the younger age groups, in particular, going on to higher education has become the norm. Although less well-educated people have not become the 'exception', they are becoming increasingly marginalised. This is the unexpected side-effect of the trend towards a meritocracy, in which everyone is judged on their own merits. If we look back to the period before the 1960s, a person's education level was determined by that of their parents and by their social position. Even highly intelligent children could end up in vocational education if their parents happened to come from a less favourable social milieu. Today too, of course, there are enormous social inequalities in terms of participation in higher education, but the system has at least become far more objective than a few decades ago. Constant evaluations and an increase in support for pupils have meant that most children are now in the most appropriate form of education for them. This means that there is often no excuse for someone who ends up in a lower education track - they simply lack academic skills. Naturally, such a meritocratic education system is highly desirable. We want people to be judged on their own abilities, not on the size of their parents' bank account. At the same time, however, this means that the boundary between those with a high and those with a low level of education has become much harder to cross. The image of the highly intelligent and promising young people who received insufficient schooling because of the poverty of their parents, but who later worked their way up through dedication and evening classes, has largely disappeared from modern society.

Meritocracy

The line separating the highly educated from the poorly educated is therefore much more hermetic than in the past, and this is reflected clearly in the political system. In the past, the socialist parties, in particular, produced a number of politicians with working class backgrounds, often recruited via the trade union movement. That recruitment channel has completely dried up today. A glance at the Dutch or Belgian parliaments reveals row after row of very well-educated ladies and gentlemen, who are, in many cases, capable of reading a legislative text or even understanding

Edelare, 1994
© Stephan Vanfleteren

a budget. The Belgian House of Representatives contains just one member with genuine experience of physical labour. At first sight, this seems to be a sign of progress; the quality of our Members of Parliament has improved considerably in recent decades. The average MP is now younger, better educated, more active and also more often female than several decades ago. At the same time, however, this stricter selection means that our politicians have lost some of their affinity with social reality. After all, we expect our Members of Parliament to genuinely represent – and therefore reflect – the population. That is the ultimate argument for having more women in senior political positions. As more than half the population are women, our assumption is that women should also have a substantial share in operating the levers of political power. However, our reasoning changes when it comes to inequality in education level. We appear not to mind at all that members of the working class have disappeared entirely from Parliament. Despite the fact that the share taken by industry in total employment has declined, there is of course

Maurice Lippens, adminis-
trator, banker, 2002
© Stephan Vanfleteren

Etienne Davignon, noble-
man, businessman, diplo-
mat, administrator, 2009
© Stephan Vanfleteren

still a large group of working-class people, and in many cases they still form the 'backbone of society'. It is just that it is no longer clear who represents them, or to whom they should turn. Should a blast furnace worker feel represented by a neatly dressed accountant who is able to explain to Parliament in fine detail the need for a new pension reform? For an office worker, having to continue working until the age of 67 is probably not an insurmountable obstacle, but someone who works as a labourer in industry probably has a slightly different take on the whole public and political debate about pensions.

This phenomenon of 'diploma democracy' has received a great deal of attention in recent years, especially in the work of the Dutch political scientists Mark Bovens and Anchrit Wille. Their thesis is that this phenomenon not only occurs among senior politicians, but is also a decisive factor in the entire functioning of political parties. Even at local party level, it is those with higher education qualifications who have the biggest say, and that means that someone with a lower education level now has virtually no means of influencing politics. Social democrats, in particular, are missing an opportunity here, because they have traditionally targeted a public which is receptive to socioeconomic policy that favours redistribution and a strong social security system. As a result, that public has become politically homeless.

Numerous studies have shown that parties on the left in Western Europe are having difficulty reaching their traditional supporters. If we just consider the socioeconomic contrasts that is a strange state of affairs. A less well-educated labour force has everything to gain from a strong social-democratic party that can influence government policy. But apart from this purely economic approach, culture and values obviously also play an important role in politics, and a broad gulf has developed in these areas between the parties of the left and their traditional supporters. That gulf is probably nowhere more evident than on the issue of integration and multiculturalism. Left-of-centre parties are generally radically opposed to racism and exclusion, and are strong advocates of a more multicultural society. That line of argument scores well among well-educated left-wing voters, who understand that society is becoming more culturally diverse and that this trend is not likely to change any time soon.

This is much less obvious to those with a lower level of education, and a clear dichotomy has accordingly developed between the 'traditional left' and the more progressive left-wing ideas that we typically find among the highly educated. In the first place, less well-educated people more often live in neighbourhoods that are regarded as less advantaged, where they are confronted more or less directly with the presence of different cultural groups in our towns and cities. On both the labour and housing markets, they are also much more exposed to competition from immigrants. There will not be many lawyers or doctors who lose their job to competition from someone from outside Western Europe, but for a lorry driver or textile worker that is part of everyday reality. This heightened competition helps explain why economically vulnerable groups more often have a negative attitude towards migration. In addition, a phenomenon that is found time and again in research is the very strong correlation between education level and racism. It is evidently much easier for someone with a low education level to harbour prejudices against groups who do not share the same culture.

When taken all together, these elements mean that a wide cultural gap has opened up between the senior echelons of the parties of the left and their traditional supporters. Those voters have accordingly turned en masse to extreme right-wing, xenophobic and populist parties, which with their direct language and uncompromising stance on migration clearly respond to the feelings of these largely less well-educated voters. The irony, of course, is that this has created yet another dichotomy: these right-wing or populist parties generally also take a negative stance on the power of the trade unions, whose job is precisely to defend the interests of the working classes. So far, however, these parties have managed to keep this dichotomy in the background, focusing in their communications almost exclusively on cultural and ethnic issues and saying virtually nothing about the economy and redistribution. Groups in society which would objectively benefit from more distribution can therefore still feel at home with an extreme right-wing or populist party.

The acceptance of inequality

Although the book by Bovens and Wille was very well received, articles in the scientific journal *Acta Politica* expressed a number of reservations about whether we are witnessing a genuinely new phenomenon. The research tradition on political participation has always pointed up social inequalities. As long ago as the 1950s, those with higher education levels participated in politics much more than the less well-educated. By its very nature, politics is about lots of meetings, debating, formulating ideas and trying to persuade others of their merits, and these are activities that more closely match the skills of those who have had a full educational career. This inequality is therefore nothing new. What is different today, however, is the public acceptance of this phenomenon. I myself have carried out research on political passivity, and among older people in particular I have often heard the statement: 'politics is not for me'. By that they meant that they do not regard themselves as competent enough to play a significant role in the political arena, partly because of their low level of education. Among the younger generation today, however, that acceptance of inequality has largely disappeared. We now assume that everyone has a right to their own opinion, and that it makes no difference whether that opinion comes from someone who has engaged in lengthy study or from someone who simply blurts out what is on their mind. The public debate has in other words become democratised, and citizens are no longer prepared to accept the diktats of a highly educated elite. It is not so much the inequality that has changed, but the fact that we are no longer prepared to accept that inequality.

Bridging this new gulf between those with a high and those with a low education level is not easy. A first option might be simply to allow the new populist parties to grow further. After all, political parties do not last forever, and it is perfectly normal in a democracy that parties created in the 19th century should disappear to be replaced by political parties which evidently reflect more contemporary sensitivities. The problem with populism, however, is that it is very difficult to reconcile with normal, sound governance of a country. The Netherlands and Belgium have each followed their own paths in this respect. In the Netherlands, the Party for Freedom (Partij voor de Vrijheid, PVV) led by Geert Wilders played a part in formulating government policy in the period 2010-2012 via a 'support construction'. This turned out not to be a great success, however, and the PVV proved not to be a very reliable or stable partner. In Belgium, the opposite strategy was followed and the nationalist Vlaams Belang party was meticulously excluded from every majority government formation. The party therefore had no influence whatsoever on policy, and has in the past even been convicted of making racist statements. Clearly, then, the big problem with populist parties is that their proposals simply cannot be carried out, either for economic or legal reasons. To cite just one example: it is legally prohibited to treat Islam differently from other religions because this would infringe the principle of non-discrimination.

Is there an answer to populism?

The other, more traditional parties will therefore have to continue playing an important role, and they will have to provide an answer to the fact that a proportion of the population is no longer represented in the value discourse of the political elite. It is for this reason that the Belgian writer David Van Reybrouck calls in his pamphlet 'Plea for populism' (*Pleidooi voor populisme*) for what he himself terms a 'healthy degree of populism'. The political elite has everything to gain from engaging with the values of the public at large, including the less well-educated section of the electorate. Van Reybrouck rightly points out that our norms and values have undergone an incredibly rapid change over the last few decades. In matters such as equal rights, non-discrimination, multiculturalism and respect for animals and the environment, both the official discourse and legislation have changed extraordinarily fast. It should come as no surprise that some groups within society have difficulty with this. Half a century ago, cigarette brands were still able to promote themselves as the 'sportsman's brand'; today, even smoking in a bar is forbidden. There is a section of the population who have difficulty keeping pace with this rapid evolution. A typical example of this type of conflict is the rise of animal rights organisations, who express concerns about traditional horse-racing on unsafe courses, bloody cockfights or the harsh way that stock are treated at a cattle market. What is striking is how much these issues inflame the emotions, and in some cases they have actually led to physical violence. Cattle dealers have always treated their animals harshly, and they feel their way of life is under attack when highly educated young urbanites suddenly come and start

Moemoe, Bruges, 2005
© Stephan Vanfleteren

telling them how they should treat a bull. This example demonstrates how difficult it is to translate that 'healthy populism' into practice. We can hardly go back
to a system where cruelty to animals was tolerated, or where the antidiscrimina-
tion laws were watered down. The European Convention on Human Rights also
stipulates explicitly that inflicting cruel forms of punishment on offenders is not
permitted, despite the fact that a section of the population would probably like to
see such punishments in some extreme cases. Moreover, our society is increasingly focused on control. Some sections of the population are undoubtedly hostile
to the smoking ban in bars, but at the same time we want the government to do
everything in its power to minimise the risks to our health. It is therefore anything
but simple to give the populist tendencies a place in policy, and given the require-
ment to adopt more and more international and European norms in the future,
that will not become any easier. The gulf between those with a high and those with
a low education level is a real problem, and there is no reason to suppose that this
new cultural divide will disappear rapidly. On the other hand, the assertion that
the recipes of populism can simply be adopted as they are is rather too simplistic.
A political system has to do two very different things: it has to interpret what
moves the people, but at the same time must possess the necessary strength to
rule. Combining these two tasks is becoming more and more difficult. As Aris-
totle remarked many years ago, a citizen is one who shares in governing and who
is willing to be governed, even if he does not agree with the ultimate decision.
Combining these two roles has never been an easy balancing act, and populism
may perhaps render it impossible. ∎

Translated by Julian Ross

FURTHER READING

Mark Bovens & Anchrit Wille (2011). *Diplomademocratie. Over de spanning tussen meritocratie en
democratie.* Amsterdam: Bert Bakker
David Van Reybrouck (2008). *Pleidooi voor populisme.* Amsterdam: Querido

The Ghent Altarpiece

Early Netherlandish, Flemish, French, German and Belgian

[WESSEL KRUL]

The monumental Ghent Altarpiece, or *Adoration of the Mystic Lamb,* painted by the brothers Hubert and Jan van Eyck and completed in 1432, is the first great masterpiece of Early Netherlandish painting. It can still be viewed in the church for which it was originally produced, St. Bavo's Cathedral in Ghent, where it attracts thousands of visitors every year. Whatever the viewer's particular interests, there is something in the painting for everybody: evidence of the great urban wealth in fifteenth century Flanders, the earliest and unequalled expression of an important and long-lasting artistic tradition, a visionary image of the Christian faith, and an artistic milestone in the development of extremely accurate realism.

One's astonishment at still finding it in its original setting is an extra bonus. Its size and age, its place and subject matter, all play their part in making the painting a highlight in the cultural history not only of Flanders but of the Low Countries as a whole. However, the impression of permanence given by the location and the painting is misleading. Although it was created specifically for the cathedral in Ghent, its qualities have not always been appreciated nor has it always remained there. Indeed, largely because of its many travels and the reunification of its widely scattered panels in 1920, the altarpiece has acquired a status far above all the other works of the Early Netherlandish School. Over the years, it has become a symbol not only of historical continuity but also of patience and suffering.

Respectful cleaning

The Adoration of the Mystic Lamb is a polyptych consisting of a number of panels or frames, which are painted on both sides so that different scenes appear according to whether it is open or closed. Tradition has it that the work was begun by Hubert van Eyck and completed by his much younger brother, Jan. On the outside the Annunciation is shown with sibyls and prophets and portraits of the patrons, the Ghent burgher Joost Vijd and his wife Elisabeth Borluut. On the inside, the upper panels show God the Father with the Virgin Mary on the left and John the Baptist on the right being sung to by angel choirs on either

side and, next to them at either end of the row, Adam and Eve after the Fall. The lower five panels show the Adoration of the Mystic Lamb near the Fountain of Life by processions of the righteous that include male and female saints, hermits and pilgrims against a background view of the heavenly Jerusalem. This last scene in particular is unusual for the late Middle Ages. It unquestionably makes reference to certain mystical traditions. The theological complexity of the work as a whole makes it unlikely that its content was thought up by the patrons or the artists themselves.

Because of its size, magnificent colouring and astonishing richness of detail, the Ghent Altarpiece soon acquired a reputation as one of the great artistic wonders of the Low Countries. On feast days, when the panels were opened, the church was so full that people could hardly move. Visitors travelled from near and far, from Germany, Italy and Spain, to view the painting and report back to those who stayed behind. In 1458, to mark Philip the Good's entry into Ghent, the St Agnes Chamber of Rhetoric modelled a *tableau vivant* on the painting. Albrecht Dürer considered the altarpiece to be one of the highlights of his journey through the Netherlands in 1521. But around the middle of the 16th century, when the painting was at least 100 years old, it began to show signs of wear. An initial attempt at restoration was so incompetent that a bottom row of panels, which seems to have included the Last Judgement, was lost. The two painters, commissioned to rescue the painting, Jan van Scorel and Lancelot Blondeel, were so impressed by what was left of the work that they kissed it reverently before starting.

King Philip II, on his departure for Spain, was so reluctant to leave the painting behind that he had a copy of it made by Michel Coxcie. The Reformation, on the other hand, had no time for such explicit Catholic imagery. During the Iconoclastic Riots of 1566, concerned burghers hurriedly removed van Eyck's altarpiece to the safety of the Cathedral's clock tower. When the Calvinists briefly came to power in Ghent, they exhibited the painting in the town hall hoping to be able to sell it. Its purchase by Queen Elizabeth of England failed to go through at the last minute. On the return of the Spanish, the work was restored to its place in the St Bavo cathedral. It is interesting to speculate whether it would have become so famous if it had simply become part of the British royal collection in the sixteenth century. Possibly it would still have done so, if only because of the exceptional status accorded to Jan van Eyck in the history of art.

Giorgio Vasari prefaced his *Lives of the Artists* of 1550 with an extensive introduction on the history of the different forms of art. It included the invention of oil paints, which he attributed to 'Giovanni da Bruggia' in Flanders. This master painter, he tells us, initiated a whole school of painting in Flanders, until Antonello da Messina went there to learn the trade and subsequently took the secret of oil paints back to Venice. In the nineteenth century, pictures were still being painted of Antonello respectfully visiting Jan van Eyck's studio. But though the Italian's work does show some affinity to early Flemish art, he clearly belongs to a later generation. The Ghent Altarpiece was not mentioned by Vasari and neither was Jan van Eyck's elder brother Hubert. These details were added in 1604 by 'the Dutch Vasari', Karl van Mander, in *Het Schilder-Boeck*, his famous handbook of painters.

According to Van Mander, Jan van Eyck was born in Maaseik, in present-day Belgian Limburg. Not only did he learn painting from his brother Hubert but he also collaborated with his sister Margareta who was a painter too. His masterpiece was the Ghent Altarpiece, which he completed after Hubert died in 1426. In Van Mander's opinion, a commission of that size must have come from the Burgundian court. For the rest, Van Mander accepts Vasari's account of the discovery of oil paint, though he attributes it to both brothers. This completed what for a long time was the accepted view of Van Eyck. Vasari's account supplemented by Van Mander survived unchallenged for centuries: Jan van Eyck was the inventor and first grand master of oil painting. That not only places him at the beginning of the Flemish painting tradition, but also of painting in the Northern Netherlands. For Karel van Mander's real subject was the blossoming of art in Holland, even though Rembrandt had not yet even been born.

From admiration to aversion

Admiration for the altarpiece continued unabated throughout the seventeenth century as evidenced by the production of yet another exact copy. However, the painting did not appeal very much to eighteenth century tastes. To supporters of enlightened rationalism it reflected an ecstatic devotion,

72

that by then had become incomprehensible. And even within the church itself, objections to it were raised. Some of the images on the polyptych no longer lived up to the newer ideals of moral edification and modesty. In the 1770s the panels with the very realistic naked figures of Adam and Eve were detached from the altarpiece and put in store where they remained, removed from the public gaze, for a very long time. The middle section was subsequently looted by the French. In 1794 the Ghent Altarpiece was removed to Paris to become part of the collection in the new national museum, later known as the Musée Napoléon.

The removal to Paris was evidence of a new appreciation of this legendary work of art. It was in this period that a serious interest started to be taken in the so-called 'primitives'. However, the main reason was without doubt the desire of the French authorities to present the painting as 'French' art. After all, it had been produced within the cultural sphere of Burgundy, which was French in language and origin. The Louvre became a treasure house of masterpieces that attracted visitors from all over Europe, especially during the short period of peace in 1802-1803. The large number of art works that it contained made it easier to draw comparisons, which led some sections of the public to conclusions that were radically opposed to those embraced by French national pride. From 1803, Friedrich Schlegel, critic, essayist and leader of the German romantic school, published a series of extremely influential articles about his visits to the Louvre. True art, in his opinion, was religious art. The proper subject matter for painting was the story of Christian redemption. He therefore rejected both classicism and realism. In the Ghent Altarpiece, to which he paid detailed attention, he particularly admired the tranquil solemnity of the subject matter. The painting was reminiscent of something ancient and original. God the Father, John the Baptist and Mary had an 'Egyptian loftiness and dignity'; they were 'stern godlike figures, as if from a misty prehistory'. Schlegel saw no connection with later Netherlandish art, for which he had little sympathy. There was no demonstrable line from Van Eyck to Rubens or Rembrandt, but Van Eyck did herald a style which reached its peak in the work of Dürer and Holbein. Schlegel therefore concluded that Van Eyck's work should be regarded not as Flemish, and certainly not French, but as German art.

Schlegel's decision to begin the history of German art with Van Eyck led to a long-lasting dichotomy in European art history. Time and again, North and South, German and Italian, Germanic and Latin culture were represented as two sharply distinguished artistic traditions and even as two different and opposing philosophies. Schlegel wanted contemporary art to model itself on Van Eyck. A scientific pioneer like G.F. Waagen, however, recognised as early as 1822 that Flemish art in the fifteenth century already represented a separate stylistic school. But even if Van Eyck was not really German, national boundaries continued to be a permanent feature of art literature. The same pattern was followed in history painting. In his murals in the dome of the Alte Pinakothek in Munich, Peter Cornelius represents Jan van Eyck as the leading old master in the North. This was echoed in innumerable similar 'parades of artists', from the Albert Memorial in London to the decorations at the front of Amsterdam's Rijksmuseum.

The centre panels of the altarpiece, which had been transported to Paris in 1794, were returned to the Ghent cathedral authorities in 1816 after the fall of Napoleon. However, far from viewing this as a restoration of Flemish, or Netherlandish, honour, the return of the painting caused some embarrassment. In the new Kingdom of the Netherlands there was little interest in early Netherlandish art. The same was true in England. Even after 1830, the new Belgian state was more attached to Rubens than to Van Eyck. In England, it was not until 1841 that the National Gallery bought its first Van Eyck. The works of Van Eyck in King Willem II's collection were auctioned off in 1850 without any effort being made by the state or any private individual to keep them in the Netherlands. The cathedral council in Ghent persisted in the indifference, even aversion, that it had shown in the eighteenth century and did everything in its power to rid itself of the work.

The side panels were sold to a London art dealer and through his mediation ended up in the Kaiser Friedrich Museum, now the Bode, in Berlin where they became one of the museum's showpieces until the First World War. The middle panels with the image of the Mystic Lamb were not well looked after and suffered fire damage in 1822. The panels with Adam and Eve remained under lock and key for several more decades because of their supposed indecency. In 1861 the church council put them on the market and they were acquired by the Museum of Fine Arts in Brussels. In this way the great polyptych was completely dismantled, with parts of it in Berlin and in Brussels and only the four middle panels, after over 20 years in Paris, back in their original place in Ghent.

National shrine

If there had not been a revival of interest in early Netherlandish art at the end of the nineteenth century, perhaps only a few art experts would have regretted this situation. But with increased public interest, national consciousness again became important. German art literature continued to regard Van Eyck and his followers as 'Northern' artists. A by-product of this was that the discovery of oil paint, traditionally attributed to Van Eyck, and even realism in painting, were also treated as achievements of German culture. Not surprisingly this viewpoint did not go down well in France. The Romantic historian Jules Michelet had already attempted to make Van Eyck a Frenchman. After 1870, French writers laid great emphasis on the French origins of the Burgundian dukes. The artistic impulse that blossomed in Flanders was in their opinion largely inspired by France.

Inevitably, Belgium was drawn into the escalating conflict between France and Germany. Belgium's intermediate position, however, could be considered to have been a positive feature. Around 1900 Belgian consciousness embraced early Netherlandish art as a legacy of Belgium's historical role as a crossroads

of cultures, a synthesis of traditions, and even a source of inspiration for the neighbouring states. The flowering of the arts under the Burgundian dukes, beginning with Van Eyck, was in its nature and originality proof of the Belgian nation's right to exist. This vision underpinned the great and extremely popular exhibition of 'Flemish Primitives' that was held in Bruges in 1902.

That exhibition was a turning point in both public awareness and scientific research. There was hardly anything on show by Van Eyck apart from the Adam and Eve panels, on loan from the museum in Brussels. Memling, whose work until then was considered to be the pinnacle of the early Netherlandish School, still was the central figure. But interest now shifted to the earlier generation and there was a growing conviction that the initial phase with Van Eyck, followed by Rogier, was also the best that this school had achieved. In fact, the organising committee had wanted, even if only for the duration of the exhibition, to bring together the entire polyptych of the altarpiece including the panels from Ghent and Berlin. They were unable to do this. But after 1902 the Adoration of the Mystic Lamb was more and more frequently cited as a national monument, as a visible memorial of Belgium's independent contribution to European culture. Reunifying the altarpiece now became an issue of the greatest importance.

The Bruges exhibition of 1902 triggered a range of reactions in neighbouring countries. A Paris exhibition in 1904 tried to prove that Van Eyck and his followers owed everything to France. However, even in France the attempt was

greeted with some scepticism. The organisers wanted to minimise the role of Van Eyck as an innovator, but at the same time maximise his fame in the interests of French culture. In Germany, the distance from France was again strongly emphasised. Although nobody any longer insisted that Van Eyck laid the foundations of German art, German publications dealing with the early Netherlandish school kept repeating that the altarpiece reflected a 'Germanic sense of form'.

In Holland no serious attempt was made to turn Van Eyck into a compatriot, though the idea that his work formed the origin of Dutch 'realism' remained a fixed tenet in Dutch art history. So Van Eyck was adopted, after all, as the source and origin of a great national tradition of painting. Even a famous historical work that at first sight was written from an opposing point of view is based entirely on this belief. In his *Waning of the Middle Ages in 1919*, Johan Huizinga presented Burgundian culture as a final phase instead of a fresh start or renaissance. Jan van Eyck's careful attention to detail did not reflect a modern approach to life but fitted completely into the world of late medieval belief. It looked as if Huizinga intended to sweep away some long cherished ideas. And yet he did so only partially. He also took for granted a direct relationship between Van Eyck and seventeenth century Dutch art, but in his opinion this was because Dutch art had remained in essence medieval, which gave it its unique character.

The peace negotiations after the First World War opened up the possibility of satisfying at least one Belgian national dream. It is revealing that of

all the Belgian art treasures in German hands, the side panels of the Ghent Altarpiece were the first to be demanded as reparation. In 1920 they returned from Berlin to Ghent where they were recombined with the St Bavo centre panels and the Brussels Adam and Eve panels. Since then this huge work of art has been the main tourist attraction in the city, for symbolic as much as artistic reasons. The Adoration of the Mystic Lamb has become a national shrine, dedicated to the suffering that the Belgian people have endured.

Final wanderings

Its exceptional status ensured that every debate on the masterpiece became a matter of great public interest. In the 1930s many learned discussions about the work took place. What exactly was the painting about? Who was being worshipped, God the Father or the Son? And who was the mysterious Hubert van Eyck? Did he really exist or was the attribution to an elder brother based on a misunderstanding? Such attention also made the work vulnerable to stunts and blackmail. In 1934 the panel with the 'just judges' was stolen in an ostentatious robbery, the purpose of which has never been made clear. The panel has never been recovered, and a copy has replaced the missing section. The return of the altarpiece to Ghent in 1920 did not put an end to its peregrinations. The Second World War ushered in a final episode of transportation and damage. The belief in the work's link with German culture was revived under National Socialism. Adolf Hitler earmarked the Ghent Altarpiece for his planned museum in Linz where it would illustrate the glories of the German artistic tradition. Pending the completion of this project, the polyptych was housed in Neuschwanstein, one of the neo-Gothic fairy tale castles built by King Ludwig II (1845-1886) of Bavaria. After all, did not Wagner's opera Lohengrin, the Swan Knight, also take place in the Low Countries? Subsequently the painting was brought into 'safety' in the salt mines at Alt-Ansee, from where it was returned to Ghent after the war. But the salt crystals had so seriously damaged the paint surface that a thorough restoration had to be carried out in 1950-51.

The polyptych has now been in St Bavo's Cathedral for over half a century, though not always in the same place. The conflicting demands of security and accessibility mean that where it should stand is a constant matter for debate. In 1986 the polyptych was placed at the back of the church, to the left of the entrance to the Villa chapel, enclosed in a bulletproof glass case. The central panels are now always left open. No-one is satisfied with this location. Restoration work on the church will be starting shortly and it is intended to rearrange the space so as to display the work in a more attractive way. Many tourists actually spend more time in front of the life-size reproduction in the Vijd Chapel, its original location. The reproduction may be photographed; the original may not.

In the course of the past two centuries the Ghent Altarpiece has been claimed by many countries as part of their cultural heritage. After 1900 it long remained a symbol of the historical origins, cohesion and fortunes of the Belgian state. In the Netherlands it has always been honoured as the first important milestone in the 'realistic' artistic tradition which emerged in the period that the Low Countries were still under a single ruler. The special reverence for Van Eyck in Flanders and the Netherlands as the founder of a national school of painting is

perhaps not as strong as it used to be. But the altarpiece still inspires great respect, as was evidenced by the wave of protest at a Flemish advertising campaign which used Van Eyck's image of paradise but replaced the lamb with a llama. Jan van Eyck's masterpiece remains an heirloom which must still be taken very seriously. ▪

Translated by Chris Emery

FURTHER READING

E. DHANENS, *Van Eyck. The Ghent Altarpiece*, Allen Lane, London, 1973.

J. GRAHAM, *Inventing Van Eyck. The Remaking of an Artist for the Modern Age*, Berg, Oxford, 2007.

C. HARBISON, JAN VAN EYCK: the Play of Realism, Reaktion Books, London, 1991.

B. RIDDERBOS, A. VAN BUREN, H. VAN VEEN, Early Netherlandish Paintings. Rediscovery, Reception, Research, Amsterdam University Press, Amsterdam, 2005.

P. SCHMIDT, Het Lam Gods, Davidsfonds, Leuven, 2005.

N. SCHNEIDER, Jan van Eyck: der Genter Altar. Vorschläge für eine Reform der Kirche, Fischer, Frankfurt am Main, 1986.

NOTE

Restoration work on the Ghent Altarpiece commenced in the autumn of 2012. It will take five years and the estimated cost will be 1.4 million euro. A team of restorers has been brought together by the Royal Institute for Cultural Heritage [Koninklijk Instituut voor het Kunstpatrimonium (KIK)]. The Cathedral has appointed Mrs Anne van Grevenstein-Kruse, Emeritus Professor of Conservation and Restoration at the University of Amsterdam, to direct the project, and an international advisory committee will oversee its execution.

The restoration of the altarpiece is necessary to prevent further hardening of the original layers of varnish which now threaten the pictorial layer of the work. The panels will be thoroughly repaired and consolidated, and earlier retouching and repainting will be treated. After that, the parts that still need it will be retouched and the panels will be given a fresh coat of varnish.

The treatment of the panels will be done in phases at the Museum of Fine Arts in Ghent and visitors to the museum will be able to observe the process. During the whole period of restoration, the altarpiece, with the exception of the panels actually under restoration, will remain in St Bavo's Cathedral and open for public viewing.

Martinus Nijhoff & Joseph Brodsky

'Harbingers of the Future'

[ANNEKE REITSMA]

Living too brief an hour
for fear or trembling,
you spin, motelike, ascending
above this bed of flowers,
beyond the prison space
where past and future
combine to break, or batter,
our lives, and thus
when your path leads you far
to open meadows,
your pulsing wings bring shadows
and shapes to air.

From The Butterfly, X, Joseph Brodsky

In the poem *The Clouds* by Martinus Nijhoff (1894-1953) the narrator recalls lying as a child with his mother in the grass: 'And mother asked me what I saw up there. / And I cried: Scandinavia, and: swans, / A lady, and: a shepherd with his sheep –'.

With a turn of phrase characteristic of Nijhoff he continues: 'The wonders were made word and drifted on'. To Nijhoff the greatest wonder is not the things the child sees in the clouds, but the fact that these figurations of the mind's eye (perceived by the child as supreme reality) can become word. He sees becoming word and becoming flesh as part of the same sacred plan. Language grants objects a second life, and it is the poet above all who enables and safeguards this rebirth.

Joseph Brodsky (1940-1996), once called 'a calm contemporary of Nijhoff' by critic Guus Middag, also repeatedly alludes to rebirth. Brodsky cherished the notion of returning as an object, once you had been dead long enough. Thus in his poem *August* he states, not without humour: 'Having made a career out of the crossroads, now the knight / finds himself a traffic signal' (translated by Andrew Reynolds). In the same vein he writes to his daughter: 'On the whole, bear in mind that I'll be around. Or rather, / that an inanimate object might be your

father, / especially if the objects are older than you, or larger.' For Brodsky even a stoplight or an armchair might be part of an animate universe, and on a metal hanger in his junk room hangs 'a white, pure-cotton angel'. Within the ideological shackles of the Soviet Union these were extremely questionable ideas.

Joseph Brodsky (1940-1996)

European culture

Joseph Brodsky, who later won the Nobel Prize, spent much of his writing life in exile. He grew up in Jewish circles in Saint Petersburg, which, though renamed Leningrad under Stalin's harsh regime, 'provided conspicuous visual propaganda for a past which had been officially renounced and for the values of European culture,' as writer and Slavicist Kees Verheul so aptly put it. (Brodsky became acquainted with Nijhoff's work through Verheul, and it made a great impression on him.) No wonder Brodsky's later descriptions of Rome, Florence and Venice always hinted at the contours of his original Western-oriented birthplace.

From Homer to Dante, from the Scriptures to John Donne, from T.S. Eliot to W.H. Auden and from Nijhoff to Achmatova, Brodsky felt bonded with European culture to the very fibres of his being. This must have required considerable effort, as almost all these names fell outside the official canon. In his *Letter to Horace*, Brodsky later said, with his characteristic irony: 'Nothing breeds snobbery better than tyranny.'

During Brodsky's sham trial in 1964 (an admirer kept notes from the court session and secretly distributed them afterwards), he was required to justify the fact 'that in failing to take up paid work he had lived at the expense of society.' The dialogue proceeded as follows:

> *Judge:* What is your profession?
> *Brodsky:* Poet. Poet and translator.
> *Judge:* Who said you were a poet?
> Who assigned you that rank?
> *Brodsky:* No one. Who assigned me to
> the human race?
> *Judge:* And did you study for this?
> *Brodsky:* For what?
> *Judge:* To become a poet? Did you try to attend a school where they train poets...
> where they teach...?
> *Brodsky:* I don't think it comes from education.
> *Judge:* From what then?
> *Brodsky:* I think it's... from God...

In order to cure himself of this gift, Brodsky was forced to carry out heavy labour 'in a remote place'. Banished to a kolkhoz near Arkhangelsk, he continued with his poetry in greatly changed circumstances. On his fortieth birthday he wrote: 'I have waded the steppes that saw yelling Huns in saddles, / worn the clothes nowadays back in fashion in every quarter, / planted rye, tarred the roofs of pigsties and stables, / guzzled everything save dry water. / (...) Granted my lungs all sounds except the howl; / (...) Yet until brown clay has been crammed down my larynx, / only gratitude will be gushing from it.' (*May 24, 1980*, translated by the author).

Tyranny is no match for human truth. Brodsky was granted early release, partly thanks to protests from abroad. He eventually received permission to leave the country, and was strenuously advised to make prompt use of it. In 1972 he emigrated to the United States, leaving behind his son, his parents and his girlfriend (to whom he would continue to dedicate poems for many years).

Ideological bankruptcy

It says a good deal for Brodsky that he never boasted of his spectacular life events, but of course these experiences shaped him. Even a poem in which Odysseus addresses his son Telemachus gains new significance from an awareness of the meaning of separation in the poet's life: '(...) away from me / you are quite safe from all Oedipal passions, / and your dreams, my Telemachus, are blameless.' (*Odysseus to Telemachus*, translated by George L. Kline.) Ithaca and Saint Petersburg become interchangeable, as a volcanic eruption

Martinus Nijhoff (1894-1953)

over Pompei foreshadows twentieth century violence. Similar connotations surface in Brodsky's biblical scenes, such as Nunc dimittis (Simeon's song of praise
to the Messiah) and *Flight to Egypt*. Reading Brodsky always involves tracing
multiple layers of meaning.

Time and again he exhibits that sense of history Eliot once claimed was necessary for anyone with poetic ambitions beyond the age of twenty-five. Brodsky's
great themes – loneliness, loyalty, betrayal, friendship, exile and fear of chaos
– rise above his personal lot and play out against a broader backdrop of cultural decline, placing him in line with the historical avant-garde, as represented
by Eliot, Auden and Nijhoff. Nijhoff writes of the crisis of the Interbellum: 'it is
an awakening to our ideological bankruptcy. The economic crisis will of course
be transient in nature (...). The psychological aspect of the crisis, however, the
ideological bankruptcy, is permanent. Never again will faith, beauty or nature
offer sanctuary (...). Humanity as a whole no longer recognises any guiding value
in these concepts and will not reconsider its position."

Contrary to later postmodernists, Eliot and his followers do not let it rest
here. In the same piece Nijhoff states (his futuristic vision agreeing precisely

with that of Brodsky): 'The human soul must adapt to that which human skill apparently innocently created. Art can play an important role in the adaptation process. Poetry must be a harbinger of the future. It must conceive the future as already existing and stake a claim for the human soul.' According to Brodsky too, the poet has an obligation to offer a final glimmer of hope along the road of poetic form.

'A great writer,' he says in the collection of essays *Less than one*, 'is one (...) who shows a man at the end of his wits an opening, a pattern to follow.' It was with good reason that he named his first poetry collection (which first appeared after his emigration to America) *A Stop in the Desert* (1972).

In *The Butterfly* Brodsky offers just such an opening, as the solo flight of a butterfly, which falls dead into his hand, is stripped of any hint of the pride of Icarus. Brodsky implies that life and death form two physical states of the same existence, in an almost Platonic pattern. It is thanks to the butterfly, loaded as it is with poetic notions, that the colourless air takes form. What form? Perhaps like the clouds it will be Scandinavia and ducks, or 'Perhaps a landscape smokes / among your ashes, / and with thick reading glasses / I'll scan its slopes - / its beaches, dancers, nymphs.' (*The Butterfly, V*)

Driven onward jubilant

Elsewhere in Brodsky's work the butterfly is accompanied by a hawk:

> *Wind from the northwestern quarter is lifting him high above*
> *the dove-gray, crimson, umber, brown*
> *Connecticut Valley. Far beneath,*
> *chickens daintily pause and move*
> *unseen in the yard of the tumbledown*
> *farmstead, chipmunks blend with the heath.*

(The Hawk's Cry in Autumn, translated by Alan Myers with the author)

In the background do we not hear Nijhoff's foolish bees, carried in on the snow motif? In Nijhoff's poem the bees are tempted by the scent of higher honey, which brings them, 'driven onward (...) jubilant, on adventure' to set course for the ice cold azure:

> *we climbed aloft and vanished,*
> *disbanded, disembodied,*
> *we climbed aloft and vanished*
> *away like things asparkle.*

This brings us to what may be the most beautiful verse in Dutch poetry:

> *It's snowing, we are dying,*
> *fluttering worldwards, homewards;*
> *It's snowing, we are dying,*
> *snowing between the beehives.*

Brodsky takes a sharper tone as he describes the hawk rising: 'Still higher! Into some blasted ionosphere! / That astronomically objective hell // of birds that lacks oxygen, and where the milling stars / play millet served from a plate or a crescent.' Finally there is an auditory shock:

And at this point he screams. From the hooklike beak
there tears free of him and flies ad luminem
the sound Erinyes make to rend
souls (...)

 (...)

(...) A piercing, high-pitched squeal,
more nightmarish than the D-sharp grinding
of the diamond cutting glass,
slashes the whole sky across.

(...)

We, standing where we are, exclaim
"There!" and see far above the tear
that is a hawk, and hear the sound that lingers
in wavelets, a spider skein

swelling notes in ripples across the blue vault of space
whose lack of echo spells, especially in October,
an apotheosis of pure sound.

Like the bees in search of 'the elusive symbol', the hawk is an alter ego of the poet, who exhibits a Mallarméan preference for 'the zenith', 'the dark-blue high of azure'. This is the deeper parallel between Nijhoff and Brodsky, as the poet rises in flight he must confront Nothingness. The butterfly formed 'a frail and shifting buffer, / dividing it from me'. After the fall from uninhabitable Nothingness, a transformation takes place. The bees are 'disbanded, disembodied' and fall in a new form, as snowflakes. In the case of the hawk, we hear 'something ring (...) like some family crockery being broken, / slowly falling aswirl, // yet its shards, as they reach our palms, don't hurt / but melt when handled.'

Bees become snowflakes and falling feathers resemble the 'curls, eyelets, strings' of Cyrillic script: 'blurred / commas, ellipses, spirals, linking / heads of barley'. They too end up where they belong, on earth.

The bees' 'foolishness' should not be confused with pride, nor should the hawk's risky adventure. It is more a case of *mania*, that higher wisdom seen as the duty and driver of poets and seers from Plato on. It is with good reason that the hawk in Homer is the messenger of Apollo, the oracle god and protector of the muses. Bees, too, are connected with poetry in classical literature.

Exile to verse

It is significant that Brodsky and Nijhoff's winged alter egos do not fly upwards entirely of their own free will: bees and hawk are *driven onward* and *propelled* respectively. They are as free or as constrained as Edgar Allen Poe's raven, Baudelaire's albatross, Mallarmé and Yeats's swans or Ida Gerhardt's kingfisher from the cycle 'Exile to verse'. All these forms, in Nijhoff's words, indicate one 'seeking superiority, and condemned to fall short.' The bees, however, have at least sniffed the scent of higher honey and the hawk has brought forth a cry which remains ringing in our ears.

The two poems reveal related notions of poetry: words too must undergo a metamorphosis, should they wish to gain poetic strength. The words must *sing themselves free of their meanings* (as Nijhoff formulated it in 'Dual death'). The snow motif has a purifying effect here, worn-out meanings can be polished up to reveal their original shine. A good example of this is in the final verse of *H Hour*, in which Nijhoff says about the trees (yet to be planted):

> *How lovely otherwise*
> *when blossoms and leaves arise.*
> *How lovely? Heaven knows how.*
> *But there it ends for now.*

According to Nijhoff even a filler can be made to sparkle like a diamond, with the requisite skill, but cold hard skill alone is not enough. There must be poetic conviction at its core. In both Nijhoff and Brodsky's work we encounter the idea, more in keeping with Byzantine than reformational thinking, that every word is divine in origin. The protestant Sola Scriptura seemed to them not so much overly restrictive as outright wrong: if God revealed himself in Word, then all ramifications of that Word must also contain the seed of the divine. Even the cry of a hawk may be a divine echo. It is the task of the poet to tap these sources, to reveal something of their sights and sounds. Disdain for everyday language has no place here - the word lives among us, after all.

Reality religion

For that reason both poets repeatedly make fascinating shifts in register. The sacred and the profane, a scooter, a kettle, a window, are naturally united in their poems. Brodsky applies this principle magnificently in the *Elegy for John Donne*, which lists every conceivable item of furniture:

> *John Donne fell asleep and all around him slept.*
> *The pictures slept, the wall, the floor, the bedding,*
> *the tables, rugs, the bolts, the latch all slept,*
> *the wardrobe, sideboard, candle, curtains, slept.*
> *All was asleep: the bottle, glass and pans,*

the bread, the bread-knife, china, crystal, crocks,
the night-light, linen, windows, cupboards, clocks,
the staircase steps, the doors. Night all-surrounding.

(Elegy for John Donne and other poems, Longman, London, 1967,
translated by Nicholas Bethell)

The image conjured up by these lines is neither the dignified 17th century pastor of St. Paul's Cathedral, nor the metaphysical poet bent over his papers, but rather one who has lived and worked among us. His universe, too, contained teacups. Nijhoff speaks of 'a sort of positive mysticism (...), a reality religion, a sensory embodiment of that which is seen'. It is this spiritual sense which Nijhoff considers essential to the 'esprit moderne'.

Within the European literary family Nijhoff and Brodsky are close relatives. They are part of a tradition as aware of its Greco-Roman as its Judeo-Christian roots. Of course there are national elements to their poetry, ranging from Bommel to one of the many bridges of Saint Petersburg, but their broad perspective prevents this from degenerating into provincialism. In Lullaby of Cape Cod Brodsky states: 'I write from an Empire whose enormous flanks / extend beneath the sea.' (VI, translated by Anthony Hecht). For centuries the same stars have shone out over this infinite empire:

Sleep, sleep, John Donne. Do not torment yourself.
Your gown is rent in holes. It hangs dejected.
Just look at it, and out the clouds will look
that star, that constant guardian of your peace. ■

Translated by Anna Asbany

NOTES

1. From *Collected poems in English (Poems written in English and Poems translated from the original Russian by or with the author, including translations by…)*, Farrar, Straus and Giroux, New York, 2000. The excerpt is part ten of a fourteen part cycle, *The Butterfly*, translated by George L. Kline.

2. Martinus Nijhoff, "On my own work". In: *Collected works 2*, Den Haag / Amsterdam, 1961, p. 1160

3. Personal communication from Nijhoff to Victorine Hefting. In: Nienke Begemann, *Victorine*. Amsterdam, 1990, p. 130

4. Martinus Nijhoff, *Collected works 2*. Den Haag / Amsterdam, 1961, p. 297

Tapestries and Racing Cyclists

Oudenaarde – a Small Town with a Big History

[DIRK VAN ASSCHE]

No matter which direction you approach the town from, the massive tower of the main church always soars up like a raised forefinger from the folds of the landscape. The town centre of Oudenaarde is so small that it needs the tower to attract attention in the rolling countryside of the Flemish Ardennes. The Scheldt is a second way of finding the town. Today, the river mostly resembles a canal, but until well into the 20th century it used to twist its way through the landscape. At one of its many bends a town came into being around the year 1000.

The town can be explored in different ways. Most visitors to Oudenaarde come by bicycle, for recently it has become the cycling capital of Flanders. However, I choose to arrive in the slowest but also the most reliable way – on foot. First through the railway tunnel and then another couple of hundred metres and I'm standing in the town centre. Until the 19th century, I would have lived outside the town walls. When the railway was established, a section of the fortified wall was demolished. This means that from my kitchen window I now see the platforms of the new station and to the right of them the small tower of the former one. This imposing structure replaced the first building as early as the end of the 19th century. It now stands empty, but it looks just like a station ought to look, with a ticket-office hall where the employees, seated behind large walls of glass, used to push a ticket through under a small hatch. It also has various waiting rooms with gleaming wooden benches and a buffet where one drank coffee out of heavy china cups. As a child I was afraid of taking the train there, because you had to cross the railway lines to get to the far platform. To help relieve me of my fear, a new station was built in 1996, with a tunnel under the tracks. But my fear has now been replaced by revulsion. Revulsion at the banality of this concrete container and, in particular, the station square in front of it. A train traveller whose first meeting with Oudenaarde takes place there will leave again by the next available train.

Standing with one's back to the old station, one looks straight at the tower of the Sint-Walburgakerk, the main church, which is visible like a beacon through the entire region. In between stands a white statue of a woman reclining on a globe and laying a crown on a grave. On this very square, in 1864, a handful of volunteers gathered who were prepared to defend the Belgian Princess Charlotte in Mexico. Her husband, Maximilian of Austria, Emperor of Mexico, was

being threatened by rebels. The result of this expedition was disastrous for the Belgian mercenaries. The Princess had to leave her husband and Mexico, and the Emperor was put to death. The name of the square, Tacambaro, commemorates this sad story.

Today, ten or so pupils are sitting on the base of the statue waiting for the bus to take them home. Close by lies the Sint-Bernardus College, the largest school in the town. In the turbulent year of 1968, a young man studied here who was having difficulty in finding his niche in life and sought consolation in poetry and drugs. After his suicide, Jotie 't Hooft became a cult figure, the first drugs suicide in Dutch-language literature, an icon of neo-Romantic poetry. He set himself up against the narrow-mindedness of Oudenaarde, but his town still reverberates with the name Jotie, a dialect form of his own name, Johan. The town's youth centre now bears the name of the youth who was expelled from school for drug abuse and who complained in a poem that in the town he is 'tolerated/as formerly the village idiot'.

The college, with its beautiful Renaissance facade, lies hardly a hundred metres from the market. This large square, at the foot of the Gothic town hall, is surrounded by scores of cafés and terraces. Here there is a suitable place for everyone to take a drink: those of maturer years drink their coffee on the terrace of the Pomme d'Or, the bikers congregate each weekend at the Carillon beneath the church tower and the younger people sit on the terrace of the Adriaan Brouwer. This 16th century painter, much admired by P.P. Rubens, is more closely associated in his native town with beer than with art. A typical Oudenaarde brown beer has been named after him – as are the annual beer festivals.

On the corner of the Grote Markt square stands a somewhat elderly man, deep in conversation. It is Freddy Maertens, one of the most controversial figures of Belgian cycle racing, who was twice world champion. Maertens is now the figurehead of the Tour of Flanders Centre that has been located in Oudenaarde since 2003. The town has invested heavily in getting the arrival of one of the most important classic cycle races on its territory, and in 2011 this also took place here for the first time. This has meant an added attraction for the town. A media magnate and avid cycle-lover purchased the race, made a TV series out of it and then shifted the arrival to his native town. Since then, Oudenaarde has become a new mecca for cycle enthusiasts from the whole world.

The Tour fits this town perfectly. The connection with the surrounding countryside is being re-established. The cyclists ride continuously through the hills of the Flemish Ardennes and almost everywhere can glimpse the top of the main church tower. While for centuries this tower was a landmark for believers in the whole surrounding area, it now serves a similar purpose for toiling cyclists.

I continue my walk past the meat market, which is now the public library, and a small beguinage until I come to the banks of the Scheldt. This is one of the most beautiful spots in the town. In front of me, on the far bank, stands the small Gothic church of Pamele. Once, this village was a proper town, like Oudenaarde. In the first half of the 13th century, the gentlemen of Pamele had a church built in the Scheldt Gothic style. It was more beautiful than the main church of neighbouring Oudenaarde and even today it still dominates the right-hand bank of the Scheldt. To the right of it stand the remains of Maagdendale Abbey, once one of the largest nunneries in Flanders and an important religious and intellectual centre. During the French era, the abbey was used as a barracks and it now houses a shooting range, the town archives and the art academy of the town. On my left, behind the lift bridge that immobilises the traffic scores of times every day, stands the Lalaing House, where an important bastard was probably born, and the courthouse, behind which lies the former gaol.

Railway station
© Dirk Van Assche.

The royal chambermaid

During an art event in 2001, the artist Johan Van Geluwe placed a sign on the right bank of the Scheldt with the text 'Achtung! Sie verlassen das Heilige Römische Reich Deutscher Nation' and on the left bank one with 'Attention. Vous quittez le Royaume de France'. He was referring to the period around the year 1000 when the Scheldt formed the border between two power blocs. On the right bank, the Emperor of the Holy Roman Empire had a fortress built in the village of Ename. Boudewijn IV, the ambitious Count of Flanders and vassal of the French King, not to be outdone by his opponent, built a tower on the opposite bank. In 1033, Boudewijn crossed the Scheldt and destroyed the fortress of Ename. To deprive the village of any future military role, an abbey was founded there. Oudenaarde, on the left bank, then became the most important settlement. Right up until the French period, the abbey at Ename, was an important intellectual and religious centre – but today it is where archaeologists conduct their investigations.

Oudenaarde rapidly developed into an important trading centre and a base for the Counts of Flanders. Jan the Fearless had a fortification built and for a while had his Council of Flanders there. Only for a short while, for neighbouring Ghent, also on the Scheldt, viewed the development of Oudenaarde with con-

siderable envy. Ghent was a self-willed town that regularly rebelled against the monarch. Oudenaarde was much more subservient and law-abiding. In the 14th century, the two towns regularly came into conflict with each other, with Ghent – the larger of the two – normally gaining the upper hand. The sympathies of the Burgundian Dukes, however, were with the smaller Oudenaarde, and they even built a residence there.

In 1521, the as yet unmarried Charles V stayed in it. His soldiers were besieging the nearby Tournai, and the governor of the town organised a feast for the young monarch. His attention was caught by the chambermaid Johanna van der Gheynst. The records state that she was extremely beautiful and was the one true love of Charles' life. Nine months later, at any rate, a daughter was born – Margaret of Parma. Charles came to acknowledge her as his lawful daughter and gave her an education suitable for a noblewoman. She thus came to play a role in the marriage politics of her father. Already at the age of fourteen she married for the first time, with a scion of the de Medici family. When he was murdered a year later, she married shortly afterwards for a second time with the fourteen-year-old Ottavio Farnese, Count of Parma, grandson of Pope Paul III. From 1559 to 1567, Margaret was the Governess of Flanders. Her son, Alexander Farnese, was later to reimpose with an iron hand the dominion of the monarch in rebellious Flanders.

During that period, Oudenaarde was a prosperous city, and this prosperity also had to be displayed to the outside world. In 1526, the first stone of a new town hall was laid. This new edifice was to reflect the wealth of the town, which is why the commission was also given to a top builder, Hendrik van Pede, who had

Alexander and the high priest (end 16th - early 17th century); 370 x 435 cm. MOU Museum Oudenaarde ©Technifoto Van Wambeke, Oudenaarde

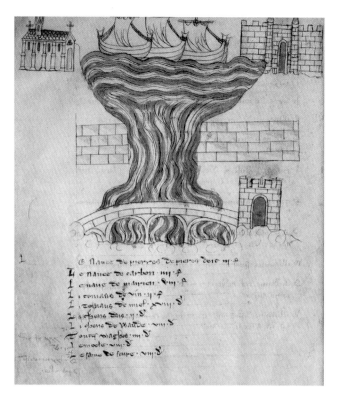

The Scheldt in Oudenaarde. On the left the church of Pamele, on the right a town gate. Royal Library, mss. 1175 © Koninklijke Bibliotheek, Brussels

earned his spurs by, among other things, building the King's House (Broodhuis/ Maison du Roi) on the Grand Place in Brussels. Right up to the present day, the town hall is one of the loveliest examples of late Brabantine Gothic architecture.

The tower of the belfry bears the imperial crown, and above it stands the statue of Hanske de Krijger (Hans the Warrior). The story is that Hanske was a watchman who was to announce the arrival of Charles V, but that he had drunk too much Oudenaarde beer and fallen asleep, which meant he did not see the monarch arrive. Charles is then said to have ordered the town to include a pair of spectacles in its coat of arms. In actual fact, it is not a pair of spectacles but the Gothic letter A of Audenaerde. According to the writer Charles de Coster, Hanske de Krijger was none other than Till Eulenspiegel himself, who lived in the town for a while and who sneaked off with the provisions of the commander of the local militia.

Purveyors to nobility

That the town could permit itself such a special town hall was due to its production of tapestries. Along with such cities as Brussels, Arras (F), Tournai, Ghent and Bruges, Oudenaarde developed into an international centre and one of the most important purveyors to the European courts. Like most Flemish towns, Oudenaarde had mainly been a producer of linen. A crisis occurred, however, and just as now innovation and specialisation were the remedy. The Oudenaarde textile sector came to specialise in the weaving of tapestries –

a luxury product. The first traces of this industry go back as far as the latter half of the 14th century. The link with the surrounding countryside was very strong. That was where most of the weavers worked. The merchants, along with the craftsmen, the tradesmen and the guilds, lived inside the town walls. In the 16th century – the golden age – more than half the population worked in the tapestry weaving industry. They mainly produced verdure tapestries (with formal designs derived from foliage), although it was in fact possible to order any genre or narrative, whether it came from Antiquity, the Bible or mythology.

Important for the tapestry industry was the relationship with Antwerp, which was then the centre of international trade. Both for the supply of basic materials and for the exporting of the finished products this seaport played a crucial role. Quite a few Oudenaarde producers sent members of their families to Antwerp, where they functioned as contacts. In 1544, Charles V regulated tapestry weaving in order to safeguard a high quality. From that time onwards, it was also compulsory to weave a town mark into the edge of the tapestry, as conclusive proof of its place of origin. In many Oudenaarde tapestries from that period we find the spectacles from the town coat of arms.

In the museum situated in the town hall some magnificent examples are on display. One of the finest is a series depicting Alexander the Great, comprising three tapestries, manufactured at the end of the 16th century. It is assumed that this series once belonged to Alexander Farnese, Count of Parma. It is thought that he received the tapestries in 1582 in connection with his ceremonial inauguration in Oudenaarde.

In the eye of many European storms

Economic success often goes hand in hand with social and political stability. From the beginning of the 16th century this was hard to guarantee. Reforms to religious services, grafted onto social unrest, obscured matters. Reformists were quickly rounded up, and the first merchants started to emigrate. Despite the harsh inquisition, the reformist movement grew increasingly stronger, and in 1572 Oudenaarde was conquered for a short period by the Wild Beggars. In 1582, Alexander Farnese put an end to this Calvinist republic, which lasted only a few years.

For the tapestry industry these times were severe. Thousands of weavers and merchants left the area and left in large numbers for the Northern Netherlands. They were to settle in Amsterdam and Delft, but Gouda in particular proved to be their preferred final destination. By around 1582-83, about 80 Oudenaarde families had moved to the city and tapestry weaving was flourishing there. But the industry back in Oudenaarde never fully recovered from this exodus. The last workshop closed its doors in 1772. Oudenaarde weavers did help lay the basis for the production of French tapestries. Today, in the Lalaing House, there is still a workshop where tapestries are restored.

From the second half of the 17th century, Flanders was at the centre of the European battlefield for many decades. Numerous conflicts were contested here and Oudenaarde, strategically situated on the Scheldt, seldom escaped acts of war. The expansionist policy of the French King Louis XIV played an important role here. In 1688, Oudenaarde came under French rule, which ushered in a brief

Church of Pamele and
St. Walburga Church
© Dirk Van Assche

golden age. But acts of war soon put an end to this. On several occasions the town suffered heavy bombardment. On 11 July 1708, the major European powers stood facing each other in Oudenaarde with enormous armies – a total of 180,000 troops. At stake in the battle was the crown of Spain. The Great Alliance, with British, Prussian and Dutch troops, was up against a mighty French army. The hilly landscape played an important role in this battle, with the French King suffering a bitter defeat. More than 6000 soldiers fell in the battle. Three hundred years later, several hundred actors from all of Europe re-enacted the battle. Once more the canons roared, but this time the battle ended with loud applause.

In the 19th century as well, the town fell on very hard times. Until 1859, people lived there under the Ancien Régime. In that year, the town authorities decided to demolish the fortresses and restrict the numbers of the permanently stationed garrisons. From that moment on, Oudenaarde cautiously sought to join the modern world.

At the end of the First World War the town was once more in the line of fire. From 31 October to 10 November 1918, one day before the Armistice, the Battle of the Scheldt was fought. French and American troops stood facing the Germans. The town was heavily bombarded and a large part of the patrimony was damaged. In addition there were many victims of German poison gas attacks. Shortly before the Battle of the Scheldt, Adolf Hitler was taken care of at a German hospital located in the local college before being repatriated to Germany.

To commemorate this battle, the Ohio Bridge was built over the Scheldt. Before the war an iron bridge stood here – it was blown up and subsequently, with the aid of the American state of Ohio, it was rebuilt. The new bridge was embellished with four American bison. They are there to this day, although now, after restoration, they mistakenly look in the opposite direction to the original one. In the town centre, the American monument in General Pershing Street reminds people of the role played by the American troops in the liberation of Oudenaarde.

The hole in the market

The Second World War also resulted in serious war damage, which was only completely repaired many years later. After this, the town wished to adapt swiftly to the new age. Everything was set in motion to bring about economic prosperity. This led to comprehensive changes to the external appearance of the town. Via various small canals, the Scheldt had had a strong presence in the townscape until well into the 20th century. For that reason, the town was also referred to as the Little Bruges. But the canals were filled in, and the twists and turns of the river Scheldt straightened out. The fact that this, among other things, meant doing away with the remains of the Burgundian citadel and a modernist artists' centre could not deter the town authorities from implementing their plans. Oudenaarde was to adapt to the modern world and to do so people were prepared to go far. So far that a large number of old houses close to the church were demolished in order to lay down a four-lane road to the Grote Markt square. This was scornfully referred to as 'the hole in the market' by the local population. At the beginning of this century, the new town authorities realised their mistake and filled in the hole once more with new blocks of flats and a cycling museum featuring the Tour of Flanders. Let us hope that the lesson has thereby been learnt that the only way of preparing a town for the future is to pay due respect to the past.

I'm still standing daydreaming a bit on the bank of the Scheldt when three men on racing bikes pull up beside me. They are apparently from Australia and have come specially to Oudenaarde from 'down under' in order to explore the area of the Tour of Flanders. They soon set off again to do some climbing in the area of Patersberg, Koppenberg and especially Oude Kwaremont, and even though they have sophisticated GPS devices with them, the tower of the church of Oudenaarde will remain their point of reference wherever they ride. ■

The Scheldt and the church of Pamele. On the left the Palace of Justice. © Dirk Van Assche

Translated by John Irons

Down and Dirty in Sheffield

What Sheffield, the once so illustrious city of steel, is lacking in monumentality or authentic little canals or charming pubs or hills where lord or sir somebody or other kicked the bucket in the umpteenth battle over one or other shire, it more than makes up for with its local colour: the residents themselves, who, as soon as the first working day is over, are already getting dressed up again for the great debauchery of Sheffield nightlife; the boozing and verbal ejaculation that can last until the end of the week and knows no bounds. When the Englishman goes on a night out he liberates himself from his class, social conventions and inherited sobriety.

The main high street is designed to accommodate the greatest number of revellers to the greatest extent. On a typical evening, the body of merrymakers takes control of this urban zone – where, on a drizzly afternoon, next to nothing happens – for the satisfaction of every base instinct imaginable; swearing, screaming, ranting, spitting, provocation, baring their teeth, cramming themselves into pubs, undressing, fighting, drunkenly loitering or throwing up their stomach contents. In short, everything an Englishman should not do. I dare say that I learned more about the English by standing side by side with them for a few evenings in the pubs than by reading endless books about the nature of English culture. Moreover, every reference book I read after that only confirmed my impressions. Whatever irony and self-control the Englishman accumulates in his little finger during the week he loses entirely as the light of Friday afternoon fades into evening.

Before Osama Bin Laden became definitively radicalized in his revulsion for the West, I imagine that he visited this alcoholic inferno on a Saturday evening. Looking through the window of an overflowing pub must have provided the ultimate nudge towards Tora Bora. Here is the West at its most vile. Everything stinks of depravity. And even if in the past this flirtation with and surrender to excess was deeply mistrusted, frowned upon, to be kept out by all those trussed up in the corset of social responsibility, the English are finished with all that now. At the weekend, the confirmation of all anthropological research, which is that only the Japanese outdo the English as far as rigidity and formality is concerned, is smashed to smithereens. Sheffield on a Saturday night is one great big crazed Manga strip!

Decadence – once a privilege of the elite to drown in the plentiful final throes of a civilization in which all that has been gained is squandered with a mere wave of the hand – is now within grasp of us all. A pauper who is married to his horse can dream fancifully all night long, only to discover the following day that he is still a pauper and his wife is still a horse.

I know all this because my apartment looks out onto the car park where the local youth leave their Japanese hatchbacks - the girls wiggling their little chicken-bottoms atop high heels as high as a hairdressers' scissors, pulling irritatingly with their sausage fingers at their far-too-short mini skirts under which the sun bed-brown legs march onwards like frankfurters, and the boys all poor excuses for British second-division footballers – to then hasten in the direction of the establishments where the drinking-bout can begin. While the situational similarities to a group of ladies-in-waiting accompanying their knights to a jousting tournament may be observed, the fact that the passing of 1,500 years of emancipation means that it is actually the women who wear the trousers now and the men who just tag along behind like a kind of also-ran.

For me, the English are the politest people in the world because they have set the standard for indirect speech. The Dutch bluntness that lends their pre-sumption of always being right about everything a crassness that sometimes leaves me reeling in disgust, would result in social suicide here. When I look at the English, I feel like I am looking at an episode of *Planet Earth* where the herd of animals being portrayed has raised the act of communication and interac-tion with each other to an art form; I can hardly contain my delight when I see a queue forming, I take pleasure in the silences that hang in the underground, silences that are the result of inner courteousness, convention and avoidance behaviour, and how in a conversation strangers always end up finding out as

little as possible about each other. At the end of the documentary I always want to watch it again as soon as possible.

At the weekend, a very different documentary is played back: the uncensored, raw version that would be better off not being shown, were it not for the fact that the participants in this joyful, hideous masquerade excel at the precise exhibition of all manner of absurdities and swearing and yelling. What struck me was the brazenness with which this behaviour is displayed - behaviour of which anyone sober would actually be ashamed. The English are not good at keeping secrets, holding things back is taboo. Privacy, yes; secrets, no. And what could be finer than, in the company of friends – those who are allowed to get close and frequent your private space – to have no secrets: 'Hey everyone, look at my tits!'

Sheffield on a Saturday night is like carnival in Maastricht: everyone is dressed for an erotic *danse macabre* and it doesn't matter what you say or who you are, the only thing that matters is where your place is in the polonaise of pleasure and jollity.

Drink is the driving force that gives this energy-devouring enterprise that pleasant mixture of recklessness and courage, and gives the English that necessary impulse whereby the consciousness is compelled to make a detour. In my eyes, this is where one ceases to be an Englishman, though I'm well aware that I run the risk of being laughed at for this. As far as I am concerned, the men and women I saw out at night have nothing to do with the men and women who climb the stairs to their office on a Monday morning; they are two beings, two different entities which are mutually exclusive. Islands apart, in fact.

Pub life in Sheffield is something special; when I walk into a cafe in the Netherlands I feel as if I am entering a space where I could possibly disturb the established order of things. Maybe it's my imagination, but this imagination is fuelled by years of walking into cafes. In a Dutch cafe you have to fight for your place, nothing is taken for granted, especially in the trendy cafes that recognize a hierarchy and a social code that usurp many a fraternity member. Fortunately the threshold in the brown cafes is a bit lower, but rules apply even there.

Coming into an English pub you feel like you were the final person that was needed to complete the party; there is an instant feeling of joviality: a convivial atmosphere that is perceptible in the faces of the customers and bartenders. When I die, let it be in an English pub. They will drink to me and if there happens to be an Irishman nearby, then there will even be singing.

Alas, at the weekend the pubs change into a frenzied blazing ghetto. The absurdly early closing times force young people to drink far too much in a short space of time, a routine that has been cultivated just as the English cultivate everything they are good at, with a pleasant form of irony. Here, standing at the bar is not so much an escape from the hard daily reality of life, as it is a social event in which class differences do not matter and, provided he shows respect for the moral code at the bar, a stranger is welcomed just as warmly as the oldest client. What was immediately evident when I made my way past a number of these pubs – there is no other form of amusement in this city – was the intimate solidarity with which young and old hitch up together side by side and, as soon as you cross the threshold, there seems to be no such thing as a generation gap or a difference between the sexes. Here it is beer that fulfils the equalizing function fulfilled in our country by football and sex.

I would be lying if I didn't say that the scenes of Sheffield nightlife shocked me. It brings home to me again the prudish background I grew up in and in which every form of nudity, the presence of sensuality or licentiousness were severely disapproved of. Although I have certainly had my fair share of nudity, sensuality and licentiousness, I can hardly abide seeing it in others. It feels like I am being shown a magnified image from the Middle Ages of all my sordid antics from years gone by. But then there will be enough people who wouldn't call this sordid, just living life.

If my colleague, the author Herman Brusselmans, were in town, he would know how to handle all this youthful abandon, he would quickly pick out a character and then transform them into the Everyman of the modern day throwaway society, a world where the individual thinks they are born to utter as many idiotic statements as possible as if they were in a reality show, where drugs are seen as medicine and are consumed as a commodity and sex fulfils no other role than to get the two airbags through the boredom.

He would sprinkle all of this with the delicate intrigue of a visiting sidelined writer – drunk every day, with stinking breath, not even capable of getting his own belt through all the loops in his trousers properly – who begins a relationship with a very young waitress. In Sheffield he would discover that there are still a few places in the world where he has sex appeal. He would of course get her pregnant only to discover that the lady in question just wants to keep the foetus and from that day onwards sees him as no more than incidental. She retreats to one of the suburbs where at the weekend all the cars are parked nicely in the street, while behind closed doors the most unbelievably sleazy goings-on play out. The author would pay for his audacity in going there to gain satisfaction with a scuffle leaving him with at least a couple of broken teeth. As he is lying in a corner coming round from the battering by her brothers, the girl would bend over him and deliver the alarming words that he needn't go thinking he has the right to anything. Luckily for him, she then tries to speak a bit of English so that he will remember it. And Brusselmans would provide all this – which now appears to the reader a tad unlikely – with the necessary injection of reality and comedy that a story like this needs. I myself don't manage that. I try to see my observations as paving the way for a razor-sharp essay in which I give a lucid yet extremely insightful glimpse into the general deterioration of the welfare state.

The notion that the parents impotently turn their faces away from so much reckless abandon is based on a wrong set of expectations. They're all getting on with it too! Before one trollop of sixteen has passed by, she is already closely followed by another slightly older one, with a slightly thicker layer of slap and often just that bit more inebriated; but also more worldly, enough to mask that exuberance with a kind of "in your dreams" attitude: the mothers. They are just as shrewd as their daughters, but more experienced, and thus smarter, and even

more desperately in search of a bit of alright. This does not necessarily have to be a man. A nice cold beer will do.

The women dress, by Dutch standards, extremely provocatively. We would say sluttishly. The average amount of material on a Sheffield wench is just enough to make a face flannel. Their bodies are sun-tanned, here and there a little ring or star or a piercing. Heels, high heels. 'People don't think the attire here is offensive or common at all. It's generally accepted.' I doubt this: it would be 'generally accepted' if newsreaders were also to wear these clothes in their professional capacity. I don't see female newsreaders doing this. Even so, it is true that this parade of flesh comes across as relatively innocent; the few times I walked up and down the main street I did not see any aggression or harassment of women.

I know it is showtime again when I wake up suddenly in the middle of the night because someone has started yelling in the car park. It's always the same. Usually a woman screaming loudly and above everything and everyone else, but not a call for help. A call to follow. A fraction of a moment later the second call sounds, usually also female. The fugue of hysteria has begun. By now, a small group of women has formed, opposite which a comparable group of male yellers assemble; significantly more enthusiastic and with louder yells, but they keep it up for a shorter time. The choir has taken over the theme. The yell of a woman has a higher frequency in any case, whereby the squeal penetrates the ear much further. Once there has been some yelling then everyone has to run after each other. At the beginning I thought there was something serious going on. A mugging. Rape. Murder. In that order. The cause was something else. Drink. Hijinks. Horniness. All that energy and no where to go with it. Whether people actually do it with each other here, I don't know. 'For the Englishman, the evening is only really a success if, to his shame, he can't actually remember the next morning what he did the night before.' So he could have done everything or nothing. Life, a black hole into which everything disappears. Drinking beer as the equivalent of safe sex.

An evening that started out nice and friendly in a local pub where at about ten o'clock all the usual golden oldies started up, where a very ordinary, straightforward type of clientele came and, in the presence of unfamiliar, let's say fresh, menfolk, the local virgins immediately started to crank up the cleavage competition, turned their gaze and let their eyes wander strategically in the direction of the table where some man had settled himself. That was the pleasant part of the evening.

At about two o'clock the decline of any common decency among young people – from which I hope they will one day come to their senses – which I don't doubt

because, as well as the capacity for complete drunkenness, people also possess a talent for self-correction – was already in full swing. Girls walked desperately through the streets with reddened eyes in search of a taxi, a bottle of vodka, a man. I saw a fat youth looking despairingly towards his girlfriend as, not that far out of view, her fat finger disappeared down her throat after which a churning, hot stream of vomit erupted like lava out of Mount Etna. She stood there vomiting with a professional nonchalance that shocked me. He was looking at her as if he were looking at a long-treasured illusion that suddenly seemed to be based on nothing other than self-delusion. What I saw in those eyes I recognized very clearly, the fear of being rejected by a girl who, once she had finished vomiting and had sobered up considerably, would come to her senses and then decide not to go with him after all so that all the time and emotional suffering that he had invested in her would have been for nothing. Nightlife conduct is governed by a very efficient and ruthless logic. I wanted to go and sit next to him and comfort him, soothe him even, but I see that he can really do without the platitudes of a stranger. What he really wants is for his girlfriend to feel better again; he doesn't even see the rip in her tights. What he was secretly hoping was that, having recovered a bit, she would decide to stay with him after all and carry on drinking for a while. Nothing is as lovely as waking up next to someone with the same dead parrot in their mouth as you.

I walked around astounded, confounded. I was astounded by everything I saw, there was so much happening and so quickly that at times I had to pinch myself to come to my senses. A group of girls walked past me who, judging by their body language, had reached that point in the evening when they were seriously getting on each other's nerves. There are three of them, two really attractive and voluptuous, the third sallow and unremarkable. The latter is showing signs of a childlike dependency which the other two shrewder girls absolutely cannot stand. And the inevitable, what the other girl was so afraid of, just has to happen and does. She is abandoned. The other two run away from her in the direction of a taxi like two cyclists in the big final stage of a tour, sprinting away from another who has been tailing them up to that point and whose role is now completely played out. Exhausted, her arms hanging helplessly by her sides, the poor young girl stands there and stares, like a lover gazing at some long-lost memory, at the friends that she so desperately wanted but are now making their getaway in a taxi. Sure enough, only to get out a few hundred metres further up where they can continue their evening as they see fit, liberated from their burden. This is where the world can be very cruel, especially on a Saturday night.

I see a group of black girls, most of them with heels as high as Cleopatra's Needle, others have bare feet, their very expensive shoes hanging loosely from their forefingers, taking turns to glug on a magnum bottle of vodka. It looks rather like a scene from a nature documentary where a group of birds are taking their fill from a flower's chalice of nectar. They are drinking with a discipline that would be more appropriate to the dragoons from Tolstoy's *War and Peace* than these savage beauties.

There are still a couple of streets before I get home. I turn the corner and, before I have chance to realize, a glass object explodes next to my ear. A bottle. I look around alarmed, at the same time extremely wary of a possible second missile that may find its way to me. Something was thrown at me with no other intention than to hit me. And so I was driven from the Sheffield nightlife and have never returned. ▪

Translated by Susan E. Holdsworth

All photos by © David Bocking

ABOUT CITYBOOKS

The Flemish-Dutch House *deBuren* invites (with the support of the Culture Programme of the European Commission) international authors and photographers to take part in a two week residency with one of the local partner organisations in various interesting European cities (Sheffield, Bucharest, Charleroi, Chartres, Graz, Turnhout, Lublin, Ostend, Skopje, Venice, Utrecht etc.).
The resulting citybook (stories, essays or poems) can be read, listened to and downloaded for free on *www.citybooks.eu*. Every citybook is available as a webtext, e-book and podcast (audio book) of thirty minutes in Dutch, English and French. The podcasts are also available via iTunes. For each city a photographer makes a series of 24 photographs, and a City One Minute video project is made.

For *Germanic Studies/School of Languages and Cultures* (University of Sheffield) Henriëtte Louwerse hosted the UK version of citybooks. She welcomed five authors (Joost Zwagerman, Abdelkader Benali, Rebecca Lenaerts, Helen Mort, Agnes Lehóczky), a photographer (David Bocking) and a video artist (Dominic Green) to create a unique portrait of the city of Sheffield, an alternative travel guide.
Abdelkader Benali visited Sheffield in autumn 2011.

'Bought by Judgement of the Eye'

Dutch Theatre Looks at the State of the World

[JOS NIJHOF]

Shakespeare's drama has in recent years been more popular than ever in the Netherlands. In the 2012-13 theatre season at least ten of his plays, some of them revivals, have been performed on the professional circuit. Ivo van Hove, artistic head of Toneelgroep Amsterdam, says: 'I see Shakespeare as a contemporary. Even though his work was written more than four hundred years ago, it always turns out to be surprisingly up to date.' It's not only Van Hove who points out this timelessness, but other theatre-makers, too, and they all seem to like nothing better than to link the social phenomena of our era with the oeuvre of the great playwright.

Obviously Shakespeare never wanted to make a statement about the enormous expansion of social media, but in a festive adaptation of *Much Ado About Nothing*, director Jos Thie of De Utrechtse Spelen very clearly wants to broach the subject of the superficiality of media such as Facebook: 'The world Shakespeare drew is still very recognisable. As a director you look for a key that allows you to shape this recognisability, and in our case it's Facebook.' In the same vein, another director links *The Comedy of Errors* to the present financial crisis, and yet others, more obviously, associate *Othello* with present-day xenophobia, and *Macbeth* and *King Lear* with the despotism and delusions of grandeur associated with certain of today's leaders.

It seems that stage directors, and not only those working on Shakespeare, are almost compulsively looking for an answer to the question of how and how much we can use the classical repertoire to portray and comment on current affairs. How can we approach today's problems by making use of plays from the past? How are we to transpose the classical masterpieces of Shakespeare, Chekhov, Euripides and so forth to the present, and how are we to make the ideas and conflicts of the past merge with those of our own era?

Between stage and society

Until about ten years ago leading stage directors, guided by an unshakeable ego, tried to make their mark on theatre very emphatically by means of unexpected angles and highly individual interpretations. That period, the heyday of

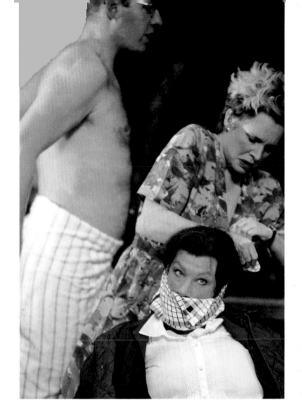

Boiling Frog © Sanne Peper

what was called 'director's theatre', gradually made way for the view that art in general, and theatre in particular, should stand up in its own right and should not have to act as a vehicle for personal obsessions. Directors faded into the background somewhat and more attention was paid to quality and the talent of individual actors and actresses.

The debate about the significance and commitment of theatre was probably cranked up again as a consequence of a number of drastic and 'dramatic' events in the Netherlands, such as the murders of the politician Pim Fortuyn and, a couple of years later, the controversial film and programme-maker Theo van Gogh and – definitely connected – the unexpectedly rapid advance of the Party For Freedom (PVV), a populist anti-Islam party whose frontman is the equally controversial and by now internationally notorious Geert Wilders. These events led to a great deal of political turmoil and debate in society, as was the case more recently with the global banking crisis, floundering European ambitions and the unexpectedly rapid ecological decline of our planet.

The directing naturally still determines the extent to which plays from the classical repertoire are geared to current affairs, and the pursuit of recognisability leaves considerable room for manoeuvre. For example, a director may be of the opinion that a production with a marital conflict at its heart can be used as a parable of a society in which people may or may not be able to accept the fact that other people are different. This is at least more or less how Ivo van Hove justified the four-part 'marriage series' (based on plays by Shakespeare, Ayckbourn, Ingmar Bergman and Charles Mee) that he directed at Toneelgroep Amsterdam between 2004 and 2006. It was a reaction to an attack made by his colleague Johan Simons, who criticised Van Hove, as head of the Netherlands' biggest theatre company, of directing noncommittal productions and thus remaining remote from the drifting society around him.

In Van Hove's view, loosely translated, the transfer from stage to society should take place in the spectator's experience, but the question is whether the existing classical repertoire is dynamic enough to generate this, even if theatre-makers expressly intend it and mould the classics to such an extent that it rubs the audience's nose in their – more or less clearly defined – intentions. They might for example direct *Elektra* or *Orestes* as traumatised African child soldiers; to contribute to the debate on integration they would have Ophelia walking around in a headscarf; they have the Cherry Orchard cut down with chain saws instead of axes, from which the audience is intended to understand something concerning current environmental problems.

Boiling Frog © Sanne Peper

It is not only the directors themselves who seem to be pretty fed up with these brilliant ideas, but audiences too. They have in the meantime been largely taken up by amateur theatre, where a new generation of directors uses every possible means to avoid giving the dreaded impression of outmoded dilettantism. Current affairs appear to be dragged in at the drop of a hat, but this does not always lead to the communication of any unusual point of view that gives cause for reflection.

To achieve the latter, one has to take a different approach, not only regarding the classical repertoire, but also when new and original plays provide the basis for the drama. An example of this was the project that the Rotterdam artist Jonas Staal launched at the end of December 2011. Under the title *Society as a Prison*, Staal presented a two-part work on the notion of a closed society versus an open one. The occasion for this was provided by a controversial 2004 architectural design for a prison designed by a PVV member of parliament. The form chosen for the piece was that of an 'all-round work of art', which included not only theatre, but also debate, reflection and analysis.

A more recent example, from March 2012, is *Breivik meets Wilders*, written by the writer and journalist Theodor Holman. It is a one-act play about a fictional encounter between the Norwegian mass-murderer, who expressed admiration for Geert Wilders in his writings, and Wilders himself, his great example. The two meet in the VIP lounge at Heathrow Airport before Anders Breivik's horrific deeds of 22nd July 2011. The discussion that follows reveals not so much the affinity between them, but the crucial difference: Breivik was not afraid of using violence to achieve his aims, while Wilders pursues his dreams through politics and democracy. The very topical subject of free speech also came up in passing. The stage Wilders says: 'One can think what one likes, conclude what one likes. That's called freedom. But one cannot do what one likes. After all, there are laws.'

The distance from reality

You cannot get much closer to the present reality than *Breivik meets Wilders*. But at the same time it raises the question of whether it can still be called a play, or is it more of an exposition in which the old rules of drama are set aside in favour of a statement that has to be made at all costs. Projects like those by Staal and plays like those of Holman appear to refer to a period when theatre productions in the Netherlands were quite often defined as current affairs programmes with a very partisan political angle.

In the wake of the *Aktie Tomaat* (Tomato Campaign) – the 1969 movement that opposed traditional repertory theatre – what were called 'informative theatre' groups popped up here and there; these were companies working on a collective basis which took a direct and confrontational look at the dubious practices of big business, from the strawboard industry in East Groningen to the DAF car factories in Eindhoven. Today's opponents of generous arts subsidies would probably call such groups as Proloog, Sater and the Nieuwe Komedie 'leftwing amateurs', and in this case it would not be entirely unjustified. According to one right-wing politician from that period, Proloog was a Marxist umbrella organisation which should not be given a single cent more subsidy. Yet, thanks to government support, 'informative theatre' survived until the eighties and this form of theatre has already been sufficiently vindicated in the chronicles of theatre history. Even now there are still productions that more or less maintain its legacy.

To give an example, this applies to some extent to *The Prey* by the Nationale Toneel, a production that attracted a lot of attention in the 2011-2012 season. At the very least it shares with 'informative theatre'a journalistic focus on current affairs and an interest in big business.The play was a dramatisation of the best-seller of the same name by Jeroen Smit, and tells the story of the downfall of ABN Amro, an institution which for almost two hundred years had played a role in the success of the Dutch economy.

Wiener Wald © Ben van Duin

Yet the need for a mission that goes further than a plain statement about avaricious bankers showed through in this production too. As the director Johan Doesburg puts it: 'The play says something about bankers, but also about every one of us. The lust for money is in our very fibre. It is the story of a struggle with no winners.' We also see this need for a transition to a more general truth, a truth that goes beyond mere anecdote, in other productions in the 2011-2012 season whose subject is the 'crisis'. For example, *San Francisco* by the young company De Warme Winkel, and *Boiling Frog* by Toneelgroep Oostpool, a play about 'the devastating power of the economy and the addictive discontent it arouses in us'.

Current affairs times ten: mightysociety

It is generally accepted that the director, Eric de Vroedt, and the changing actors and staff of mightysociety are among the best-known makers of contemporary politically-engaged theatre. They have made a series of ten productions since 2007, with management and publicity support from Toneelgroep Amsterdam. This series is very prosaically numbered, from *mightysociety1* to *mightysociety10*. Since the start in 2004, they have dealt with a varied range of subjects including terrorism, globalisation, the fear of Islam and the war in Afghanistan.

The penultimate production, *mightysociety9*, a three-part play 'on life and love in an era of poison scandals', was based on the notorious Probo Koala case. The story of this 'chemical odyssey', with the Panamanian ship the Probo Koala in the leading role, is extremely complex and the last word on it has not been written yet. To summarise, it describes the illegal dumping of four hundred tons of poisonous waste at various tips in Ivory Coast, for which the Dutch Trafigura company was responsible. This had disastrous consequences. According to some reports, hundreds of people suffered as a result of the dumping of this waste and there were at least ten fatalities. The incident led to the fall of the Ivory Coast government in 2006 and the legal aftermath is still continuing today.

The first of the three parts of the play shows how much the media manipulate so as not to disappoint the public, which has particular expectations. The cliché of the African biting the Western benefactor's feeding hand is overturned because this supposedly primitive being now has a mobile phone and a laptop, and in addition there is also an unwelcome love affair with a Dutch presenter. The second part takes us to a press conference given by the management of a Dutch multinational. The meeting gets completely out of hand, partly as a consequence of the director's dark-skinned wife making an appearance, and they get caught up in a heated dialogue that contains references to the myth of Jason and Medea. In the third part the play reaches a climax when two actors perform a competitive dance - a white office worker versus an inexhaustibly energetic African.

This summary shows how reality increasingly fades from sight in the course of the play, and how the initially realistic settings and chance occurrences dissolve into stylised artistic abstraction. The play ultimately breaks away completely from the Probo Koala issue and concerns itself only with the machinations that underlie certain political-economic developments. As the makers of *mightysociety9* themselves say: 'For quite some time, the whole Probo Koala debate has no longer been about people killed by poison. It is about greed, at the expense of everything else'.

The final part of this huge project, *mightysociety10*, which premiered in January 2013, zooms in on Indonesia, the country where De Vroedt's mother was born and where his father died. This instalment covers the time from a perfect youth spent in Batavia to the commercial nightmare of a luxury resort in Bali. But here, too, it is not essentially about the minor drama itself, but about the big story behind it. Against the backdrop of a vigorous, advancing Asia, it takes stock of a bankrupt Europe at the start of the second decade of this century.

Wiener Wald © Ben van Duin

The eye of the beholder

In the end, the main thing in current politically-engaged theatre is to find the right balance between realism and abstraction, fact and fiction, reality and imagination. Theatre-makers who, rather forcedly, try to mould the classical repertoire to fit their own insights and put great emphasis on the here and now run the risk of ignoring the difference in time and thereby generating a performance practice that is not rooted and which will float somewhere in an unrecognisable universe.

I have seen a few of the Shakespeare productions I mentioned above and to be honest not one of them gave me the slightest new insight into today's world. Conversely, not long ago I saw a version of Chekhov's *The Cherry Orchard* by the Arnhem company Keesen&Co that touched me to the quick. The acting and directing were outstanding and this play, more than a hundred years old, suddenly shed new light on the political division into left and right, which, as I realised, is all to do with ideals on the one hand and vested interests on the other, but probably also vaguely had something to do with lethargy and vigour. The world shifted a fraction and life briefly became a little more complex. And this happened at a more or less hallucinatory moment, without feeling that the director and actors were deliberately trying to push me in a particular direction.

In summer 2012, I saw one of the annual open-air performances in the Amsterdam woods. It was *Wiener Wald* (Vienna Woods), based on *Tales from the Vienna Woods* by the German-Hungarian author Ödön von Horváth. A play about Germany in the thirties, it was populated by a procession of characters from the petit bourgeoisie. On closer examination, the play has hardly any points of contact with the present, although a link can of course be made between the years of crisis at that time and our present financial malaise. The director allowed the script to do its job and did not make any radical changes to the historical dimension. The result, again, was a performance that touched me and taught me something about the vexation a society lapses into when money – or rather the lack of it – dominates life and love.

What determines the power of theatre is the appeal to one's own imagination and the individual potential for identification. Theatre should leave the audience room for its own, original, unforeseen insight into current events. Or, as Treplev, the young writer in Chekhov's *The Seagull*, says: 'You shouldn't portray life as it is, nor as it ought to be, but as it appears in your dreams'. I can't formulate it any more concisely and effectively than that.

In the second decade of this century, many theatre-makers have fortunately shifted the accent from the bare reality (or one larded with brilliant ideas) to the dream. It would not surprise me to learn that this development had been brought about precisely by the changes in the political climate and the debate in society. After all, it is only dreams that offer any way out of such tumult. However much an artist does his best to extol the virtues of his goods, in the end it is only the spectator's imagination that will be able to settle the dispute. To quote the Princess of France in Shakespeare's Love's Labour's Lost: 'Beauty is bought by judgement of the eye, / Not utter'd by base sale of chapmen's tongues'. So it is an indisputable truth that the transfer from the stage to society has to take place in the mind of the spectator. And theatre-makers have to be dreamers and share their dreams with the audience. ■

Translated by Gregory Ball

www.jonasstaal.nl
www.debalie.nl
www.nationaletoneel.nl
www.dewarmewinkel.nl
www.oostpool.nl
www.toneelgroepamsterdam.nl
www.mightysociety.nl
www.keesen-co.nl
www.bostheater.nl

Anna Bijns (1493-1575)

A Poetess in Antwerp

1528 saw the appearance in Antwerp of a remarkable collection of refrains. Among its novel features was its attribution to a living writer. Furthermore, the author turned out to be a woman, the 'honourable and ingenious young lady, Anna Bijns'. That this need be no obstacle to excellence was proclaimed at length on the title page. The book claimed to contain beautiful, refined texts, to be religiously orthodox and to offer a host of artistic refrains in line with the literary fashion of the age. This was all the more astonishing since women were not admitted as official members of the chambers of rhetoric. That was reserved for men. Yet Anna mastered like no other the art of the rhetoricians, who were the first to design a literary language and try their hand at new kinds of text.

That judgement was a contemporary one, since at least five editions of this first collection appeared during her lifetime. What is more, a Latin translation appeared as early as 1529 – virtually unheard of with literature in the vernacular – which actually gained her a European reputation. In addition, new collections appeared in 1548 and 1567, and were also reprinted. This was further proof that she had rightly been labelled ingenious in 1528, blessed with a talent inspired by the Holy Ghost irrespective of sex.

Fearing the charge of pride, Anna began her book with a dedicatory poem which immediately acknowledged her readers as her equals: 'Artistic spirits, who long for art', that is, we are all connoisseurs together, thirsting for good literature. She had not produced these texts out of vanity, but as a loyal daughter of Mother Church. And should anything have gone amiss with the style, 'tell yourselves, it's all just woman's work'. Women were intellectually less capable than men, as science had shown, and Anna did not question this. There was no question of irony, however much she might relish using it in other places. Still, this demonstration of humility after the fanfares to her genius was also very sophisticated. One did not need to be a connoisseur to see that her refrains were far superior to anything one might have read and heard up to then.

Anna Bijns, who lived and worked in sixteenth-century Antwerp, is one of the Low Countries' major authors. Yet her work is little known. But in her own time her texts were widely disseminated in manuscript and print. She was in fact the first writer in the vernacular to achieve widespread fame through the printing press. Everything she experienced in her city was material for her sharp pen. Nothing was taboo: badly thwarted love, the vain illusions of Luther and his followers, the threat of freebooters from Gelderland at the city gates, the insufferable policy of tolerance pursued by the city council, deceit and conflict within marriage, the sad but well-deserved lot of hen-pecked husbands and the need to relax with the hilarious nonsense of the repertoire of popular festivals.

She is able to express all that excitement with a verbal dexterity almost unequalled in Dutch literature. Complex rhyme-schemes, alliterations and neologisms gave her texts an irresistible cadence, while the subtly orchestrated passion still came across as natural. She was also the first author in Dutch literature, to present herself emphatically as an individual with personal views and emotions of her own. That was undoubtedly due in part to her being a woman, which meant that the rules of public life did not apply to her and to a large extent she was able to be herself.

The family Anna grew up in must have started her on the path to literature. Her father, a successful breeches merchant, moved in rhetoricians' circles, since at least one refrain by him is known. Probably he awakened Anna's interest in the new literature, which proved exceptionally congenial. She definitely participated in the competitions between members in the chamber of rhetoric. Talented women operated quite often in these male literary preserves, but always had to do so anonymously.

Was she not the fifteen-year-old girl from Antwerp who won a prize at a poetry festival in Brussels in 1512 with refrains in praise of the Virgin Mary? Unfortunately the age does not tally, since Anna Bijns was already nineteen at the time. But 'maiden' and an age of fifteen might well be an estimate in describing a teenager, as yet unmarried and still without a fixed position in society, who had been allowed to compete with the eminent gentlemen. With her younger

Anna Bijns grew up in the direct vicinity of the old town hall, which was demolished in 1564. Print from 1561. City Archives, Antwerp

'Den Bistro', then the 'Cleyn Wolvinne', is Anna Bijns's birthplace, at 46 Grote Markt. The property next door was later bought by her father too.

brother Maarten she ran a primary school, and after his marriage in 1536 set up in business for herself: she was now officially enrolled in the teachers' guild.For many years, until 1573, she continued to teach the simple catechism, alongside reading, writing and arithmetic. Finally, at the age of eighty she was no longer able to continue. Two years later Anna died, and was buried on 10 April 1575 after a pauper's funeral that was definitely not in keeping with the reputation she had acquired in the course of a long life.

Attacking the Reformation

Besides the three printed volumes, three bulky manuscripts of her work have been preserved, having been collected between 1540 and 1550 by the Antwerp *frater minor* Engelbrecht van der Donck. In addition, refrains by Anna are found in some fifteen manuscript collections of rhetoricians' work. All in all this dis-tribution in manuscript form points to great popularity in rhetoricians' circles, where a repertoire of such manuscripts circulated. The work that has been preserved consists almost solely of refrains, a genre that seems to have been invented with her in mind. Modelled on the French ballad, such poems had at least four verses, with a recurring line (or refrain) at the end of each verse marking the theme. Each verse, with an identical rhyme scheme, contained an exposition with varied arguments, which always culminated in the repeated conclusion in the refrain. This made the form admirably suited for persuasion and provocation, like an axe with a repeatedly chopping blade.

Anna's approach was far from dainty. With unequalled mastery of form and virtuosity she succeeded in raising the refrain to the level of a seemingly natural mouthpiece for the heights of indignation and the depths of feeling. The impact was all the greater because of the oral nature of the literary form. It involved emotionally-charged recitations to gatherings that were frequently not predisposed to share the opinions being expressed. Many rhetoricians had Erasmian sympathies or were even bold enough to take an expressly Reformist stance, while her merciless satires of family life were not calculated to please every head of household or lady of the house in her audience. Her refrains were built on such public confrontations. The audience was often addressed in so many words, as were those at whom a refrain might be strictly aimed: Luther, his foolish followers, lax monks, deceitful lovers, bossy women and hen-pecked husbands.

The first collection of 1528 consisted almost entirely of fierce attacks on the Protestant heresy, which she invariably saw as the aftermath of Martin Luther. The Lutherans were sneered at, derided and blamed for all the misery on earth. There was scarcely any reasoned argument, for which Anna anyway lacked the intellectual baggage. She had an impressive knowledge of the Bible, but at the level of the catechism lessons she gave to primary school pupils. She simply reiterated the traditional articles of faith of the Mother Church, but now allied bizarrely with the new literary genre and quasi-realistic street language.

As a result Protestant theology was reduced to the arrogant populism of conceited laymen who thought they could take charge of their own salvation: 'Scripture these days is read in the ale-house, / With gospel in one hand, in the other a pint.' Even women believed that they were capable of teaching the gospel to scholars – what drunken idiots! They were leading the world towards a new Flood, since 'Man wallows in evil like pigs in the sty'. This tone was tempered somewhat in the second volume, to make way for moralising, self-examination and meditation. In the third volume militancy faded into the background and resignation and praise of the Creator predominated.

Maarten van Rossem as a treacherous scoundrel. Woodcut from soon after 1542. Rijksprentenkabinet, Amsterdam

Crossed in love

Her refrains on worldly love, marriage and the family were very different, both serious and sarcastic. These are found only in manuscript form. Anna was sceptical about all aspects of earthly love. Lovers were faithless, marriage led directly to slavery and bred battle-axes and hen-pecked husbands, leading to complete chaos in the family. This was her variation on a set of literary themes that were almost de rigueur in the chambers of rhetoric and hence cannot simply be taken as an idiosyncratic preference. Still, Anna's almost obsessive choice of these themes is striking. She herself never married, though she did remain focused on the world, which at least leads one to assume that she did not want to exclude the possibility of marriage. At any rate deep disappointments in her personal love life may well have triggered these literary settlings of account.

The refrains with the recurring lines 'You are what you are, I've come to know you well' and 'Although I don't say much, I think no less for that' are telling. But elsewhere, too, the deep amorous wounds are repeatedly mentioned. Precisely that fixation on cheating in love create the impression that she is definitely making use of her own experiences, no doubt distorted and exaggerated, since we are after all dealing with literature. Besides, private situations and current affairs also prompt her to write in other situations too. That is the purpose of poetry: to give depth to the particular, individual and private and convert it into emotions and more general messages. That is also achieved by fitting these events into significant historical contexts.

That is why she opens a refrain with Jason as the archetypal love cheat, drawing a parallel between the deceitful lover and the faithless Christian, and hence making her personal experiences an integral part of God's scheme of salvation:

View of Antwerp as the trading metropolis on the Scheldt. From: *Lofzangen ter eere van keizer Maximiliaan*, printed in 1515 by Jan de Gheet. Facsimile edition, 1925

The one who believed so devoutly in me,
Now proves false. But I clearly see
How his passions fade.
Though once for my love he fervently prayed.

It is not even beyond the bounds of probability that she is trying to communicate directly with her ex-lover in this way, making it appear that he is still within reach. In the other refrain she addresses him directly as 'O love', and the emphasis in the whole poem is on humbly enduring the pain he has inflicted on her. She even reveals that she constantly bombards him with (literary) texts:

What good are my poems, all I write or say?
My lover thinks that they're hot air anyway.
Even if I read him this pretty wee refrain,
I'd declaim it in vain.

In such repeated assertions and laments there is a single message, only comprehensible to the intended recipient, which other readers and listeners cannot make head or tail of:

Princely love, it still makes my heart bleed,
That you should deceive me so: you know when indeed.

We know that Anna actually corresponded in refrain form, so that such remarks have a definite meaning. However, in this case, it can only apply to the deceitful lover. Such a clause is meaningless to an anonymous readership: the secret is not solved in the text, the unsuspecting reader or listener cannot help feeling excluded. Or is this a way of reinforcing the illusion that the listener is privy to private business?

This literary game is best understood as a personal formal expression of deep hurts, whether or not at the invitation of friends, a chamber of rhetoric or a printer. After all there is no real reason to leave such deeply-felt, intensely emotional sentiments hanging in the air as superior exercises in the art of rhetoric. The formal professionalism need not be at odds with personal motives. On the contrary, it provides the right platform for giving private sorrow literary shape according to the rules of art and the taste of the time. However, we know nothing concrete about Anna Bijns' experiences in love. She does, though, write about them continually. And we find that she is capable of establishing intimate relations with a small number of monks, who act as confessors, spiritual guides, literary admirers and editors.

There's nothing worse than Luther

She also had a number of personal friends among the Antwerp *fratres minores*. Brother Matthias Weijnssen in particular seems to be the person who encouraged her to write. Elsewhere too, the *fratres minores* were known to be fervent opponents of the Reformation. And literature in the vernacular

Even in 1520 Luther's work was still published openly in Antwerp: *Van den tien gheboden*, printed by Claes de Grave. City Library, Antwerp

was one of the ways they used to wage a propaganda war and reach as many people as possible emotionally. Very probably Anna allowed herself to be used for their purposes from the very beginning. Her themes matched their ambitions completely: fighting heresy, satirising marriage, and monastic entertainment in silly refrains with scores of names for anus and a farting competition among beguines – people were fond of combatting the dreaded melancholy, which could lead to suicide, with the crudest form of scatological folklore.

Her best known refrain concerns the (ironic) question: which is preferable, Martin Luther or Maarten van Rossem? This was prompted by the frustrated assault on Antwerp by the freebooter from Gelderland in 1542. In fact she used his violent actions to argue yet again how much more harmful the actions of Luther were. Van Rossem tormented bodies, but Luther sent souls to perdition. If destruction by the robber baron meant a passport to heaven, the price of selling one's soul to Luther was eternal damnation. Hence Van Rossem was after all the better of the two.

Van Rossem might be a villain, yet he had the 'advantage' of not being a heretic and therefore exercised some restraint with clergy and church property – at least so Anna maintained, before letting rip at Luther again. And for the umpteenth time she drew on her arsenal of terms of abuse, traditionally disguised as arguments. In view of his sermons no one could be sure of their own possessions any longer. And what's more Luther had set his sights particularly on the plundering and destruction of church property and egging people on to disobey the clergy. As a result of all those atrocities there had already been 200,000 deaths in the Peasant War in neighbouring countries.

Tsijn bede schrofte schapen we Christus cope
Der hepligher kercken weerd ich gheslotē
Niet eenen sope zijnse ouergoten
Tgheloove der kercken si bepde vertijen
Men soudtse wel ghelijcken met eender roten
Hoe de Lutheranen de herdoopers benijen
Sy zijn selue so vrij van ketterijen
Recht als tkerckhof vrij is van dooden lien
Want alle ouerhden seiten si besijen
En eens anders goep wercke en muege sp niet sien
Allet iammer datmen heenldaechs siet gheschien
Dat de stede verraden werden van binnen
Luther is de sake/ick blijfs bp dien
Aen de miraculen leert de sancten kinnen.

Refereyn. --- 13.

O God wat hooren wp nv al rumoers

In the final verse she reached the high point of her indictments of Luther, which though familiar were expressed with surprising originality. First she dubbed Van Rossem and Luther the prince of all 'highwaymen' and all 'false prophets' respectively. But why should she waste any more paper lamenting their atrocities? Actually both belonged in the company of Lucifer, whom she introduces at the last moment as the unexpected member of the trio: 'which of the three is best?' But even then she continued to give precedence to Van Rossem. She was most afraid of Luther's poison – Lucifer is obviously in a class of his own. And she concluded with a vulgar image that put things in perspective: she didn't give a 'squashed pear' for the choice – after which she wrote the recurring line for the last time.

Anna Bijns is the first author in Dutch literature to reach a wide readership thanks to the printing press. Her talents were fully recognised, used and exploited. The fact that she excelled in a literary form, which as a woman she was debarred from practising in the context of a chamber of rhetoric, makes it all the more piquant that in the view of her contemporaries she far surpassed all her male colleagues. ∎

Caricature of Anna Bijns in a copy of a 1541 reprint of the first collection of refrains. Royal Academy of Sciences, Amsterdam

FURTHER READING

Herman Pleij, *Anna Bijns, van Antwerpen*, Prometheus, Amsterdam, 2011.
Herman Pleij's anthology of her verse will appear shortly under the title *Meer zuurs dan zoets* (More Sour than Sweet).

Translated by Paul Vincent

Refrains

By Anna Bijns

Dedication

Artistic tempers, with art on your minds
Nothing here but what in good faith was done.
Now knowing this, relish its affection even more. [1]
And in case of a fault, well, 'tis a woman's work!

Bright spirits, to learn from you what's right
I am prepared to do; let your wisdom join mine.
In technique my skill, I know, is poor,
Not masterly yet; hence my teachers I praise highly.
So, eagerly, by artists I'll be taught.

For love of Truth, for an ever stronger Faith
I have blithely worked and shed no tears. [2]

[January 11, 1528]

1. The affection with which she wrote the poems.
2. This dedication (with acrostic) opened Anna's first book (1528).

Artificiael geesten, die na conste haect,
Niet en is 't gemaect dan uut rechter trouwen sterck.
Neemt hieraen gemerc, opdat ghi die jonste smaect.
Al esser yet misraect, peinst: 't is al vrouwenwerc.

Bequame sinnen, onder correctie reene
Ic mi stelle: mach wijsheit in mi vermeert sijn.
In consten kenne ic mijn perfectie cleene,
Noch leerkint, dus meesters moeten geëert sijn:
Seer geerne wil ic van constenaers geleert sijn.

Liefte totter waerheyt om 's geloofs verstercken
Heeft mi sonder verdriet uut jonsten doen wercken.

Unyoked Is Best! Happy the Woman Without a Man

How good to be a woman, how much better to be a man!
Maidens and wenches, remember the lesson you're about to hear.
Don't hurtle yourself into marriage far too soon.
The saying goes: "Where's your spouse? Where's your honor?"
But one who earns her board and clothes
Shouldn't scurry to suffer a man's rod.
So much for my advice, because I suspect -
Nay, see it sadly proven day by day -
'T happens all the time!
However rich in goods a girl might be,
Her marriage ring will shackle her for life.
If however she stays single
With purity and spotlessness foremost,
Then she is lord as well as lady. Fantastic, not?
Though wedlock I do not decry:
Unyoked is best! Happy the woman without a man.

Fine girls turning into loathly hags -
'Tis true! Poor sluts! Poor tramps! Cruel marriage!
Which makes me deaf to wedding bells.
Huh! First they marry the guy, luckless dears,
Thinking their love just too hot to cool.
Well, they're sorry and sad within a single year.
Wedlock's burden is far too heavy.
They know best whom it harnessed.
So often is a wife distressed, afraid.
When after troubles hither and thither he goes
In search of dice and liquor, night and day,
She'll curse herself for that initial "yes."
So, beware ere you begin.
Just listen, don't get yourself into it.
Unyoked is best! Happy the woman without a man.

A man oft comes home all drunk and pissed
Just when his wife had worked her fingers to the bone
(So many chores to keep a decent house!),
But if she wants to get in a word or two,
She gets to taste his fist - no more.

And that besotted keg she is supposed to obey?
Why, yelling and scolding is all she gets,
Such are his ways - and hapless his victim.

And if the nymphs of Venus he chooses to frequent,[1]
What hearty welcome will await him home.
Maidens, young ladies: learn from another's doom,
Ere you, too, end up in fetters and chains.
Please don't argue with me on this,
No matter who contradicts, I stick to it:
Unyoked is best! Happy the woman without a man.

A single lady has a single income,
But likewise, isn't bothered by another's whims.
And I think: that freedom is worth a lot.
Who'll scoff at her, regardless what she does,
And though every penny she makes herself,
Just think of how much less she spends!
An independent lady is an extraordinary prize -
All right, of a man's boon she is deprived,
But she's lord and lady of her very own hearth.
To do one's business and no explaining sure is lots of fun!
Go to bed when she list, rise when she list, all as she will,[2]
And no one to comment! Grab tight your independence then.
Freedom is such a blessed thing.
To all girls: though the right Guy might come along:
Unyoked is best! Happy the woman without a man.

Prince,
Regardless of the fortune a woman might bring,
Many men consider her a slave, that's all.
Don't let a honeyed tongue catch you off guard,
Refrain from gulping it all down. Let them rave,
For, I guess, decent men resemble white ravens.
Abandon the airy castles they will build for you.
Once their tongue has limed a bird:
Bye bye love - and love just flies away.
To women marriage comes to mean betrayal
And the condemnation to a very awful fate.
All her own is spent, her lord impossible to bear.
It's *peine forte et dure* instead of fun and games.
Oft it was the money, and not the man
Which goaded so many into their fate.
Unyoked is best! Happy the woman without a man.

1. Prostitutes.

2. Compare Shakespeare, *The Merry Wives of Windsor*, II.2: "Never a wife in Windsor leads a
better life than (Mrs. Page) does. Do what she will, say what she will, take all, pay all, go to bed
when she list, rise when she list, all is as she will. And truly she deserves it; for if there be a
kind woman in Windsor, she is one."

Het es goet vrouwe sijn, maer veel beeterheere.
Ghij maegden, ghij weduen, onthoudt dees leere:
Niemandt hem te zeere om houwen en spoede.
Men seijdt: daer geen man en es, daer en es geen eere.
Maer die gecrijgen can cost en cleere,
Niet haest haer en keere onder eens mans roede.
Dit es mijnen raedt: weest op u hoede,
Want zoo ic bevroede, ic zie 't gemeene,
Als een vrouwe houdt, al es se eel van bloede,
Machtich van goede, zij crijcht aen haer beene
Eenen grooten worpriem. Maer blijft zij alleene
En zij haer reene en zuver gehouden can,
Zij es heere en vrouwe: beeter leven noeyt gheene!
Ic en acht niet cleene 't houwelijck, nochtan
Ongebonden best, weeldich wijf sonder man.

Proper meijskens werden wel leelijcke vrouwen.
Arm danten, arm slooren, hoordt jonck metten ouwen,
Dit sou mij doen schouwen 't houwelijckvoorwaer.
Maer, wachermen, als zij den man eerst trouwen,
Zij meijnen de liefde en mach niet vercouwen,
Dan ees 't hem berouwen eer een half jaer.
Och, het pack des houwelijcx es al te zwaer!
Zij weten 't claer, die 't hebben ghedraghen.
Een vrouwemaeckt door vreese menich mesbaer,
Als de man hier en daer gaet druck verjagen,
Drincken en speelen bij nachte, bij dagen.
Dan hoort men beclagen dat men 't oeyt began.
Dan en muegen u helpen vrienden oft magen.
Dus hoordt mijn gewagen en wacht er u van:
Ongebonden best, weeldich wijf zonder man.

Ooc compt de man somtijts droncken en prat,
Als d'wijf haer gewracht heeft moede en mat,
Want men moet al wat doen, sal men 't huijs bestieren.
Wilt zij dan eens rueren haer snatergat,
Zoo werdt sij geslagen met vuijsten plat:
Dat droncken vol vat moet se obedieren.
Dan doet hij niet dan kijven en tieren,
Dat sijn de manieren, wee haer die 't smaeckt.
Loopt hij dan elders bij Venus camerieren,
Peijst wat blijder chieren mebn thuijs dan maeckt.
Ghij maegden, ghij weduwen, aen ander u spaeckt,
Eer ghij ooc gheraeckt in zelcken gespan.
Al waer 't dat ghij mij al contrarie spraeckt,

Mij en roeckt wie 't laeckt, ic blijv' er weer an:
Ongebonden best, weeldich wijf zonder man.

Een vrouwe ongehoudt moet derven 's mans gewin:
Zo en derf zij ooc niet wachten zijnen sin.
En, na mijn bekin, de vrijheijdt es veel weerdt.
Zij en werdt niet begresen, gaet si uutoft in.
En al moeste zij leven op haer gespin,
Voorwaer veel te min zij alleen verteerdt.
Een ongebonden vrouwe werdt alom begeerdt.
Al ees 't dat se ontbeerdt eens mans profijt,
Zij es meester en vrouwe aen haren heerdt.
Te gane onverveerdt, dat 's een groot jolijt.
Zij mach slapen en waken na haren appetijt,
Zonder yemandts verwijt. Blijft ongebonden dan:
De vrijheijt te verliesen, geen meerder spijt!
Vroukens, wie ghij sijt, al creeg dij eenen goeden Jan,
Ongebonden best, weeldich wijf zonder man.

Princesse
Al es een vrouwe noch zo rijck van haven,
Veel mans die achten se als haer slaven.
Ziet toe, alse u laven met schoonen proloogen,
En gelooft niet soo saen, maer laet se draven,
Want mij dunckt, de goeij mans sijn witte raven.
Acht niet wat gaven zij u bringen voor oogen.
Alse een vrouwe hebben in 't nette getoogen,
Es liefde vervloogen, dit sien wij wel.
In 't houwen werdt menige vrouwe bedroogen,
Die moeten gedoogen groot zwaer gequel.
Haer goedt werdt verquist, de man valt haer fel.
't En es vrij geen spel, maer noeyt zwaerder ban.
't Es somtijts om 't geldeken en niet om 't vel,
Dat dezelcke zoo snel liep dat hij stan.
Ongebonden best, weeldich wijf zonder man.

Yet, When Compared, Martin Rossom Comes Out Best

1.
Lately, melancholy's weight was hard to bear,
Made sore my mind, chased phantoms throbbing through my head,
Kept me brooding over oh so many things.
Just considering the world's present course,
What was there to brighten up my mood
With nothing but sorrow to spare - and I was sad.
And then my weary fancy in its rambling
Called forth a pair of men
With names the same but not much else.
One, Martin Luther, whose error spawns and spreads;
The other, Martin Rossom, whose cruel sword
Proved far too sharp for many far and near.
Rossom racks the body, Luther lays waste the soul,
So what's up! "Evil creature" fits them both.
To choose between these two? Waste of time.
Still, since Luther through his error kills your soul,
When compared, Martin Rossom comes out best.

(...)

4.
Martin Rossom, nobleman by birth,
As Emperor's renegade also his honor forsook;
But Luther betrayed the Lord Supreme
To whom his allegiance he had pledged
And put a nun's coif above his own.[1]
A nun who had promised God the same!
Why, Rossom spurns Emperor, but Luther's evil tongue
Wags at Pope and Emperor alike,
Teaches subjects' revolt against their betters,
Spreads defamatory libel of kings and princes,
Flings filth at church lords just the same.
Rossom wrought havoc fierce in Brabant's land
But his flaming fury did most often
Leave the Church alone, at least.
And blessed maidens he didn't even touch
(Though 'tis rumored that he did, here and there).
Martin Rossom: model of the tyrant harsh?
When compared, Martin Rossom comes out best.

5.

Where Martin Rossom's crime was treason,
Martin Luther's was double so foul,
For many a Christian soul his evil kiss
Slammed heaven's gate forever shut. Thus,
The Desecrator of Our Lord must have sent
This double plague to infect the Christian world.
Rossom a killer? Luther through his actions
Sent two hundred thousand peasants to their graves.
Blood of men and women freely flowed, with
Water and fire curbing his heretic's views.
So, he has butchered both the soul and body.
Martin Rossom merely racked the latter.
Now, he's just as cruel to the meek and lowly,
But through his hand, if they're patient, they'll soon be placed in God's.
Not that this would make his guilt seem less -
I'm not excusing him, I'm not washing him white!
Yet, though both be venomous vipers,
When compared, Martin Rossom comes out best.

(...)

7.

Martin Rossom and Martin Luther,
The best of both still a mutineer.
'Tis not strange that Rossom knows no fear,
For he's a soldier, a worldly cavalier.
But Martin Luther, that braggart, claims, he dares,
To comprehend Scripture down to its least detail,
With the Holy Ghost leading him on the way.
If supposedly he knows the way, his erring sure looks weird
But of course the ghostly spirit that guides him most
Has firmly wrapped its tail round Dymphna's painted feet.[2]
Martin Rossom sacked Brabant for tons of loot,
A sad affair which many still deplore,
But Luther himself has hands none too clean.
Monasteries were emptied by apostates on his command
Of their treasure and holy vessels. God will find out
If he didn't get a share himself. How about that?
Satan clasps both Martins in a tight embrace,
Yet, when compared, Martin Rossom comes out best.

8.
Martin Rossom, Freebooters' Prince,
Mastermind in stealing and plunder;
Luther, all false prophets' Prince,
If your histories I'd set out in full,
The reader would be much distressed, I guess –
'Twould also be a loss of time and paper.
Thus for now I hold my duty excellently done.
Allow me to defer the sequel to some other time.
Luther, Rossom, and Lucifer (for he fits in real well),
I wonder who's worthiest of the three.
Rossom piles much gruesome plunder in his lair,
Luther is conniving night and day,
Intent on poisoning our Christian lands.
So, this couple is wicked, very clearly so.
But Luther's venom most of all I fear,
For eternal damnation follows in its rear.
Even though the choice of either isn't worth a rotten fig,
When compared, Martin Rossom comes out best.[3]

1. Viz. Katharina von Bora's, whom he married on July 13, 1525.
2. The devil, who in paintings of Saint Dymphna crouches at her feet.

1.
Onlancx bezwaert zijnde met merancolijen,
De sinnen becommert, 't hooft vol phantasijen,
Van als overlegghende in mijn ghedachte,
Quam mij weijnich tevoren dat mocht verblijen.
Aensiende de werelt nu ten tijen,
Zijnde vol verdriets, des werdt mij onsachte.
Dus dinckende mij phantazijevoortbrachte:
Twee manspersoonen mij haest invielen,
Ghelijc van name, diversch van gheslachte.
D'een was Merten Luther, die dolinghe doet krielen,
D'ander Merten van Rossom, die 't al wil vernielen,
Die veel menschen bracht heeft in zwaer ghetruer.
Rossom quellet lichaem, Luther heeft de zielen
Deerlijc vermoort, dus esser cleijnen kuer
Tusschen hen beijen: elck es een malefactuer.
Ic en gaef om den kuer niet mijnen minsten teen.
Maer want Luther de zielen moordt duer zijn erruer,
Noch schijndt Merten van Rossom de beste van tween.

(…)

4.

Heeft Merten van Rossom zijn eere verloren,
Afgaende den keijser, hooghe gheboren,
Luther es den oppersten Heere afghegaen,
Die hij hadt gheloeft en trouwe ghezworen,
En heeft voer zijn cappe een nonne verzoren,
Die God ooc gheloefte hadde ghedaen.
Versmaet Rossom den keijser, merct Luther saen:
Hij spreecft van paus, keijser beijde veel blamen
En leerdtd'ondersaten teghen d'oversteopstaen.
Van princen en vorsten scrijft hij veel diffamen.
Prelaten, bisscoppen hoort men hem misnamen.
Al heeft Rossom veel quaets bedreven in Brabant,
Men sach hem niet veel kercken oft cloosters pramen
Met enighen brande aen gheenen cant.
Aen gheestelijcke maeghden en stack hij gheen hant,
Alsoo 't tot sommighen plaetsen wel scheen.
Al heet Merten van Rossom een quaet tijrant,
Noch schijndt Merten van Rossom de beste van tween.

5.

Es Merten van Rossom een verradere,
Luther es ooc een, en zooveel quadere.
Hij berooft met verraet van der hemelscher erven
Menich kerstenziele, dus Gods versmadere.
Lucifer heeft dees twee ghesonden tegadere,
Omdat zij heel kerstenrijc souden bederven.
Es Rossom moordadich, Luther heeft doen sterven
Tweehondertduijsent boeren duer zijn bedrijf.
Veel esser onthooft, verbrandt, ghesackt menichwerven
Om zijn valsche leere, beijde man en wijf:
Dus es hij een moordenaer van ziel en lijf.
Merten van Rossom mach meer d'lichaem hinderen.
Al mach hij d'onnoosele quellen even stijf,
Zijn zij patient, hij maect se Gods kinderen.
Dit en sal zijn sonde niet verminderen,
Ic en wil 't 's niet excuseren oft maken reen.
Al zijn 't beije twee venijnighe slinderen,
Noch schijndt Merten van Rossom de beste van twee.

(…)

7.

Merten van Rossom en Merten Luthere,
De beste van hem beijen es een mutere.
Maer 't en es niet vrempt, al es Rossom onghevreest,
Want 't es een crijchsman, een weerlijc rutere.
Maer Merten Luther vermeet hem, deesstutere,
Dat hij scriftuere verstaet na den rechten keest
En dat hij es vervult van den Heijlighen Gheest.
Die den wech dus wel weet, 't es wonder dat hij dwaelt.
Maer het schijndt wel den gheest regeert hem meest,
Die men onder Sint Dignen voeten maelt.
Al heeft Merten van Rossom veel roofs ghehaelt
In Brabant, d'welck noch veel menschen bequelen,
Merten Luther in dit stuck ooc niet en faelt.
Hij heeft d'apostaten uuijt cloosters doen stelen
Kelcken, ciboriën, ic wil 't God bevelen.
Oft hij niet mede en paert, elck knaghe dit been.
Al heeft de duvel dees twee Mertens bij der kelen,
Noch schijndt Merten van Rossom de beste van tween.

8.

Merten van Rossom, Prince van den snaphanen,
Die om stelen, om rooven zijt cloeck ter banen.
Luther, prince van alle valschen propheten,
Soud ic u legende gheheel vermanen,
't Sou den leser verdrieten, soude ic wanen:
Den tijt en 't pampier werd ermede versleten
Dus voer eens heb ic mij ghenouch ghequeten:
Tot op een ander tijtborcht mij de reste.
Luther, Rossom, Lucifer daerbij gheseten,
Mij twijfelt wie van drien es de beste.
Rossom sleijpt veel quaets aest'zijnen neste,
Luther es nacht en dach in de weere
In kerstenrijck te stroijen een dootlijcke peste.
Dus haer beijder boosheijt blijct in 't cleere.
Maer voer Luthers venijn ic mij meest verveere,
Want de menschen brenght in d'euwich ghleween.
Al en es den kuer niet weert een platte peere,
Noch schijndt Merten van Rossom de beste van tween.

Translated by K.P.G. Aercke.

Building an Open Horizon

The Vision and Work of Landscape Architect Adriaan Geuze

[JAN-HENDRIK BAKKER]

The stretch of water called the Vlaarding Vaart is spanned by a statement called the Twist. This bicycle and pedestrian bridge connects the new urban residential area with the Broekpolder nature reserve and recreation domain, with its tennis and hockey, which serves as a starting point for city residents who might like to take a long walk through the bird-rich peat fields and new nature areas. The bridge consists of a conventional path for walking and cycling, encased by an unorthodox robust steel frame. Just like the design for railway bridges at the beginning of the last century, but now a little more honed, in red, and sporting a cheeky twist halfway across; this is what gives the bridge its name. The local people used to call the bridge "*De Wokkel*" (a spiral-shaped crisp), but you won't hear that mocking tone these days. The Twist has become a defining part of the local community; it marks the transition from the city to the outside world. Much of the work and ideas of landscape architect Adriaan Geuze (1960) are characterised by robustness, sympathy for craftsmanship, and love for landscape and nature.

The Twist is one of the smaller-scale projects by West 8. This Rotterdam firm is currently one of the most well-known and successful design agencies in the Netherlands. It was set up by Adriaan Geuze in 1987 after he graduated from Wageningen. The firm combines landscape architecture with urban planning and has had some success in this area, with commissions for the major Dutch cities and also high-profile projects abroad, where West 8 usually works with local firms. As far as international fame is concerned, Geuze and his office seem to be on their way to succeeding Koolhaas and his office OMA, but with an entirely different approach. West 8 provided the Canadian city of Toronto with a new Waterfront on Lake Ontario, replacing the former industrial harbour site with a lively public area. Next to the New World Symphony Building in Miami Beach, a small, open palm garden grew up, and now serves as a podium for performances, as well as being a place where you can wander around a mosaic of paths. And since last year the Spanish capital Madrid has had a ribbon of green space and a recreation area in the heart of the city above the motorway along the Rio Manzanares. West 8 took part in an ambitious project to rejuvenate the river banks.

There is an increasing need for designers who can adopt a practical and integrated approach to urban chaos. Urban design needs landscape architecture.

There was once a world in which romantic designers busied themselves with gardens, estates and parks, while in another urban planners earned the money with their grand artistic developments. Now these two worlds are joining forces. The combination is relatively new. What is remarkable is that there are more landscape architects than urban architects working at West 8. This also reflects the realisation that the gap between town and country is being bridged.

Governor's Island New York
©West8

Catastrophic idleness

The career of Adriaan Geuze (1960) is a result of this development. He is a typical 'doer', but one with ideas about nature and landscape. Geuze combines a love of land and nature with modern urban design and planning. He and his firm radiate optimism and confidence in their own abilities. The optimism is a well-considered component of the ideology. As far as Geuze is concerned, this ideology is accompanied by sharp criticism of the lack of spatial planning, systematic thinking and cultural awareness of the generation that changed the face of the Netherlands after the post-war reconstruction period: namely, the baby boomers. Geuze holds this generation responsible for a catastrophic idleness which, chiefly in the Randstad, destroyed both urban and rural areas. More about this later.

The intellectual status that he enjoys seems to suggest that Geuze's integrated approach works. A professor at TU Delft and Harvard, he is often asked by the media to explain his vision of urban planning and cultural developments. His work has won several prizes. But he was also the leader of a group of critical architects and property entrepreneurs who united under the name *"Laten we Nederland mooier maken"* (Let's make the Netherlands more beautiful) to take a stand against the laissez-faire policy in spatial planning.

Waste processing

One of Geuze's most prominent and high-profile projects to date is the Schouwburgplein in Rotterdam. Later there was much criticism of the way the square functioned, but the bold Rotterdam-ness of it, with allusions to the intensive work in the harbours, was praised. The idea of combining housing and a waste-processing company on one site won him the Prix de Rome. Geuze continued to make a name for himself with the idea of transforming the Amsterdam neighbourhood of Borneo/Sporenburg into a compact residential area by moving the cars underground, exposing the open water of the IJ to everyone, and allowing a whole host of different building styles to preserve the openness of the public space as much as possible. Other projects that set him apart include the Leidsche Rijn Park (now Máxima Park) in Utrecht and the park on Governors Island in New York. In 2007 West 8 won a competition with the design for a 'world park' on the island, which is a national monument eight hundred metres off the coast of Manhattan. In 2005 Geuze was the curator of the Second International Architecture Biennale in Rotterdam. The Dutch polder was the central theme of this event. Previously, at the Venice Biennale, he had taken a critical look at the Vinex culture in the Netherlands.

Geuze's international successes seem to run contrary to his thoroughly Dutch orientation. But it doesn't matter, because, as Geuze himself constantly reminds us, it was in Holland that the *landschap*, whence the English word landscape

derives, was more or less discovered; first by the great hydraulic engineers, who slowly but surely drained the marshland delta, and then quickly thereafter by great painters like Rembrandt, Ruysdael, Potter and others, who went about portraying this new country. From a Dutch point of view, the landscape is something to be constructed. And that's also how Geuze sees his task as a landscape architect. Geuze has no qualms about contributing to a major symposium entitled *Towards the Megacities Solution*, with a talk that focused mainly on the landscape artists of the Dutch Golden Age. Moreover, Geuze is a direct heir of Dutch polder country. He was born there, in Dordrecht.

Governor's Island New York
©West8

Adriaan Geuze comes from a family of engineers: people who make things. His grandfather was an important man at the Lopikerwaard district water board. His father, a mechanical engineer, often took him and the other children to the mud-banks, the dike areas and the pastures around Dordt. 'He taught me this: the landscape is yours', a key notion in Geuze's world view, as was to be seen later. The expression makes a strong claim about being rooted, and it also reflects an active attitude. Reporters have often asked Geuze if he isn't a little too attached to the landscape of his youth, and whether his stance against the looting of the countryside is not just a bit idiosyncratic. He tells these reporters that a man has a right to be rooted and that the profound indignation that resonated throughout the Western world when the Taliban desecrated old Buddhist statues in Afghanistan should likewise greet the building over of the Netherlands' Green Heart. In his view, this is an equally huge cultural crime.

Footloose

Geuze's diagnosis of the current discomfort in Dutch culture is that the suburban person has become footloose. Unable to identify with the city, he sees less and less of the landscape of the surrounding areas. He is not at home anywhere. 'People don't function well if their social and physical environment caves in... It is a fact that people panic when their spatial orientation is turned upside down.'

Waterfront on
Lake Ontario Toronto

Although Geuze likes to provoke, the comparison to the Taliban is fairly close to the mark. The Green Heart of the Dutch 'Randstad' makes up a considerable part of the urban and personal identity of North and South Holland. Cities like Gouda, Haarlem, Dordrecht, Leiden and Delft have always been halfway houses in an area of water and pasture. It is a collection of cities around emptiness and openness. The filling in of the Randstad, as is happening now around Gouda with the construction of a second new town like Zoetermeer, called Zuidplas, is the worst of all possible urban planning scenarios and not even necessary if better use were made of the inner urban space, according to Geuze. 'Who decided on our behalf that the empty space is up for grabs? Did you read about it in a memorandum? Were you consulted about it? We, the makers of landscape, have allowed this happen to us!' he says in a conversation with colleagues.

There is a lot at stake for Geuze. 'The landscape that was shaped on the sea-bed forms the soul of Dutch culture. In this country with its polders and water cities, a unique landscape has developed: the 'Randstad'. Without the presence of an effective urban planning strategy, this metropolis will lose its vitality and, as a consequence of an inexplicable self-loathing, its magical empty centre with its horizons and low overcast skies. Without the panoramic polder land, the inhabitants will be spiritually lost, powerless like the Swiss without mountains and lonely like Italians without their culinary culture', says Geuze in his *Megacities* lecture.

Identity

Geuze is convinced that there is a close bond between people, culture and landscape. Dutch history is one of land-makers. Famous hydraulic engineers, polder pumping stations, low horizons, heroic projects such as the *Afsluitdijk* ('enclosure dam' that closed off the former Zuiderzee to form the IJsselmeer) and the Delta works, landscape builders, long skating and cycling trips into a headwind: they're all part of the Dutch identity. According to Geuze, this heritage has been lost because of two interrelated factors: the laissez-faire mentality of the generation that took control in the post-war period, and immigration.

As far as the baby-boomers are concerned, Geuze is convinced that they are to blame for cluttering up the Dutch polder landscape and selling it off at knockdown prices. Those responsible are a large group of administrators and politicians who, from the eighties onwards, refused to believe in the dynamism of the forefathers. In their soft, anti-authoritarian meeting-based culture they demonstrated that they were pampered and lazy, and had no intention of imposing any further visions from above. In the spirit of Thorbecke, the federal government left spatial planning to the provinces and municipalities, so that every village got its own industrial park and Vinex neighbourhood. Short-term vision and specific interests ruled public affairs. The bill for all this was presented in the nineties, when the cluttering of the Dutch man-made landscape spread all over. This sums up Geuze's vision of the generation before him.

Green heart

Geuze denounces these predecessors as the large group who took early retirement and are now enjoying the peace and quiet of their second homes in France, which they earned by ruining the peace and quiet of the Randstad. And those who saw Geuze recently in a VPRO documentary in conversation with Wim Derksen, director of the Spatial Planning Bureau, will have seen how the relatively young – or at least young-looking – architect heard from a former administrator that the Green Heart no longer exists, except in Geuze's romantic imagination. This cynical argumentation confirms Geuze's picture of a generation conflict. It is as if Derksen is retrospectively legitimising the lack of vision and drive of his generation. But in the same 2010 documentary, Geuze also met the young Dutch Minister of Logistics and Environment, Melanie Schultz van Haegen: 'Adriaan, it's not my job to make the Netherlands more beautiful,' she says. Apparently the problem is not just a generation conflict.

Vlaarding Vaart ©West8

Here we see two views of the task of government in conflict. One, that of Schultz van Haegen, holds that the government must ensure that business and citizens can get around as easily as possible in order to earn money, while the other believes in a totality of economy, ecology, climate and landscape. In his polemic, Geuze emphasises the value of the open character of the Randstad for the purposes of setting up business there. If the Randstad is going to end up looking like Los Angeles, international institutions and businesses, and the more highly educated inhabitants of the country, will no longer show any interest. In addition to that, he proclaims, filling up the low-lying land is about the most stupid thing you could do at a time when the sea levels are rising and the major rivers are facing more and more intensive rainy periods.

For Geuze it goes without saying that the quality of the surroundings, city and landscape has an impact on the human condition of the (post-) modern Dutchman. In his analysis he traces a lot of the current unease back to the immigration of foreigners in the sixties and seventies and the consequent departure of the middle classes from the cities. They left the inner cities and went to suburbia. The inner cities lost their diversity, but Vinex developments also lack vitality. Furthermore, every day commuters have to travel long distances, losing valuable time that could be spent with family and friends. Geuze reiterates this sort of analysis again and again. His architectural attitude is holistic.

Miami Beach
©Robin Hill

Maximá Park

This integrated approach can be seen in the Leidsche Rijn Park project, which connects the Vinex area of Leidsche Rijn in the west of Utrecht with the history and culture of the place. Alongside existing elements it also introduces new features such as a Victorian teahouse, a pergola wall, sports fields and a Japanese garden. The whole project is still ongoing, but even on a wet and windy day in January you can see that it works. It is the kind of park, at the crossroads of urban functions (living, working and recreational activity), for which Jane Jacobs – the advocate of the living city – would gladly have returned to earth: a couple of walkers from adjacent neighbourhoods, school kids on their way home, a little activity on the peripheries, a group of joggers braving the weather. You can reach it by bike from the centre of Utrecht in ten minutes.

Now called the Maximá Park, it is the size of Central Park in Manhattan, with its three hundred hectares. It creates an enormous free space in an area which would otherwise have soon fallen victim to urban sprawl. In fact it is made up of a great many snippets of residual waste ground and hamlets. It runs under the railway line and motorway, giving the impression that it is divided again. Geuze's invention is to hold all this together by means of a huge walkway and cycle path meandering for eight kilometres like a ribbon around the whole area.

The 'Ribbon' is an open invitation to joggers, cyclists, skaters and walkers. In the park itself old elements of the landscape from its polder history are combined with new elements. Original historical building meets nostalgic construction. Geuze also opens up the course of the Rhine bed, along which the Vikings entered Utrecht long ago. This Viking Rhine, which will eventually be openly connected with the Leidsche Rijn, is a vital section of the park; it invites people to go boating, but also reminds visitors of the old stories from Carolingian times.

In conclusion: Adriaan Geuze is a leading proponent of a new movement in urban

Madrid
©Jeroen Musch

planning, in which the concern for space as a totality is key. Not the single iconic building as an autonomous artwork or the garden as its rural counterpart, but the interplay of the two. In Geuze's book, city and country are no longer at loggerheads. Attention to the social and cultural aspects of living, such as connection to place and history, is a constant theme. Openness and horizon are key concepts that Geuze has brought with him from his own life in the Dutch polders. ∎

www.west8.nl/adriaan_geuze

Translated by Gregory Ball

FURTHER READING

Adriaan Geuze, 'The Necessity of Melting Polar Ice', *Towards the Megacities Solution* no. 10, TU Delft, 2008

'I Continue Where the Text Ends'

The Wondrous World of Illustrator Carll Cneut

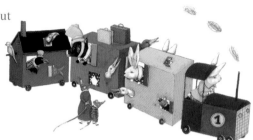

[ANNEMIE LEYSEN]

In 2011 Carll Cneut celebrated fifteen years as a professional illustrator. An exhibition, four new books and enthusiastic media attention put him and his work constantly in the spotlight. This attention and appreciation are totally appropriate. Cneut is an illustrator through and through, a craftsman with a passion for the book as an object and an obsession for drawing and painting. Together with a number of other talented illustrators of the so-called new 'Flemish School' he re-invented the picture book. With his typical, unmistakeable style, Carll Cneut has become well-known in recent years, both at home and abroad. His books have been translated all over the world into more than thirty languages and also received many prestigious prizes and other honours. At first glance, this success doesn't seem inevitable. Cneut's characters aren't creatures you'd want to hug or stroke. The often abstract style demands an attentive viewer, with imagination and empathy, and stimulates one's creativity. His pages are filled with grotesque, silent creatures, often against a sober, almost stylized background. Cneut is especially masterful in his eccentric compositions and his arresting use of colour, which create striking images and powerful narratives.

Commedia dell'arte

Carll Cneut (born in Roeselare, in 1969) studied graphic design at the Sint-Lucas Institute in Ghent. After a short career in the communications sector he became a full-time illustrator. He also teaches illustration at the Royal Academy of Fine Arts in Ghent. Since 1996 he has illustrated more than twenty children's books, of which a great number have found their way abroad. He works for the major British publisher MacMillan and has done illustrations for The New York Times. For *Dulle Griet* (Mad Meg) and for *Mijnheer Ferdinand* (Mr. Ferdinand) he was awarded a golden plaque at the Biennale in Bratislava. The French Prix Octogone was given to *Rougejauneblancnoir* (Redyellowblackwhite; orig. title: *Roodgeelzwartwit*) and he received a Special Mention at the Bologna Ragazi Awards for *Woeste Mie* (Wild Mie). Time Magazine named *City Lullaby* one of the ten best American children's books of 2007. *Het geheim van de keel van de nachtegaal* (The Secret of the Nightingale's Throat) received nearly every prestigious prize in the Low Countries. In 2010 he became one of the five illustrators nominated for the distinguished Hans Christian Andersen Award.

Carl Cneut is an illustrator who is not afraid to experiment. He paints a world that is related to the world of the commedia dell'arte, where surreal and lifelike elements blend harmoniously. His figures often look like caricatures, as he plays around with traditional proportions, perspectives and ways of expression. In his first books the settings were mostly reduced to the bare essentials. Later on the backgrounds became more exuberant and colourful. He is constantly experimenting with innovative techniques. Acrylic paint is used a lot in his drawings. He mostly puts down several layers in different colours and then adds pastel, pencil, wax pencil or ink. His brushwork and style have become more delicate and precise over the years. Composition is his forte, the way he is able to suggest an unfinished world that continues beyond the page. His work is constantly evolving. His mastery of form, colour and layout increases all the time, and he uses these three basic elements brilliantly to visualize emotions.

Carll Cneut never allows the written story to limit or constrain him. Strict instructions from the author would be wasted on him. His imaginative pictures add a new and free dimension to the text and an original interpretation. 'I continue where the text ends', he has said in an interview.

Left:
Whistle as You Are
© Carll Cneut

The Secret of the Nightingale's
Throat © Carll Cneut

Cneut made his debut in 1996 as the illustrator of *Varkentjes van marsepein* (Marzipan piglets), a book of poetry by Geert de Kockere. He immediately demonstrated his surprising personal style. You didn't see the usual adorable piglets on the cover, but a joyful tangle of pink energy. In another book by Kockere, *Een straatje zonder eind* (A little street without end), the illustrator lays the foundation for what will remain a stroke of genius: an original composition that takes the viewer far beyond the pages of the book. With *Willy*, Cneut makes a real breakthrough. A clumsy elephant that has become a target of abuse because of his plump legs, his big flapping ears and dangling trunk, discovers that his flaws are also his greatest strengths. In 2000 the book received the Flemish Peacock Award.

The first picture in *Roodgeelzwartwit* (Redyellowblackwhite) is intriguing to say the least. Four cube-shaped blocks seem to be floating against a yellow background. You only partly get to see the massive figures. The four colours subtly hint at the rest of the story. For *The Amazing Love Story of Mr. Morf* (*Het ongelooflijke liefdesverhaal van Heer Morf*), Carll Cneut also provided the story. It's about a circus dog, on a hopeless quest to find his true life's partner. Cneut lets his sad, yearning hero almost literally step off the page, at the top of which only the legs of his paired-off colleagues are shown. A very inventive device that makes words unnecessary.

Carl Cneut portrays emotions through the postures of his characters and a suggestive page layout, rather than by explicit facial expressions. "The postures tell you more about the characters in my work than their physiology or their expressions. (...) When you put all the expression into the face, the character becomes complete. He has become who he is and that creates a distance." That is also the underlying strategy in *Zie ik je nog eens terug?* (Will I See you again?), in which a tense little girl slowly thaws out by relinquishing her secrets bit by bit. Slowly but surely the illustrator brings little Sara out of her isolation by making her more and more dominant on the page.

Mijnheer Ferdinand (Mr. Ferdinand), a poetic story by Agnes Guldemont, is again an example of a successful symbiosis of colour, composition and form. The story is as follows: Mr. Ferdinand has lost something, but he doesn't know what it is. He is overcome by a kind of midlife crisis and he doesn't feel like doing anything anymore. In vain he starts looking for what he has lost. In one moving picture you see the poor fellow on a park bench, sliding into total apathy. His posture suggests more than words can ever convey. Gradually Mr. Ferdinand discovers that it is all a question of looking. A book to read slowly and to look at closely.

Willy © Carll Cneut

With his striking illustrations for *Dulle Griet* (Mad Meg), Cneut's drawing technique and use of form and colour reaches an impressive height. The book is inspired by the intriguing painting of the same name by Pieter Brueghel the Elder. The illustrator wanted to give this bizarre, apocalyptic scene his own interpretation. To this end he has lifted Mad Meg from the Brueghel painting and given her a new life and a different background. She is no longer the warrior woman in helmet and breastplate, but a vulnerable and at the same time recalcitrant female, who, because she has been cast out by her community, tempts fate and presents herself to the devil. Brueghel's full, turbulent background has been replaced by random snapshots of people and composite, hallucinatory monsters with fish heads and bird bodies. The book becomes grimmer with each new page, with hatred, envy, spite and despair on the large faces, reminiscent of those by Ensor. Good and evil, hypocrisy and ruthless cruelty are all given timeless expression in toothless skeletons and abhorrent monsters. The tone is black, both on the intriguing cover and in the images full of war, hell, rage and madness. In this book, Cneut ingeniously connects the Flemish present with its past, through images and themes, and boldly shatters the dividing line between minor and major literature. Like no other he is able to give expression to the deeper meaning of the story. His daring interpretation caused a lot of commotion, especially in Italy.

His masterful juggling with proportions and blown-up details turn *Monster, Don't Eat Me* (*O monster, eet me niet op*) into an ingenious picture book. It was published in 2006, in eleven languages and fifteen countries simultaneously. It's about eating and being eaten, with once again a greedy pig as its main character. Here Cneut uses, for the first time, busy, colourful backgrounds, with lots of attention to detail.

In *Een miljoen vlinders* (One million butterflies), a story by Edward van de Vendel, ethereal butterflies of every kind and size and colour can be seen flying around. The little elephant Stach is being harassed by whole swarms of them, which disappear when he gets company. He can't understand it. To his resigned parents, however, it is all too clear. "Oh, our very own big boy ... the time has come." With a knapsack, tears and wishes for "the very best" he is sent on his way to figure things out. Cneut has drawn this colourful butterfly universe with a flourish; you can nearly hear the rustling of their wings. The different compositions into which he has placed his characters are again masterful: for example, a whole throng of animals, with Stach in the middle, is spread over four pages, as the illustrator typically goes beyond the boundaries of his page. Other pages project emptiness and loneliness. Again, with such an abundance of colourful, intriguing characters, you are reminded of paintings by Ensor, Brueghel and Bosch.

On the cover of the collection of animal poems, *Fluit zoals je bent* (Whistle as you are), compiled by Edward van de Vendel, there is also a colourful animal parade going by. The drawings inside are sometimes mere illustrations, but just as often add something to the poems they accompany. Cneut has dressed up the animals in bright clothes, in keeping with each character, and has given them human traits and postures. Immediately the dividing line between the species becomes blurred. Human or animal, what is the difference actually? It isn't really important in this wonderful 'carnival of the animals'.

One Million Butterflies
© Carll Cneut

For his many adaptations of world literature classics, Ed Franck found the perfect visual interpreter in Carll Cneut. In *Hou van mij. De mooiste verhalen over liefde* (Love me - the most beautiful love stories) with six adapted stories by Franck about famous couples and their tragic loves, Carll Cneut succeeds in evoking the spirit of the time in which the story is set and palpably bringing the passion, tragedy, sorrow and desperation of those loves to life. Downright masterful are the drawings Cneut made for the book *Te veel verdriet voor één hart* (Too Much Sorrow For One Heart), published in 2008, a re-telling of four tragedies by Shakespeare. For each character the illustrator had an interpretation and a separate technique. Collages, photographs and acrylic drawings alternate. Hamlet remains a shadowy face against a black background, while Ophelia's pale face nearly disappears into a black dress that becomes part of a dark background. King Lear is shown in profile in a black collage, while his beloved daughter Cordelia emanates tragedy and fragility in her white dress. Once again, Cneut leaves a lot to the imagination of the viewer. Black and blue are the dominating colours in the drawings for *Nachten vol angstaanjagende schoonheid* (Nights Full of Terrifying Beauty), an adaptation of stories by E.A. Poe. Here, too, Cneut is able to subtly capture the eerie atmosphere of the texts retold by Ed Franck, with spectres, shadows and skeletons looming out of the darkness. More colourful shadowy images illustrate *Verboden liefdes* (Forbidden Loves), Franck's adaptation of stories from *The Decameron*. Cneut shows himself a master in the art of suggestion in this book.

For his adaptation of the fairy tale *The Nightingale*, by H.C. Anderson, Peter Verhelst insisted on having Carll Cneut as his collaborator. The effect of this joint venture, *Het geheim van de keel van de nachtegaal* (The secret of the nightingale's throat), is overwhelming. In a perfect combination of text and images, author and illustrator put their own artistic signatures on the fairy tale. They wanted to make a book for people "to feast on" and they have certainly achieved their goal. It's hard to take your eyes off the more than forty small and lavish paintings. Cneut doesn't fall into the trap of using an obvious and affected oriental-looking style. Again he makes use of his strengths and turns the whole book into a masterful symbiosis of colour, form and composition and adds his original take on a different culture. Busy, dynamic images alternate with more intimate scenes that closely follow the rhythm of the story. He creates a beautiful play of light and dark and experiments with new techniques like Chinese shadows and with colours that are unusual for him. Blue, yellow and green dominate here. His typical red is hardly used. The brushwork

Monster, Don't Eat Me © Carll Cneut

of the backgrounds is rough. Carll Cneut clearly enjoyed himself painting the imperial Garden of Gardens, an abundance of wild flowers and plants, in lavish colours and a thoughtful layout. The clothes and attributes of the imperial household also turned out to be right up his alley. Each costume and object has the proper cut and texture, with beautiful hues and patterns. This delightful book was given nearly every prestigious prize. And it seems to mark a new direction in Carll Cneut's work, as can already be seen in *De blauwe vogel* (The blue bird). In this fairy tale full of symbolism by Maurice Maeterlinck and adapted by Do Van Ranst, the use of dark colours, the fascination with textures, the silhouettes and the eerie magical atmosphere continue.

Always pushing boundaries

Ten Moonstruck Piglets (*Tien bolle biggetjes keken naar de maan*), a cheerful cardboard book for young children, seems to be a recapitulation and finalization of fifteen years of illustrating. The fat, sleepy-looking piglets, the enormous moon, the suits in all colours and sizes, the house with windows open to the whole world, they all make reference to earlier picture books. Is it time for something else, a new beginning, surprising perspectives? The upcoming projects leave no doubt about that. A second collaboration with Peter Verhelst, a book with the Italian author and illustrator Anna Castagnoli and another with Saskia De Coster, plus illustrations for Ed Frank's adaptation of *The Canterbury Tales* are all in the offing.

With his unique style, Carll Cneut has definitely pushed the boundaries – in every sense – between literature for children and for adults, between local and distant cultures, between humour and emotion, between tradition and renewal. His work has given children's literature new colours, forms and structures in recent years, as well as breathing refreshing new life into it. ■

Translated by Pleuke Boyce

SELECTIVE BIBLIOGRAPHY

M. Maeterlinck, Do Van Ranst, *De blauwe vogel*, De Eenhoorn, Wielsbeke, 2012

Lindsay Lee Johnson, Carll Cneut, *Ten Moonstruck Piglets*, Clarion, Boston, 2011

Lindsay Lee Johnson, Joke van Leeuwen *Tien bolle biggetjes keken naar de maan*, De Eenhoorn, Wielsbeke, 2011

E.A.Poe, Ed Franck, *Nachten vol angstaanjagende schoonheid*, Davidsfonds, Leuven, 2011.

Ed Franck, *Verboden liefdes. Verhalen uit Boccaccio's* Decamerone, Davidsfonds, Leuven, 2011

Edward Van De Vendel, *Fluit zoals je bent*, De Eenhoorn, Wielsbeke, 2010

Peter Verhelst, *Het geheim van de keel van de nachtegaal*, De Eenhoorn, Wielsbeke, 2008

Ed Franck, *Te veel verdriet voor één hart*, Davidsfonds, Leuven, 2008

Eward Van De Vendel, *Een miljoen vlinders*, De Eenhoorn, Wielsbeke, 2007

Carl Norac, *Monster, Don't Eat Me!*,Groundwood Books, Toronto, 2007

Marily Singer, Carll Cneut, *City Lullaby*, Houghton Mifflin Harcourt, Boston, 2007

Carl Norac, *O monster, eet me niet op!*, De Eenhoorn, Wielsbeke, 2006

Ed Franck, *Hou van mij! De mooiste verhalen over liefde*, Davidsfonds, Leuven, 2006

Geert De Kockere, *Dulle Griet*, De Eenhoorn, Wielsbeke, 2005

Edward Van De Vendel, *Zootje was hier*, De Eenhoorn, Wielsbeke, 2004

Agnes Guldemont, *Mijnheer Ferdinand*, De Eenhoorn, Wielsbeke, 2003

Ed Franck, *Zie ik je nog eens terug?*, Querido, Antwerpen/Amsterdam, 2003

Carl Norac, *Een geheim waar je groot van wordt*, De Eenhoorn, Wielsbeke, 2003

Brigitte Minne, *En toen kwam Linde*, De Eenhoorn, Wielsbeke, 2003

Carll Cneut, *The Amazing Love Story of Mr. Morf*, Macmillan children's Books, 2002

Carll Cneut, *Het ongelooflijke liefdesverhaal van Heer Morf*, De Eenhoorn, Wielsbeke, 2002

Danie Billiet, *Een wereldkaart op ware grootte*, Averbode, 2002

Brigitte Minne, *Roodgeelzwartwit*, De Eenhoorn, Wielsbeke, 2002

Geert De Kockere, *Woeste Mie*, De Eenhoorn, Wielsbeke, 2000

Brigitte Minne, *Heksenfee*, De Eenhoorn, Wielsbeke, 1999

Geert De Kockere, *Willy*, De Eenhoorn, Wielsbeke, 1999

Geert De Kockere, *Ik heb een idee!*, De Eenhoorn, Wielsbeke, 1999

Geert De Kockere, *Niel*, De Eenhoorn, Wielsbeke, 1998

Geert De Kockere, *Straatje zonder eind,* De Eenhoorn, Wielsbeke, 1997

Geert De Kockere & Annemie Van Riel, *Koetje in de klaver*, De Eenhoorn, Wielsbeke, 1997

Geert De Kockere, *Varkentjes van marsepein*, De Eenhoorn, Wielsbeke, 1996

I Found a Form

Hubert Van Herreweghen: Seventy Years a Poet

[PIET GERBRANDY]

How much room for manoeuvre do we have? We are born with a genetic coding, we are shaped by the environment we grow up in, society conditions us, in order to eat we have to work, we reproduce, we experience war and grief and finally our powers decline and we disappear into the abyss. Isn't freedom a spurious concept? Isn't everything we think, say and do determined by forces which we not only cannot control, but of which we are not even aware?

One could see the last few centuries of Western culture as an attempt to escape from the restrictions of origin and nature. In science, philosophy, art and literature, as in politics, there has been an urge towards emancipation and liberation, in which, since every revolution creates its own dictatorship, every victory is a Pyrrhic one. Technology offers both mobility and control, God's laws have been exchanged for those of Darwin, visual artists have obeyed the decree that abstraction and conceptualism have made the depiction of reality redundant, those who left the church were converted to nebulous something-ism or aggressive consumerism. We'll never get any further, while, in the meantime, neglecting valuable traditions and exhausting natural resources.

And what about poetry? Although many wild experiments have come and gone, from Ezra Pound's intertextual fireworks to the hermetic linguistic implosions of Hans Faverey, from the politically charged expressionism of Van Ostaijen and Lucebert to the elusively evolving on-screen word formations of Tonnus Oosterhoff, basically little seems to have changed. All poets still celebrate, to use an old word, the inexorable progression from birth to death, while focusing en route on love, beauty and life's horrors. They try to give their words a pregnancy that does not work in prose, making grateful use of the universal fact that language is built of sounds. Poems are concentrations of music and meaning. Poets have been doing that for thousands of years. How much variation can you expect? And isn't poetry so precious precisely because it always does the same thing?

Despite the power of tradition many poets begin as revolutionaries and rabble-rousers. Everything must change, and what Harold Bloom calls the anxiety of influence drives them to assassinate their intellectual fathers, but as soon as they are admitted to the establishment a kind of ossification generally appears. What was once startlingly new becomes a party trick. The freedom of the

Hubert Van Herreweghen (1920)
©Anne Van Herreweghen

adolescent was a rite of passage. Almost no one manages to remain an innovator all through their life. Perhaps that is not even necessary. Gerrit Kouwenaar, once a distinguished champion of an alternative poetics, has been writing the same poem for the last thirty years, but it gets better each time. H.H. ter Balkt repeats himself in every collection, but sparks and crackles as noisily as he did half a century ago.

Focused on harmony

Hubert Van Herreweghen (1920), revered in Flanders as a master but unknown in the Netherlands, has been through an extremely interesting development in his seventy years as a poet. Although as a journalist and television programme-maker he was in close touch with current affairs and he must have closely followed the technological innovation of what we today call 'old media', as a poet he was always averse to publicity and avant-gardism. In his retreat in the Brabant countryside the poet went entirely his own way. Hugo Claus and Hughes Pernath, Herman de Coninck and Eddy van Vliet came and went, but Van Herreweghen seemed completely unconcerned. Brought up in the ancient Catholic faith, with a strong bond with the countryside and familiar with the long history of Dutch, he made his debut in 1943 with poems that in terms of both form and content might just as well have been written several decades previously. His second collection, *Liedjes van de liefde en de dood* (Songs of Love and Death, 1949) opens as follows:

The words that hold each other dear
And glisten in the self-same glow,
group into sentences so clear,
and dance out the poem in a row.

Although in the second verse the anguish of a poet can be heard, even that dissonant note cannot conceal the fact that this poetry is focused on a harmony that is sometimes difficult to reconcile with the turbulence of post-war culture. Old social structures decay and crumble, the colonies fight free of the rule of their exploiters, women fight for emancipation and Charlie Parker's alto sax explores every nook and cranny of tonality, but Van Herreweghen picks a lily-of-the-valley 'to show a girl plain/that no words can explain/ how my heart longs for her'. Nor does he shrink from writing a verse such as this that belongs in the darkest misogynistic tradition of Christianity:

Women are like a keg that's cursed
if from the dregs you try to drink
next morning you'll be full of thirst
and your breath will stink.

The poet is totally anachronistic when, as late as 1953, he appears to sub-scribe without the slightest doubt to the archaic dogmas of original sin and damnation. At least, this does not look like irony:

Like boils that burst and pus and ordure leak,
death breaks us open when we are bursting quite
with viciousness and sin, and with a heretic's shriek
our souls are lost for good in evil's dreadful night.

In the margins of prayer books

But lo and behold, the poet matures, and as he grows older does not cling to what is so familiar, but instead undergoes a step-by-step process of poetic liberation that I find fascinating. In one of his less lucid moments Herman de Coninck called him 'Flanders' most recalcitrant, language-grinding innovator'. That is nonsense, since Van Herreweghen is in no way an innovator and his language does not grind, but sings and dances. But the older bard definitely reinvented himself. Although there has been no shift to speak of in his themes and he remains true to the prosody copied from fifteenth-century rhetoricians like Anthonis de Roovere, his work gradually opens up in a way that allows the wealth of phenomena to speak for themselves. Perhaps even the older Van Herreweghen finds it hard not to preach, yet he observes the world with a de-tachment that some years ago I described as Buddhist. The seasons pass as they always have, the farmer goes on ploughing, the hops are added to the fermenting beer, children are born and the old return to the earth. The poet looks on and smiles.

In 'Jug', from the collection *Aardewerk* (Earthenware, 1984), he speaks about form. Discovering is not invention but recovery:

I found a form that many found,
a space that fire and clay surround,
a wall of mud from ploughed-up land.
Its stone-like fullness filled my hand.

The image of an earthenware jug for poetry is of course not new; one has only to think of John Donne's 'well-wrought urn' and Keats' 'Ode on a Grecian Urn'. However, it is striking that Van Herreweghen stresses the earthly origin of the clay and the simplicity of form, which is expressed in the repetition of the rhymes. The jug contains nothing but water, with which the poet refreshes himself. But even the absence of living water does not detract from the value of the earthenware:

Thirst quenched, your virtues I expound:
your belly's curvature rings out
up to your rim, all hollow and round.
The vacuum leaves your beauty safe and sound.

The virtues are not those of some divinity, but of the poem itself, as a self-contained artefact enclosing an emptiness full of meaning. That is a modernist principle.

If the form of 'Jug' is still evocative of the poet's late-medieval models, he also began gradually to experiment with typography. Indentation and extra spacing between lines create air and space, creating a visual rhythm that suggests an interplay of voices. The poems seem to become a series of responses, in which the right-hand side of the page enters into dialogue with the left-hand side. Dialectic would be too ponderous a word, since Van Herreweghen is seldom concerned with conflicts, but he does create a musical question-and-answer dynamic which is in search of a new equilibrium. There is a nice example of this in *Een kortwoonst in de heuvels* (A Smallholding in the Hills, 2002):

Flowers after the lightning
>*terror's allowed*
>*and thunder all night long*

>*Peonies irises unopened*
>*the sensitive membrane*
>*too tender to touch*
still stand next day
>*disarmed and terrified*
>*glad that they're alive*
and feel the tepid light upon their eyes...

Though I tremble too
>*we can still laugh together.*

In the first two verses, if I can call them that, the three lines that begin at the left-hand edge indicate steadfastness in difficult circumstances, while the indented lines evoke rather the vulnerability of the flowers. Even the happiness at still being alive issues from the fear that has been endured. Since the right-hand side has more than twice as many lines as the left-hand side, in the last verse the speaker tries to restore the balance by placing his concern on the left and his relief on the right, and in addition neutralises the 'night' of the first verse with 'laugh'. Over and against this there is the fact that in a musical sense the trembling of the 'I-figure' constitutes an answer to the survival of the peonies. The initially separate characters – since the flowers are personified – are united in the final four words. A provisional state of harmony has been reached.

In 'Still Life' culture and nature enter into a dialogue. On the left we read about an elderly couple that are on the point of dissolving back into the landscape from which they emerged, on the right their situation is related to old prayer books and still lifes. At the same time there is a suggestion that we're not dealing with wild nature but with farmland that has been rather left to its own devices, while on the other hand the above-mentioned art objects derive their beauty from the vegetation:

> Though crops we'd long been, grown wild
> just like woad plants, we,
> two death's heads seemingly,
> we blend along the lea
> with the blue of chicory,
> clay's multiplicity
> and, more real than a painting compiled
> > in the margins of missals,
> > of ancient epistles,
> > to princes or abbeys supplied,
> serrated silverweed,
> > > beside.

> Wild life mild
> > in the oval of an afternoon
> > made a mild
> > > still life.

The rhymes 'wild', 'compiled' and 'mild' are telling: rough is opposed to civilised, until in the final word they merge in a kind of Hegelian synthesis, which does not represent a compromise or an Aristotelian golden mean, but a new phase at a higher level. The princes recall the famous medieval song of the two royal children, who are contrasted with the old lovers who *did* find each other. The phrase 'serrated silverweed' is striking – 'serrated' refers to the leaves of this member of the rose family – which both through the suggestion of a carpentry operation (sawing, fretting) and the material silver, seems to belong more in the world of applied art than at the edge of a meadow. However, the fact that the plant is more real than 'painted' suggests mainly the realism of the illumination in the margin of the manuscript. The longer you look at this tranquil scene, the livelier it becomes.

The gestation of the poem

Van Herreweghen is by no means blind to events in the wider world. In *A Small-holding in the Hills* he refers several times to military action, while in *Webben en wargaren* (Webs and Tangles, 2009) he reacts subtly to the xenophobia that seems ineradicable even in highly civilised Western Europe. But this poet is not a troublemaker, his way of criticising is to show an alternative, a world of care and attention, where man forms part of a landscape that he has come to know thoroughly over the centuries. He looks with love and compassion at the most unsightly insect, the humblest plant, the most fleeting raindrop. It is the look of a walker aware of the history of the path he is on, who experiences his transient presence as a kind of grace.

Language is one component of the natural environment that through its history carries with it a knowledge of the world from which we can learn a great deal: 'The words that know more about things / and more of life long before my time'. This is why Van Herreweghen is fond of rehabilitating words and showcasing elements of his own dialect. These are often terms from agriculture, nature and local crafts. You won't find such words as 'kaamsel' (froth on beer or wine), 'sas' (punch [tool]), 'har' (hinge), 'keest' (germ, bud), 'schokkeloen' (barley) in everyday Dutch. Although it is of course worthwhile looking up words like these if you don't know them, which in itself is a kind of craft activity, they also generate through their rarity an almost autonomous music, which has an evocative effect even apart from meaning. In his celebrated 'Lyric Poetry - Instructions for Use', an essay by which Van Herreweghen admitted he was influenced, Paul van Ostaijen says:

Where both meaning and sound value operate together, I speak of the sonority of the word, and by that I mean, as in painting, the vibration of interacting values, the imponderable that lies in the tension between two words, a tension which, without being represented by any particular sign, produces nonetheless the essential vibration.

We find the 'sonority of the word' in what Van Ostaijen calls 'pure lyricism' in a poet like Rimbaud ('Voyelles'), but particularly in the predecessor who is probably Van Herreweghen's main source of inspiration: Guido Gezelle. A precursor of the modernists in his language-oriented constructions, Gezelle was first and foremost a lyricist who praised God's creation. Both aspects are also markedly present in Van Herreweghen. We hear pure sound in 'Toe':

Toe 't plezier te zeggen toe
            (eerst de tongtop tegen tanden
            dan het blazen van de oehoe)
liet me dikwijls open zwijgen
zonder dat ik daarom hoe
toe dan ook 't gerucht 't gedicht
dat de zotte zinnen richt
in zijn rotten dicht kon rijgen.
(...)

Do the pleasure of saying do
            (first your tongue-tip tight on teeth
            then expelling the ooh hooh)
often paralysed my tongue
leaving me without a clue
how to keep the poem's sounds
that hold the crazy words in bounds
within its ranks securely strung.
(...)

(Note: 'toe' can be used in Dutch as an encouraging, inviting, mocking interjection (Compare: 'Do come in, vicar'). It also means 'closed'.)

The interplay of sounds acquires biblical associations in 'Rattle':

The man who held together
            the shabby lamb
that came from its mam
            in his arms crammed
            before it could be a ram
                        or a wether
            or a ewe
            I stared after him:
                        A-
                  bra-
                              ham?

So lame so tame
            so blade so male
            so meek a fine view.

In the second half of the poem, as in Jan Hanlo's 'Oote', only ostensibly meaningless syllables are left (ra, ta, ram, ma), scattered casually over the page. But a note informs us that 'tarara' is the Spanish word for 'winnow', and if one looks further one sees a tame lamb (*tam lam*) emerge, a mother, the Indian god Rama and the holy month of Ramadan. What does all this suggest? The holiness of all creation, for which one is required to sacrifice new-born children? The magic of old syllables? Whatever the case it is a poem that one can listen to for a long time.

Listening is probably Van Herreweghen's greatest virtue. In 'Wang' he says: 'my writing is more wordless listening / than saying what I may know'. In a wonderful, not too serious prose text of 1955, the poet describes his visits to Brabant breweries where special beer was maturing. After pointing out the earthy smell of the fermenting brew he describes its auditory aspects:

Sometimes the beer spits like an angry cat, and you can hear it doing its best and making an effort, and on a lukewarm summer's evening, as you walk through the galleries with slow cautious steps, you hear, not without a surge of strange and altruistic emotion, how the beer is tiring itself out for you. Sometimes you hear it squeak like a nest of young mice.

Is this not a splendid image for the fermentation of the poem? ▪

Translated by Paul Vincent

Six Poems

By Hubert Van Herreweghen

The poem

The words that hold each other dear
and glisten in the self-same glow
group into sentences so clear,
and dance out the poem in a row.

A poem can start just like the rain
or swaying like snow, and light.
All at once in the chorus's train
you hear the poet's sobbing plight.

You hear him under the to and fro
of the words imbued with pain
because no sultry phrase can flow

over March leaves like rain,
because no word can weigh like snow,
no sound make flowers smell again.

Het gedicht

De woorden die elkaar beminnen
en glanzen in hetzelfde licht,
rijen aaneen tot zuivere zinnen,
dansen de rei van het gedicht.

Als regen kan een vers beginnen
of wiegend als de sneeuw, en licht.
Plots hoort gij in de rei daarbinnen
de dichter die te schreien ligt.

Gij hoort hem onder het bewegen
der woorden, waar 't verdriet in vaart
omdat geen zin zo zoel als regen

kan ruisen op het loof in maart,
omdat geen woord als sneeuw mag wegen,
geen klank de geur der bloem bewaart.

From: *Songs of Love and Death* (1949)

Uit: *Liedjes van de liefde en van de dood* (1949)

©Anne Van Herreweghen

And you

If to death you're blind
in the child in the wife
all you love in life
you can't read my mind

    if you can't hear or see
    in the water and wind
    in the eyes of a friend
    in words, melody

shy things that portend
the swift flight is through
the child starts to bend

    earrings' tinkles end
    you want to call that friend
    but he's dead. You too.

En gij

Wie de dood niet ziet
in de vrouw in het kind
in al wat hij bemint
die begrijpt mij niet

    wie niet hoort en ziet
    in 't water en de wind
    in de ogen van een vriend
    in het woord en 't lied

het schichtige het te snelle
de vlucht het is voorbij
het kind gaat overhellen

    stil vallen de orenbellen
    de vriend wilt gij nog bellen
    maar hij is dood. En gij.

From *Poems IV* (1967)

Uit: *Gedichten IV* (1967)

Source

The water that's in love with life
      long yearning must learn to bear
      till the appointed day is there
it came towards me from its cave
      always cheerful and pious
          wildly composed
      it looked at me up close
      my eyes in its eyes
and I said good day mr water,
          liquid lady,
having come to greet the sunrise
on this holy day
      from a thousand deep nights
and I said lick me lick
          my hand, I said
and it licked me and blessed
          the deeply reverend
and where it flowed
      and tried to fall
      we laughed, we all
      willow, alder and grass,
      the herbs that were there
the sun and I, the cloud and the earth.

Bron

Het water op het licht verliefd
      moet lang verlangen dulden
      tot de dagen zijn vervuld en
't kwam uit zijn grot naar mij gelopen
      het altijd vrolijke het vrome
          het wild bedaarde
      het keek mij aan dichtbij
      mijn ogen in zijn ogen
en ik zei goedendag heer water,
          vochtige vrouw,
naar de opgang van de zon gekomen
op deze heilige dag
      uit duizend diepe nachten
en ik zei lik me lik
          mijn hand, zei ik
en 't likte mij en zegende
          het diep eerwaarde
en waar het liep
      en wilde vallen
      lachten wij allen,
      wilg en els en gras,
      van kruiden wat er was,
de zon en ik, de wolk en de aarde.

From: *Basket and Trough* (1993)

Uit: *Korf en trog* (1993)

Stubborn day

The stubborn day beech hedge and holly
  all sullen wood with knots in
    from the shadows of
      bristly bushes in the verge
        and thorny undergrowth
          wrests the green night forth
            and wounds me as it feels
              the tender epidermis
                with its scored bark
the soul a membrane of nerves
            with its rock-hard grooves
              and ridges of displeasure
            greys the light
and in horror he retreats.

Like this love might begin
a lick of love's what we lack
but time is short

      it's freezing within
      at noon the sky's black.

Stugge dag

De stugge dag haagbeuk en hulst
  van nukkig hout met kwasten
    wringt uit de schaduwen van
      borstelig bermgewas
        en doornig onderhout
          de groene nacht naar buiten
            en kwetst mij als hij tast
              de tedere opperhuid
                met neuten van zijn basten
bezenuwd vlies de ziel
            met zijn steenharde groeven
              en ribben ongenoegen
            vergrauwt het licht
en gruwelend wil hij weg.

Liefde zou zo kunnen beginnen
er is een lik liefde vandoen
maar tijd te kort

      het vriest al binnen
      het avondt op de noen.

From: 'Uncollected Poems' in: Dirk de Geest (ed.),
Bloemlezing uit de poëzie van
Hubert Van Herreweghen (1999)

Uit: 'Ongebundelde gedichten' in: Dirk de Geest (ed.),
Bloemlezing uit de poëzie van
Hubert Van Herreweghen (1999)

The great schools

One who paints the sea as a white plane
knows that the moon beneath the tiles
                    of the roof
                        rules the hard roe
                            and soft.

Then great schools move south
                        the armies of clones
                        homeless, alone
                        banished from sea to sea
along with the ancient law
                        of moons

there goes what longs for deep and dark
there that raging silver churns

they turn north
                        drilled into a single sect
where the maternal net
silences the writhing of the death urge.

From: *A Smallholding in the Hills* (2002)

De grote scholen

Wie de zee schildert als wit vlak
weet dat de maan onder de pannen
                        van het dak
                        regeert de kuit
                            en hom.

Dan trekken grote scholen zuid
                        de legers klonen
                        die zoeken waar te wonen
                        van zee tot zee verbannen
met de oude wet
                        der manen mee

daar gaat wat diep en duister wil
daar gaat dat woedend zilver om

en keren noord
                        tot één sekte gedrild
waar 't moederlijke net
't gespartel van de doodsdrift stilt.

Uit: *Een kortwoonst in de heuvels* (2002)

Tangle

I can't get a comb through my hair anymore
I hold a thing and let it go,
Things' existence is absurd,
people's helpless gesturing.
I am the wind, I romp with leaves
I hold a thing and let it go,
it's caught in a wild tangle,
fingers don't know where to begin,
it doesn't stick out, it doesn't stick in.
I held a thing and let it go,
with the wind it's gone to sail.

My ma'd have wound it without fail
round her wooden reel just so,
which she to the last would not let go.

Wargaren

Ik krijg geen kam meer door mijn haren,
ik heb iets vast en laat het los,
der dingen zijn is zonder zin,
der mensen 't hulpeloos gebaren.
Ik ben de wind, ik stoei met blaren,
ik houd iets vast en laat het los,
't verstrikt in een wild warregaren,
de vingeren vinden geen begin,
't steekt er niet uit, 't steekt er niet in.
Ik had iets vast en liet het los,
't is met de wind gaan spelevaren.

Mijn moeder vroeger zou 't wel klaren
en winden op haar houten klos,
die liet ze voor de dood niet los.

From: *Webs and Tangles* (2009)

Uit: *Webben en wargaren* (2009)

All poems translated by Paul Vincent

Dreams and Achievements

Theo Jansen's Beach Creatures

They loom on the coastline: huge monsters resembling gigantic crabs or elephants. With their yellow bones these arthropods have a timeless, prehistoric-looking form. They move, driven by the wind, between seawater and loose sand. Sometimes they are solitary colossuses; sometimes there are whole herds of them together. They have no need of food; they derive their energy from the wind.

The likelihood of your coming across them next time you visit the beach is small, but if it is up to the artist Theo Jansen, sometime in the future our beaches will be populated by herds of 'beach creatures' living and propagating completely independently. This new species has sprung from his imagination. Since 1990 he has worked in his studio in Ypenburg, a district of The Hague, on new, increasingly intelligent generations. Every now and then a new specimen is tested or you can visit an exhibition of beach creatures as it travels the world. But the easiest way to see these intriguing creatures at work is to see them on the Internet. Both on the artist's website and on YouTube you can watch films of beach creatures in action. They are amazing. They are not only beautiful to see but they really look alive, though they are actually made of yellow PVC tubes. The technical genius of the artist is amazing too; the fact that he has the knowledge of mathematics and physics to produce such an effect on those who see these creatures and knows which materials to use.

Trial and error

Some of this is a result of Jansen's education. In the seventies he studied physics at the Technical University Delft. He very quickly abandoned his studies, however, to concentrate on his artistic activities. From the start he combined these activities with science. In 1986, for example, he developed a *Painting Machine*. A paint-spraying machine moves in horizontal lines from top to bottom in front of a canvas, measuring the amount of light with an electronic sensor. The darker the spot detected the more paint the machine sprays on the canvas. This enables the painting machine to make an almost photographic replica of the people and objects in the room. A few years previously he had constructed a flying object, which he sent into the sky above Delft, without notifying the inhabitants. Then he went to gauge the reactions. Some of these can be seen on the DVD

Theo Jansen. Works of Art. Flabbergasted inhabitants find the UFO "really scary". One woman is extremely shocked: 'I thought my days were over'. With visible enjoyment Jansen continues his questioning; he shows the front page of a local newspaper the following day: 'UFO spotted over Delft'.

The artist tries to move his 'creature' on the airfield Valkenburg.
© Loek van der Klis

Causing amazement and recreating nature: two elements that Jansen would continue to develop in the oeuvre he began in 1990. It started, writes Jansen in his monograph, *The Great Pretender*, with a book by the British biologist Richard Dawkins. Jansen remembered a passage from it about how stick insects have become what they are now through natural selection and evolution. He found a second germ of an idea for his new oeuvre in an old column he had written in de Volkskrant – Jansen was a columnist for the newspaper for a long time. In it he wrote about the rising sea level. It can be prevented if we manage to raise the height of the dunes: 'There really should be creatures that constantly loosen lots of sand and then throw it into the air so that it blows towards the dunes'. Together these germinal ideas would result in the beach creatures as we know them now and have done for more than twenty years. But the process started on a computer screen. *Artificial life* was in its heyday at the time; software that allowed a self-created world of virtual 'creatures' to evolve. Jansen designed little 'creatures' himself on his PC, in the form of lines which he subjected to evolution and selection. The next step consisted of virtual creatures with four legs on their bodies.

But the beach creatures only actually became real when Jansen translated his ideas into material form. He came across the appropriate material very quickly - cheap, readily available, yellow PVC electrical tubes that are resistant to wind and weather. Just as protein is the building block of every form of life on earth, so the PVC tube is the building block of his universe of beach creatures. By trial and error he searched for the strongest and most effective tube constructions. First

he bound them together with tape, later with nylon cable ties, and later still he tried bending the tubes with hot air. That turned out to provide the best result. In fact Jansen has divided his beach creature era into different periods according to these construction techniques. Just as in geology we have the Palaeozoic and the Mesozoic eras, so the beach creatures lived successively in the Pregluton (the creatures on the computer), the Gluton (the period during which he used tape), the Chorda (nylon cable ties), the Calidum (hot air) and the Tepideem (tepid air, which reduces the risk of the tubes breaking). In this way the artist reinforces the idea that he has created a whole new world with the beach creatures, a world that evolves according to the scientific laws of the world we know. The creatures' names contribute to that idea too. Inspired by the Linnaean method of categorising and naming species, which still frames our biological knowledge of the world today, Jansen created a taxonomy of "Animaris" creatures, a species he baptised with a name formed by the contraction of "Animal" and "Mare" (sea). The very first actual beach creature, which was developed in the Gluton, was given the name "Animaris Vulgaris". It could not walk. The subsequent development of the legs was a very crucial step that helped the species to survive. Here, too, Jansen used computer models. Starting with a crankshaft with a diameter of 15 centimetres to drive the legs, the computer calculated the ideal measurements for the rods that formed the legs. This series of 12 'sacred numbers', as Jansen calls them, forms the 'DNA' of the beach creatures. This is passed on from one generation to another. In the meantime there are eight generations, including, after the Tepideem, the Ligna-tum (in which Jansen abandoned the electrical tube and started experimenting with wood and steel), the Vaporum (during which the creatures' movements generated compressed air, so that they could move forwards even when there was no wind) and the Cerebrum, the phase we have been in since 2006. In this present period Jansen has developed so-called 'nerve cells', constructions that allow the beach creatures to start thinking independently. In practice what it comes down to is that the artist invented a sort of step counter. As soon as a creature reaches the tideline a mechanism is activated that makes it turn around and go in the opposite direction till it reaches the loose sand on the other side, at which point it walks in the other direction again. Thanks to this ingenious intervention the creatures 'remember' how far they can move forward. Their advanced form of intelligence prevents them getting stuck in loose sand or being carried away by the waves. For Jansen leaves no doubt about it: 'I'm not trying to make beautiful creatures. I'm working on survival - damned hard.'

Wriggling on their own square metre

In earlier generations some of the beach creatures developed other characteristics that were intended to increase their chances of survival. There is the Animaris Sabulosa, for example, a creature from the Calidum. Large parts of the body of the Sabulosa are stuck with tape. That is good for the sturdiness of the construction, but it also has a handy side effect. Grains of sand get stuck to the creature's 'skin', so that it takes on the colour of its environment and is therefore less visible to any natural enemies. A form of mimicry that occurs frequently in existing nature, too. The Animaris Rigide Ancora (Tepideem), on the other hand, had a sort of tail with an anchor on the end of it. The anchor ensured that the creature always stood with its propeller-side in the wind, so that it had a constant supply of energy. And the Animaris Arena Malleus (Calidum) had a trunk with a little hammer on the end that attempted to knock a peg into the sand, which meant the creature could prevent itself being blown away.

The 'Rhinocerae' are outsiders in the land of the beach creatures, too. Jansen designed them in the Lignatum. They are massive, robust creatures with a sort of cockpit so that they can transport someone. There are specimens in cardboard and in wood (pallets), but the most impressive rhinoceros is definitely the Animaris Rhinoceros Transport. This creature's skeleton consists of steel and the skin is made of polyester, which gives it a greyish, rhinoceros-like colour. The monster weighs a good 3.2 tons and is nearly 5 metres high. Nonetheless it can run with the wind. During a trial on an old airfield this rhinoceros creature ran so fast that its joints

Animaris Geneticus
© Guus Dubbelman

gave up. After repair, the Animaris Rhinoceros Transport was given a place in a pond in Amsterdam. Jansen dreams of taking the creature off its base once a year and letting it walk through the streets of this city on the Amstel. It would give his art a new, social dimension. But it hasn't happened yet.

Smaller in size than the Rhinocerae are the Vermiculi. Jansen developed these worm- and caterpillar-like creatures in the Vaporum, the period in which he experimented with stored air. The worms and caterpillars had a system of muscles – defined by Jansen as 'things that get longer or shorter on command' – that sent a surge through their bodies, a vigorous horizontal or vertical wriggling. Only they didn't manage to propel themselves forward, they remained on the spot in their peristalsis and were limited to rather charming wriggling on their own square metre.

Convinced deep down that he's a god

In 2011 Jansen tested the most recent offspring of the family of beach creatures on the beach south of The Hague. The Animaris Gubernare, the 'steerable beach creature', was the 38th manifestation of the species since its creation - and we do not know how many more manifestations there will be. Nor do we know whether the artist will achieve, before he dies, his dream of developing a beach creature family that lives completely autonomously, reproducing itself and able to survive quite independently of him on beaches all over the world. We do know that in the meantime his creatures have attracted attention from journalists, art lovers and aficionados worldwide. Major broadcasters from Japan, the US and South Africa have devoted reportages to Jansens' oeuvre. Top magazines like *Wire* have made space to present his creatures and comment on them. So though Jansens' creatures have not yet succeeded in propagating themselves, his ideas certainly have. But why? What is it about the beach creatures that appeals so much to us - and to the world?

First of all there is the form and appearance of the beach creatures. They are biomorphic, they move like 'real' animals move; we recognise their 'bones' in the yellow PVC tubes and we recognise wings, tails and skin. The fact that dead matter looks alive like that creates bewilderment and amazement.

Secondly there is the idea of imitating nature. More than once Jansen points in his book to his own role as that of the Creator of the universe. He is, to quote a well-known Dutch line, convinced deep down that he's a God, who is not content with his place in the present reality, but wants to create a physical – in all senses of the word - world himself. Ever since the myth of Icarus the idea of rivalling nature has appealed strongly to the human imagination. In ancient Greek times it led to hubris: the overconfident human burned

Animaris Rectus. © Loek van der Klis

Animaris Ancora.
© Theo Jansen

his wings and hurtled into the sea destroyed. But in modern times mechanics and technology have increased confidence in human capacities exponentially. *Uomini Universali* such as Leonardo Da Vinci, who operated at the cutting edge between what were then the less strictly divided fields of art and science, developed all sorts of apparatus and instruments, the usefulness of which increased their beauty. The useful and the pleasurable combined. Jansen has positioned himself as an extension of this centuries-old tradition.

Thirdly, Jansens' beach creatures pick up on many current trends in science and deal with issues that define the social debate in the early twenty-first century. There is the question of the rising sea level, for example, which was at the origin of Jansens' beach creature production, linking his oeuvre to contemporary ecological issues. In addition, it refers to and makes use of concepts from mechanics and physics, as they have been developed since the Renaissance in Europe, but it couples these disciplines with more recent scientific trends such as Linnaeus' biological taxonomy, Charles Darwin's Theory of Evolution, Richard Dawkins' genetics and artificial life models from computer science. In this respect Theo Jansen's beach creature project synthesises a whole host of scientific knowledge from various disciplines.

Survival of the fittest

It does it with art disciplines too, which is the fourth reason why Jansens' oeuvre strikes a chord with us today. Jansens' special focus on the material is related to Arte Povera, his choice of the beach as the primary habitat for his beach creatures (and not a gallery or a museum) is reminiscent of land art, his focus on movement links him to the kinetic art of Tinguely and Calder. And what's more, his technical knowledge means that his oeuvre does not get stuck in the poetry of dreams, like that of the Belgian artist Panamarenko.[1] The latter is satisfied with machines that *could fly*, and as such are no more than expressions of Panamarenko's *will*. As an engineer Jansen, in contrast, looks further for means of survival. His beach creatures are attempts to formulate an answer to a *biological* question. Yet it could perhaps be interpreted as inconsequence in his oeuvre that he prefers to approach his work by trial and error rather than with study and planned experiments, possibly in cooperation with specialists in the matter. 'In my self-imposed isolation I lacked the knowledge. I wanted to invent it all again. That takes time. That isolation was not a conscious choice. I'm just not the sort of person who drops into the library before I start on a project. My tendency to do everything alone is probably due to laziness or shyness.' In that sense Jansen still shows himself to be a very romantic artist, who hopes, in self-imposed isolation, for (divine) Inspiration. And that is where a weak point in his oeuvre is exposed: that the categorisation of the beach creature family into periods, the whole DNA terminology, muscles and nerve cells are ultimately mainly a matter of metaphors, a linguistic game with science as its frame of reference, when it could just as well, if Jansen were less lazy or shy, use scientific methods. It does not make the beach creatures any less beautiful, but it does show that his oeuvre could be stronger if it were less naive and had a better theoretical underpinning.

In other areas Jansen shows himself to be considerably less naive. In 2006 the German car manufacturer BMW sent a new advertisement spot into the ether worldwide.(2) But there is no sign of a car in the picture. For sixty seconds we are served up pictures of beach creatures, alternated with shots of Theo Jansen, 'kinetic sculptor', explaining what he does as an artist and engineer, and why. 'The walls between art and engineering exist only in our minds', he claims. 'And few have the imagination to see beyond them', adds BMW in bright white letters, followed by the slogan: 'BMW. Defining innovation.' This spot has undoubtedly increased Jansen's international recognition exponentially. But the way in which, without any hesitation, he allows his own message to be taken over by a commercial company, which can add extra lustre to his image, is witness either to infinite cynicism or an extremely opportunistic spirit of salesmanship which, in my opinion, seriously undermines the authenticity of his artistic project. Though Jansen has realised, perhaps, that the survival of the fittest has become the guiding principle even in artistic circles in these neo-capitalist times. And that his own survival as an artist is the best guarantee that there may yet be autonomous herds of strange yellow creatures living on our beaches one day. ■

Translated by Lindsay Edwards

© Loek van der Klis

www.strandbeest.com

FURTHER READING

Theo Jansen, *The Great Pretender*, Uitgeverij 010, Rotterdam, 2007, 235 p.

NOTES

(1) See Ilse Kuijken, 'A Naïve Engineer. Panamarenko's Art.', in: *The Low Countries*, nr. 2, 1994, pp. 181-185; Joost de Geest, "Panamarenko. 30 years of thinking about space', in: *The Low Countries*, nr. 1, 1993, pp. 307-309

(2) You can find the BMW commercial on YouTube: http://www.youtube.com/watch?v=a7Ny5BYc-Fs

'Deeper, Deeper, to the Bottom, Paula'

The Prose of Mensje van Keulen

A middle-aged lover of literature asked to place Mensje van Keulen in time would probably think of the seventies, a period long past but still very much alive in literary terms. It is time we re-evaluated certain writers of the period torn to pieces in Jeroen Brouwers' defamatory pamphlet *De nieuwe Revisor*. 'Boys' literature' was not the only genre he objected to which would come to be declared outstanding upon its revival. Other authors, more focused on story telling than literary design, were valued less in criticism at the time. These authors included Mensje van Keulen, pseudonym of Mensje Francine van der Steen (The Hague, 1946).

Narrators of the time such as Maarten 't Hart and Mensje van Keulen, though generally judged by critics to be less important than the largely academically trained postmodernists clustered around the fashionable journal *De Revisor*, have matured to be great writers. Van Keulen's work has a timelessness about it. It would not surprise me if she fed on the literature of 'past' authors such as Angus Wilson or Lawrence Durrell. At the same time her prose is deeply anchored in the seventies when she made her debut. This applies as much to the genre of Dutch parlour realism, her longstanding niche, as to the widely professed literary preferences of the time, Nescio and Elsschot's melancholy. The influence of the naturalists of the early part of the last century and before also features prominently in her work. The way she incorporates these literary influences into her prose has changed over time. Mature writer as she now is, she no longer needs shock tactics such as those in an early novel like *Van Lieverlede* (Little by little, 1975), in which a snack bar manager throws hot chip fat at the crotch of a difficult customer. Even without such theatrics she succeeds in furnishing reality with a sense of doom.

What is literary criticism other than a series of argued choices? I consider *De Gelukkige* (The happy one, 2001) to be Van Keulen's crowning glory. Here she rose above parlour realism, making a laudable stab at the threatening, morose, Calvinistic tone of Arthur van Schendel's novels. De Gelukkige deserves to be a classic. Sadly in the public memory it is a long forgotten incident in a constantly growing supply of books.

Van Keulen started writing her most important prose in the nineties: the novels *De rode strik* (The red snare, 1994), *De Gelukkige* and *Liefde heeft geen*

hersens (Love has no brains, 2012), and the collections of short stories *Het andere gezicht* (The other face, 2003) and *Een goed verhaal* (A Good Story, 2009).

Mensje van Keulen (1946)
© Mona van den Berg

The great strength of her short stories is the penetrating power of the tragedy and horror, often combined. Van Keulen's skill is apparent in the effortlessness of even her prose, like the work of a chess master approaching her endgame. 'Doris lived alone,' reads the opening of one story. It could not be starker. Another, 'Thieves were lurking everywhere, said her mother.'

Van Keulen follows two thematic lines within the short story genre, sometimes even within a single story. She has a penchant for homely gothic in the style of Roald Dahl's *Tales of the Unexpected*. This is exemplified to insane extremes in 'Zand' (Sand), where a woman bitterly accuses her husband of past unfaithfulness. The husband, locked in a magnificent, desperate monologue, goes to the beach to escape, only to be interminably raped by a big black man, the incident described to the last dysfunctionally sick detail. The second line is that of slice of life literature, in which silent despair and irrational internalised grief lie in wait, as in the exemplary prose of Raymond Carver, the Edward Hopper of the pen. I believe Van Keulen could afford to develop the slice of life line further, leave behind the frills (a contrived plot, overly conspicuous peculiarities) and describe her human characters' inner struggle straight up. Taking a step in this direction, in her latest collection *Een goed verhaal* (A good story) her expert use of the inner monologue and monomaniacal stream of words raises all six stories from sketch status to a professional expression of the human condition. She cuts deepest when she adds irrational behaviour, as in 'Pilgrimage', when Paula, drunk, paws at a urinal: 'She draws her fingertips through the yellow syrupiness, which creeps under her nails. Deeper, deeper, to the bottom, Paula.'

Everyone grasps, gropes and screws

Van Keulen's best novels exhibit remarkable stamina. The modern fairy tale *De rode strik* (The red snare, 1994), set probably in the fifties, plays out in a provincial street in The Hague, full of petty hidden sorrows. Abandoned by her husband, the mother of Maria and Bee, both still children, starts seeing her husband's older cousin, 'ninety-seven kilos as nature intended him'. Initially all that alerts the sisters to Uncle Leen's existence is the presence of a bottle of Dutch gin in a cupboard, but that soon changes. He burps and farts out loud, has a 'nasty' way of doing up his flies, talks at length about his tattoos, suggests calling the rabbit 'Christmas', and, more disturbingly, ventures into very adult forms of harassment. After telling a bloody story he takes to using the ominous nickname Bambi for Maria. While wandering in a graveyard he says, 'Here's a children's corner. Seven years old, ten. (...) nine, two. There's a little girl called Maria as well.' Shortly after his violent death Maria sighs, 'I think the evil has left the street.'

According to Maarten 't Hart, an expert on the subject, Mensje van Keulen's work springs from two motives working in opposition. 'In her work the shop is the positive pole, blood the negative pole', he writes in his collection of essays *A Tie Pin from Tula*. Blood inspires disgust in her characters, while a shop offers comfort. According to 't Hart, the choice of the butcher Engelbert as the main character in the novel of the same name is Van Keulen's attempt to unite these poles.

't Hart's insight applies only partially in *De rode strik* (The red snare, 1994). Blood flows abundantly, as the title implies. 'The poacher's snare. When he catches a fox or a rabbit, it turns red.' Uncle Leen, who uses this threatening language, owns a shop himself, but it is not a pleasant place to be, let alone comforting. To eleven-year-old Maria and nine-year-old Bee's horror Uncle Leen trades in pest control products and writhing maggots. Maria also sees her mother and Uncle Leen 'doing it' in the back of the shop. The tradesmen Leen and Engelbert are certainly related figures in their oppressive grubbiness, but there is a more interesting correspondence between *Engelbert* (1987) and *De rode strik*. As Van Keulen makes the abject Engelbert increasingly more human and less hateful in the course of the novel, she presents the murder of the 'beast man' Leen by the two sisters in De rode strik as an entirely just act, something wholly natural. This follows from the narrative perspective, that of Maria, the main perpetrator.

This kind of lead character is vintage Van Keulen. In her narrative people are always somewhat unfathomable, never one hundred percent good. As she puts it in her Künstlerroman *De laatste gasten* (The last guests, 2007), 'There is no virtue, everyone grasps, gropes and screws.' Van Keulen is at her best when she writes about crooks, who appear surprisingly charming and positive compared with their insidiously malicious fellow human beings, prattling on about moral values.

Shocking mortality

In this shady setting a title such as *De gelukkige* (The happy one) is atypical. It is, moreover, an imperative: the issue of the main character's happiness or lack thereof is settled immediately. The title suggests an association with naturalist novels, a genre which laid more emphasis on the 'weakness' of failing characters in the past than it does now. But Van Keulen's approach does not differ that much, as her first person narrator is far from happy.

Nora is a middle-aged woman who married the local car mechanic, Martin, when she was young. The marriage has endured through many years, in spite of Martin's unfaithfulness. Inspired by Martin, who is excited by the idea, Nora takes a lover, the architect Daniel. However, Martin fails to foresee the consequences. Nora, whose first and only love was Martin and who has always seen sex as a chore, falls head over heels for Daniel. She even follows him to Islamabad in Pakistan. In this repressive country, the situation goes swiftly downhill. Daniel drinks like a fish and takes to lashing out. So after three weeks Nora flees the country, back to her familiar haven, where Martin awaits her hopefully. In sum, Nora chases after her 'happiness' and returns disoriented.

This barebones summary captures the anecdotal themes, but does not do justice to the drama or the scope of a notion such as happiness as conceived within the novel. Fortunately Van Keulen does not provide a ready made answer to the question of whether Nora's happiness is attainable. There is something to be said for the various viewpoints expressed by the characters in question. Martin, the sober realist, is driven to desperation by Nora's ambivalent behaviour after her adventure in Pakistan: 'You think you had something beautiful. All women in love think so. But love isn't beautiful.' A village woman is also critical: 'You've no right to complain, Nora. You had it all. (...) You, you were the happy one.'

Van Keulen does not reply directly, but implies a great deal, the flood of suggestion forming the backbone of the novel. Nora's story might be explained with reference to her mother. As a doctor's wife from the city, she felt displaced in the oppressive Christian village where she was forced to live for the sake of her husband's honourable profession. Van Keulen plays extensively with narrative motifs, which all appear to lead to a sombre finale: death by one's own hand. There are multiple references to cats, a catlike smile, until it transpires that Nora's old furry friend was killed by a hail of shot – from Martin's gun? - during her adventure in Pakistan. No nine lives, just shocking mortality.

The enticing water swells continually in the background of Nora's adventures. 'Water is a gentle accomplice.' Other villagers too turn out to have sought death by drowning. In the end, mentally fragile as she may be, Nora chooses life. As for other hints contained within the novel, no clear resolution is forthcoming. After Nora's flight, Daniel seems to disappear off the face of the earth; perhaps something happens to him in Pakistan, but Nora cannot find out the truth. Together the strategically placed loose ends form a stifling web.

It is the details which are so effective. Even a teapot is sufficient for Van Keulen to conjure up a spirit seething with jealousy. In the summerhouse, where Martin has presumably been with his mistress, Nora finds her teapot: 'It was in the middle of the table, a withered bunch of wild flowers in it. Broom, dwarf aster, cornflowers, sage, thyme: grey and drooping, in my English teapot, the one I'd always used exclusively to make tea.'

A detail to conjure up the world

In her latest novel, *Liefde heeft geen hersens*, Van Keulen places even greater demands on the title, the one explicit point in the novel, also stated in the first sentence: 'love has no brains'. The expression is repeated throughout the story, to ensure that we understand the animal instincts driving people in Van Keulen's everyday horror world.

With a few elegant strokes of the pen, Van Keulen moves from that first sentence to invoke a scene reminiscent of Maria Callas, faded glory, a boudoir and Puccini's aria 'Vissi d'arte' from *Tosca*. We find ourselves in the apartment of the aged ballerina Irma in The Hague. As we know from the author Helga Ruebsamen, a literary relative, The Hague is not only pure brilliance, the better classes, pearl necklaces around wrinkled necks and the refined life of times past, it is also the scum of the earth and the little people of the servile working classes. Crime lurks in the background, base meanness. Illusions are stranded in prosaic reality. It is already embedded in the name of the young widow who comes to her neighbour Irma's apartment in the first scene to pay her respects. Romy she is called, after Romy Schneider, the film diva who played Sissi and met a grim end, with her son speared on a fence, and her subsequent suicide with sleeping pills. Her fate is commemorated in *Liefde heeft geen hersens* (Love has no brains), but really this is unnecessary. Van Keulen's gift is the chaining of associations, summoning up a world with a single detail.

Romy works as a tea lady at a funeral home and moonlights as a cleaning lady. Among her clients is Irma, who does not give a kick for the entire novel because she is stone dead. What does a normal person do on encountering one who has passed away? She telephones close relatives and the doctor. Not Romy. She is frightened by the dead woman's facial expression and suspects murder. 'This isn't a peaceful face with old, familiar lines. Not an empty face, but one still gripped with a spasm of horror.' Romy remembers Irma complaining about valuables disappearing from her house and immediately suspects her own son. So she patches up the body a little ('The most gruesome bit is the tongue, which bulges behind the teeth') and when she is finished it looks as if Irma has choked on a sandwich.

A little strange, to say the least. But there are no normal characters in Van Keulen's work. The horror is anchored in the very things that signify ordinary life. No one, it is impressed upon us, can be completely understood. Everyone has a screw or two loose. That is a theme throughout her work, which swarms with colourful, disturbed characters and eccentrics. The novel introduces a caretaker, Harro, who still lives with his elderly mother and in many ways resembles Norman Bates from Hitchcock's *Psycho*. There is a great deal not right with him, we soon realise, but we do not discover exactly what. It remains suspicion, inflamed by a well chosen detail, the odd half remark. We learn that there was a woman in Harro's past, that she has a scar on her collarbone, a souvenir of him. Exactly how remains unclear, but it is enough to suggest that Harro is a freak, who presumably needs all these self-imposed rules and rituals in his life to keep himself in check, to say nothing of his tendency to stalk the object of his desire.

Van Keulen employs this kind of suggestion throughout *Love has no Brains*, to great effect. Virtuoso monologues and streams of consciousness suck us into the characters' lives, raising the relentlessly increasing tension to fever pitch. Everything and everyone is significant. In the end it no longer matters whether Irma was helped towards her end, or by whom, for we are busy following the creepy Harro as he approaches Romy; we want to know what is happening with Romy's daughter and her grossly obese friend; we are curious as to what Romy's disturbed, bisexual son will make of his life. Moreover, where is Irma's cat Freddie? And isn't Romy's new flame Eric just a little too perfect?

The horror of provincial life

Once again we cannot afford to make light of the power of Van Keulen's details. They reveal her razor-sharp eye for the horror of provincial life. Even in an apparently innocent paragraph the gaze is drawn towards a couch kept covered in plastic, 'so that in the summer you had to peel your bare legs free with a sucking noise'. The smell of overcooked sprouts rises straight off the page.

Van Keulen uses details to give shape to the two other pillars of her prose: her exceptional psychological insight into human relationships and her fascination with death. Given a funeral home setting, you know Van Keulen will really let rip. We read of a corpse that jumps up during cremation, 'when the furnace was stoked from 800 to 1,000 degrees'. We discover that the remains from cleared graves end up in the 'bone pit', 'Brown bones, shreds of clothing still hanging from them'. At the funeral home we also encounter a necrophilic employee, reminiscent of a similar character in just such a situation in Herodotus' *Histories*.

A single detail of Romy's memories of domestic violence reveals the true horror: 'a dishcloth stuffed in my mouth'. As stated above, Van Keulen does not do ordinary people. In itself that is nothing special. The deviant, the unusual, the accidental, these are standard ingredients in the literary test tube. What is special in Van Keulen's work is that her damaged, insane characters are such convincing creatures of flesh and blood that, engrossed in our reading, we accept them as normal. Van Keulen intentionally creates this illusion: her prose reads as a resounding 'no' to judging one's fellow human beings.

Viewed through this writer's lens the world is an ocean to be drawn on, an inexhaustible source. As we have seen, every detail counts. Take the incident at a famous actor's funeral: 'Beer', shouts a heavy voice. 'Where is the beer? Why isn't there beer?' Loading every detail like this is risky. If the target is missed, an expression out of place, it is conspicuous. Perfection is largely unattainable, but near-perfection, such as the gifted author Van Keulen seems constantly and effortlessly to exhibit, is worthy of admiration. ▨

Translated by Anna Asbury

FURTHER READING

Mensje Van Keulen, *Liefde heeft geen hersens*, novel, 2012

Mensje Van Keulen, *Een goed verhaal*, short stories, 2009

Mensje Van Keulen, *De laatste gasten*, novel, 2007

Mensje Van Keulen, *Het andere gezicht*, stories, 2003

Mensje Van Keulen, *De gelukkige*, novel, 2001

Mensje Van Keulen, *De rode strik*, novel, 1994

Mensje Van Keulen, *Engelbert*, novel, 1987

Mensje Van Keulen, *Van Lieverlede*, novel, 1975

All Mensje van Keulen's books are published by Uitgeverij Atlas, now Atlas Contact, in Amsterdam. For a complete bibliography see www.mensjevankeulen.nl

Two Stories
By Mensje van Keulen

Prima la Musica

Gerrit had been drinking and he walked home along the canal, singing loudly. First he sang, with a catch in his throat, a hit song that had been playing in the bar and was still sounding in his ears, then a children's song that always made him feel sad though he didn't know why, then a tear-jerker about two sailors, and by the time he entered the alley, it was Figaro's opening aria from *The Barber of Seville* that reverberated between the walls of a warehouse and a former girls' orphanage.

From the other end of the alley a woman was coming towards him. The only available light came through the cracks of a rollshade that covered the window of a flowershop, but it was enough to see that she wore an old-fashioned coat with a hood and that she was hiding her hands in her sleeves as though she felt cold. Convinced that she was going to ask him for money, Gerrit checked his pockets.

'Too bad,' he said when she had come closer, 'I'm clean out. I don't even have enough to pay for a small glass of beer.'

'I don't need money,' the woman said. 'But it's very kind of you to offer it.' She hesitated for a moment and then asked: 'You like to sing?'

'Oh yes,' Gerrit said. 'But I'm absolutely no good at it. That's why I only sing when I've had a few. My father was a piano tuner, and many's the time, when I was a kid, that I lay under a piano, listening to the music being played on it and the songs being sung to the music. Oh, how I'd like to sing the stars down from the sky, that must be the most marvelous thing there is.' And he looked at the sky high above the alley and sang, belting it out in a way that once upon a time would have awakened all the orphans most unpleasantly from their sleep: '*Bravo, bravissimo! A te fortuna non mancherà!*'

The woman did not let on that she knew how dreadful it sounded. She produced a small bottle from her sleeve and gave it to him, saying: 'A single drop, and you'll have a golden voice all day long.'

Gerrit laughed and said: 'Just one drop, while I've been drinking big glasses of beer to cheer me up?'

'It's enough for your entire life,' the woman said, 'but be careful not to waste it.'

And she put her hands back in her sleeves and disappeared in the dark alley.

Continuing his drunken medley of songs, Gerrit weaved his unsteady way home.

The next morning, as he picked his clothes up off the floor and the bottle slid out of his pants pocket, he remembered the nocturnal meeting. It can't have happened, he thought. One of my friends must have put the bottle in my pocket, and I dreamed the rest.

'Whatever,' he said hoarsely. 'I'll have a drop. Who knows, maybe it'll lubricate my poor dry throat.'

The fluid in the bottle was odour- and colourless, and when he let a drop slide over his tongue it seemed to be tasteless as well. His throat was just as dry as before, and his thirst was so great that he guzzled straight from the tap until he was gasping for breath. He did not look forward to his job in the big, crammed kitchen, the cook's pants he had to wear, the plastic-wrapped foodstuffs floating in boiling hot water, the odours that escaped when the bags were cut open. His stomach protested and he said: 'Oh, I shouldn't have drunk so much last night!'

He then looked around in surprise. Who had said that? Whose was that melodious voice?

'Was that me? Was that, is that my voice?'

And once again the gorgeous full baritone filled his room.

For the first time in his life Gerrit had the feeling that his chest was swelling and was actually a sound box. But his room was too small for all the sounds that were welling up within him, and he opened his window and let them take flight, clear and exceptionally beautiful: 'Deh, vieni alla fenestra ...'

After this serenade he sang an exuberant aria. People stopped to listen, they applauded, they asked for more.

'Come on down,' shouted a man who had been a stagehand with the local opera company for the last thirty years. 'Come, and I'll guarantee you a bright future.'

That same afternoon Gerrit sang for the musical director, the artistic director, and the business manager; and that same week he stood in for Giovanni Terracini, who had broken an ankle while singing in Tosca, and Friedrich Bruno von Knabe, who had come down with hay fever just before the opening performance of Die Meistersinger.

It did not take long before he was in demand everywhere – Bayreuth, Milan, New York. People spent the night outside box offices and offered scalpers huge sums of money so they could be enchanted by his voice. Rigoletto. Otello. Falstaff. But also Bluebeard's Castle, Wozzeck, L'Orfeo and La Damnation de Faust, in which his performance as Mephistopheles was so overpowering that the audience wanted to sell him their souls en masse.

Even greater was the effect of his voice when he sang the title role in Don Giovanni. People almost fainted with delight, and when one evening he drank not one but several drops from the bottle, numerous women in the hall jumped to their feet, eager to throw themselves into the abyss with him.

One triumph followed another, and Gerrit couldn't get enough of it. But as his star rose, in so far as it could still rise, the bottom of the bottle came in sight, and one day he anxiously added a bit of water to the last drop.

Right in the middle of *Capriccio* his voice broke.

The newspapers reported that the demi-god had been brought low by a sudden throat infection, but when Gerrit woke up the following morning in his king-size hotel bed, he knew he had to return to his home town and would never enjoy the celebrity life again.

He started drinking, night after night. And one November evening, as a biting wind blew through the alley next to the girls' orphanage, the woman in the hooded coat came towards him for a second time.

'Oh,' he said, sobbing, 'I'll never sing again. So if you want to give me a bottle, please just make it beer. Or something stronger, something stronger would be okay, too.'

'You've been too greedy,' she said. But she was not insensitive to his tears, took another small bottle from her sleeve and said: 'This is for eternity. But you're going to need patience, and you're going to have to work hard.'

The next morning Gerrit unscrewed the top of the bottle and saw that it contained ink, pure, black India ink. He dipped his pen in it and began to write. He wrote about love and death, heaven and hell, poverty and riches, desire and drunkenness, about his childhood and his father, the piano tuner. And the people who read his stories said: 'Everything comes alive before your eyes. And it's beautifully written as well. I'll be damned if it isn't true, but sometimes it's just like the words are singing to you.' ∎

Translated by Michiel Horn

Two Versions of Proceedings
For Herman Franke

1

As he locked his bike, his front wheel swung and touched hers. There was something intimate about it, would she notice? Don't get too close, she had said. Not too close: how did you judge the distance?

This street was quiet. The only noise was from a few houses along where there were building works, a whine as if iron or a hard type of stone were being ground. Once he was inside, in his own stairwell, not even this could be heard. He blinked momentarily at the dark and retrieved the paper and advertising brochures from the mat. He took the first steps cautiously, as if in a game without amusement: do I want to go upstairs? Yes, I do. No, I don't.

Had she heard him come home? Yes, she'd heard. No, she hadn't realised yet.

She worked half days, but perhaps she wasn't home yet. She might be at a friend's. Or in town. Recently she had started visiting her sister again, the sister who liked hearing things were going badly. He hadn't looked to see whether the car was there.

He stopped and it was as if he could hear his rapid heartbeat bouncing off the walls. He wondered whether his father had ever been in such doubt when he got home. Across the pavement between the playing children, past the box and hydrangeas in the front garden. A staircase was not the only thing that made footsteps heavier.

He could turn back. No. Yes. No, he wanted to go upstairs. Whatever she said, whatever she did.

Perhaps she had gone, really gone.

He climbed two more steps, closed his eyes and saw much more. An unaddressed envelope on his keyboard. Against the black pen tidy. In front of the books in one of the middle sections of his bookshelf. On a pile of books in the living room. On the table, in the place where his plate usually stood. Against the teapot. On the floor, right behind the sliding door, where their flat began.

The paper almost slipped out of his hands, one of the advertising brochures fell. He read:

For all your odd jobs: PERFECTO

Three more steps in the dark.

The door slid open and there she was with her flaming hair in an ambush of light.

2

Angry. Even as a child she had wondered why a single word could carry such weight. You look really angry. When someone said that, though she was just lost in thought or in a pleasant state of blankness, anger automatically came rushing along. Is something wrong? And she would make 'something' up. You look tired. And she would let her shoulders droop, and try to hide her face.

She had seen him cycle off this morning. He had a train to catch. Where to? A place she thought was in Brabant, but turned out to be in Noord-Holland. As soon as he was out of sight, she had called in sick. Sick. Another command, but she didn't give into it, she just had swollen eyes. Lie. A word to run away from.

She didn't run away. She went back to bed, fell asleep and was woken up by the sun on her face. She went round the flat, looked at the objects he loved and those they both loved or had acquired out of necessity. The oblong table could have been round, the floor not careful grey but red, or would that have made their rows fiercer? A question generated other questions, questions that tired you out. She took a small book out of his bookcase and sat down in his chair, leaning on the arms with her elbows. She leafed through the book. She read: 'One day soon he would reach her hiding place' and shivered. A line further on caught her eye: 'Even her pubic hair was orange.' And then: 'He had left a nice painting behind.'

She heard him locking his bike and went to the window. She saw him bend forward and pull his bike wheel clear of hers. Leave it, she wanted to call out to him when he bent over again. The wheel would not budge and after the fourth attempt he gave up.

It took him a long time to get upstairs. Had he turned back? Had he gone away again? She slide the gleaming white door open. She forgot everything she had wanted to say, and she did not hunt for words. 'I'm glad,' she said. 'I'm glad you're back.' ▪

Translated by Paul Vincent

'The Paint is the Message'

The Physical Painting of Sam Dillemans

[ERIC RINCKHOUT]

Sam Dillemans has painted boxers, nudes and couples making love. In the last few years he has got his teeth into portraits of writers – all exceptional people whom he admires. Before that he took direct inspiration from the great masters: he transposed Rubens, Giotto, Grünewald and El Greco into his own forms and paint. It was not imitation, but creative reinterpretation. 'Lots of contemporary artists think they are the be-all and end-all. They are wrong. You need the old masters to be able to put yourself in context,' says Sam Dillemans.

Dillemans, born in Leuven in 1965, is a painter in whom past and present coincide: his painting is somewhere in between the figurative and the abstract. In his work there is a thin line between form and dissolution. Love and hate, reconciliation and conflict merge with one another too.

Dillemans is a physical painter, he lives in paint, he is paint. He does actually live in his studio, surrounded by hundreds of canvases, tubes of paint and brushes. His paintings are evidence of his struggle with the material: they are challenges and conquests in paint, layer upon layer. Paintings full of churning, quivering paint. Paintings full of life and bodies. It is his form of expressionism.

'My ambition is to become ninety years old – to realise as much as possible of my painterly dream. I still have so much to do.'

August 2012. In Sam Dillemans' studio, the spacious back of a house in Antwerp, there are more than a hundred portraits on the wall. Expressive and sketchy. Most in black and white, sometimes with sparse touches of blue, green and red. Their dimensions vary from 30 by 24 to 50 by 60 centimetres. Men and women. Mainly writers, such as James Joyce, William Faulkner, Raymond Carver, Emily Dickinson, Charles Bukowski and George Sand. Composers, philosophers, singers and sportsmen too - Eddy Merckx, Jacques Brel, Schubert and Mozart. Occasionally a painter. They are the great figures whom Sam Dillemans hugely admires.

'There are so many writers amongst them because I have been reading non-stop since I was twelve,' he says. Reading has consoled me. The Russians! I devoured Dostoyevsky. In fact I think you ought to read him when you're young. Yes, most of them are dead writers. They are certainties, they are world literature. You're not wasting your time with them. I've postponed reading Céline for a while

because I knew he was difficult and pessimistic. But what an author! It's no co-incidence that the real greats, like Céline, Chekhov and Schnitzler, all three of them, were doctors. They've had their hands on flesh, they know what death is.'

Dillemans has been working on this extensive series of black and white portraits since January 2012. They are powerful close-ups. He uses a dry brush for its dynamic line and sometimes uses his fingers too. In some places he applies the paint so thinly that the texture of the woven cloth shows through.

Large parts of the canvas remain unpainted. 'I call it etching with paint,' he says. 'It's sink or swim. If I want to correct something I can always try erasing it with white paint or white spirit. But that doesn't always work and even when it does the corrections stand out. That's why these portraits are a leap in the dark. I can allow myself to do that because I've been doing portraits in colour for more than two years.'

Dillemans does not start with a white canvas for these colour portraits, but uses a wide variety of supports, including landscape paintings he buys in the recycling shop. 'These little paintings make a fantastic ground. I sensed that I could really use works like that. It all went very intuitively. I turn the landscape painting 90° or upside down. A rowing boat or a piece of a tree might become an eye. I don't search, I find. Yes, I've overpainted a lot of works by Sunday painters.'

Sam Dillemans, *A Kiss*, 2007.
Oil on panel, 40 cm x 50 cm

Sam Dilemans, *Lovers*, 1999.
Oil on canvas, 200 cm x 200 cm

Since 2010 he has turned more to black and white, again intuitively. 'The last six months I've painted hardly anything else than portraits in black and white. But I don't start from a concept, if I did it would just get screwed up. It's purely about the experience: I have fun doing the hundredth nostril. My brush wanders and I follow. There's nothing cerebral about it.'

Dillemans paints these portraits while sitting in the lotus position on the floor. A photo of the author or composer in question sits on a chair in front of him. 'It doesn't even have to be a good photo.' The white canvas lies in front of him. He does not do any preparatory drawings. 'The white canvas is the worst thing there is. It was Picasso who said that, not me. And if even he thought so, what must it be like for us? I have to persuade myself that the portrait I'm working on is both important and unimportant. I have to deceive and fool myself, otherwise the fear of failure would be too great and I couldn't get started.'

When the painting doesn't go smoothly, he glances at a big photo of Eddy Merckx, the great Belgian cyclist. To recharge his batteries. 'He is my crucifix. That man knows what solitude is too.'

Dillemans paints his portraits hovering between flamboyance and restlessness. 'I always start with the eyes. They are the most important.' Sometimes chance interferes: on one occasion Dillemans' dirty trouser-leg rubbed against the side of a canvas with a portrait of the American author Theodore Dreiser. 'I left the mark as it was, as a demarcation. The portraits shouldn't be too clean.'

Dillemans puts music on when he's painting. ABBA, Vivaldi, Mozart... 'But I don't put Verdi on when I'm painting Verdi's portrait. I don't go that far.'

Should the portraits resemble their subjects? 'That's a fascinating problem. There should of course be a certain resemblance.'

It's typical of Dillemans that as he works on a series of portraits they become more and more abstract. The same thing happened in his series of nudes and boxers. 'But Orwell's face should still be Orwell. To me the bone structure is essential. And then come the emotions. I'm much freer, of course, when I paint a self-portrait or the portrait of a model than when I paint a well-known figure.'

Dillemans wants to keep on surprising himself. 'I'm afraid of repetition. I want

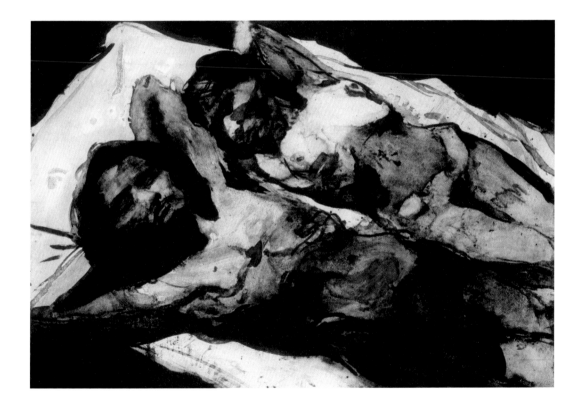

to keep on discovering things. How can I paint a nostril so that I surprise myself, so that it doesn't look like the nostril that it nevertheless clearly is? If painting becomes too much of a routine, I change format or choose another subject.'

That is why Dillemans recently started on some large-format landscapes. Two by two-and-a-half metres. Wild, bright, colourful spaces. Not a figure to be seen. 'I wanted to work on a large scale. I needed that physical effort. I wanted to paint standing up again, not sitting down. With broad gestures and thick blobs of paint.' For these works Dillemans relies on photos from magazines or his own shots. 'I have them enlarged until the details disappear. I don't want any anecdotes in these landscapes.'

A haystack, a river, a tree. Colour, paint, matter. Dillemans is clearly enjoying himself.

A meteorite strikes

It all started for Sam Dillemans when his mother gave him an art book on Vincent van Gogh for his 14th birthday. 'Van Gogh is the source of everything. He was a lucid man, a commonsensical Dutchman. He knew very well what he wanted. Not a lunatic, as people often like to portray him. I'm fascinated by Van Gogh, I've made forty copies of his work. Look closely at his paintings: it's a single layer of paint and it's right first time. That's phenomenal. Just try it. And you have to realise that in the meantime his works have lost 60% of their luminosity. What a shock those paintings must have been for his contemporaries. Vincent was a meteorite that struck the world.'

Dillemans started copying old and modern masters to learn their techniques: Van Gogh of course, and Schiele, Beckman, Soutine and Kokoschka. At a later stage he took lessons. He studied at seven art colleges, including

Sam Dillemans, *Selfportrait*, 1997.
Oil on canvas, 90 cm x 60 cm

Sam Dillemans,
The Left Hook, 2006.
Oil on canvas,
95 cm x 130 cm

Antwerp, Ghent and Brussels, but wasn't happy with the teaching anywhere. In the end he graduated from the Academy in Tourcoing in northern France.

For Dillemans, drawing has always been the basis of his painting: drawing from a plaster or living model or copying the masters. 'The hard business of drawing has to be learnt. Most art colleges don't teach it anymore and that's completely wrong. Degas copied half the Louvre! And when Ingres saw him there, he said: "Que des lignes, monsieur Degas, que des lignes!".'

'I have learned to draw a skull, a larynx and a cheekbone perfectly. You have to know your anatomy. You have to learn to draw with pencil when you're young and make sure you've got drawing in your blood. As a child I drew myself with my eyes shut. At a later stage you can completely forget your knowledge and skills. But you have to be able to draw a foot before you can break it apart. Picasso could draw better than anyone by the time he was 12. As an artist you have to start where Picasso started.'

The old masters

In 1995 Sam Dillemans met Lizy. For five years she was his one and only model, fulltime, 30 to 40 hours a week. This yielded some marvellous nudes, at various stages of distortion. Sometimes only a nipple or an eyebrow is recognisable, or a lock of hair in a single sweeping, virtuoso brushstroke. 'One model, a thousand paintings,' says Dillemans. 'In the end I knew Lizy through and through. What her collarbone and her cheek looked like. I was able to abandon realism. I could pull her apart and put her back together again. I really polished

Sam Dillemans, *Tempest*, 2011.
Oil on canvas,
240 cm x 140 cm

her off as a model, I didn't know I would maul her that much. In my studio I painted almost without light. So she asked me whether she really had to keep on coming, but I needed her, in the end, just as a source of energy.' Dillemans was looking for that one, ultimate image. An unattainable goal.

There are a handful of paintings from 1999 entitled *Lovers*. *Lovers* I is an overwhelming canvas. A naked man is lying on a naked woman. They are staring at each other. The woman's eyes are both predatory and sensual. Her nostrils are slightly flared, the teeth clamped together. The man has a calm look, almost unmoved. They are floating in a white vacuum, outside time. But this relative calmness does not extend to their bodies, which are a tangle of robust black strokes. The paint twists, the colours are formless. The bodies lose themselves on the battlefield of love.

After Lizy, the painter returned to another old love: the great masters. This is not an obvious choice at the end of the 20th century, but in Dillemans' view the old masters are beyond time. 'When I see a Rembrandt, I have a sense of panic. Rembrandt is not the past, like many people think, Rembrandt is not yesterday, Rembrandt is tomorrow.'

'In my eyes, Tintoretto and Rubens are alive. When I look at a Rubens, it's as if I'm looking at a beautiful woman. For me it's the same. The old masters comfort me. They paint the great ever-recurring emotions – and that affects me. But above all it's the way they paint: it's the hand of the painter that consoles me.'

'Any confrontation with the old masters is lost before you begin. They thrash you, force you into a corner. It's a lesson in humility.'

Unlike the copyists of the 19th century, Dillemans never intended to get as close as possible to the original. 'You shouldn't try to copy them, that's pointless. I just wanted to declare my love' Dillemans is above all concerned with their style and technique. 'Rubens painted the shadow on a thighbone in blue. So in certain senses he was already an impressionist. If you look at every square centimetre, Goya turns out to be an expressive revolutionary.' 'A lot of people wonder why they have to look at all those Madonnas and all those cherubs yet again. You have to look at 'how' the light falls on the wing of one of Rembrandt's angels. Look at 'how' the Madonnas are painted. It doesn't really matter whether it's Christ or a bunch of bananas. Cézanne turned art history upside down with his peaches. The paint is the message, nothing else.'

In 2005, Sam Dillemans showed his 'creative interpretations' at the Rubens House in Antwerp: Rubens, Van Dyck, Velazquez and Titian. According to Dillemans, the Descent from the Cross hung in the middle of Rubens' studio. The silhouettes of Jesus and Mary are still vaguely recognisable, but within these outlines the paint churns and squirms. It is applied thickly, in 8 to 10 layers. The longer Dillemans works on a painting like this, the more it changes from innocent to evil. Ultimately it becomes a revenge. The paint explodes, the forms disintegrate.

Dillemans painted his version of Christ's descent from the cross on the floor. 'I dance around the canvas as I paint. Yes, that does make you think of Pollock. The most important thing is that there is no top or bottom because the painting is lying flat. There is no more normal perspective. I almost gave up, I couldn't get an overview of it anymore.'

Endurance is essential

Dillemans was tired after the old masters. He had done 300, possibly 350 copies. A series, which is the way Dillemans works. He works all the time, too. 'If I don't paint for two days, I feel bad. No, I don't see it as work, I'm permanently on holiday. I tackle a particular painting depending on my mood – rage, sadness, jealousy, a sense of eternity. Painting is like the hundred-metre hurdles. You have to be in condition, otherwise you won't succeed.'

And Dillemans does work on his condition, and also unremittingly. He learnt boxing from the Belgian light-heavyweight champion Freddy De Kerpel. Dillemans still boxes, but no longer at the club. He has a punch bag in his studio and practices on his own. He also does an hour of skipping every day. 'Endurance is essential.'

At a certain moment Dillemans realised that he could also use the boxers in his work. 'Boxers or Rubens, it's actually the same. I'm always involved with bodies. And with pain. A large part of a boxer's body is naked. It's all well developed. You can clearly see the muscles and bones, as in Rubens' paintings.'

He paints anonymous boxers, but also a fight between such resounding names as Sugar Ray Robinson and Carmen Basilio, a portrait of Rocky Marciano, or Archie Moore knocked out on the floor.

The boxer paintings are explosions of power. Sweat and blood spatter around. A left hook is applied vigorously to the canvas. These are fights in and with the paint. Snapshots, film stills, frozen movements and strength.

Translated by Gregory Ball

In these boxer paintings there is also an evolution from expressive realism to an almost Bacon-like abstraction. In other cases the figures seem to dissolve into the whiteness of the canvas. A boxing match is an image of the human condition, life between pain and ecstasy. There's not much difference between this and lovers kissing. In Dillemans' work a kiss often looks like a bite and a chew, as if the lovers were going to tear each other apart. 'Boxing and kissing are both physical confrontations,' reacts the painter. 'I'm concerned with the bodies. How do they relate to each other, how do they clash?'

Dillemans considers painting to be an endless quest and an unceasing struggle. And he paints with utter dedication. 'There is no such thing as a part-time painter. There are no compromises in art, there is only sacrifice.'

When he's really stuck, Dillemans starts on a self-portrait. It is rarely flattering. 'A self-portrait is like going back to the source. I know myself through and through – from the outside. That's where I start from. Then all my knowledge and experience go into a new self-portrait.'

Paint becomes skin, and through this tight skin the skull is dimly visible. As if every portrait is ultimately a vanitas painting. Dillemans is painting against time. ▪

FURTHER READING

Marc Ruyters & Jozef Deleu, *Sam Dillemans* (Rubenshuis, Antwerp, 2005) (bilingual Dutch-English edition)
Jon Thompson, *Sam Dillemans* (Ludion, 2007) (English edition)

Statements are taken from:
Luc Lemaître & Sam De Graeve, *Sam Dillemans: De waanzin van het detail / The Madness in the Detail* (Dutch, with English subtitles) (DVD, Woestijnvis, 2007)
Eric Rinckhout, 'De mep van Rubens. Schilder Sam Dillemans met boksers, vrijers en naakten in Antwerpen', in *De Morgen*, 3 October 2005
Eric Rinckhout, 'De uppercut van Dillemans. Schilder brengt overrompelende tentoonstelling in garage op Antwerps Eilandje', in *De Morgen*, 5 October 2009
Conversation with Sam Dillemans, 21 August 2012

www.samdillemans.com

Sam Dillemans, *W. Somerset Maugham*, 2010.
Oil on canvas, 24.5 cm x 22 cm

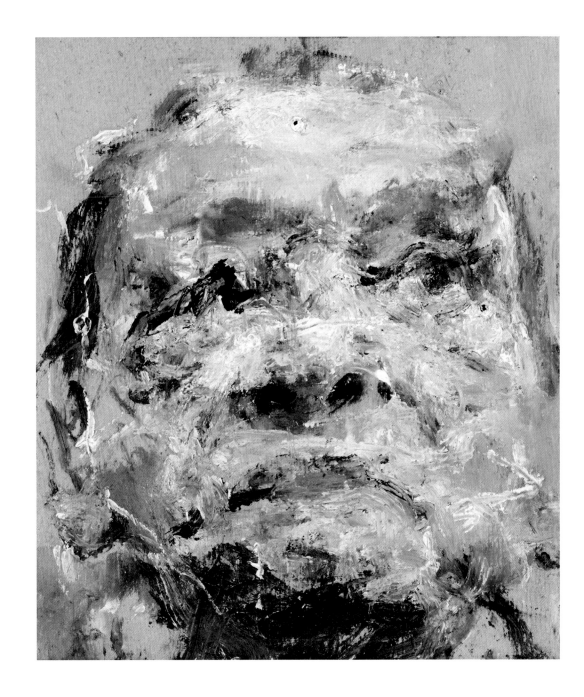

'In the Silence between Words Hides a Little Poem'

The Fascinating Sound Universe of Spinvis

[DIRK STEENHAUT]

In the past decade, Spinvis has stood out as one of the most original musical voices in the Low Countries. The songwriter and musician, born Erik de Jong, was 41 when he made his debut in 2002 with an untitled album that fused lo-fi, experimental indietronica and well-crafted pop tunes, accompanied by wistful, often melancholy lyrics.

Spinvis lives in Nieuwegein, a town just south of the Dutch city of Utrecht. His stirring first album was a distillation of hundreds of cassette tapes he had recorded over the years, by himself, in the attic of his family home. His off-kilter yet familiar sounding songs, created on a computer using a copy-paste technique, struck a chord with the public right away. The collection of songs found some twenty thousand buyers overnight, and within a few months it was featured on numerous 'best of 2002' year-end lists.

Why did it take Spinvis more than forty years to rise to the surface? 'Some people are fast, others slow. Apparently I belong to the latter category', the singer offers. 'I needed time to develop my technical skills and to carve my own path. I would have preferred to remain anonymous. Like *'Here is the record; beyond it I do not exist'*. Unfortunately I had underestimated the power of the media. I'm as vain as the next man, but all I really want to do is to bring comfort by creating something beautiful.'

The wheat and the chaff

Spinvis is more than just a musician. He is a collage artist who constructs his multi-layered songs by manipulating loops and samples. This process makes him a kindred spirit of indietronica artists such as Air, Beck, Grandaddy and The Notwist. To him his studio is a laboratory where, like some sort of alchemist, he can mix up ingredients that seem unlikely or impossible to combine. That does not necessarily mean Erik de Jong is bored with traditional ways of making music. 'The adrenaline rush you get from a real band is unbeatable. But making music with other people always demands compromise. The discipline I have attained is comparable to a writer's: every day you add something or cut something out. The whole thing primarily takes place in my head. Working on your own, you tend to have more doubts, but that's fine: an artist who ceases to doubt is creatively dead.'

Around the time of his debut, Spinvis decided it was important for the sound and feel of his original demos, with all their faults and shortcomings, to be preserved. The album sounds like an aural diary in which his family life is deeply embedded. The careful listener can pick up the sound of a vacuum cleaner in the house, a moped driving by or De Jong's bickering children. It gives his work an almost documentary feel. 'These elements crept in purely by coincidence, but they made the music sound vulnerable and authentic. So yeah, that record is me, albeit in a carefully distilled form. Emotions are bottled up and deliberately moulded into a particular shape. On a computer, you can change things up until the very last minute, so there's the danger that a song will never be finished. I can spend ages fiddling around with details. You can only be sure that all the parts are in the right place if you rely on your instincts. There are no certainties.'

© Tibor de Jong

© Keke Keukelaar

Although Spinvis always uses laptops and samplers, his records (three studio albums, half a live CD and a collection of rarities) also feature guitar, bass, drums, keyboards and flute. 'I can play a little bit of everything, but I'm not especially good at anything,' he explains modestly. 'I guess my "punk attitude" is to blame for that. Virtuosity or technique is not that important to me. Even if you can only play four notes on a single string, what matters is you can come up with them at the right moment. I am not a musician per se. I paint with sounds and always think of the whole picture. Minimalism breaks things open. Even the things you might miss out on the first time you listen are in there somehow.'

It may come as a surprise, but Spinvis insists that his music has been shaped partly by chart friendly acts like ABBA and The Bee Gees. 'You might really hate a particular song, but the next day you find yourself in your car, the sun is shining, and all of a sudden you're hooked. Anyone not open to this sort of experience, for example because he is hiding behind his good taste, narrows his own world. Sometimes you just need to look beyond the packaging. What I love about pop music is that no one can expropriate it. Every morning, when you get up, you will notice the rules have changed. Yesterday's chaff is tomorrow's wheat. This endless succession of tastes, fashions and opinions is quite appealing to me.'

Spinvis has never regarded himself as a performer and readily admits that he is a mediocre singer. But following the success of his first CD, the demand for concerts became so overwhelming that this DIY merchant ultimately decided to trade in his safe domesticity for a place in the spotlight. As there is nothing duller than watching a figure fiddling around with knobs all evening, he decided to re-shape his songs entirely. On the album he had used samples from different genres, cultures and periods, so he developed the concept of the 'time machine', where he surrounded himself with musicians from different generations and with widely divergent backgrounds. The nine-strong Spinvis Orchestra consisted entirely of seventy-somethings from the worlds of classical music or jazz, and the songs were re-arranged for harp, vibraphone, Turkish saz and accordion. 'The book has already been written, so this is the film adaptation,' the singer would mumble during every concert. The metamorphosis was drastic, the difference between the live versions and the recorded ones spectacular. But Spinvis was not afraid of taking risks and proved that a great song can assume many different guises. Some of the reinvented live versions would find their way onto the 2003 album *Nieuwegeinaan Zee*.

Mother tongue

To Spinvis it seemed self-evident he was going to sing in his mother tongue. 'If I were to use English, it would be artificial, it wouldn't be me. I'd have to sing in a language I know exclusively from films and TV. Luckily, in Dutch, you can only imitate yourself,' he explains. Writers and poets from his own country, like Gerard Reve and Gerrit Achterberg, are every bit as important to him as The Beatles or The Beach Boys. 'I've always been interested in literature, but I certainly don't claim to write poetry. If a particular word perfectly expresses what

© Erik de Jong

I want to say, but it doesn't fit into the flow of the music, I will definitely take the scissors to it. Lyrics and music must combine to create perfect harmony. I guess you could say I'm operating an audio typewriter: I'm typing with sound.'

Spinvis almost always uses colloquial speech in his lyrics. Back in the days when he still worked in factories, he would patiently observe the way his colleagues interacted and would pay attention to the things they said – or didn't say – to one another. Their unspoken thoughts, unfinished sentences, pauses and hesitations eventually found their way into his songs. 'I always carry a notebook and write down things I hear other people say. If you gather up all these unconnected sentences into a kind of bouquet, they start to spontaneously suggest a story. It'll be a plotless one, of course, but that's what life is like. It's all about context. At least, until we manage for ourselves to make some sense out of it.'

In 'Smalfilm', one of the five protagonists says: *'When I go out, I become a photographer / When I visit some friends, I turn into a writer.'* The latter is also true of Spinvis. If anyone around him says something he can use, he absorbs it like a sponge and eventually it pops up in his writing. As he's not a fan of one-way traffic, listeners are given plenty of space to infuse his lyrics with their own meaning.

De Jong deliberately keeps things mysterious. 'Blurred photographs are often the most beautiful, because they seldom show what you think you see. I love that ambiguity, that sense of suggestion.' Furthermore, he manages to conjure up a whole world in a few pithy words: *'The city is undressing / It's drinking like*

a bride', he sings in 'Ik wil alleen maar zwemmen'. 'Herfst en Nieuwegein' has a lot in common with a subtly impressionistic painting, in which time seems to have frozen and everything is standing still. And in 'Club Insomnia' the lyrical and the prosaic flow into one another almost seamlessly: *'In the silence between words hides a little poem / About now and never, about dream and death / About you and I, about cunt and prick.'*

Spinvis's lyrics, usually written using a stream of consciousness technique, have a highly sensory quality, even though the artist will sometimes turn things on their heads. He 'breathes with his eyes', describes planets that *'sing'* and a motorway that *'rustles'*. The singer views the world with a childlike naiveté, but discovers that he doesn't actually see things any differently from anyone else. 'There are many who silence the child within them, because they are convinced that naïve astonishment is no longer appropriate at their age. Me, I'm just less embarrassed about writing what I think. As a schoolboy, I gave free rein to my imagination. Until I discovered that reality doesn't easily allow itself to be moulded. Becoming aware of that really hurt.'

Occasionally, in songs like 'Smalfilm' and 'Astronaut', you will find a science fiction component; a vision of the future straight out of boy's fiction. In their teens, Erik de Jong and his older brother would read cheap fifties pulp fiction, by writers like Jack Vance. The singer still has pangs for the romantic futurism and unconditional belief in the future that emanated from those books at the time. Even to the extent that the title of his album *Dagen van gras, dagen van stro* (2005), was taken from the Dutch translation of *Ringing Changes*, a volume of short stories by science fiction author R.A. Lafferty.

This second record sounded more organic than his first. Spinvis was intelligent enough not to make a carbon copy of his successful debut album. This time around he was inspired by the dynamic of his live band and he carefully allowed his songs to find their own direction. Judging by the long-drawn-out spoken word piece 'Lotus Europa', De Jong's literary aspirations had evolved as well. The track was somewhere between a fever-induced dream and the absurdist interior monologue of a man in a swimming pool who, to his horror, discovers that his limbs are dying off and disappearing one by one. At the same time, he is witness to a cruel game in which one of the bathers is constantly having someone push his head under water. Some see this as a metaphor for the old Europe which, due to the economic rise of Asia, is being slowly but surely suppressed. Here, the words take precedence; the music does little more than set the tone.

Eye contact of the loneliest kind

In recent years, Spinvis has significantly expanded his artistic vocabulary. He has created theatre performances, worked on a radio musical and came up with music for radio plays and the TV series *Najib & Julia* and *Medea* by the Dutch film producer Theo Van Gogh, who was murdered on the street in Amsterdam by a Muslim terrorist in November 2004. Furthermore, he has written soundtracks for Belgian films like Miel Van Hoogenbemt's *A Perfect Match* and Hans van Nuffel's *Oxigen*. A few of his side projects were compiled on the 2007 album *Goochelaars en geesten*. A year later, Spinvis made another EP with the

poet Simon Vinkenoog, while in 2010 he formed the Dorléac duo along with singer Geike Arnaert from the popular Belgian triphop band Hooverphonic.

De Jong was so busy with various kinds of commissioned projects that it took him more than six years to come up with a new Spinvis record. On *Tot ziens, Justine Keller* (2011), his most straightforward piece of work to date, he chose a middle path between catchy synthpop, intoxicating Krautrock and subdued acoustic ballads where the proportion of electronica had been reduced to near nonexistence. The narrative voice on the album is that of an adult man who continues to long for the illusion/fantasy of the woman with whom he was in love as a twelve year old boy. He is obsessed with an ideal that does not exist and therefore seeks solace in nightlife. A second central theme on the album is the role of alcohol in our society. Spinvis calls it a substance which is both good and bad: it detaches, anesthetizes and makes people happy, but also brings out the worst in them. Hanco Kolk has produced a graphic novel version of the album, having previously created a cartoon based on the song 'Voor ik vergeet'.

What is also striking is the re-appearance of a character called Ronnie, who featured for the first time on Spinvis's debut album. In his songs, the singer often portrays fragile, damaged characters who struggle to fit into mainstream society: a boy in a psychiatric clinic, a lonely man in an old people's home, dreamers too fragile for this world. 'Voor ik vergeet' articulates a fear of dementia. 'There's no doubt that Alzheimer's is everybody's nightmare', Spinvis says. 'But that particular song is also about the transitory nature of happiness. For example, you might go for a bike ride on a beautiful day and realize that there will come a time when you'll no longer remember it. That's okay. Some things are just pre-destined to evaporate. But that doesn't change the fact that they are significant in the course of a human life.'

Although in Spinvis's universe the role of reminiscence should not be underestimated, the artist is all too aware that memory cannot always be relied upon. '*Those were good times, if I'm not mistaken*', he sings at one point. 'Isn't it strange that you keep on changing your interpretation of particular moments in your life? Autobiography is fiction, while what is intended as fiction often betrays a whole host of autobiographical elements. At the end of the day, you can only make up what's already inside you.'

Despite his understanding that he is only a speck of dust in history, the idea of 'back then' has an irresistible allure for Spinvis. And one way or another, he experiences his own transience as a relief: '*I was waiting on the edge / On the banks of time / And everything passed me by / Lost its name / And drifted ashore*'.

Spinvis does not really write protest songs as such, yet for those who can read between the lines there is a thread of social commentary running through his work. He has criticized vivisection, irresponsible parenthood, people devoid of civic responsibility, a society that carelessly shoves older people aside, and television game shows that play on the lowest and greediest of human impulses. 'Het voordeel van video' is about the media's voyeurism and the ubiquitous cameras that invade our privacy on a daily basis. Such a far-reaching indiscretion is symptomatic of the loneliness in our society: we think we know all there is to know about someone else, but actually we know nothing. Even parties rarely succeed in cheering Spinvis up. Because: '*The last thing you get / The best you can score / Is eye contact of the loneliest kind.*'

The singer stresses that, unlike politicians, he does not have an all-embracing vision. 'I am a kind of filter. I write about small things, about subjects that everyone knows and understands.' If there is any sense of outrage in his work at all, it is expressed in a poetic or surrealist manner. No one is interested in a run-of-the-mill pamphlet anyway. Or as Spinvis likes to remind us: 'If it's not beautiful, there's no point at all.' ▪

Translated by Gregory Ball

DISCOGRAPHY

Spinvis (2002)

Nieuwegeinaan Zee (2003)

Dagen van gras, dagen van stro (2005)

Goochelaars en geesten (2007)

Tot ziens, Justine Keller (2011)

All these albums were released by Excelsior Recordings.

Jozef and Isaac Israëls

Realist and Impressionist Painting

The writer Frans Erens wrote of Jozef and Isaac Israëls, father and son: 'Being the great son of a great father is a rare occurrence in history, and especially in the history of art.'[1] Both were prominent artists: one in his realism, while the other broke with this in favour of a vigorous, impressionistic approach to his subjects.

Jozef Israëls (1824-1911)

Jozef Israëls was born in 1824 in Groningen, the third of ten children. In his childhood years there was great emphasis on the Jewish religion and art. Already in his early teens he took drawing and painting lessons in Groningen, before leaving in 1842 for Amsterdam to work at the studio of the renowned portrait painter Jan Adam Kruseman (1804-1862). Israëls had this to say about how the master interacted with his pupils: 'Sometimes he allows 1 or 2 days to pass before he comes to look at our work, he mostly allows his pupils to work in their own way, only drawing their attention to truths.'[2] A year later he was admitted to the capital's Royal Academy, where he was taught by Jan Willem Pieneman (1779-1853), among others. He also took lessons in Paris from artists including Paul Delaroche (1797-1856) and Horace Vernet (1789-1863).

Painter of life in fishing communities

During the initial period as an artist, Jozef Israëls searched for a style and genre that suited him. His early works, informed by his education, were in the Romantic tradition. Critics of these paintings have already observed that Israëls 'is a sensitive artist'. [3] Sentiment is indeed clearly evident in works such as *Meditation* (1850), in which a young woman is depicted staring melancholically into the water. The image and composition are strongly reminiscent of *Young Woman in Tears by the Sea* (1823-1827) by Ary Scheffer (1795-1858), a painter in the Romantic style whom Israëls admired. After painting a number of historical pieces, Israëls turned his attention to genre painting, in which he found a

theme that was to become his speciality: depicting the life of fishing people. Increasingly he moved away from Romanticism, though the realism that replaced it was always rendered with a degree of sentiment.

Israëls was not the only painter to work in the fishing genre. Other nineteenth-century artists worked on this theme too, including the artists of the Düsseldorfer Schule, whom Israëls probably met during a visit to Düsseldorf in 1850.[4] The theme is also related to depictions of labourers and peasants, as painted by French Realists such as Gustave Courbet (1819-1877), in which the lives of ordinary people were portrayed. Israëls' paintings likewise evoke nineteenth-century poetry, in which the life of fishing communities was a popular subject.[5]

It is not only in terms of theme that parallels can be seen between Israëls' painting and the poetry of his contemporaries. He gave poetic titles to his depictions of ordinary people, and the feeling he brought to his paintings was often compared to poetry. *Passing Mother's Grave*, in which a fisherman who has just returned from the sea is passing by the grave of his late wife with their two children, was acclaimed with the words 'insightful poetry'.[6] The painting marks a turning point in Israëls' oeuvre. One of his first fishing scenes, it is exceptionally large for a genre piece and takes on a different meaning because of its size. This was probably inspired by a visit to the World's Fair in Paris, where Realists had presented images of working-class people depicted on a monumental scale.[7] The image of the humble, barefoot fisherman is life-size, and the low position from which the painting is viewed lends a sense of the majestic and heroic. The drama of the image is enhanced because the viewer knows that a fisherman's return usually means a joyful reunion with loved ones. Moreover, in art and literature it is usually the fisherman's wife who waits anxiously for her husband to return. The painting was well received. Today it is still regarded as one of the most important works in the oeuvre of Jozef Israëls.

His next major success came in 1861 with *Fishermen Carrying a Drowned Man*. The style of this painting is more realistic than *Passing Mother's Grave*, but equally emotive: a procession of people carries home the body of a drowned fisherman. The small group in the foreground – the grieving wife and children –

Isaac Israels, *Military Funeral*, 1881-1882, oil on canvas, Collectie Gemeentemuseum Den Haag.

Jozef Israëls, *We Grow Old*,
1883, oil on canvas,
Collectie Gemeentemuseum Den Haag

is particularly poignant. Israëls omitted the histrionic element and depicted the characters' grief with restraint and empathy. The painting received an honourable mention at the Paris Salon and was shown at the World's Fair in London. Israëls' sister, who lived in London, informed him: 'You're famous! [...] Your picture is the talk of the town!'[8] It was indeed extremely well received, with words such as 'the most touching picture of the whole exhibition'.[9]

After his breakthrough in the mid-1850s, Jozef Israëls exhibited at several major exhibitions every year, such as the 'Exhibitions of Living Masters' in various Dutch cities, the Paris Salon and the International Exhibitions. His fame also grew internationally. He painted several variants on the fishing theme, such as fishermen's wives waiting for their husbands to return and elderly people living out their days in poverty. More light-hearted themes included children playing on the beach. Many of his paintings are set in the humble interiors of fishermen's homes, which Israëls initially used as an example. In 1879 he had a fisherman's interior built in his studio, and it was described in 1906 in The Pall Mall Magazine: 'there it was – his "binnenhuisje" – the background for so many of his pictures. A low dark cottage window, with rough, small panes, white halfway curtains, and oaken shutters [...] matted peasants' chairs stood in the shadow; the screen lent possibilities of corners.'[10]

Israëls was famous and made an excellent living from his art. The business sense of his wife Aleida Schaap (1843-1894), whom he married in 1863, certainly contributed to his success. The fact that, from 1859 onwards, his art was often compared to that of Rembrandt, also did much to enhance his reputation. The artist himself encouraged this myth-making by writing a book about Rembrandt in 1906, and later in his career he even painted similar themes, such as *The Jewish Wedding*.

Isaac Israels (1865-1934)

By the time Isaac Israels[11] was born, in 1865, his father had become one of the most prominent artists in the Netherlands. In 1871 the family moved to The Hague, where art was flourishing. Artists were inspired by the city's location between the sea and the polder landscape, which offered many artistic possibilities. The work of a number of young artists in The Hague was heavily influenced by Realism, and in 1875 the art critic Van Santen Kolff coined the term The Hague School,[12] to which Jozef Israëls was considered to belong.

Isaac Israels grew up in his father's studio, which was not only the place where his paintings were created, but was also a meeting place for artists, writers, art dealers and collectors. It was almost inevitable that Isaac would become an artist too. In 1871, when his son was only six years old, Jozef Israëls wrote of him: 'he is a clever animal painter and with the aid of the lord he will be a better colourman than his father' [13]. Indeed, Isaac indicated at an early age that he wanted to become an artist. His parents supported him in this, and decided that, after completing his basic education, he would focus fully on his career as an artist. His command of languages was excellent, due to his interest in literature and to the fact that the family travelled extensively abroad. From 1878 they attended the Salon de Paris

Isaac Israels,
Maids on an Amsterdam Canal,
ca. 1894, oil on canvas, 60
cm. x 80 cm. Groninger
Museum, Groningen

every year, which meant that Isaac encountered new tendencies in art from an early age.

He learned perspective drawing from his father and in 1880 he became a pupil of the Academy of Art in The Hague. Just one year later his work was shown at several exhibitions. He achieved his first successes with realistically painted military subjects. *Military Funeral* (1881-1882) was highly praised in 1882 at the Paris Salon. The title of the painting suggests a connection with his father's oeuvre, but Isaac's approach to his subjects was different. He observed the scene and painted what he had witnessed, without the intention of arousing emotions or telling a story. Jozef Israëls also noticed the difference in approach: 'My Zon paints the Varriors going to the Var and I paint the Veeping Vidows'.[14] He probably wrote this with regard to the painting *Transport of Colonial Soldiers* (1883), which earned his son an honourable mention at the Paris Salon of 1885. Whereas his father's aim was to stir the viewer's emotions, Isaac favoured a more objective observation, leaving out the narrative element as far as possible.

Isaac Israels achieved major successes at a young age and his future as an artist appeared secure. But he wanted to go his own way and break away

Isaac Israels, *A Sunny Day on the Beach, Viareggio*, oil on canvas, private collection, previously in the collection of Simonis & Buunk Art Gallery, Ede

Jozef Israëls, *Passing Mother's Grave*, 1856, oil on canvas. Stedelijk Museum, Amsterdam

from parental authority and his father's artistic influence. In 1886-1887 he took lessons at the Rijksacademie voor Beeldende Kunsten in Amsterdam, together with George Hendrik Breitner (1857-1923). Israels and Breitner already knew each other, because Breitner – who was slightly older than Israels – had visited Jozef Israëls' studio in 1879 and was impressed with the young Isaac's paintings. Both artists quickly abandoned their studies at the academy, because they felt it had little to teach them. Entries for both artists in the Academy's register note that, since they were trained artists, the Academy was a 'totally inappropriate' place for them.[15] Israels did settle in the capital, and took the time there to develop his own style.

Letters written by Isaac's mother reveal that his parents were extremely concerned about him: '[...] when he was 17 years old, he was the brightest of all the young painters in our country – he could have remained so, but did not – why? Now he has killed his talent, he is on the wrong track with his art – he is in the mire, and it will be the end of him'.[16] Israels' Amsterdam friends, on the other hand, had every confidence that it would all turn out well. The writer and psychologist Frederik van Eeden wrote to Aleida Israëls-Schaap: 'He is quietly going his own way, as he always has. He does not want to be under anyone's influence and I assure you [...] that, with someone like Isaac, all will soon turn out well.'[17]

Isaac spent several years working mainly on sketches and experimenting. It was not an easy time, as he himself records: 'Every morning I rise, determined to prevail, and every evening I give up. *Vaincu!*'[18] But he persevered and found new subjects that interested him, such as dance halls and coffee pickers. This long quest suggests that he shared a trait with his father, who was once described as an example of 'self-assured strength, of relentless zeal, of a persistent will to overcome difficulties – in flagrant contrast to the sitting down in despair, the fretting and complaining, that a dealer is often obliged to witness in so many other artists.' [19] In the first half of the 1890s, Isaac Israels revealed his new style, characterised by a vigorous, impressionistic touch that came to typify his work. The first paintings in this style include 'snapshots' of city life

in Amsterdam, such as maids walking along the canals, whom Israels painted
en plein air. In general, his new approach was well received by the exhibition
reviewers. Israels' work sold well during his life, and continues to do so today.

Sadly, Aleida Israëls-Schaap did not live to see her son's renewed and hard-
won success; she died in 1894. In order to raise Jozef Israëls' spirits, father and
son went on a long trip to Spain, accompanied by the writer Frans Erens, who was
Isaac's best friend. According to Jozef, Erens was a valued travel companion: '[...]
painters see everything in terms of outward appearance, and that is how it should
be because that is their field. But it is a privilege to be accompanied by a philosopher and poet to observe and hold onto the deeper significance of what passes.' [20]
The trip does not appear to have had a great deal of influence on either artist's
oeuvre. Although Jozef found the inspiration for a painting and travel journal, he
had long since found his style and theme, and Isaac too had only recently mastered
a new style. By contrast, his extensive travels later *are* reflected in his paintings.

Isaac Israels painted a range of subjects, almost always with the emphasis
on people, in particular women. Apart from the servant girls he painted in his
early period, his oeuvre includes busy city scenes, seamstresses, mannequins in
fashion houses, dancers in the theatre and people at leisure in parks. His beach
scenes were often created in the company of his father and the German painter
Max Liebermann (1847-1935), a friend with whom he often painted on the beach at
Scheveningen, near The Hague, in the summer. Whereas Jozef was mainly interested in the local fishing community, Isaac painted the worldly bathers, from children on donkeys to women in the latest bathing fashions.

Isaac Israels is regarded as one of the Amsterdam Impressionists and, like his
father, had a great deal of contact with fellow artists. But unlike his father, who
was involved in artists' societies and the founding of the Hollandsche Teeken-
maatschappij (Dutch Drawing Society), Isaac was more of an *Einzelgänger*. He preferred to go his own way, his freedom from ties enabling him, whenever the mood
took him, to pack his things and leave for destinations such as Paris or London and
spend as much time there as he chose.

Father and son were both among the most prominent artists of their time.
Although their respective oeuvres differed, they admired each other's work.

It is often said of Isaac Israels that he chose a more 'distant' approach. If we compare his cheerful depictions with his father's sensitive work, this is indeed the impression we gain. Yet his sketches and portraits of people reveal a talent for capturing the subject's character with just a few lines. Here, perhaps, we can see traces of the 'deep human feeling' for which his father was known, albeit expressed in a completely different way. ■

Translated by Yvette Mead

NOTES

1. F. Erens, *Isaac Israels*, Amsterdam 1912, p. 9.

2. Letter from Israels to Mr Essingh, 16 July 1843, A.S. Kok archive, Rijksdienst voor Kunsthistorische Documentatie. A passage from the letter is included in: D. Dekkers, *Jozef Israëls 1824-1911*, Groningen/Amsterdam 1999, p. 362.

3. Darie Wetan (Joh.C. Zimmerman), 'Adagio con espressione. (De laatste gedachte van Weber)', *De Gids*, 15 (1851) deel 1, p. 630. Quoted in: D. Dekkers, *Jozef Israëls* 1824-1911, Groningen/Amsterdam 1999, p. 20.

4. D. Dekkers, *Jozef Israels, een succesvol schilder van het vissersgenre*, diss. University of Amsterdam 1994, pp. 41-63.

5. Examples are 'Heugenis van Zandvoort' by E.J. Potgieter and 'De gewone mens en de gevoelige mens te Zandvoort' by J. van Oosterwijk Bruyn. See also D. Dekkers, *Jozef Israëls 1824-1911*, Groningen/Amsterdam 1999, pp. 21-22.

6. 'De twee Amsterdamsche tentoonstellingen van Kunstwerken in 1856', *Algemeene Konst- en Letterbode*, 1856, p. 378, quoted in: D. Dekkers, *Jozef Israëls 1824-1911*, Groningen/Amsterdam 1999, p. 22.

7. D. Dekkers, *Jozef Israëls 1824-1911*, Groningen/Amsterdam 1999, pp. 137-138.

8. A. Luden, 'A New Royal Academician. Josef Israels: His Life-story and his Art', *The Pall Mall Magazine*, May 1906, vol. XXXVII, No. 157, pp. 527-537.

9. Quoted without a reference in: A. Wagner, *Isaac Israels*, Rotterdam 1967, p. 6.

10. A. Luden, 'A New Royal Academician. Josef Israels: His Life-story and his Art', *The Pall Mall Magazine*, May 1906, vol. XXXVII, No. 157, p. 530.

11. In the case of Jozef, the surname Israels is usually written with two dots over the 'e'. In the case of Isaac, the dots are usually omitted.

12. R. de Leeuw, J. Sillevis and C. Dumas, *De Haagse School: Hollandse Meesters van de 19de eeuw*, The Hague 1983. The artists of The Hague School included J. Israëls, H.W. Mesdag, J. Maris, M. Maris, W. Maris, J. Bosboom and J.H. Weissenbruch. In general their art is characterised by realism, but on closer consideration it is highly diverse in terms of subjects and style. The name 'The Hague School' therefore denotes the location in which all these artists worked, rather than a shared artistic vision.

13. Letter from Jozef Israëls to his friend and collector John Forbes White, dated 23 February 1871, Aberdeen Art Gallery collection. Quoted in: I.M. Harrower, 'Jozef Israels and his Aberdeen Friend', *Aberdeen University Review* XIV, March 1927, pp. 112-113.

14. Fragment from a letter from Jozef Israëls to the collector John Forbes White, quoted in: I.M. Harrower, 'Jozef Israels and his Aberdeen Friend', Aberdeen University Review XIV, March 1927, p. 112.

15. A. Wagner, *Isaac Israels*, Rotterdam 1967, pp. 16-19.

16. Letter from Aleida Israëls-Schaap to Albert Verwey, 12 December 1888, quoted in: J. Sillevis et al., *Jozef en Isaac Israëls, vader & zoon*, Zwolle/The Hague 2008, p. 35.

17. Letter from Frederik van Eeden to Aleida Israëls-Schaap, 20 June 1888, quoted in: J. Sillevis et al., *Jozef en Isaac Israëls, vader & zoon*, Zwolle/The Hague 2008, p. 35.

18. Described by Jan Veth in *De Taak*, 1922, quoted in: A. Wagner, *Isaac Israels*, Rotterdam 1967, p. 22.

19. *Een halve eeuw met Jozef Israëls*, 's-Gravenhage (Boussod, Valadon & Cie.) 1910, p. 10.

20. J. Israëls, *Een reis door Spanje*, Utrecht/Antwerpen 1989, p. 14 (original edition: 's-Gravenhage 1899).

The Establishment of
the Orange Monarchy in 1813-1815

A National Myth

[MATTHIJS LOK]

Every day hundreds of passers-by, cyclists, trams and cars pass the imposing nineteenth-century monument on the stately Den Haag square, 'Plein 1813'. Most of these passers-by are probably unaware of its significance as a memorial to the restoration of Dutch independence after the fall of the Napoleonic Empire and the establishment of the Orange monarchy in 1813-1815. The relative obscurity of the monument – before the national commemoration of the bicentennial in 2013-2015, in any case – illustrates the fact that these events have been forgotten by the great majority of the Dutch population.

The relative obscurity of the monument cannot be attributed to its form. Due to its impressive size the monument towers high above the square. On top there is the figure of a maiden, representing the Dutch nation. In her hands she holds the seven arrows of the seven provinces of the old Republic. Beside her sits the Dutch lion symbolising resurgent courage. Beneath her feet lie the broken chains of French tyranny. On the city side we find the statue of William I (1772-1843), swearing the oath on the constitution. On the seaward side stand the statues of the triumvirate that formed the interim government in November 1813, Van Hogendorp, Van der Duyn van Maasdam and Van Limburg Stirum. The founding principles of the Dutch state, religion (biblia) and history (historia) are represented on either side. The collapse of Napoleonic rule and the arrival of the Prince of Orange on the beach at Scheveningen, welcomed by the cheering population, are depicted heroically in relief.

The monument was intended, as stated, to be a reminder of annexation by the Napoleonic Empire and the establishment of the Orange monarchy in the Netherlands. A short summary of these events goes as follows: in November 1813 Napoleonic rule in the Dutch provinces, which had been annexed to the Napoleonic Empire in 1810, collapsed after the defeat of the imperial armies by an international coalition near Leipzig on 16-19 October 1813. French officials started to flee the country and a power vacuum threatened. The Rotterdammer and former regent, Gijsbert Karel van Hogendorp (1762-1834), who had not held any important posts since the Batavian revolution in 1795, but had forged plans for the restoration of an independent Netherlands, seized his opportunity and on 21 November he proclaimed himself, in the name of the Prince of Orange, together with Van der Duyn van Maasdam and van Limburg Stirum as the country's

Monument 1813, The Hague

interim government. Van Hogendorp's independent behaviour came to an end when the Prince of Orange himself, returning from England, where he had been exiled from the Continent for years, landed on the beach at Scheveningen on 3 November 1813.

At first the Prince of Orange appeared to be hesitant about taking the lead in setting up the new state formed under the protection and patronage of Great Britain. As his position had not yet been established, William was initially given the rather vague title of 'Sovereign Monarch'. A constitutional commission was set up by the Prince under the chairmanship of the inevitable Van Hogendorp. On 29 March 1814 the constitution was approved by a 'Meeting of Notables', personally selected by William and his close associates, who had come from every corner of the land to the *Nieuwe Kerk* (New Church) in Amsterdam. A day later William I took the oath on the brand new constitution, giving his rule a legitimate basis. On 2 May that year he opened the sitting of the Estates-General, the national parliament of the Northern Netherlands.

The formation of the young kingdom ended with the merging of the Northern and Southern Netherlands, which had gone their separate ways after the Revolt in the sixteenth century. In August 1814 the Prince was given interim authority over the Austrian Netherlands. With the approval of the European powers, William assumed the title of King on 16 March 1815, just as the new state came under threat from Napoleon's unexpected one hundred day return to France from exile on Elba. The defeat of the Napoleonic armies near Waterloo on 18 July, however, secured the survival of the young kingdom. On 21 September of that year William I made his ceremonial entrance into Brussels as King of the United Kingdom of the Netherlands, a state which, as we know, would not last fifteen years.

Monument 1813, The Hague. Detail. The triumvirate that formed the interim government on 20 November 1813

Like all monuments, the monument on Plein 1813 says more about the time when it was erected, around 1860, than about the time that the edifice was supposed to commemorate. Fierce political strife preceded the erection of the monument, including even death threats against Minister-President Thorbecke. Besides being a symbol of the political strife round 1860, this monument also represents a more durable phenomenon in Dutch history – the national myth of '1813'. According to this myth the establishment of the Orange monarchy was the result of a national struggle for independence in which the population of the Netherlands united to drive out the foreign tyrant and his servants under the leadership of the returning 'father', William I, a descendant of *pater patriae* William the Silent (1533-1584). The classic national image of '1813' is of a new beginning and a national 'liberation' and 'deliverance' after a dark period of occupation. This image was created immediately after 1813 by contemporary historians like Van der Palm, Boscha and Konijnenburg with the aim of legitimising the establishment of William I's regime by presenting the new state as a return to the traditions of the fatherland and creating a sharp contrast between the tyrannical Napoleonic rule and the freedom-loving, patriotic government of the Orange monarch.

Source of embarrassment

It is striking that this image of '1813' persists even today. The official committee appointed by the Dutch Council of Ministers on 1 July 2011 to organise the commemoration of the two hundredth anniversary of the events of 1813-1815 is following the classic concept too. On the committee's website (www.200jaarkoninkrijk.nl, as viewed on August 1, 2012) the establishment of the monarchy is also presented as a national liberation after a period of foreign domination. Following a period of dark tyranny William I brought national independence, Dutch freedom combined with the constitutional guarantee of human rights and burgeoning democracy. That the commemoration committee propagates this type of historic image is in itself very understandable. By presenting '1813' as a national independence struggle following grim foreign domination, the distant events of the early nineteenth century, which do not as such evoke strong images, can be dramatized for more Dutch and brought alive in the eyes of the inhabitants of the twenty-first century. The official representation of '1813' seems to echo the commemoration and conceptualization of the liberation after the Second World War, a memory that still has a big impact on Dutch conceptions of the past.

The existing national image of '1813', however, is founded on a myth. To start with, the characterisation of the regime preceding the 'liberation of 1813', the period of annexation to the Napoleonic Empire, between 1810 and 1813, as 'foreign occupation' is anachronistic. Many members of the Dutch administrative elite – right up to the highest level – had participated in the annexation government, partly out of pragmatism but also because they – like the head of the Imperial Court and foremost Dutch legal officer, Cornelis Felix van Maanen (1769-1846) –felt that in so doing they could carry out the much needed reform of the Dutch governmental and legal system. In contrast to the German domination of 1940-1945 the Napoleonic Empire wanted to integrate the local elites of the annexed territories into the administration. Dutchmen could be found at every level of imperial rule, from the lowliest *Maire* to the State Council and the Senate in Paris, not just many former Batavian revolutionaries but moderate Orangists who had shown their loyalty to Emperor Napoleon after 1801 too. Although some of the Batavian revolutionaries, like Anton Reinhard Falck (1777-1843), had refused to work for the annexation government, many Dutch administrators agreed with Napoleon's position, that the former Dutch republic was simply too small to continue to exist independently and had therefore been added to the *Empire* out of 'compassion'. In 1810 the disappearance of the Netherlands as an independent political unit was a realistic future scenario. That the Netherlands is still alive and thriving as a nation state now has more to do with the French Emperor's strategic military mistakes than with the patriotic sentiments of the Dutch population - but that is not the subject of this article.

After 1813 the major role played by Dutch officials in the imperial government naturally became a source of embarrassment and the significant Dutch contribution to the annexation government was hushed up and explained away. After 1813, government during the annexation became, retrospectively, cruel foreign domination by the Corsican monster Napoleon ('the bloodthirsty predator' according to one Dutch pamphlet) and his fickle Frenchmen, ancient enemies of the Dutch. Insofar as Dutch notables had served Napoleon, they did it, according to their own apologias and Dutch historians, only because of their desire to alleviate, as far as possible, the brutal measures the 'French authorities' were inflicting on the troubled population of the Netherlands. The publicist Jacobus Scheltema wrote that prefects from the Southern Netherlands, such as Celles and de Stassart, 'honed and exacerbated the cruelty of the imperial regulations, rubbing salt and pepper into the open wounds, while prefects [from the Northern Netherlands] applied oil and balsam'. The whole period from the Batavian revolution to the annexation was excluded from Dutch history after 1813 and characterised in national historiography as the 'French period', as if it had no place in national historiography.

Monument 1813, The Hague. Detail. The landing of William I (30 November 1813) at Scheveningen beach, only a few metres from the place where he had left the country with his father eighteen years previously

Dynastic interests

Whether or not the main actors during the 'liberation of 1813' were motivated by love of the fatherland, as is so beautifully portrayed in the reliefs on the monument, is also questionable. The actions of the Prince and the Stadholders' family themselves can certainly not be called purely nationalistic in the period 1795-1813. On 26 November 1801 the Prince's father and last Stadholder, William V (1748-1806), who lived in exile, had, partly under pressure from his son, given up his rights to the Netherlands in return for the payment of damages because the return of the Stadholders' family no longer seemed to be a realistic prospect. Having bowed to Napoleon, William I was given the tiny German principality of Fuldato to rule in 1802, though the Emperor took it from him again in 1806. The Prince then went to run his properties in Silesia and Posen as an ordinary country gentleman. His endeavours in the period 1795-1813 seem to have been aimed mainly at getting some territory to rule over somewhere – anywhere – in Europe. Thanks to his mother, Wilhelmina of Prussia, William realised that his best chances lay in Great Britain, and in the spring of 1813 he left for the island state to work for the restoration of the Orange dynasty in the former Republic. It was then that it became clear that the Napoleonic Empire was less invincible than had hitherto been thought. As far as the later William I was concerned, dynastic interests prevailed over Dutch nationalist feelings. Obviously, though, after his accession to the throne in 1813-1815 the Prince did not want to be reminded of his – quite understandably – pragmatic behaviour in the period preceding his return to the Netherlands.

Large sections of the Dutch population seemed, then, to have more or less forgotten the stadholders' family in the early nineteenth century. The death of the last Stadholder, in 1806, passed largely unnoticed. The Orange sentiments of the 'ordinary folk' seem mainly to have been activated when the Napoleonic Empire, coming under increasing pressure as a result of its military defeats from 1812 onwards, began to take on a more and more repressive character. National sentiments certainly existed before 1813 and were reinforced by resist-

Monument 1813, The Hague

ance poetry such as J.F. Helmers's *De Hollandsche natie* (the Dutch nation; 1812) and the experience of annexation. Nonetheless, the revival of Dutch nationalism in the years 1813 to 1815 as expressed, for example, in the many pamphlets and poems written at the time in honour of the nation and the Orange dynasty, was certainly just as much a result as the cause of the events of 1813-1815.

Indeed, the attitude of the majority of the Dutch elite can definitely not be characterised as patriotic. For fear of a not entirely unrealistic military resurgence of the Empire, many members of the Dutch political and professional elite advocated a 'system of neutrality' in October and November 1813, whereby they took no sides, neither Napoleon's nor the Prince of Orange's. Some officials, such as Cornelis Felix van Maanen, only stopped reporting to the Minister of Justice in Paris after he had himself seen the Cossacks on the Malieveld in The Hague. The uncomfortable truth, from the perspective of the current commemoration, is that in general the Northern Netherlands' elite was more afraid of chaos and plundering by its own 'ordinary folk', as a result of the power

Monument 1813,
The Hague. Detail

vacuum that had developed after the departure of the French military, than it was of the 'foreign' annexation regime. When the revolution turned out to be irreversible, many officials attributed an important role in the 'national liberation' to themselves – with retrospective effect, of course.

A creation *ab ovo*

The portrayal in national historiography of 1813 as the start of the modern Dutch state and monarchy is incorrect too. In terms of his monarchy, William I was able to build, to a large extent, on the example of the first King of the Netherlands, Louis Napoleon (1778-1846), who had been appointed by his brother, Napoleon I, as the King of Holland from 1806 to 1810. In pamphlets after 1813 Louis was jeeringly referred to as the 'shadow King' of his brother Napoleon, but Louis was just as much the shadow King of William I. Louis made the monarchy acceptable to the citizens of the country, with its long republican tradition, by visiting the victims of national disasters such as flooding and gun powder explosions (and by having these visits recorded in many poems and pictures). After 1813, however, William I never mentioned the first King of Holland and Louis Napoleon was not given an official reception when he visited the country in 1840.

Furthermore, it is a myth that William built his state – in the words of the British Ambassador, Clancarty – *ab ovo* (from the egg, or from scratch). Very soon after his return William realised that he had more in common with the professional and centrist-leaning former Napoleonic civil servants (who had been mainly moderate revolutionaries during the period 1795-1798) than with the regents left over from the Old Republic. In the constitutional commission of 1814, powerful men such as Van Maanen, Elout and Roëll were able to influence Van Hogendorp's draft to suit the Napoleonic centrists. The archaic constitutional terminology from the republican period obscures the extent to which William I's state 'lay in a bed made by Napoleon'. By historicizing the institutions created in the period 1795-1813 the Batavian-Napoleonic heritage was 'nationalised'.

Joseph Paelinck, *William I, King of the Netherlands* (1819). Rijksmuseum Amsterdam

What is also striking is the high degree of continuity in terms of the senior official apparatus between the 'cruel foreign annexation' and the liberated Netherlands. William I wielded his power over a kingdom of real political weathercocks, who had transformed themselves expertly from servants of the Empire to loyal officials of the fatherland between 1813 and 1815. In the period 1814-1830, for example, two thirds of the State Councillors in the Northern Netherlands had already held office during the Kingdom of Holland and half during the annexation. A similar pattern held for the ministers too. The administrative continuity with the Batavian and Napoleonic periods had major consequences for Dutch administrative practice after 1813. The establishment of the Orange monarchy was, in short, to a large extent the work of the Napoleonic administrative elite, though obviously there was little mention of this in the nationalist version of events. In my opinion, then, there is a scene missing from the monument on Plein 1813 – that of Cornelis Felix van Maanen as the impersonation of administrative 'weathercocks' (to use the language of his contemporaries) and their important role in the construction of the Kingdom of the Netherlands.

The international dimension

Another aspect of the distorted national memory of 1813 is obviously the denial of the international dimension of the events of 1813-1815. Although it cannot be denied that the headstrong behaviour of the triumvirate, or that of William I, influenced the outcome of the regime change in 1813-1815, the events of those years in the Netherlands must be put in perspective. Developments in the Dutch provinces during those years were only a sideshow compared to developments on the broader European scene. Without the arrival of the mounted Cossacks on the Malieveld in The Hague, William I could not have established his national monarchy. And the Prince's landing and the establishment of the state in the Northern Netherlands, in 1814, would have been no more than the first act of a process that would result in the founding of the United Kingdom of the Netherlands, a bi-lingual state with The Hague and Brussels as dual capitals. This 'amalgamation' was not only 'forced' on the country by the international powers, as the official rhetoric would have it, but was also very deliberately sought after by William I and company (including, initially, the father of the constitution, Gijsbert Karel van Hogendorp). Despite the national rhetoric, William I's endeavours were aimed primarily not at national but at dynastic interests. It was not the landing at Scheveningen, on 30 November 1813, but the Battle of Waterloo, on 16-18 July 1815, that was the most important national historical event of this United Kingdom. Only after the separation of the Kingdom, in the revolution of 1830, did the 'national memory' of 1813 acquire a purely Northern Netherlands colour and would William I's Benelux be referred to as a bizarre experiment, doomed to failure, in both Dutch and Belgian national history.

The official 2013 commemoration committee seems to want to add a new dimension to the already layered national myth of 1813. William I is also presented – on the commemoration website mentioned above, for example – as the bringer of parliamentary democracy and defender of the values of democratic pluralism. But William I would turn in his grave if he knew that two hundred years later he would be depicted as a democrat. William I's system was actually aimed at restricting the influence of the people as much as possible and leaving the administration of the country to 'self-possessed' ('bedaard') gentlemen of standing, property and morally irreproachable behaviour. Indeed, the French terror had made it very clear to many contemporaries exactly where unbridled people's power could lead: to anarchy and bloody despotism.

To sum up, the national memory of '1813' as a national liberation from a brutal foreign tyrant and the start of modern Dutch political history and democracy is founded on a myth. In reality the transition was much more chaotic and messier, and the behaviour of the protagonists much more pragmatic and not what could be called heroic. The myth of the 'national liberation' was created by contemporary historians and publicists after the facts, in 1813-1815, with the aim of legitimising the new state of the Orange monarchs. That myth still exists and, as the website of the commemoration committee shows, is constantly being fed. That this version of events is incorrect, however, does not of course mean that the myth is by definition harmful. Every political establishment creates – deliberately or imperceptibly – its own 'historical regime' to justify its own existence and there is nothing wrong with that per se, as long as critical voices are not excluded. Conceptualization of the national liberation struggle against a foreign tyrant can also be very useful in arousing or keeping alive, in people who are not professionally involved with the period, a historic interest in relatively distant events. Successfully familiarizing a broader public with complex historical events from a distant past always requires simplification and thinking in strong contrasts. National memories that have been created, like those of 1813, may possibly even increase social cohesion in a society that feels threatened by either imagined or real social and political fragmentation. But if the Netherlands is really the full-grown democracy that it pretends to be, according to the commemoration committee, then there must also be historians who have the thankless and perhaps rather disagreeable task of researching national memories as far as possible outside the national context and ultimately subjecting them to the critical examination of scholarship as well. ■

Translated by Lindsay Edwards

NOTE

For a more detailed exposition and substantiation of this interpretation of the events of 1813-1815, please see my book *Windvanen. Napoleontische bestuurders in de Nederlandse en Franse Restauratie (1813-1820)* (Amsterdam: Bert Bakker 2009; includes summary in English; EN title: Political weathervanes. Napoleonic officials under the Dutch and French Restoration monarchy (1813-1820)). *Windvanen* was defended as a doctoral thesis on 17 April 2009 at the University of Amsterdam. It can be consulted digitally via the catalogue of the University of Amsterdam (http://dare.uva.nl/record/300419).

During the memorial year 2013 various commemorative collections and other works on the period 1813-1815 will be published (including three new scientific royal biographies of William I, William II and William III).

FURTHER READING

Aerts, R. e.a., *Land van kleine gebaren. Een politieke geschiedenis van Nederland* 1780-1990 (Nijmegen/Amsterdam 1999).

M.J. van der Burg, *Nederland onder Franse invloed. Culturele overdracht en staatsvorming in de Napoleontische tijd,* 1799-1813 (Amsterdam 2009).

Joor, J., *De Adelaar en het lam. Onrust, opruiing en onwilligheid in Nederland ten tijde van het Koninkrijk Holland en de Inlijving bij het Franse keizerrijk (1806-1813)* (Amsterdam 2000).

Jourdan, A. (ed.), *Louis Bonaparte, Roi de Hollande* (Paris 2010).

Lok, M. and M.J. van der Burg, 'The Dutch case: the Kingdom of Holland and the imperial departments'. In M. Broers e.a. (Ed.), *The Napoleonic Empire and the New European Political Culture.* (England: Palgrave Macmillan 2012), 100-111.

Lok, M. and N. Scholz, 'The Return of the loving father. Masculinity, legitimacy and the French and Dutch Restoration monarchies (1813-1815), *BMGN/The Low Countries Review* 127.1 (2012), 19-44.

Rooij, P., *Republiek van Rivaliteiten. Nederland sinds* 1813 (Amsterdam 2005).

N.C.F. van Sas, De Metamorfose van Nederland. Van Oude orde naar moderniteit, 1750-1900 (Amsterdam 2004)

W. Uitterhoeve, *Cornelis Kraijenhoff,* 1758-1840. *Een loopbaan onder vijf regeervormen* (Nijmegen 2009)

J.C. van Zanten, *Schielijk, winzucht, zwaarhoofd en bedaard. Politieke discussie en oppositievorming* (Amsterdam 2004).

The Underbelly of the New Century

On the Remarkable Novel of Manners *Bonita Avenue*

Siem Sigerius, the vice-chancellor of a university in Enschede in the Eastern Netherlands, is busily pressing the flesh at a reception, when he suddenly recognises his daughter. Nothing special about that, except that he recognises her as the nude model on his favourite porn site.

That in itself is a good starting point for a novel of manners, but for Dutch readers there was another reason why *Bonita Avenue* attracted attention. The author incorporated the Enschede firework disaster into his book: the explosion of a firework storage depot on 13 May 2000, which wiped out an entire neighbourhood and caused hundreds of casualties and 23 deaths. In *Bonita Avenue* the explosion coincides with the moment when Siem Sigerius' happy, perfect family is torn apart.

In the course of 2011 Peter Buwalda, previously a journalist and a publisher's editor, metamorphosed from an unknown beginner into a best-selling author. The novel of manners, which took him four years to write, was on the Bestseller 60, the official Dutch list for book sales, for over a year. A number of awards and nominations completed the wealth of acclaim.

Explaining the success of *Bonita Avenue* is not that easy a task. Certainly Buwalda writes powerful, graphic prose that does not pull its punches. One reviewer talked of a style that was 'cutting edge (...), rich, vivid language, charged with testosterone.' (*HP/De Tijd*, 6/10/2010) A catalogue of all the ingenious turns of phrase in this book, always surprising but not so thick on the ground that they get in the way of the plot, would be going too far. In addition the novel, because of its rock-solid structure full of cliff-hanging moments, is quite simply compulsive reading.

A winner

Yet it is mainly the characters that make *Bonita Avenue* unforgettable. In an interview Buwalda stated: 'I'm fed up with wimps in fiction'. That is why Siem Sigerius, the main character, is a winner, someone who has proved his exceptional qualities both physically and intellectually. In the distant past he played competitive judo and would have taken part in the Olympic Games if he had not

Peter Buwalda (1971)
© Klaas Koppe

been ruled out by an untimely injury. While he was recovering from that injury his talent for mathematics was discovered. His mathematical studies won him a Fields Medal. In the course of the novel the very media-friendly vice-chancellor will also receive an attractive offer from the world of politics.

However, Siem inevitably has an Achilles heel: his children. In the first instance the trouble seems limited to Wilbert, the son of a previous marriage, who has become mixed up in crime. Wilbert is 'a criminal who had worked his way into crime like a corkscrew'. But that is not all. Sigerius suddenly sees a shocking likeness between his foster-daughter Joni and a nude model. In the course of the novel it becomes his mission to find out whether or not he is wrong. Is Joni really using her body as a commodity?

Buwalda tells the story from three perspectives. The chapters narrated from Sigerius' point of view take place in 2000. The others are set (mainly) in the present. The focus is on Joni (who has become a successful businesswoman in the porn industry in California) and on Aaron, Joni's ex, who has retreated to a village near Brussels following a psychotic episode. He does not know the course of events in Enschede and tries to fit the pieces of the jigsaw together.

Bonita Avenue appears to be first and foremost a novel about sex, and about how two successive generations deal with it. For Sigerius and his contemporaries sex is a rather embarrassing necessity, preferably indulged in in silence. For Joni and Aaron sex has in fact been split in two, there is the role that it plays in a relationship, but besides that it is simply merchandise. Joni is not a sad prostitute-by-necessity, but a smart young woman. All she does is to play the cards dealt her by nature to the greatest possible advantage. Aaron is halfway between Joni and Sigerius. He has no problem with photographing his girlfriend for a porn site, but blows his top in a big way when he suspects she is about to ditch him as her lover. That dichotomy proves fatal. However, in the figure of Siem Sigerius, Buwalda broaches a second theme. Siem Sigerius has broken free of his working-class roots, has climbed the social ladder, and loses his self-control when his origins rear their heads. Here Buwalda touches on a very sensitive issue. In the 1990s the Netherlands saw itself as a model state, a finished project whose main features were open-mindedness and professional political administration. But in the twenty-first century the breakthrough of populist politics obliged the nation to take a painful look in the mirror. The Netherlands consisted not only of a head, but also of an underbelly, which was constantly making itself felt. Sigerius' struggle is the conflict that seized hold of the Netherlands in this new century: the head that realises with dismay the existence of the rest of the body.

The nice thing about *Bonita Avenue*, nevertheless, is that Buwalda never forces his theme too crudely down the reader's throat. The picture (political, social, erotic) that he paints of the period is not a vehicle for an unambiguous message. Ambitious novels sometimes have the pernicious tendency to reduce everything that takes place within their covers to a single moral, a single line of thought. In *Bonita Avenue* readers are allowed to interpret and, if they wish, judge for themselves.

The following excerpt from Bulwada's novel immediately precedes the moment when Sigerius makes the fateful discovery about his daughter. During a ceremony at the university his two lives collide: his ex-brother-in-law seizes this perfect moment to tell him that his son Wilbert has been released early from prison. The suppressed aggression implicit in this passage foreshadows the blood-curdling hand-to-hand fight between father and son later in the novel.

America is mentioned in this excerpt. Sigerius and his family lived there for several years, while he was writing his doctoral thesis. Their house, on *Bonita Avenue*, gradually becomes a symbol of a moment when their lives were perfect. A moment in the past, of course. ■

Translated by Paul Vincent

An Extract from *Bonita Avenue*
By Peter Buwalda

Once Tineke had dropped him off at Enschede station, as soon as the strain of the college's anniversary week slid off him, he started fretting about what he had seen. All the way to Schiphol Airport he'd asked himself questions, absurd questions (were they the same size? were they the same age? the same build?), after which he reprimanded himself (it just can't be, it's too much of a coincidence, this is what psychiatrists mean by paranoia), checked in relatively calmly, and without slipping into outrageous fantasies browsed through the bestsellers in the bookshop display, only to catch himself posing even more absurd questions while boarding (is she capable of this? is this *in* her? in her genes?) — a steady tidal motion, panic and calm, panic and calm, that had possessed him for the past three days.

Tubantia's fortieth anniversary celebration had gone as these kind of public events usually did: it washed over him, it was as though he had dreamt the past few days; and just like in a dream, there was no opportunity to look either forward or back. Pampering four honorary doctorates and their spouses; rewriting, rehearsing and reciting his keynote speech on nanotechnology, hardly the meatiest of subjects; breakfasts, lunches and dinners with his guests, the endless chitchat, that tedious blather, good god, he might just drop dead in the middle of his speech.

It was Thursday afternoon, during the closing reception, when things started coming undone. After he'd draped the Tubantia regalia onto his four honourees at the Jacobuskerk, the whole circus moved to the Enschede Theatre. He, Tineke and the four honorary doctorates and their spouses mounted the raised black-velvet platform in the foyer, ready to be fêted by the hundreds of schmoozing guests who snatched glasses of wine and fancy hors d'oeuvres from silver platters, or took their place straight away in the discouragingly long reception line. He must have stood there for three hours, shaking hands, exchanging witty repartee, the long garland of patience reflected in his patent leather shoes.

About an hour into the handshaking he spotted Wijn. Menno Wijn, his ex-brother-in-law and former sparring partner, towering head and shoulders above the hundreds of students and almost exclusively toga-clad professors, inconspicuous at first, clearly ill at ease, glancing around awkwardly with a mineral water in his fist, almost, it seemed, on the verge of leaving. When he looked again five minutes later, Wijn was standing in the queue like a clay golem. "Psst, look, two o'clock," he whispered to Tineke. Her chubby hands released the arm of a professor's wife and she turned towards him. "To the left," he said. Mildly amused, she scanned the queue and froze. "Well, I'll be goddamned." She lifted her shoulders and shook her freshly coiffed hair that smelled of cigarettes and pine needles.

Wijn had the expression of someone sitting in a dentist's waiting room. Before he had arrived, the foyer was the picture of diversity, so many different faces, so many nationalities, but since noticing his ex-brother-in-law Sigerius realized that every academic looked like every other academic. Back when he and Wijn were in their twenties, he had a rough but rosy face and a ready laugh, preferably and most boisterously at someone else's mistakes, until those mistakes started to close in on him. Those mistake-making others were his sister Margriet and his nephew Wilbert, but most of all him, Siem Sigerius, traitor, the cause of Margriet's undoing. According to Wijn. What on earth was he doing here? He hadn't been invited, he must have read about the reception somewhere. Had he come all the way from Culemborg for this?

While Sigerius planted kisses on powdered cheeks and endured flattering small talk, he could feel the brother of his late ex-wife gaining ground. Vengeance and venom filled the foyer like fumes. It was twenty-five years ago, damn it. In the first few months after the divorce, his old pal just ignored him, but once Margriet and Wilbert had moved into the attic of Wijn's sports school in Culemborg, things turned bitter. Hostile. For years, Margriet let her stable but angry brother do her dirty work for her: sis needed money, sis had to go to the liquor store. And for Wijn – by that time landlord, lawyer and foster parent all rolled into one – what was one more nasty telephone call? Sigerius was already in America with Tineke and the girls when, right around Wilbert's birthday, an envelope arrived with a greeting card – "congratulations on your son's birthday" – accompanied by a typed sheet of expense claims: bills from the glazier, fines, medical expenses, sessions with the juvenile psychologist, you name it, and at the bottom, the bank account number of Menno Wijn Martial Arts Academy. It was the prelude to a few phone calls per year, collect calls of course, fault-finding tirades in which Wijn, in his crude redneck lingo, filled him in on what that "punk" had gotten up to now, which school he been kicked out of and why, about the pulverized liquorice cough drops the "fuckwad" sold as hash, how Menno had to throw out the "scum" that came round to the house for payback, about the brawls at the carnival, the shoplifting – so when you coming back to Holland, Pop? Menno was down on that whole America thing. But when Sigerius himself phoned, Wijn gave him the cold shoulder, let the deserter know in no uncertain terms that he had no business with them, and via lengthy monologues rubbed it in that Wilbert had settled in just fine with his dutiful uncle. "He ain't a bad kid, you know, all of a sudden he got twenty-four canaries up in the attic. Loves 'm, y'know. Gerbils too, hamsters, it's a regler zoo up there."

He always just let it go. Of course he was worried. You're here now, Tineke would say. We are in California. Menno only quit haranguing him after Margriet died. After that there was only the occasional telephone conversation, Menno grousing about his role as Wilbert's guardian, he as the disillusioned father trying to get out of his alimony obligations. Businesslike exchanges, the enmity of the past electrically dormant on the phone line.

Here he comes. His ex-brother-in-law, backlit by the glare cutting in through the tall front windows of the theatre, climbed the broad steps to the podium and stopped in front of him. You'd almost expect to see him holding a UPS clipboard, or wonder whose chauffeur he was, what was this guy doing coming after his boss? Straight as an arrow, arms dangling alongside his bony body, his weight on the balls of his feet, just like he used to take his place on the mat: here I am, just try me. No handshake.

"Menno," said Sigerius.

Wijn pulled in his chin. "Doin' all right for yourself, I see," he said with the exact same tacky accent they spoke back on their old stomping grounds, Wijk C, forty years ago. "I was passing by. I've come to tell you your son's free."

Sigerius cleared his throat. *"What?"*

"Reduced sentence. On accounta good behaviour. He's already out."

At times, language could have a physical effect on him, like ice cold water being dumped on his head from several metres above. "Oh no," he muttered. "Now that is news. Bad news."

Wijn picked at a penny-sized scab on his cheek, no doubt the remnants of a blister he'd got himself scraping across a judo mat, a self-conscious gesture that made him look, for a brief moment, like his dead sister. His middle finger was missing its nail. A blind finger.

"Just thought I'd let you know. And tell you that I wash my hands of 'm."

"He was supposed to be locked up until 2002." Tineke said that. She stood glowering at Wijn with eyes like barrels of a pistol, but he ignored her, just like he'd been ignoring her for the past twenty-five years.

"Where's he going to live?" Sigerius asked.

"Dunno. Don't give a shit."

Then they stood there looking at each other in silence, the rector and the gym coach. Two middle-aged men who used to stand in the shower room to-gether, three times a week, year after year, after having mixed their sweat on dojos all over the west coast of Holland. It hadn't been of any use. Suddenly, without provocation, Wijn raised his hand and jabbed Sigerius on the forehead with that nasty mole-finger of his.

"Dog," he snarled.

Before Sigerius could realize he *mustn't* respond, before he realized he was *not* in the position to hoist the man up high and crosswise by his polyester col-lar, hurl him back down and, growling, yank him back up again – strangle him on the spot, as big and nasty as he was – Wijn walked off. Without looking fur-ther at anyone, he shambled in his cheap, ill-fitting suit past the row of laure-ates and stepped off the podium with a hollow thud. ■

From *Bonita Avenue* (Amsterdam: De Bezige Bij, 2010)

Translated by Jonathan Reeder

From Bruges to Amsterdam

The Roots of Stock Exchange Trading in the Low Countries

[LODEWIJK PETRAM]

Since the onset of the present financial crisis, the financial markets have dominated the news, especially since the focus of the crisis has shifted to the sovereign debt of a number of countries in the euro area. Every statement by European politicians or central bankers brings an immediate response from the news media wondering how 'the financial markets' will react. Did yields on Spanish government bonds fall during a speech by European Central Bank president Mario Draghi? If so, his words evidently conveyed hope. Did the euro weaken following the announcement of figures on consumer confidence in the eurozone? That will be a sure sign that confidence has fallen.

A lazy journalist could get away with simply glancing at the share price ticker for an interpretation of the news. And that interpretation would probably not be too far from the truth, because prices are determined by the innumerable transactions of dealers from all over the world, and the way in which all those dealers interpret the news is priced in to those transactions. The most important prices and exchange rates are updated every second of the day – there is always an exchange open somewhere in the world where dollars are being traded for euros. Yet a certain amount of distrust is called for in using price data. Market dealers famously do not always act rationally, and we also know that many transactions are executed by pre-programmed computers – systems which, however clever they may be, cannot be trusted when it comes to interpreting the news.

Price data were already being used as a means of interpreting the news before the arrival of the Internet, when it was not yet possible for enormous quantities of data to be uploaded onto a computer screen within a fraction of a second. In fact, it was already happening more than three centuries ago. In the summer of 1688, Daniel Petit, the English Consul in the Dutch Republic, regularly reported in his correspondence with London the price at which shares in the Dutch East India Company (VOC) were currently being traded. Petit saw a very large fleet being assembled in the Dutch Republic during that summer, but had no idea what its purpose was. Official reports from the Admiralties in the Dutch Republic asserted that the ships were intended to fight piracy in the Mediterranean region, but Petit doubted the truth of these statements: was the fleet not rather large for a pirate mission? To be on the safe side, he kept a close

eye on the price of Dutch East India Company shares. If the fleet really was to be deployed against pirates, the share price would hardly respond; however, if the fleet was being readied for war with England – a not implausible notion, given the three recent Anglo-Dutch wars (1652-1654, 1665-1667 and 1672-1674) – the share price would plummet: war with England represented a huge risk for the East India Company, with its richly laden ships making attractive spoils of war.

Antonius Sanderus, *Flandria illustrata*, Coloniae [Amsterdam], 1641-1644. The Stock Exchange square in Bruges

When the share price suddenly took an enormous dive at the end of August 1688, Petit immediately drew his conclusions and warned his homeland. It was not the fault of Petit that England was unable to prevent the Dutch Stadholder William III from landing at Brixham in Devon, on England's southwest coast, in early November 1688, from where he made haste to London and ascended the throne on 13 February 1689. What Petit was unable to pick up through diplomatic channels, he learned at the stock exchange.

Petit was fortunate that he was based in Amsterdam. In any other city in the late seventeenth century, he would have had to make more effort to determine the reasons for equipping a battle fleet. The Amsterdam exchange was the only one in this period to resemble a modern stock exchange. Traders from all over Europe carried out innumerable transactions there daily. The large exchange building, designed by Hendrick de Keyser, with its rectangular inner courtyard and roofed gallery, was a centre both for trade in commodities and financial transactions. On every day of the week except Sunday, traders could go to the exchange to obtain the latest exchange rates for foreign currencies, the price of East India Company shares, the level of maritime insurance premiums and the price of all manner of commodities. They could also go to the exchange to perform more complex derivatives transactions. If a dealer wished to be sure of securing a consignment of grain from next year's harvest at a fixed price, for example – no problem. Or if he wished to buy an option as a hedge against a fall in the East India Company share price, that too was easily arranged in Amsterdam.

225

Daily trading on the exchange was not an Amsterdam invention. That honour goes to another city in the Low Countries: Bruges. From the middle of the four-teenth century, trading in the city took on characteristics which were akin to modern stock exchanges. In and around the inn owned by the Van der Beurse family, situated in what is today Vlamingstraat, traders of many different na-tionalities came together to perform transactions. Initially the foreign traders left Bruges in the winter, the low season for mediaeval trade, but it was not long before a group of traders settled permanently in the city.

Trading at the Bruges inn, the name of which still lives on in several lan-guages as the name for the stock exchange (Dutch – *beurs*, German – *Börse*, French – *bourse*), was a marked contrast to the way in which international trade had been organised up to that point. Until the fourteenth century, long-distance trade in Europe took place mainly overland. Merchants from northern and southern Europe came together at annual fairs, the biggest and best known

The Stock Exchange
in Antwerp

of which were in the Champagne region of northern France. The concentration in one place of merchants from every corner of Europe made these fairs highly suited to international trade. However, during the fourteenth century the political situation in Europe became unstable – among other things, this was the era of the Hundred Years War (1337-1453). Land-based trade became risky and therefore expensive. Merchants increasingly preferred transport by sea.

In this situation, Bruges was in the ideal position to grow into Europe's principal trading centre: it was close to the sea, had long played a pivotal role in the northern European Hanseatic trading network and had a hinterland in Flanders and Brabant where cloth was produced for export, making it an attractive place for Castilian wool traders to set up business. It was not long before Italian merchants also began to see that Bruges was the ideal city from which to export luxury goods from southern Europe and to import cloth from northern Europe. The level of commercial activity in Bruges grew at lightning pace, and was of course not limited to the trade in goods. Italian bankers followed in the wake of the merchants and introduced their financial techniques to the north. Bruges grew into a centre of the trade in bills of exchange, the primary means of payment for international transactions. And in contrast to the annual fairs, trade in Bruges took place every day, summer and winter.

Antwerp as a world city

Bruges remained the principal trading centre in Europe for around 150 years, but in the sixteenth century lost its primacy to Antwerp. Bruges had lost its appeal, partly because of the silting up of the harbour and the waning importance of the Hanseatic League. At the same time, Antwerp succeeded in attracting merchants by imposing less stringent regulations. Antwerp grew into an even bigger trading centre than Bruges had been – so big, in fact, that the city administration decided to build an exchange, just behind one of the most important streets in the city, the Meir. Where merchants in Bruges had been forced to do their deals in a family inn and in the square that fronted it, and in Antwerp had initially traded in a row of adjacent houses, for the first time they now had their own building, specially designed for commercial trade.

Midway through the sixteenth century, Antwerp was a world city by early modern standards, but later things went decidedly downhill, and to make matters worse the city became a political football of the opposing sides in the Dutch Revolt. In the 1570s, Antwerp had taken the side of the rebels, who were demanding that the Spanish King Philip II allow them a degree of freedom of conscience and some influence over the administration of the Low Countries. However, the King was naturally not about to allow Antwerp, the largest city in the Low Countries, to slip through his fingers without a murmur, and in 1584 he laid siege to the city. The siege lasted almost fourteen months before, on 17 August 1585, the city surrendered to Alexander Farnese, later Duke of Parma. The long siege was disastrous for Antwerp trade, but it was the rebels who really sounded the death knell. They controlled the area around the mouth of the Scheldt, the river linking Antwerp to the sea, and closed it off to all shipping to Antwerp. It would be well into the nineteenth century before the Scheldt opened again, but by then, of course, international trade had long since moved on to a new location.

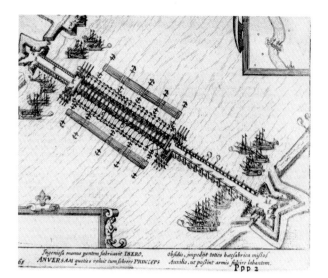

Parma's bridge over the Scheldt in 1584, built of ships. The bridge closed the access to Antwerp and was the beginning of the end for the city

Ingeniosa manus pontem fabricauit IBERO.
ANVERSAM quoties voluit cum soluere PRINCEPS
Obsidio, impedijt totres bærsfabrica missos
Auxilio, ut possint armis figere labantem.
65
Ppp 2

Share dealing in Amsterdam

That location was Amsterdam, a city which in the sixteenth century derived its success principally from trade with the Baltic region, and which during the Dutch Revolt had responded best to shifts in the trade flows in northwestern Europe. Within a short space of time, Amsterdam grew into a hub of trade routes, just as Bruges and Antwerp had done before it, and found it had struck gold. Henceforth, ships no longer sailed to the Baltic laden with worthless ballast in order to return with their holds full of grain and timber, but instead carrying luxury goods imported from southern Europe on the outward voyage. International merchants flocked to the city and the city walls reverberated from the number of commercial transactions. The city administration, though, apparently needed a little time to realise fully what was going on in its city. It was not until 1607 that the city fathers gave instructions for the building of an exchange, at a time when London and Rotterdam – cities which, not entirely without justification, saw an important role in international trade for themselves – had long had such a building. The design of all these exchange buildings was greatly inspired by their Antwerp predecessor: with their open inner courtyards and roofed galleries, they all resembled a walled market square.

Until 1611, when Hendrick de Keyser's *beurs* was taken into use, trade in Amsterdam was an open-air affair. Initially it took place in Warmoesstraat, the most important street linking the port and the Dam, Amsterdam's central square. On busy days, this narrow street was sometimes so full of traders that it was impossible to walk through it. For this reason, in 1561 the city administration designated the Nieuwe Brug – the most northerly bridge over Damrak, situated right on the IJ, the sea inlet which formed Amsterdam's natural harbour – as the new location for trade. In good weather this was an excellent spot, but when the weather was bad, with a raw wind blowing across the IJ making it feel bone-chillingly cold, the merchants were completely unprotected. On such days, they returned to the Warmoesstraat, where they found shelter under the awnings of the shops. So, when it was raining or cold they still blocked all commercial activity in this little street. To resolve this problem, in 1586 the merchant community was given permission to use Sint Olofskapel (St. Olof's Chapel), a stone's throw from the Nieuwe Brug. The Chapel had stood empty since 1578, the year in which Amsterdam sided with the rebels and embraced Protestantism, and was owned by the city. Now it became Amsterdam's first exchange building.

Today the average tourist in Amsterdam walks past the Nieuwe Brug and Sint Olofskapel without a second glance. That is a pity, because history was written here. These are the places where for the first time in world history, trading in an exchange was extended to include the trade in shares. These were the same shares which in 1688 warned Daniel Petit of the preparations for war with England: shares in the Dutch East India Company (VOC). Like Amsterdam's success in international trade, the VOC was a child of the Dutch Revolt. As a result of the war with Spain, the rebellious regions, later united to form the

Jacob van der Ulft, The Dam, Amsterdam, 1659. Gouache on paper. Musée Condé, Chantilly

Dutch Republic, dared to break the Treaty of Tordesillas. Under this Treaty, signed in 1494 and sealed by Pope Alexander VI, Spain and Portugal divided the known world between themselves. Spain received America, apart from part of present-day Brazil, while Asia and Africa were for Portugal. Other countries had not signed this Treaty, but the papal seal of approval meant that it could

not simply be ignored without compunction. And since Spain and Portugal were the two most powerful nations on earth at that time, no one considered infringing the Treaty and risking war as a result. But once the rebellious regions of the Low Countries had become embroiled in war with Spain for other reasons in the sixteenth century, they had nothing more to lose. They scented their opportunity for a share in the lucrative long-distance trade.

As luck would have it, from 1580 Portugal fell under the power of the Spanish crown. As a result, the rebelling regions of the Low Countries, and later the Dutch Republic, were effectively catapulted into war against Portugal. This offered opportunities to send expeditions to the crown jewel of the Iberian colonies, the East Indies, and specifically the Moluccas, where under the Treaty of Tordesillas only Portugal was permitted to trade.

The VOC and the birth of share dealing

The first Dutch ships set sail for the East Indies in 1595. The vessels were owned by the Compagnie van Verre (lit.: long-distance company), a privately owned company which had raised the capital needed to build the fleet by recruiting investors. This expedition was not especially successful, but it did demonstrate that it was possible to trade with the Indies without being overcome by the Portuguese. The initiative accordingly mushroomed and in the years that followed dozens of ships, owned by a variety of companies, set sail from the Dutch Republic to the East Indies.

All these companies were in fierce competition with each other. The States-General, the supreme authority of the Dutch Republic, was not happy with this situation, feeling it would be better for the country's economy if they were to compete with Portugal instead of with each other. Moreover, a strong, united company could also come in very useful in the war.

That united company, the VOC, was formed in 1602. It acquired a monopoly on trade from the Dutch Republic with the East Indies. In exchange, the VOC was

Philipp von Zesen, Picture
of the city of Amsterdam.
New bridge

expected to represent the interests of the Republic in the East Indies. In practice, this meant that the VOC had to take on the war against the Portuguese in Asia.

The VOC also raised its initial capital from private investors. Unlike its predecessors, however, the East India Company organised a public subscription. 'All residents of these Countries', declares the 10th article of the deed of incorporation, 'may participate in this Company.'

The offering was a great success. In Amsterdam 1,143 persons subscribed for more than 3.5 million Dutch guilders. Naturally, they hoped that they would earn a return on their investment, but for many this was not the only reason for subscribing to the Company's initial capital. The VOC was not simply a company which would send ships to the East Indies to bring back spices. The VOC was more than that: it was a prestige project for the Republic. The idea that the young Republic could be supported by investing in the VOC also played a role - it was still only 21 years since the States-General had renounced Philip II as their King, and in 1602 the Republic was not even recognised internationally as a sovereign state.

In addition to the public subscription, there was another way in which the VOC set itself apart from its predecessors. The Company not only had to steal away as many spices as possible from under the noses of the Portuguese, but also had to ensure that the Dutch presence in the Indies would be a lasting one. The VOC built forts at strategic locations and actively engaged in the battle with the Portuguese. In view of this, the VOC was incorporated for a period of 21 years – a very long time compared with the average of three to four years for which its forerunners had been in business. The authorities realised that investors might hesitate to tie up their money for so long, and the first page of the subscription register accordingly included an additional provision: 'Reassignments or transfers [of shares] may be effected by the bookkeeper of this Chamber.' In other words, subscribed capital could be transferred to someone else! For investors, this provision meant that they did not need to wait until the VOC was wound up before being able to recover the capital they had contributed. They could simply sell on their share before that time. This would go down in the annals of world history as the start of share dealing.

Emanuel de Witte, *Interior of the Stock Exchange in Amsterdam,* 1653. Oil on panel, 49 cm x 47,5 cm. Museum Boijmans van Beuningen, Rotterdam

The first transactions date from the moment when, a few months after the subscription register had been closed, the VOC asked its investors to pay the first instalment of the capital to which they had subscribed. One investor, Jan Allertsz., realised that he did not have enough money to pay this first instalment. He sold his share and so became the person who performed the first ever share transaction. After Allertsz. came more – many more – transactions. And because most of the shareholders were merchants, the share dealing took place in the same locations where the merchants had become accustomed to performing their goods transactions and settling their bills of exchange: Nieuwe Brug (New bridge) and Sint Olofskapel.

The red tape that accompanied share transactions – shares had to be officially transferred from the seller's account to the buyer's account in the VOC books, something for which transaction fees also had to be paid – quickly took traders in search of simpler ways of dealing in shares. In 1607, just five years after the founding of the Company, forward contracts ('futures') for the delivery of shares were already being concluded. This was the beginning of derivatives trading – trading in contracts which were associated with shares and the stock market, but in which no shares were traded directly. This trade took off rapidly. As early as 1608, a group of merchants sold large numbers of forward contracts for the delivery of VOC shares which they did not even possess. Their intention was to engineer a fall in the share price and to generate profit from this. Today, they would be called naked short sellers. A few years later, share dealers began trading 'repos': they pledged shares to lenders as collateral for loans which were used to buy those same shares. Investing in this way – using borrowed money – meant that even people with little capital could acquire large positions in VOC shares. Finally, from the middle of the seventeenth century onwards, a lively trade in options got under way. Around this time, the community of share dealers had become quite large and diverse, with speculators on the one hand and on the other investors hoping for a positive return in the longer term. This meant that there was a ready market for the transfer of risks, something for which the option is a very suitable instrument. Long-term investors were only too keen to transfer their risks in respect of short-term price fluctuations to speculators, who conversely were willing to take on those risks.

Three centuries after the start of daily exchange trading in Bruges, the Amsterdam exchange had taken on much of the élan of Wall Street today. The trade in futures, options and repos was the bread and butter of Amsterdam traders. One only had to step inside the exchange, or to accost a broker, to learn the latest exchange rate in any number of foreign cities. And there was another similarity with today's world, in that the exchange regularly played host to a crisis. Where wars were the agents of those crises in the seventeenth century, in the eighteenth century the crises were taking place in the exchange itself. So the Low Countries were present at the birth of all facets of modern stock market trading. ▨

Translated by Julian Ross

Drawing the Line

The Serious Art of Joost Swarte & Ever Meulen

[DEREK BLYTH]

The comic strip started in daily newspapers as a funny story at the back of the paper. But it has evolved in the Netherlands and Belgium into a subtle and subversive art form.

The people who drew the first comic strips worked at large tilted drawing boards in newspaper offices. Some still do. But others have branched out into record album covers, posters, postage stamps and postcards.

Comic strips are taken seriously in the Low Countries, much more seriously than in Britain or the United States. You realise their cultural weight when you visit the Belgian Comic Strip Centre in Brussels, which is housed in a beautiful Art Nouveau building. As soon as you enter the vast entrance hall, once a department store, you realise that this is not a museum for children, but a temple of fine art where drawings by Jijé or Franquin are treated with the reverence of a Picasso sketch.

The comic strip is deeply embedded in the culture of the Low Countries. Almost every house in the Netherlands or Belgium will have a tall stack of old comic strip albums sitting around. The comic book sector is a major industry in these countries, providing work for dozens of freelance comic strip artists. In Brussels, bookshops are closing because of competition from the internet, but comic bookstores are still flourishing, along with shops selling Tintin merchandise or Smurf figures.

It doesn't take long in this region to realise that Hergé is the most important comic strip artist the Low Countries has produced, on a level with some of the region's great artists. In 1929, when he launched the first Tintin book, Hergé was just another illustrator working in a newspaper. In 2012, when the Paris auction house Artcurial sold the original hand-drawn cover of '*Tintin en Amérique*', it fetched the record sum of €1.3 million.

Hergé began his career as a comic artist drawing in the rough, sketchy style of American newspaper comics, but he gradually developed a clean, precise style that became known as ligne claire, or clear line. This allowed him to create vivid images on the page in which every element is sharply defined by clean black lines and strong colours.

© Ever Meulen

Hergé's style has had an enormous influence on illustrators working in the Low Countries. The first generation mainly worked alongside Hergé in his Brussels studio, but a second wave emerged in the 1960s and 1970s. These artists, led by Ever Meulen in Flanders and Joost Swarte in the Netherlands, took ligne claire in an entirely new direction.

Happy Ever After

'I love beautiful things; cars, houses, women,..' Ever Meulen declared in a recent interview. His offbeat enthusiasm for automobiles and modern architecture may seem a little dated, his fondness for leggy blonde women even mildly incorrect, but this modest Flemish illustrator is much loved for the way he brings lightness and humour to modern times.

He was born Eddy Vermeulen in Kuurne, a village in West Flanders, in 1946. The war in Europe had recently ended and there was an infectious mood of optimism in the air. The postwar sense of innocent optimism reached its purest expression at Expo 58, when 50 million people flocked to northern Brussels to see the latest ideas in architecture, transport, furniture, food and music.

The mood of the age was captured by the Atomium, that strange building in the form of a molecule of iron. With its nine spheres of gleaming steel, it looked rather like a space craft that had landed from another planet. Everything at

Expo 58 was fun and futuristic, from the cheerful cable cars that floated above the site, to the fragile architecture of steel and glass.

Vermeulen was just 12 at the time, but he was profoundly influenced by the spirit of '58. After studying graphic design at the Sint-Lucas Institute in Ghent, he moved to Brussels in the late 1960s and slowly picked up design commissions for record sleeves and posters.

His career began to take off in 1970 when his graphic art began to appear on the covers of the Flemish TV listings magazine *Humo*. At the time, this was one of the most popular magazines in Flanders, admired as much for its radical journalism as its TV coverage. By getting onto the cover, Ever Meulen's joyful images could be admired on coffee tables throughout Flanders.

Eventually, Vermeulen's drawings began to appear on the cover of *De Standaard's* weekly magazine, taking his art to a new audience. He also designed posters for the Beursschouwburg theatre in Brussels and the Brussels metro system, as well as creating artwork for records by the Belgian group Telex.

Covers for *The New Yorker*
Left © Ever Meulen
Right. © Joost Swarte

Ever Meulen's style owed a great deal to Hergé's clear line, but he also found inspiration in the whimsical cartoons of Saul Steinberg. Like the American cartoonist (whose mural *The Americans* appeared at Expo 58), Meulen liked to show people in modern environments where they were not entirely comfortable. But the Belgian was more than just a funny cartoonist. As Paul Gravett argues in his essay *In Search of the Atom Style*, he also found inspiration in contemporary artists such as Giorgio de Chirico, Magritte and Picasso.

Ever Meulen's illustrations continue to capture the sheer optimism of the postwar world, his precise drawings representing a seductive 20th century utopia of shiny cars, glamorous women and neat apartment buildings.

He illustrated this modern world with an enormous sense of affection along with a certain cool humour. His art might in fact be defined as a comic response to Belgian Modernism. Look, he seems to say, the modern movement is smart and cool, but the people are vague and awkward.

His style found an enthusiastic audience in the United States after the illustrator Art Spiegelman invited him to contribute to his alternative comic magazine *RAW*. 'I wish I could live in Ever Meulen's garden,' Spiegelman wrote in the foreword to *Verve*, a compilation of Ever Meulen illustrations. 'Witty, cool and somehow sensual, these images offer a place that overflows with whimsyness, harmony and intelligence.'

Meulen was later commissioned to design *New Yorker* covers by Spiegelman's wife, Françoise Mouly, art director at the magazine. 'His lines quietly call attention to themselves,' Mouly observed.

Now regarded as Belgium's greatest living illustrator, Meulen has exhibited in New York, Amsterdam, London, Helsinki, Angoulême, Tokio and Geneva.

© Ever Meulen

Yet he lives a rather quiet life in a Brussels suburban house with his wife and four cats. Here he works in a bright studio filled with drawings, framed posters, books and drawing instruments. He also has several antique cabinets filled with shiny model cars. In an interview, he confessed to a fondness for the fast streamlined cars of the Fifties, like the Citröen DS, the Lancia Aurelia B20 and the Oldsmobile Rocket V-8. But his favourite, he said, was the 1950 Studebaker.

In the 1980s, the owner of the Brussels art shop Plaizier spotted Ever Meulen's work and brought out a series of postcards. In 2012 he created a series of stamps for the Belgian post office. Illustrating the theme 'visit Belgium', the stamps are gently mocking of famous Belgian motifs, like Magritte's pipe and

Groucho © Joost Swarte

rainy skies. The Atomium is placed in the middle, with the spheres redesigned with comic symbols like Tintin's quiff.

It might seem as if Ever Meulen's time is over. We are no longer obsessed with sleek jet planes or modernist skyscrapers. The world has grown old. But Ever Meulen remains the eternal optimist, the child who never grew up, still in love with fast cars and unattainable women.

The art of Swarte

'I try to combine the freedom of the underground movement with the craftsmanship of the old masters,' claimed Joost Swarte in his book *Bijna compleet*. His graphic finesse has earned him many admirers and countless awards, including most recently the Marten Toonder Prize, awarded to a comic artist who has made an exceptional contribution to graphic storytelling.

'There is no one in the Netherlands who hasn't seen a drawing by Joost Swarte,' the jury said. 'He has designed postage stamps, posters, watches, houses, stained glass windows and phone cards. He combines a very creative approach to content with a strongly traditional graphic style.'

Born in Heemstede in 1947, Swarte is just one year older than Ever Meulen. They both share a passion for streamlined cars, cool modern buildings and the lifestyle of the 1950s. They might almost be brothers.

After studying industrial design in Eindhoven, Swarte took up comic illustrations in the late 1960s. He launched his own comic magazine *Modern Papier* in 1971 and built up a young fan base with his stories involving Jopo de Pojo, a hopeless musician with an enormous quiff that looked like Tintin in a rock'n'roll phase.

During the big Hergé exhibition *Kuifje* in Rotterdam in 1976, Swarte coined the term *ligne claire* to describe Hergé's distinctive style. His own style drew inspiration from Hergé's technique, although Swarte eventually went in new directions that no other comic illustrator had ever attempted.

The Dutch comic artist first gained an international following in the 1980s when he exhibited at the Angoulême international comic show. His reputation grew further in 1984 when the French publisher Futuropolis brought out the first survey of his work. One year later, Swarte set up the publishing house Oog & Blik and began to publish his own books. In 1992, he founded the annual comic strip convention Stripdagen in his home town of Haarlem to promote comic art in the Netherlands.

Like many comic illustrators, he has provided covers for magazines like the Dutch *Vrij Nederland* and the Flemish *Humo*. He has also turned his hand (like Ever Meulen) to record covers, posters, cards and even postage stamps.

In the 1990s, Swarte developed a new audience in the United States after his cartoons began appearing in the alternative comic magazine *RAW*. Like Ever Meulen, he raised his Transatlantic profile further by providing cartoons and cover illustrations for *The New Yorker*.

Like Ever Meulen's, the world according to Swarte is a cool modern environment where the individual seems to have lost his way. Swarte once said that his favourite film was *Playtime*, the 1967 Jacques Tati classic in which Tati plays a helpless individual in a modern world that he is powerless to control.

At a certain moment, Swarte's career path began to veer off in a different direction from Ever Meulen (or any other comic artist, for that matter). In 1991, Swarte turned his hand to music in an unusual collaboration with the Dutch experimental singer Fay Lovsky. For her album *Jopo in Mono*, Lovsky composed a series of songs inspired by Swarte's Jopo de Pojo. Swarte designed the CD cover and inside illustrations, but he also helped to compose the track 'Appellation contrôlée' as well as providing the vocals for two other tracks.

Ever Meulen was obsessed with the mechanical world, but Swarte had a softer side. In many of his drawings, he betrayed a fondness for books and bookish people. In 2009, he created a striking cover for the summer issue of the Canadian magazine *The Walrus* in which a single car stands out in a traffic jam. The other cars are rendered in dark grey wash, but one car is bright yellow. The reason? Books, of course. They are strapped to the roof in a tall pile, and lined up on a bookshelf attached to a trailer.

© Ever Meulen

Swarte returned to his love of books in a series of drawings for a publisher's calendar on the theme 'Reading can damage your health'. One drawing illustrated the health warning by showing a car driver so engrossed in a book that he doesn't notice a train approaching down the line.

The bookish people in Swarte's drawings are often solitary souls in a forbidding grey environment. For a 2007 *New Yorker* cover, he drew an isolated woman sitting in a Manhattan street with a book on her lap. It is a gloomy city, but the woman is illuminated by a single shaft of brilliant sunlight that passes between the skyscrapers.

Swarte is constantly experimenting with new ideas and overturning conventions. In the full-page comic strip *Incredible Upside Down!* he created a conventional strip which ended in the last frame with the instruction to turn it upside down. The reader is then immersed in an entirely different story that explains certain details that seemed puzzling on the first reading.

In 2012, Joost Swarte published a book titled *Is that all there is?* This brought together in 120 pages all his comic art from 1972 onwards. But the title was misleading. It was far from everything.

Is that all there is?

In Swarte's work, a fondness for modern architecture and transport permeates every frame. He lovingly recreates the progressive modernism that emerged in European avant-garde circles in the 1930s and returned on a mass scale in the postwar boom of the 1960s.

In 1996, Swarte made the leap from the page to reality when he was commissioned to draw a design for the Toneelschuur theatre building in Haarlem. In a single sketch, he created a complex building with bold colour accents and modernist details like ladder windows and thin concrete struts. The Delft architects Mecanoo carefully followed the drawing to create the final building, which in photographs looks very like a comic book illustration.

Such was its success that other architecture commissions came his way. In 2001, Swarte was asked to take charge of the interior design of the new Tintin Museum in Louvain-la-Neuve. For the next eight years, he planned out the different rooms where Hergé's comic art would be displayed.

In 2010, Swarte added to his architecture portfolio by designing a low-cost housing project on Willemstraat in Amsterdam's Jordaan district. Here he created a witty modernist building with a bright yellow stairwell and bathrooms fitted with an odd jumble of exposed pipes.

Is that finally everything? Not quite. In 2010, Swarte was commissioned by the French publisher Glénat to design a series of stained glass windows for the old Sainte Cécile chapel in the heart of Grenoble, which was to serve as a library for the publisher. Here the bookish Swarte was in his element. He designed eight allegorical scenes representing 'the life of the book,' the first showing a book lying in a cot while the parents, both with books for heads, admire their offspring.

There is still more. Swarte has also designed furniture for children, including a brightly-coloured stool with two seats. Turn it one way, and it is the right size for a small child. Turn it the other way, and it is perfect for an older child.

But possibly his most pleasingly absurd design is a table with four enormous carrots as legs. Like Ever Meulen, Swarte is slowly transforming the world, one frame at a time. ■

Reading may reduce
the blood flow and
cause impotence

© Joost Swarte

The Mirror © Joost Swarte

Writer in the Public Debate

On Stefan Hertmans

[ANNE MARIE MUSSCHOOT]

Since he was first profiled in this yearbook (*The Low Countries* 1998-1999), the Flemish-Belgian writer Stefan Hertmans (born 1951) has developed significantly as an artist. Hertmans started out as a poet but came to the attention of the general public primarily as a novelist, with books such as *Terug naar Merelbeke* (Back to Merelbeke, 1994) and *Als op de eerste dag* (Like the first day, 2001). He went on to add theatre texts to his multi-award winning oeuvre, and the poet and prose writer is now mainly active as a prominent essayist, well-known in the public sphere for his opinion pieces. His work as a whole is characterised by an unusual degree of erudition and by a rapid evolution in which he, as a critical intellectual, constantly questions and comments on himself and the culture in which he lives. He perpetually pushes back boundaries, and, like all strong personalities, resists all forms of limiting labels.

Yet it is possible to see a development in this many-sided and multiform oeuvre. In the first books of poetry and the early prose, Hertmans used a hermetic form indicative of the need of 'high modernism' to construct a purely linguistic, 'depersonalised', objectified or autonomous world. However, gradually the poet and prose writer moved towards a more open, melodic, flowing and communicative verse and a more recognisable, communicative narrative method. Nevertheless, the world that he evokes continues to explore the boundaries between fantasy and reality, and his linear narrative method is increasingly splintered into fragmentary, often diary-like mosaic structures.

As in the work of Wallace Stevens, considered an important benchmark by Hertmans, one can see also in Hertmans' work a transition from modernism to postmodernism, and a reflection of the climate of the time in which he lives. Most recently he has adopted the critical stand that results inevitably from the non-committal scepticism of postmodernism. The absolute relativism of this movement marginalised late capitalist culture and led to the loss of the public function of literature. The complaint that 'literature no longer matters' was (and still is) widely heard. Not surprisingly, many writers have gained a fresh awareness of their role in social debate - including Hertmans. He remains of course a writer of poetry, novels and theatre texts first and foremost, but he is now also a writer who fulfils his role as a public intellectual with conviction.

The past occupies a significant place in the poet's consciousness. Not just the cultural past, with the heritage of all the art forms with which lyrical subject he, as a teacher of philosophy of art, is very familiar, but also the personal past, with the poet's own memories. *Goya als hond* (Goya as a dog, 1999), in which the long, eponymous title poem pays homage to the Spanish painter, is the first collection in which Hertmans gives equal prominence to autobiographical elements. The lover is present, as is the young son who places a 'finger in the palm of his hand' that 'fits perfectly'. As in the earlier poetry, the poet enters into a dialogue with several artists who have gone before him; there are just as many confrontations with and projections of himself, always with a strong philosophical bias. In the title poem, which is based on the painting commonly known as *The Dog* (1821-23), by which Hertmans was transfixed during a visit to the Prado in Madrid, he sees how the painter processes his memories, and this 'releases the things that he himself remembers'. It is also a poem about the passing of time, about his own dog in former landscapes, which in particular evokes an awareness of the threat of 'the end times', of hellhounds swimming against the current, and of drowning in the present. In the present, that which has foundered and sunk comes back, and time 'is against him'; the dog continues to drown.

Hertmans' maturity as a poet was confirmed with a substantial collection that – rather confusingly – was given the same title as an earlier collection: *Muziek voor de overtocht. Gedichten 1975-2005* (Music for the crossing. Poems 1975-200, 2006), a title that incidentally demonstrates the same fascination with the end, the crossing. This collection also includes a few stray poems not published previously, but fortunately does not mark the end of Hertmans' work as a poet. In 2010, another new volume appeared, *De val van vrije dagen* (The fall of free days), which again deals with the themes of the present melting into the past, cultural tradition, and reflection on what has come to an end but which is at the same time also a portent of what is to come. Time passes and is always an uncertain 'interim'.

Vital melancholy

In his prose of recent decades, it is noticeable that the fantastic, sometimes burlesque and grotesquely magnifying element has been suppressed. However, although Hertmans' prose seems to have become more realistic, the narrative is still far from traditional. In *Het verborgen weefsel* (Hidden fibre, 2008), for example, the narrator crawls as it were into the consciousness of an outwardly very tough, but inwardly very vulnerable woman, and experiments further with ways of expressing the inexpressible. There is a lot of Hertmans himself in this highly empathetic portrait of an extremely sensitive woman. The name of the main character is Jelina, with a nod to the Austrian writer Elfriede Jelinek, a passionate feminist. But Antigone was also a source of inspiration, and of course Emma Bovary is not far away. This *journal intime* contains references to the cultural past, and the author also brings in a familiar topic: he condemns the constant failure to write and speak. Things evade the consciousness. The 'hidden fibre' that Hertmans describes in this book resembles another analysis of what he described in an earlier essay as 'vital melancholy': a fundamental discontent that preserves itself through an ever-present will to survive.

This oppressive, strong poetic prose was preceded by the remarkable *Intercities* (Steden, 1998), which has since been translated into several languages and has contributed greatly to the writer's international reputation. The subtitle of the book is 'Stories on the Road' ('Verhalen onderweg'), but it could be equally well described as a book of essays. Hertmans even shifts or modifies the boundaries of the genres within which he chooses to write. This book marked the definitive end of the image of a rather other-worldly writer and intellectual who stood out high above the rest of society. The essays about cities such as Sydney, Tübingen, Trieste, Dresden, Vienna, Bratislava and Marseille, but also Amsterdam and Brussels and his former, 'indescribable' home city of Ghent, are not travelogues but rather commentaries on what the traveller sees and thinks. They mark the first steps towards the new role that the writer has taken upon himself, that of providing an open, critical reflection on reality. The fact that he has gained great erudition over the years, which he also uses in his analyses, does not stand in the way of subjective involvement with what he sees and experiences. For here, too, he is seeking to grasp the (always shifting, impossible) essence of things, the intangible Idea beneath and behind things. In so doing, concrete perceptions repeatedly form a mirror in which the I can discover itself. Even the smallest detail can be of significance in this: 'Voices, things and faces [are] linked to an understanding of life'.

Nomadic involvement

Hertmans' growing involvement in public life is evident from a rich collection of volumes of essays in which the leitmotiv is closely connected to the body of ideas contained in the creative, non-reflective work. 'Creative people sail without a compass', Hertmans let slip in passing, as it were, in an essay entitled 'Een vergeten oratorium van Hindemith en Benn' ('A forgotten oratorium by Hindemith and Benn', in *Fuga's en pimpelmezen* (Fugues and blue tits, 1995). The reason for this remark was the indefiniteness he observed in the course sailed by the artist, or of the erratic significance attached to the artist's experiences. The remark as such can also be applied to Hertmans himself: he too chose not to choose, to sail without a focal point. His thinking always fans out; he offers 'open' criticism which provides a commentary without a fixed point. He is a critic of the centrifugal, meandering movement.

In fact, Hertmans' positioning as an 'open' and 'creative' critic goes back to 1988, when he published his first book of essays about literature in *Oorverdovende steen* (Deafening stone). At the time, he noticed when editing or updating his essays that his previously expressed views could quickly acquire a 'completely different meaning', which served to increase yet further his fascination with the 'paradoxes in everything we know and think about literature'. In later volumes of essays, *Sneeuwdoosjes* (Snow globes, 1989, with essays about literature, music and film) and the above-mentioned Fuga's en pimpelmezen ('about current affairs, art and criticism'), the writer broadened his outlook even further. Not only does he do away with the linearity of time in his reflections, but this leads to an 'inherent infinity of possibilities', a space in which it becomes possible to consider all art from all time periods. The search for the absolute and for truth is experienced as impossible and abandoned in favour of multiple perspectives, relativism and scepticism. But Hertmans has left postmodernism behind: he has rejected nihilism and lack of commitment and replaced them with prompt reactions to political, social and cultural current affairs.

This development also includes resistance to 'closed' theories and dogmas. In a sound, philosophical consideration of Peter Sloterdijk, the author of among other things the bestselling book *Critique of Cynical Reason* (*Kritik der zynischen Vernunft*), Hertmans discusses the new eclecticism in depth (in *Oorverdovende steen*). Recurring subjects and motifs include an interest in Rilke and his attempt to 'say the unsayable', and renewed attention to the translation of poetry, with the associated problem that the essence of poetry is not apprising and therefore also not translatable. There is a preoccupation with the immovability of things (a focus he shares with Walter Benjamin) and with his own past and memory, which of course brings him to the greatly admired Proust: Proust, who composed his sentences in circular motions and in accordance with musical principles.

Hertmans, himself a creditable jazz musician, is one of the few essayists able to write in depth and inspiringly about music, preferably classical music.

In *Fuga's en pimpelmezen*, Hertmans makes a definitive break with focusing solely on the literary. This is a 'creative' intellectual speaking who connects everything to everything else, cuts across all art forms and, freewheeling, with free associations based on his broad cultural baggage, sets about tackling literary and philosophical texts, music, contemporary politics and social issues. The book begins and ends with essays in which the writer positions himself as a 'courageous' intellectual. In a response to the – for him outmoded – nihilism of the twentieth century, the essayist posits that the guarantee of a liveable society lies in learning to live as individuals, i.e. in a non-egocentric way, and in continuing to think along the lines of the current philosophy of doubt. But in the concluding essay, about the French philosopher Bernard Henri Lévy, Hertmans redefines the task of the critical intellectual within 'the philosophy of action'. Not choosing is replaced here by militant reflection and positioning. And that does indeed require courage.

The essay on George Steiner, a philosopher and critic once held in high esteem by Hertmans but against whose *Real Presences* he reacts vigorously, fits into the same framework of thinking. The existence of God (the 'real presence') is impossible according to Hertmans, nor has he, as a reader and critic, any need of an explanatory model. Steiner's condemnation of deconstructionist reading is disregarded as conservative and authoritarian. 'Real' readers are those 'who are not afraid of the thought that the job is never done and never can be done.' What is necessary is 'the courage of the critical intellect' that holds the uncertainty of deconstructionist, never-ending reading in creative esteem 'in a never-ending, nomadic criticism.' Hertmans is in fact himself a nomadic critic: he reveals himself in this book as a critic who sails without a compass, an attitude which he retains in his later essays too, with his finger on the pulse of current affairs, but also with very personal testimonies of his musical experiences. The expression of his personal preference for string quartets (in a piece on Leoš *Janáček's Intimate Letters*) is a dazzling ode to the genre almost certain to move every music-lover.

Against entertainment

The 'nomadic criticism' continues in *Het putje van Milete* (The well of Miletus, 2002), in which Hertmans combines essays on philosophical debates and current affairs with essays on literature. The writer had by this point begun teaching philosophy of art, and this has left its mark. He published a guide to the agogics of art *Waarover men niet spreken kan* (Whereof one cannot speak, 1999) and a comprehensive discussion of the obscene in art, Het bedenkelijke (Dubious matters, also 1999). In *Het putje van Milete*, the 'shuttling between study and world' is visible within a single book. The essayist follows the debates and controversies in and around the thinking of Martin Walser, Martin Heidegger and Peter Handke, Th.W. Adorno, Peter Sloterdijk and Ludwig Wittgenstein, and switches with ease to enthusiastic reflections on political and social current affairs in the Netherlands. It is clear from the title, a reference to the paradigmatic joke about the foolish philosopher Thales of Miletus, who fell into a well while gazing at the stars, that Hertmans' border crossings are figurative as well as literal. According to Hertmans, this incident expresses 'perfectly the greatest risk of lofty thoughts: that you lose sight of concrete situations.'

Hertmans will not fall into a well like Thales of Miletus while he is philosophising about art. His focus on concrete reality is stronger than ever, and he is 'passionately involved' with the world, as one critic put it in a recent portrait. It was only with the publication of *Het putje van Milete* that the true breadth of Hertmans' range emerged. In the space of a single book, he sweeps breathtakingly through the oeuvres of Beckett, Yeats, Borges and a number of important Flemish writers such as Hugo Claus, Maurice Gilliams, Herman de Coninck and Peter Verhelst, and is able in many cases to compare their work with his own work and development. The essay on the dramatic works of Hugo Claus is particularly revealing in this context, leading as it does to a probing consideration of the recent disappearance of writers' theatre and theatre texts recognised as literary. The new relationship between text and director is a development in which Hertmans himself played an important role, with the prominent dramatic text *Kopnaad* (Suture). *Mind The Gap* (2000), in which the audience gets to hear the viewpoint of three women from ancient Greek tragedies, is another impressive example of new theatre practice. In connection with these two texts and the subsequent *Empedokles* (Empedocles), Hertmans also wrote a series of inspired reflections on working with Greek tragedy in our time. They were compiled in *Het zwijgen van de tragedie* (The silence of tragedy, 2007).

Yet Hertmans still continues to surprise. In 2011 he published a new collection of essays, *De mobilisatie van Arcadia* (The mobilisation of Arcadia), with further lucid, sharp and always highly erudite analyses of the spirit of the age and contemporary art in his own country. This time he is fulminating against the lack of 'real' commitment on the part of artists. He unleashes an eloquent tidal wave of outrage over what he calls emotional sensationalism and the runaway hedonistic economy for which the media are responsible. Where the focus has shifted 'from the artist and the work of art to the public', art has become chiefly 'an entertaining, easily consumable art'. However, the *locus amoenus* and 'Arcadian existence' do not belong to our reality, the teacher points out, and art must remain free from general condescension. Once again, Hertmans explores the ambivalence surrounding the status of the artist accused of elitism. Or: how the centuries-old relationship between artist and society can still provoke elevated and profound discussion, perhaps today more than ever. With Hertmans as an inspiring guide. ▪

Translated by Rebekah Wilson

An Extract from *Intercities*
By Stefan Hertmans

Sydney: Parallel Worlds

It is as if for centuries a substance has flowed from the human eye that affects and changes the world, a glue that binds places and things. That substance doesn't really exist, things are not joined together into a meaningful whole by any glue. And yet it is our eyes that bind things together, that give them a place in the whole; a look that hesitates between understanding and incomprehension, as if we intuitively want to assign things a place in an otherwise chaotic world by the simple fact that we see them; though without necessarily having the guarantee that we can actually place them.

However, the human eye certainly does put the whole world into a meaningful context: all urban and rural landscapes have been formed, determined and constructed by concepts from geometry and perspective. Nothing is simply there. What we see is always determined by what others before us have seen in it. We, who stand there and look on, as the popular Dutch song says, link things when we see them; not a single landscape in which man has intervened escapes this linking look, which connects things, glues them back together again and interprets them as a coherent whole - a bridge, a tunnel, a tower, a bend in a road - as if we are forming sentences, 'making syntax' of the discrete things around us. The open places in urban landscapes are the most far-reaching example of this binding, this assigning-of-a-place by the human eye: we immediately fill the emptiness with the meaning of a square. These open places suggest spatial continuity without our actually seeing it or being able to say much about it, but which we nevertheless recognize immediately and intuitively as a common experience.

Seen in this way, the desolate plain around the Berlin Potzdamer Platz before 1990 wasn't simply an empty site, but a scar full of meaning, a story about war and cities, and what might seem empty was immediately glued together by the eye into an historical site in which each thistle shooting up could acquire a meaning of its own.

In the film *Der Himmel über Berlin*, the old Homer, a leather cap with earflaps on his wrinkled head, stumbles across the immense fallow field through the overgrown grass:

I can't find Potzdamer Platz! No, here I thought ... No, that's not it! Potzdamer Platz, surely that's where Café Josti ... So this can't be Potzdamer Platz! And no one to ask ... It was a district full of fun! Trams, buses with horses and two ears ... Tell me, Muse, of the poor immortal precentor ...

This twentieth-century Homer staggers past rubbish through the grass that has grown grey with urban dust and slowly the vanished square looms up in the mind of the viewer. As he talks of them blindly, the things rise up and walk in the midst of old paper, condoms and greasy chip papers, between the garbage and the signs of a space left to its own devices. The fallow field again becomes a square, the bell of the tram rings, the coffee in Café Josti regains its aroma and the first cars draw up. Time's arrow is reversed for a while. Then the old man sinks into a dilapidated sofa and gets his breath back as he sadly meditates. In the background, we see the ugly improvised pedestrian bridge that, in the meantime, has disappeared.

The Campo dei Miracoli in Pisa, the Piazza dell'Unità d'Italia in the glittering bay of Trieste, the canal basin like a square of water in front of San Giorgio Maggiore in Venice, the vague (disquieting) open space in front of the Kremlin or behind the Hermitage in St Petersburg, the unforgettable bleakness around the Brandenburg Gate in Berlin, the ancient emptiness of the great Roman sites; but also the new emptiness deliberately filled by architecture with nothing but the potential of the human eye, the deserts of suburbs. This eye immediately fills with memory and makes the new into something that can be understood in a different story. Take Sydney harbour, with its twentieth-century version of what Venice must once have been, in which the famous shell-shaped

Opera House contrasts with the tall metal bridge, the park with its white ibises and corellas, and the quay with the metro line above it - all these things that were placed in a different perspective by the intervention of that most recent building, the Opera House. Such open spaces are linked together by the subtle adhesive of the human eye, which sticks contrasting elements together; even through the arbitrariness of pleasant diversion, they interact and complement each other, in turn forming the glue through which the eye goes exploring and assigns a place to the skyline, the water, the arc of the iron bridge or the kissing couples, the same the world over, in the warm dusk by the railing of a ferryboat that is just leaving.

The human eye knows about proportions and plays with them consciously but, at the same time, absent-mindedly, looking with a detached emptiness that prevents the viewer from being pinned down by a single object or focus.

The same emptiness that activates the glue of the eye assails you all the time in Australia. It begins the moment you start flying over the outback for hour after hour, the monotonous landscape intersected by heat and vague dream lines, the empty heart of this continent, like a huge deserted square around which the cities have assembled like buildings and through which the central emptiness acquires a meaning that cannot be found anywhere else; for example, this meaning remains noticeably absent when you fly over the Siberian steppes – here there is no longer any boundary, only centripetal emptiness, far below zero.

On Circular Quay, the bow-shaped quay around which Sydney's waterfront square lies, a *Writers Walk* has been set up - about 40 brass plates with quotations from authors like D. H. Lawrence, Robert Hughes, Eleanor Dark and Charles Darwin, David Malouf, Jack London, Rudyard Kipling, Mark Twain and Arthur Conan Doyle. They are all quotations which in a strangely varied way evoke a fascination with what has been forgotten, hidden under the shuffling feet of laughing tourists who, without one look at the plates, are far beyond

the Oyster Bar on their way to something undefined, which they hope to find in Botany Bay.

'Silence ruled this land,' it says on Eleanor Dark's plate. 'Out of silence mystery comes, and magic, and the delicate awareness of unreasoning things.' (from *The Timeless Land*, 1941)
The rollerbladers whizz across the words.

Would Australians have done anything differently if their country had not been settled as the jail of the infinite space? Certainly they would. They would have remembered more of their own history. (from Robert Hughes, *The Fatal Shore*, 1987)

Nearby sits an Aborigine, dressed up and decorated with what was once a unique heritage but has now degenerated into its own exotic form of kitsch, playing his sonorous didgeridoo. Fascinated by the primeval power of this spectacle, the rhythm and the sound, more and more clusters of people stop. Then the man, who is at least six feet tall, takes the instrument out of his mouth, and with a smoky voice says in broad Australian, 'Well, if ya like ta hear what I play, why don't ya put some money in here?' He points contemptuously at the bowl by one of his knees and goes on playing. The primeval sound that left his listeners free to think their own thoughts has suddenly acquired a voice straight out of a soap opera, but with a tone that frightens the anonymous public to death, a direct challenge to its non-committal attitude. This is more than a walker out in search of the exotic can bear. Immediately the ogling group disperses, the man is alone again and behind their backs the monotonous ancient rhythm begins again - as the fascinating bad conscience of the exotic dream. ∎

From *Intercities*, Reaktion Books, London, 2001
(*Steden. Verhalen onderweg*, Amsterdam/Leuven, Meulenhoff/Kritak, 1998)

Translated by Paul Vincent

Two Poems
By Stefan Hertmans

The Free Fall of Days

There is in intervals of expectancy
no pit so shallow that the soul
fails to tumble in: the phlox that are no roses,

cloudlessly raining, bronze that crumbles
like stale cakes, empty portraiture
before a breathed-on mirror,

your pale eyes which, said Baudelaire,
convey the tempest of a passion in a stain,
more insignificant than you or I,

because our dying is announced
in someone else's clothes,

the interval in which you are no more
expected, a hole in which
your life once lay,

as night draws in your neighbour whistles low
'No milk today', or for tomorrow anyway.

De val van vrije dagen

Er is, in tussentijden van verwachting,
geen gat zo ondiep of de ziel tuimelt
erin: de floxen die geen rozen zijn,

wolkeloos geregen, brons dat tot
koek verkruimelt, lege portretkunst
voor een beademde spiegel,

je bleke ogen die, zoals Baudelaire,
het onweer van een passie in een
vlekje dragen, nietiger dan jij en ik,

want aangekondigd is ons doodgaan
in andermans kleren,

de tussentijd waarin je niet meer
wordt verwacht, een gat waar
ooit je leven zat,

tegen de avond fluit de buurman zacht
No milk today, alvast voor morgen.

The Jerónimos Monastery in Belém

You can start your life all over
any minute by wanting nothing
other than this now:

blue and yellow, aerolite and sand,
the shadow of a column and
voices in an arcade.

Look at the transient:
the airplane humming lazily in
the flawless day glides
with swallows and seagulls
above the roof.

A child summons you to these hours,
imagine trickling water,
centuries without people.
Be still as ancient stones.

It is now.

Klooster San Jeronimo, Belém

Je kunt je leven elk ogenblik
opnieuw beginnen door niets
meer te willen dan dit nu:

blauw en geel, luchtsteen en zand,
de schaduw van een zuil en
stemmen op een gang.

Kijk naar het vluchtige:
het lui zoemende vliegtuig in
de smetteloze dag glijdt met
zwaluwen en meeuwen
over het dak.

Een kind roept je naar deze uren,
denk aan druppelend water,
aan eeuwen zonder mens.
Word stil als oud gesteente.

Het is nu.

From *The Free Fall of Days* (*de val van vrije dagen*,
De Bezige Bij, Amsterdam, 2010)

All poems translated by Donald Gardner

Mastering the Brush like a Singer his Voice

On Jean Brusselmans, the Painter

North Sea, 1939. Horizontal grey brown strokes alternate with careful white lines that, without transition, unite in the middle to form a broad street: the reflection of light on water. The foaming waves curl against the bottom edge. Round shapes float in the air, ever bigger, more irregular, more quickly executed. Three boats sit on the horizon. The overwhelming sky, which extends over two-thirds of the canvas in forceful lanes of blue, white and a paler grey than the sea, is separated from the water not by a straight line but a confident curve. The sea – a challenging theme that implies both depth and perspective and which, in its emptiness, also resembles abstraction – is boldly set down in planes and stripes and without any unnecessary ceremony. The painting can be read as a lesson in composition by Mark Rothko, but without strata, impetuous, square. The clouds, tiny boats and the sea barely conceal the painter's pleasure. His name, written in proud calligraphy in the left hand corner, reads 'Jean Brusselmans, 1939'. It is reminiscent of the signature of another autodidact, Henri Rousseau *'le douanier'*. His name is the sign that the work is 'finished'. It is missing from some of his intriguing, complex works (*The Bathing Women* from 1935, for example), as though the painter is trespassing on forbidden terrain, or the canvas is not yet complete.

In another seascape, *Blue Sea* (1932), which contains the shadow of a single lost boat, the water and air are calm and the painting is yet more abstract. A beige strip, as wide as the blue of the high sea that it borders, floats between the water and the sky, a sky that is full of clouds and always moving. The beige area above the horizon divides the canvas into two equal rectangles. It suggests a foggy sunset but this is by no means certain. Two white streaks against the bottom edge also require an explanation: 'The painter must see nature in new ways. He must find the technique that expresses this way of seeing and will therefore be different than the previous one ... What the artist regards as a clear expression will remain a mystery for most of us.'

Brusselmans' seascapes are as immediately recognisable as all of his other work, even though they are so different. He painted the sea for thirty years, always including ships. Two of them dance on the rolling waves in *Storm* (1936).

A dramatic fan of sunlight, painted in rigid strokes of alternating light and dark yellow, falls upon the horizon from two heavy, yellow ringed clouds. The clouds drift off from a peaceful baby blue sky. The storm is almost over. Or is it approaching? Time and motion submit to the brush. On the grey-green sea, which is as stylised as wallpaper, broad foaming waves are juxtaposed with the harsh mountain of sunlight above. This fiery bundle of rays resembles the fan in some of his still lifes, another genre that Brusselmans constantly practised. In *Rainbow* (1932), the white waves roll up to the horizon, which is exceptional. The rainbow itself is drawn with firm hand, a few narrow, concentric half-circles in the uniformly dark air. The rainbow starts at the right hand side of the horizon and is suspended halfway above the left hand side. In this part of the picture, a curtain of rain in bold, sloping stripes shimmers overhead. Time and movement are once again united with air and water.

Jean Brusselmans, *North Sea*, 1939. Oil on canvas, 66.5 cm x 64 cm, Collection Royal Museum of Fine Arts, Antwerp. © Sabam Belgium 2013

By contrast, his interiors and busy still lifes are motionless. The four elements – Earth, Fire, Water and Air – animate the banal objects arranged neutrally next to each other in a cosmic rebus. Painting is the creation of an enigma. Brusselmans does this systematically. Yet it is also an adventure: 'I never know in advance how I'm going to start a painting and I never seem to manage to finish it: in that respect I'm like Titian.'

Stubbornly figurative

His idiosyncratic exploration of the no man's land between figuration, abstraction and idea, makes Jean Brusselmans (1884-1953) an *artist's artist*. He seeks geometric patterns in seascapes and landscapes. His approach to interiors and still lifes is conceptual and he chooses everyday objects not just for their material, but also their metaphorical, significance. He remains stubbornly figurative and always shows things just as they are. A vase is a vase, a shell is a shell, a house is a house and a field – ideally the undulating Brabant field – be it a square, a rectangle or a diamond, remains a field. He paints the horse or the human figure as though with a stencil. He never succumbs to the temptation of virtuosity. The trivial objects in his still lifes, which recur so persistently, come from his immediate environment. The brass oil lamp is one of his earliest motifs. He associates himself with the petroleum can with its broken spout, one of his best-known fetishes. The matchbox speaks for itself. With these symbols for Fire he combines those for Water. Herrings refer to poverty but perhaps also to Catholic rituals, although Brusselmans was born an anarchist. Scallops allude to restlessness and the pink conch shell evokes exotic dreams. The fan refers to Air and the wicker basket, the fruit and the flowers to the Earth. The chessboard, the vase, the painted china and the few sticks of furniture belong to the little man that he himself is, and from whose perspective he paints the world.

Sometimes he juxtaposes these objects with a complicated Oriental textile pattern – a piece of the original covering of his sofa. It must have cost the painter a great deal of time and patience, relatively speaking, to depict this object amongst the familiar simplicity of the others. As a consequence, there is something particularly mysterious about it. Over the years, Brusselmans detached the textile fragment from the sofa, which finally got a new cover, and it became an independent part of his large still lifes. According to his friend, the critic Paul Haesaerts, the discovery of the 'embroidery' was a revelation. 'The painter seems to be saying: 'so is the inner composition of my universe' and it's not only through this piece of embroidery that he speaks to us in this way...' In *Still Life with Slices of Sausage* (1936) the carpet pattern conquers the entire upper half of the canvas like a kind of wallpaper or firmament, but when he paints his renowned *Lady on a Sofa* the following year, the upholstery on the sofa is plain. The attention is drawn to another piece of fabric: the black and white checked dress of Mrs Brusselmans who, like *Olympia* by Manet or *Madame Récamier* by David, is reclining on the day bed. Her face is schematic and still. There is no expression in Brusselmans' portraits. The rhythm of her dress is quietly continued in the dotted linoleum of the floor. Perhaps the most

Jean Brusselmans, *Woman at the window*, 1917. Oil on canvas, 100 cm x 90 cm. Collection Groeningemuseum, Bruges. © Sabam Belgium 2013

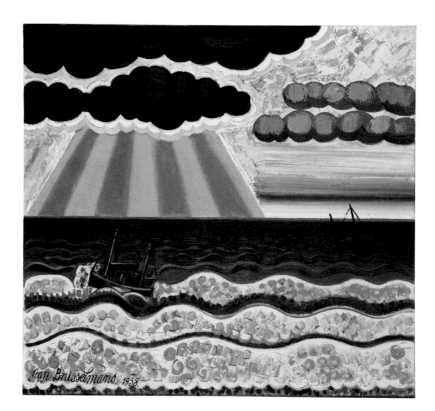

enigmatic thing of all in this painting is the 'mirror' on the wall behind her. Like an abstract painting, it is divided into two unequal, even rectangles.

A similar abstract composition is integrated into *Woman with Lamp* (1938). Brusselmans quotes abstract art almost carelessly. The Persian pattern jostles with the checked dress of his wife, which he continued to paint until long after her death in the famine of 1943. Brusselmans is not on a quest. He makes sovereign use of what life hands him and gives each new element its place in an ordered world. Within it, the focus is derived from the tangible to the invisible, which is as abstract as the tiled floor, the dress, or the mirror in *Lady on a Sofa*. It is a world in which poverty reigns, although he doesn't stress this. The deprivation is not a theme but more of a reservoir of motifs that have a deeper meaning. The human figure is a decorative object, the shell a world. The Persian textile motif in the 'wallpaper' of a still life foreshadows the black and white dress, but also the abstraction of the trees and shrubs in his landscapes, or the stylised bustle of *Gulls* (1949), which prefigures Hitchcock's *The Birds* (1963). In the same way that an Easterner knots a carpet or paints a miniature, Jean Brusselmans is consciously two-dimensional. And it is because of this that he comes into conflict with the Western pictorial tradition. The influence of the Orient is not to be excluded by this voracious autodidact. Hanging in *Large Interior* (1936) is the almost life-size portrait of a Chinese official that the artist was given by Luc Haesaerts. The Chinese man is the only 'presence' in the room. Three years later he paints his wife, amongst his familiar objects, reading against the same wall. She is wearing the famous dress, which reduces her, like the print of the Chinese official or the cast of Michelangelo's *Head of a*

Slave facing her, to part of the collection of flowers, vases, displayed plates and jugs, the fruit basket and the large hinged shell from the Caribbean. There is no hierarchy, emotion or emphasis.

One can trace the spots where Brusselmans placed his easel. For his landscapes, this was at the window on the first floor of his house in the then still rural outskirts of Brussels. As 'painter of the Brabant landscape', he was incorporated into the Flemish Expressionists, albeit struggling. His favourite interiors are the attic, with its imposing triangle of roof timbers, and the living room. In Ostend, he painted opposite the lighthouse at the harbour channel or straight in front of the anonymous, universal sea. Sticking to the same viewpoint, the reduction and the repetition of his subjects suggests that what he paints is subordinate to a metaphysical message. 'In my paintings a line remains a line and touches of colour and impasto stay what they are. The true painter renounces *trompe l'oeil* in search of a higher truth. What counts is the inner colour of a painting, which reveals its whole meaning. That colour is not only the result of inspiration but also of a mental process. Making art is giving light to all kinds of things, including the most ungrateful and pernicious.'

Angular and obstinate

A pedestrian bridge in Anderlecht, whether or not with naked swimmers, inspired him for at least twenty years and is another persistent motif. It is his most important cityscape and relates closely to a late group of mythological and religious paintings, the themes of which are rather surprising. The anarchist Brusselmans doesn't flatter. He is angular and obstinate. He refuses to meet expectations. As a consequence, there were no ovations for his work. He was reproached for painting too flatly, too stiffly and without depth, content or atmosphere. To some of his contemporaries, his work was no better than the wallpaper of his interiors. There were attempts to link him with the Brabant Fauvists, an ill-defined group, or, to his horror, with the Flemish Expressionists. Brusselmans, who saw himself as a Flemish painter, remained unruly and wanted to fit in nowhere: 'Initially, I was influenced by Gustave Courbet and Van Gogh. It was only later that I understood Van Eyck, the Greeks and the Egyptians. However it is thanks to the so-called folk art that I've found the path that leads to the true tradition of Flemish art and the essence of our people.'

To this folk art belonged the prints of Epinal, which he copied in his youth. Brusselmans had only attended primary school and never learned to write without mistakes. This reinforced the headstrong stubbornness that he had inherited from the modest but artistic environment in which he was raised. He came from a very musical family and had sung in the children's choir of the Brussels Opera House, La Monnaie / De Munt. He was averse to pathos and chose the implicit over the explicit, suggestion over caricature: painting was a matter of 'mastering the brush like a singer his voice.'

The components of his landscapes are equivalent, in the same way that those of his still lifes and seascapes are. Brusselmans depicts the simple, new, interchangeable homes on the Kapellekensbaan that he saw from his window. After the First World War, Belgium was filled with these uniform working men's houses that always tended to stand in rows. The novelist Louis Paul Boon evoked

Jean Brusselmans, *Grey Winterlandscape*, 1935. Oil on canvas, 86 cm x 57 cm. Collection Groeningemuseum, Bruges. © Sabam Belgium 2013

them in his famous *Chapel Road* (Dutch title: *Kapellekensbaan*). Brusselmans bought one himself, after having moved ten times between 1911 and 1924. It was located in Dilbeek, near his hometown of Brussels, on a hill in the area of Koudenhaard. And it was this name that he adopted, with a sense of irony, for his residence [it literally means 'Cold Chimney']. For twenty years, denial and deprivation constantly haunted him there. Since nobody had a taste for Brusselmans' work, there was more than one occasion when he was forced to sell some of his modest furnishings in order to survive. He didn't completely lack influential defenders – there were the Haesaerts brothers – and in the 1930s and 1940s he began to receive cautious acceptance. His diffidence stood in the way of success. This increased over the years instead of abating, but it also protected his radicalism. And this is precisely why, today, he is recognised as a pioneer.

Brusselmans was not always a recluse. In his hopeful youth, he was a fellow student of other loners: Edgard Tytgat, with whom he shared his love of folk art, and Rik Wouters with whom he took an attic studio on the Twaalf Apostelenstraat in Brussels in 1907 (nine years before Wouters' untimely death). By that time, Brusselmans was twenty-three, and it was already obvious to him that his path would not be strewn with roses. His painting, *The Vale of Sorrow*, was refused for the Godecharle prize. He destroyed it. That same year, he met the woman whom he would marry in 1911, after she had become the mother of his only child, Armand. The musical Marie-Léonie Frisch shared his poverty and was his greatest model. During this promising time, Brusselmans searched for the support of artists' fellowships. Sometimes he founded these himself, like the *Clan du Parruck* in 1912, the year of his debut in *Les Bleus de la G.G.G.*. This exhibition included, amongst others, Spilliaert, Tytgat and Permeke and was held at the Georges Giroux gallery, the new Brussels sensation on the Koningstraat. Giroux had recently opened its doors with a startlingly cutting edge exhibition of Italian Futurists. "*J'étais en plein enthousiasme, en pleine production et aussi en pleine misère.*" ['I was full of enthusiasm, in full production and also full of misery']. In 1914, he participated in the last exhibition of *La Libre Esthétique*, the successor of the famous artists' group *Les XX*, the members of which included Ensor, Rops, Khnopff, Rodin and Signac. The First World War quickly dispersed the young generation of Belgian artists. Permeke and Tytgat arrived in England and Wouters never returned from the Netherlands. Brusselmans moved around the outskirts of Brussels like a restless nomad.

No tralala

Three years after the war, he was given his first solo exhibition. It was not in the capital but at the Breckpot Gallery in Antwerp. For Breckpot, it was the first exhibition in a historical series, but it didn't prove to be a breakthrough for Brusselmans. He was twenty when he'd chosen to be a full-time artist. He was now thirty-seven. One after the other, his contemporaries from the School of Latem had all won recognition. This they owed to the critics André De Ridder and Paul-Gustave Van Hecke, who had established the Sélection gallery and the eponymous art journal in Brussels, and who had presented the Expressionists alongside Picasso, Matisse and Chagall. Belgian painting wouldn't be seen on such an international stage again until the Belgian World Expo of 1958, a setback that is still felt today. For Brusselmans, the Sélection gallery was hardly a blessing. The Van Hecke-De Ridder duo considered him to be second class. Georges Giroux, who had exhibited him before the war, died two years after Brusselmans' solo debut. There was, however, one remaining influential friend from the pre-war period: Hippolyte Fierens-Gevaert, the curator-in-chief of the Brussels museums between 1918 and 1926. But even this connection yielded little. His work became increasingly sober, his palette sparser, his position ever more isolated. He did odd jobs in advertising to keep his head above water.

But when the financial crisis of 1931 put an end to the boom in the Belgian art world, Brusselmans, who was nearly fifty, stood on the brink of the decade in which he was to flourish. The Fascist wave engulfed Europe, but the Nazis didn't find the Flemish Expressionists, Brusselmans included, 'degenerate'. On the contrary, they were 'interpreters of the fundamental traditions of the race'. Again, there was a protector: Robert-Louis Delevoy, who had opened the Gallery Apollo in Brussels in 1941. As the founder of the *Jeune Peinture Belge* prize and director of the Ecole Supérieure d'Architecture et des Arts Visuels (La Cambre) he had remained influential after the war. In 1972, he edited the *catalogue raisonné* of Brusselmans' work. Just as important was the interest of the art historian and senior civil servant, Emile Langui. Finally, there was the interest shown by Tony Herbert, a Kortrijk industrialist, supporter of the Flemish movement and member of the resistance. In a short period of just a few years, he had purchased sixty paintings and watercolours from Brusselmans. In 1952, a year before the artist's death, he threw a huge party for Brusselmans and invited three hundred prominent guests. Herbert saw many similarities between the wiry artist and himself. 'That hardness, the sharp line, the orthodoxy, no tralala', said his son Anton. Herbert could not understand why he was the only collector of Jean Brusselmans. In his eyes, he was even more important than the celebrated Constant Permeke, of whose work he also possessed a large collection.

At the end of his life, Jean Brusselmans saw the beginnings of recognition. Since his death, it has continued to grow in fits and starts but he is still virtually unknown abroad. It will therefore be many more years before he acquires the place in art history that he so rightfully deserves. ■

Translated by Helen Simpson

What's in a Name?

Changing Labels for the Dutch Language

[ROEL VISMANS]

The naïve language user (and foreign language learner) has good reasons to feel confused by the names for the Dutch language, both in English and in Dutch. There are two sources for this potential confusion. One lies in the English word *Dutch* itself and in its history, the other in the variety of names that have been given to the language by its own speakers over the centuries and which persist to the present day. The English word *Dutch* is similar to German Deutsch, but they refer to different languages, a state of affairs that English learners of German in particular have to learn to live with. The official name for the Dutch language is *Nederlands*, but many Dutch people refer to it as *Hollands* and many Flemish people use the word *Vlaams*. In this article I will discuss these issues in order to throw some light on them.

The English word *Dutch* is cognate with the German word for 'German', *Deutsch*, as well as its Dutch equivalent *Duits*, i.e. the Dutch word for 'German'. All three words stem from an earlier Germanic word, *theodisc* [1], meaning 'popular, of the people', which was used in the early middle ages throughout the West-Germanic language area to distinguish the spoken language from Latin (and French and other non-Germanic languages). In Dutch the word developed into various forms, most notably Middle Dutch *dietsc* in the south-west and *duutsc* elsewhere. In Dutch, present-day *Duits* developed from the latter form, whilst the word *Diets* is now archaic, although sometimes still used in non-technical references to Middle Dutch. Moreover, regional names like *vlaemsc* or *brabants* were also used in the Middle Ages, evidence of the sensitivity for regional differences that existed at the time. At the time, some of these regional labels also occurred in the surrounding languages, for example in English (e.g. Flemish) and in French where the word *flamand* appears to have been more widely used than *thiois*, the (medieval) French translation of *dietsc*.

In the course of the 16th century, as standard languages began to develop, the term *Nederduits* (again with various spellings) gradually entered the language as a way of distinguishing Dutch from (High) German. The overlap between this development and the emergence of a Dutch political entity with its own national identity is certainly no coincidence. This was soon followed by the introduction of the word *Nederlands* alongside *Nederduits* in some official texts and in books about the Dutch language. Gradually *Nederlands* began to replace

Nederduits and by the end of the 19th century the word *Nederduits* had almost completely disappeared. It is now only used to refer to the Low German dialects (*Plattdeutsch*) spoken in Northern Germany. Regional labels also continued to occur, however. Of some interest in this context is the title of a Dutch grammar by W.G. Brill that appeared in 1946 as *Hollandsche spraakleer* and was later reprinted as *Nederlandsche spraakleer ten gebruike bij inrichtingen van hooger onderwijs* ('Dutch grammar for use in institutions of higher education'). This shows that the label *Hollands*, in essence a regional reference, was also being used to refer to standard Dutch in much the same way as it is today, certainly in colloquial language. We shall return to this issue below.

Other languages soon began to copy the formal distinction between Dutch and High German with direct translations of the word *Nederlands*, for example into French *néerlandais* and German *Niederländisch*. Just as in Dutch, however, forms like *hollandais* and *Holländisch* also occur and are reserved for more colloquial speech. In English, meanwhile, *theodisc* developed into Dutch which was first used to refer to all precursors of present-day Dutch and German. However, the English word *German* already existed as well, so from the late 16th century onwards English also began to distinguish between Dutch and German in line with the political and sociolinguistic developments on the continent but with different words than in Dutch or French and German:

Woordenboek der Nederlandsche Taal (WNT), the greatest dictionary in the world (1864-2001) © Jonas Lampens

In the 15th and 16th c. 'Dutch' was used in England in the general sense in which we now use 'German', and in this sense it included the language and people of the Netherlands as part of the 'Low Dutch' or Low German domain. After the United Provinces became an independent state, using the 'Nederduytsch' or Low German of Holland as the national language, the term 'Dutch' was gradually restricted in England to the Netherlanders, as being the particular division of the 'Dutch' or Germans with whom the English came in contact in the 17th c. (OED)

However, in English there is no equivalent of the label *Hollands* as there is in, for example, German or French. It is noteworthy that in the early modern period some authors tried to incorporate the prefix *neder-* in their names for the Dutch language, e.g. Thomas Basson's *Coniugations in Englishe and Nether-dutche* (Leiden 1586) and William Sewel's *A compendious guide to the Low Dutch language. Korte wegwyzer der Nederduytsche taal* (Amsterdam, 1700). However, such sensitivity may have been due to the fact that Basson was an English immigrant and Sewel the son of an English immigrant. The latter was not consistent in his inclusion of *Low* alongside *Dutch*, witness the title of his dictionary: *Nieuw woordenboek der Nederduytsche en Engelsche taale .... A New dictionary Dutch and English* (Amsterdam, 1691).

English also has one other term for the Dutch language, *Netherlandish*. However, it is rarely used, even by linguists and it is significant that in four of the seven quotations for its entry in the OED, the word *Dutch* is added by way of explanation, e.g. 'The origin of new Netherlandish or Dutch is to be found with the *Rederijkers*', a quote from the 1890 Chambers Encyclopedia. In other contexts, the adjective *Netherlandish* tends to refer to art from the Low Countries.

Confusion

An added complication is that words like *Dutch* or *English* are not only nouns referring to languages, but also adjectives denoting political entities and especially nations. This is true for English as much as it is for Dutch, e.g.: *het Nederlands elftal* ('the Dutch eleven'), *the English football team*. Moreover, in English the names for some languages are also used as nouns referring to people, e.g.: *the Dutch lost spectacularly*. This link between language and nation, fundamentally a 19th-century concept, continues to shape much of our thinking about language and the way we speak about it today.

One way of speaking about countries is the *pars pro toto* in which the name of a small area of a country is used to refer to the whole nation. Thus, many British people say 'Holland' when they mean 'the Netherlands', in much the same way as many continentals say 'England' for 'Great Britain'. Indeed, during the Olympic Games in London in 2012 many English people could be heard celebrating 'English' successes, even if the other UK nations (Scots, Welsh, Northern Irish, Manx, etc.) would have said 'British'. The Dutch are less particular, not only when it comes to football (they all sing *Hup Holland Hup*), but often also when they refer informally to their own country (*Nederland*) as 'Holland'. Even so, regional sensitivities sometimes become apparent, because strictly speaking 'Holland' only refers to the two western provinces of North and South Holland.

Along similar lines, 'Flanders' now usually refers to the entire Dutch-speaking region of Belgium, even though the term originally only denoted the county of Flanders, the present-day provinces of West and East Flanders. However, a slightly different situation pertains to 'Flanders' than to 'Holland', as 'Flanders' (*Vlaanderen*) is actually also the official name for the region.

These differences between formal, official, and informal, colloquial naming conventions for the Netherlands and Flanders are reflected in the present-day names for the Dutch language. Officially and even legally, the name for the language is *Nederlands*, but Hollands is often used by Dutch people to talk about their own language, e.g. in the phrase *praat gewoon Hollands* ('just speak Dutch'). In many ways this phrase means more than it says, because it can be used as an admonition to anyone acting above their station. Here, *Hollands* is equivalent to 'normal', 'ordinary', 'everyday'. Similarly, people in Flanders regularly refer to Flemish Dutch as *Vlaams*, reserving the term *Nederlands* for official and formal usage. What is referred to as *Vlaams* and *Hollands* covers a wide range of speaking styles, from standard language, through colloquial speech, to dialect. In particular, *Vlaams* as a general label can also be a cover term for the colloquial Flemish variety known as *tussentaal* (lit. 'in-between language' a.k.a. *verkavelingsvlaams*) which combines a number of features from dialects, supra-regional speech and standard Dutch.

In Flanders, *Hollands* refers to Dutch as it is spoken north of the border, and likewise in the Netherlands people refer to Flemish Dutch as *Vlaams*. However, the label *Belgisch* (lit. 'Belgian') can probably be heard just as frequently in the Netherlands to refer to Dutch spoken in Belgium, but never in Belgium. When Dutch and Flemish people use these terms to refer to the language from the other country, they have a set of characteristics in mind which is perhaps not clearly defined, but on which there is a general consensus. By and large, these characteristics comprise a combination of phonological and lexical features, predominantly the quality of the consonants 'g' and 'w' (in Flanders 'soft', voiced /ɣ/ and bilabial /w/, in the Netherlands 'hard' voiceless /x/ and labiodental /w/) and a limited set of words. These features are also frequently used to draw unflattering caricatures of each other.

Although the labels *Vlaams* and *Hollands* are frequently used for Dutch in general, they can also be applied in their much stricter sense to provincial dialect from East or West Flanders and North or South Holland. Other provincial dialects are usually labelled similarly, although there are further sub-divisions of the Dutch dialects (see the maps on http://www.streektaal.net/). Thus, we can have for example *Gronings, Drents, Brabants, Zeeuws* or *Limburgs* referring to dialects from the provinces of Groningen, Drenthe, Brabant, Zeeland and Limburg. Only *Fries* refers to a distinct language, Frisian, spoken in the Dutch province of Friesland and recognised in law as an official language there.

Some order

My brief for this article was to 'create some order in the confusion' of the nomenclature for the Dutch language. On the one hand, there is 'confusion' about the English word Dutch. This is quite easily explained by historical developments, although it is not helped by the existence of a term like Pennsylvania

Dutch, the name for a variety of High German spoken in the American state Pennsylvania by the descendants of German settlers. Nevertheless, the differentiation between 'Dutch' and 'German', which has existed in English from the 17th century, mirrors quite neatly the differentiation between Nederduits/Nederlands and Duits which developed in Dutch a few decades earlier.

On the other hand, there is 'confusion' in Dutch due to the existence of various colloquial and regional labels alongside the formal name Nederlands. From the outside, e.g. for English-speaking learners of Dutch, this may indeed seem confusing, but it points to the different and complex realities that exist for speakers of Dutch and how they express those realities. In addition to the (generally accepted) existence of standard Dutch (Nederlands), they have different perceptions of other speakers of the language. More importantly, they need to be able to express their sense of linguistic identity: as speakers of Hollands, Vlaams or Surinaams-Nederlands, or none of these; perhaps as speakers of a regional variety, of an 'ethnic' variety or of straattaal ('street language' or 'youth language'), or as speakers of standard Dutch who wish to reject variation. More often than not, that identity is a complex one in which several factors interact, such as regional origin, nationality, level of education, age and gender. In today's globalised world, the linguistic identity of speakers of Dutch is also frequently shaped by language contact, not only with English, but with a wide range of other languages from around the world. It is a complex reality that also exists elsewhere, even if it is not expressed in quite the same way.

The following table is offered as a first guide through the labels discussed in this article. ■

NOTE

[1] There are various spellings for this word depending on the source consulted. Here I use the modern English version, which would in Old English have been written with the character thorn: þeodisc. For further etymological information, see the *Oxford English Dictionary* (OED), the *Woordenboek der Nederlandsche Taal* (WNT) and the *Etymologisch Woordenboek van het Nederlands* (EWN). I have consulted the online versions of OED and WNT.

FURTHER READING

Bakker, D.M. & G.R.W. Dibbets. *Geschiedenis van de Nederlandse taalkunde*. Den Bosch: Malmberg. 1977. (Digitale bibliotheek voor de Nederlandse letteren, http://www.dbnl.org/tekst/bakk-005gesc01_01/).

Daniëls, Wim. *Talking Dutch*. Rekkem: Stichting Ons Erfdeel. 2005.

Oxford English Dictionary. Oxford: OUP. Online version June 2012.

Philippa, M. *et al.Etymologisch woordenboek van het Nederlands*. Amsterdam: AUP. 2004-2009.

Sijs, Nicoline van der, ed. *Wereldnederlands. Oude en jonge variëteiten van het Nederlands*. The Hague: SDU. 2005.

Toorn, M.C. van den *et al. Geschiedenis van de Nederlandse taal*. Amsterdam: AUP. 1997.

Woordenboek der Nederlandsche Taal. Leiden: Instituut voor Nederlandse Lexicologie. Online version 2007.

Dutch label	English label / translation	gloss
	Dutch	everyday English word for the Dutch language
	Netherlandish	learned English word for the Dutch language
Belgisch	Belgian	used esp. in the Netherlands to refer to Southern (Flemish) Dutch and distinguish it from Northern (Netherlands) Dutch
Diets		archaic word for Middle Dutch
Duits	German	
ethnisch Nederlands	ethnic Dutch	variety of Dutch resulting from language contact between Dutch and another language (cf. van der Sijs ed., 2005)
Hollands	Hollandish	colloquial term for Northern (Netherlands) Dutch; also dialect from the provinces North or South Holland
Nederduits	Low German	in the early modern period also used to refer to Dutch, now only used for the Low German dialects spoken in Northern Germany (*Plattdeutsch*)
Nederlands	Dutch	the formal Dutch name for Dutch, in existence since the 17th century. The official name for the standard language in both Flanders and the Netherlands
Straattaal	street/youth language	variety of Dutch spoken by young people with influences from English and other languages, esp. Sranan
Surinaams Nederlands	Surinamese Dutch	variety of standard Dutch spoken in Suriname
tussentaal	in-between language	colloquial variety of Dutch spoken in Flanders combining features from dialects, supra-regional speech and standard Dutch
verkavelingsvlaams	in-between language	= *tussentaal*
Vlaams	Flemish	colloquial term for Southern (Flemish) Dutch; also dialect from the provinces West or East Flanders

Roger Raveel
Garden Wall (detail), 1964.
Oil on canvas, 120 x 150 cm
© Sabam Belgium 2013

Chronicle

Architecture

The Lurie Garden in Chicago

The 'Primal Feel of Nature'
The Gardens of Piet Oudolf

Piet Oudolf (° 1944) was in his thirties when he and his wife Anja started the nursery in Hummelo in the province of Gelderland. His first important garden, the Dream Park in Enköping in Sweden, dates back to 1996. The following year his book *Planting the Natural Garden* was published in the original Dutch edition, showing Oudolf's work alongside that of twelve other garden designers from the Netherlands, Belgium, France, Germany, England and the United States. Innovative use of perennials and ornamental grasses was the overarching theme.

Oudolf's ideas were picked up by several young garden designers and journalists in England as a welcome rejuvenation of the English flower garden. In 2000 he was invited to design a garden for the prestigious Chelsea Flower Show, which was promptly crowned Best Show Garden. This brought Oudolf important work in England, including jobs at Scampston Hall and at Trentham Hall, a historical park in Stoke-on-Trent. The Royal Horticultural Society (RHS) even asked him to make two large flower borders at Wisley Gardens, the RHS showpiece. He also arranged the planting of the prestigious Potters Fields Park by London's Tower Bridge.

In 2001 the well-known American landscape architect Kathryn Gustafson asked Oudolf to work on the Lurie Garden, a large roof garden next to famous architect Frank Gehry's concert hall in Chicago's Millennium Park. Oudolf's definitive US breakthrough came a year later, when he was asked to come up with a master plan for the private institution behind The Battery in New York, a park on the banks of the Hudson River at the southernmost tip of Manhattan. On the back of this, in 2003 New York City Council asked him to make a memorial garden on the edge of the park for the victims of the attacks on the Twin Towers. These Gardens of Remembrance immediately made him famous.

In 2005 Oudolf was asked to collaborate on the High Line, a new city park on an old railway line ten metres above the ground, crossing trendy Chelsea and the rundown Meatpacking District. The High Line was a huge success: the park has become one of New York's most important tourist attractions, reviving the Meatpacking District, and Oudolf is currently working on extending it. Still in New York, he recently designed the gardens for Goldman Sachs' headquarters and Frank Gehry's new Beekman Towers too.

How can we explain Oudolf's phenomenal success? And what's so special about the New Perennial

Movement of which he is the figurehead, also known as Dutch New Naturalistic Gardening and New Wave Planting? His marked preference for naturalistic use of hardy perennials and ornamental grasses is a key part of this. This approach not only strikes a sensitive chord with traditional garden lovers, it also allows Oudolf and his supporters to bridge the gap between ecology and design. It all started in Oudolf's Hummelo nursery. With a few like-minded Dutch and German gardeners, he experimented with a new plant palette: strong, hardy plants which require little care and look natural, preferably single flowered varieties in warm shades of purple, red and brown. Following a few legendary German cultivators, such as Karl Foerster and Ernst Pagels, Oudolf also became a great advocate of ornamental grasses. Colour is of secondary importance to Oudolf, who prioritises plants' shape and structure, along with the way they die back and their winter look.

In addition to innovative choices of plants, Oudolf is also original in his combinations of large groups of plants and his overwhelmingly naturalistic approach. 'I want the plants to look as they do in nature,' he says. This is not about copying nature, which can only lead to disappointment. 'Studying the details of beautiful landscapes can show us how to use them successfully in the garden.' Nature as a source of inspiration for artistic form.

Several developments explain Oudolf's success in artistic circles. The Venice Biennale commissioned him to create a new flower garden in the Giardini, at the request of the Kunsthalle Bielefeld he designed an artistic garden in the German spa town of Bad Driburg, and renowned Swiss architect Peter Zumthor called on him to design the garden inside his temporary pavilion in London's Serpentine Gallery.

Plants don't need to be pretty or special in themselves, says Oudolf; the important thing is their role in the bigger picture. It is not the individual character of the plant which counts, but how they come together. Oudolf likes to compare his work to composing music. 'As in music, rhythm,

The High Lane in New York

repetition, coherence and scale play an important role in forming a fluent whole.' He also talks about complexity and creating order in chaos. 'A garden is a metaphor for nature. My gardens aren't wild gardens, but they do evoke the primal feel of nature. This is a gardening style for people who love nature, not for cowards or those who cling to traditional notions of orderliness.' By bringing the focus back to plants, Oudolf blows new life into landscape gardening. Plants are more than decoration or filler, they are an essential part of the design.

Perhaps the best word to describe Oudolf's gardens is 'sublime'. His flower gardens evoke images of nature, prairies and alpine meadows, unexpected images in the city. 'When you visit a garden or park, it should make you think. I want to touch people, I want them to respond to what they see, to be surprised or moved.' Perhaps this is the key to Oudolf's success: the residents of cities such as London and New York need more than good architects and designers, they need sublime images to move them too.

PAUL GEERTS
Translated by Anna Asbury

www.oudolf.com

Film and Theatre

A Finger on the Pulse
The Choreographer Meg Stuart

The American choreographer Meg Stuart illustrates the openness of contemporary dance in Flanders better than anyone. After training as a dancer at the renowned Tisch School of the Arts in New York, in 1991 she was noticed by Tine Van Aerschot, a talent scout for the cutting-edge Klapstukfestival in Leuven, while Stuart was working at 'The Kitchen', an interdisciplinary melting pot for the arts. The immediate outcome was an invitation to a six-week residence in Flanders.

Both the audience and critics in Leuven were unerring in judging the importance of what was her first full-length production. This was not self-evident, because in this piece – Disfigure Study – Stuart found what she was looking for: a break with the postmodern idiom of American dance as practised by Trisha Brown and Lucinda Childs. It was precisely these two who had helped define the style of the early works by Anne Teresa De Keersmaeker, one of the figureheads of the innovative trends in Flemish dance in the early 1980s. Ten years after the first Flemish Wave, Meg Stuart ushered in a second wave of renewal, all on her own in Leuven. Now, after thirty productions and a series of site-specific and improvisation projects, she is still one of the most innovative and influential choreographers in Flemish and international dance.

In Disfigure Study, Stuart showed fragmented and distorted dancing bodies, driftwood left by the ruthless machinery of progress. She refers to Francis Bacon as a source of inspiration: 'I would look at his paintings and see how he pulled the bodies apart, and I wondered how far I could go in that direction.' At the same time she wanted to show the dancer as a human being. 'I didn't just want to impose stories on my body, but instead show those stories that live in the body.' Disconnection, failure

Meg Stuart © Chris Van der Burght

and vulnerability are still current themes in Stuart's work, though now in more complex contexts than in the past.

Encouraged by her positive reception, Stuart opted for Flanders as a base for her nomadic projects. In 1994 she set up her own company in Brussels, Damaged Goods, a name inspired by a review of Disfigure Study. In The Village Voice, Burt Supree wrote that 'everyone is shown as damaged goods'. The Flemish authorities awarded Stuart an operating subsidy; she was the first foreign choreographer to receive one. Although her office is still in Brussels, Meg Stuart has for some time been living in Berlin, where she has been collaborating closely with the Volksbühne am Alexanderplatz for the last six years. But her latest piece was produced under the wing of the Münchner Kammerspiele.

This absence from home is not so odd when you consider that Stuart has played a pioneering role in stimulating collective projects and interaction between arts disciplines – in inverse proportion to the 'disconnection' she shows on stage. As early as 1994 she presented a 'dance installation' amidst works by Louise Bourgeois, Luc Tuymans and others in This is the Show and the Show is Many Things at the Museum of Contemporary Art in Ghent (SMAK). Between 1996 and 1999, in various cities including Lisbon and Moscow, she put on six versions of her Crash Landing improvisation project, with the assistance of Steve Paxton, one of the founders of dance improvisation. Highway 101 (2000-2001), a 'blending & merging' site-specific project in five European cities, was considered by critics to be just about the most interesting work of that period, worldwide. With a variable team of performers and artists, Stuart followed a route through a variety of dance spaces, in each case prompting the audience to view the space in a new way. For example, in the Centre Pompidou in Paris, the dancers hid amongst the audience and stared at the spectators as they waited for the performers to appear.

In the meantime, Meg Stuart continues more than anyone to keep her finger on the pulse of artistic and societal trends. In Blessed (2007) an ecological apocalypse takes shape in a cardboard set, around a man (performed by Francisco Camacho, one of Stuart's original company) who is out of balance with himself and his surroundings. With agonisingly slow inevitability his world degenerates into a shapeless mess of pulp. Stuart thereby delivered an all but political message, but without preaching. A year later she was awarded the prize of the French critics for this compelling work. In 2012 she also won the German Konrad Wolf Prize for the same production, and the set designer Doris Dziersk received a New York Dance and Performance Award (aka a 'Bessie') for what was described as a 'brilliant technical achievement that perfectly matched the artistic intent of the work'. In 2008 the choreographer herself also received a Bessie Award for her entire oeuvre, and in the same year she was awarded the Flemish Culture Prize for the Performing Arts.

In her most recent piece, Built to Last (2012), Meg Stuart establishes a link with history for the first time in her career and also uses existing musical scores for the first time. She questions the impact of music on Western utopias and ideals, on the basis of works by such great composers as Beethoven, Schoenberg, Xenakis and Monk.

Meg Stuart has developed her own special dance idiom in Flanders, but her impact also extends much further: flexible multidisciplinary joint ventures, research-oriented work, an interest in work processes, and social engagement have all become self-evident concepts for young choreographers. This is largely due to Stuart's indefatigable drive to keep on expanding her horizons.

LIEVE DIERCKX
Translated by Gregory Ball

www.damagedgoods.be

JEROEN PEETERS (ed.), *Damaged Goods: Meg Stuart: Are We Here Yet?*, Les presses du reel, Dijon, 2010, 256 p. Available in English and French.

Exception or Rule?

The International Rise of Dutch Children's Films

Since its world premiere at the International Film Festival in Berlin in February 2012, *Kauwboy*, the film debut of Boudewijn Koole, has swept all before it. After being awarded the top prize for best children's film by the international jury in the Generation programme and taking the prize for best film debut in the entire festival, *Kauwboy* went on to scoop awards at an array of other national and international festivals. *Kauwboy* was chosen as the Dutch entry for the Oscars, and in 2012 was voted the best European debut during the European Film Awards, the 'European Oscars'.

The film (about a ten year-old boy who is trying to come to terms with the loss of his mother and strikes up a friendship with a jackdaw which he keeps hidden from his volatile father), marks a high point in a trend that has been under way for some time, namely the international rise of Dutch children's films. The Dutch Film Festival celebrated the importance of the genre in 2012 by opening with *Nono, the Zigzag Kid (Nono, het zigzagkind)*. This film portrayal of David Grossman's novel is a Dutch-Belgian co-production, directed by the Fleming, Vincent Bal, and featuring Isabella Rossellini in a major supporting role. The film tells the story of a 13 year-old boy trying to find out who his dead mother was because his father refuses to tell him anything about her. The film premiered at the International Film Festival in Toronto, and has also been selected for the children's section of the 2013 Berlinale.

The first prize awarded to a Dutch film at the Berlin Children's Film Festival dates from 1989, when *Mijn vader woont in Rio* (My father lives in Rio) was awarded a prize by the children's film jury. The film (about a girl who does not know that her father is in prison) was produced by Burny Bos. With his company BosBros, he was in at the birth of the genre of Dutch family films that has now become immensely popular. The genre is typified by an often adventurous quest told from the per-spective of a child which, with its nostalgic undertone, serious themes and humour, also appeals to adults. Bos broke with the tradition of somewhat moralising and rather artificial children's films that had been the norm until then and replaced them with realistic dramas with scope for fantasy and imagination. More attention was paid to acting skills, thematic development and hefty budgets. Bos also formulated ambitions which looked beyond the national borders, towards Berlin and towards Disney, which he was aiming to trounce at the box office. He succeeded in 1998, when the American distributor Warner financed the large-scale distribution of the BosBros production *The Flying Liftboy (Abeltje)* in Dutch cinemas.

Since then, Dutch children's films have become a regular fixture in Berlin. *De Tasjesdief* (The Bagsnatcher, 1995), *Mariken* (2000) and *Bluebird* (2004) all won Crystal Bears there. Maryanne Redpath, director of the Generation children's section of the Berlinale, says the following: "What makes *Kauwboy* special – and this applies to lots of Dutch children's films that we select – is that it deals with very human issues. These films are shot from the perspective of the child, and describe in detail

Stills from *Nono,*
the *Zigzag Kid*
© Walther Vanden Ende &
BosBros / Daniël Bouquet

how that child deals with the fact that his mother is absent, for example."

Redpath finds it difficult to list the general characteristics of Dutch children's films, because the output is so diverse. "It's a mixed industry that covers an enormous range, as regards topics, with something for everyone from age 4 to 16, and as regards form; from big-budget fairytales and adventure films to raw, documentary-style films such as *Snackbar* [a story about kids hanging around on the streets: KW]; from classical works to art house productions."

Dutch children's film has grown since 2002, with at least four titles being released every year. In fact, in the last five years this has risen to an average of eight films a year, roughly a quarter of the total annual Dutch film output. Half the 16 Dutch films which attracted more than 100,000 visitors between September 2011 and September 2012 were children's films: *Bennie Stout* (Bennie Brat), *Razend* (Furious), *Sinterklaas en het raadsel van 5 december* (Sinterklaas and the Mystery of 5 December), *Dolfje Weerwolfje* (Dolfje the Werewolf), *Achtste-groepers huilen niet* (Big Kids Don't Cry), *Tony 10*, *Sprookjesboom de film* (Fairy Tale Tree: the Movie) and *Brammetje Baas* (Fidgety Bram). These are not necessarily the films that go abroad, though that happens regularly, too. *Kauwboy* drew only 20,000 visitors in the Netherlands, because this idiosyncratic film was out of step with most Dutch people's expectations of children's film and therefore proved more difficult to market.

Looking across the annual crop and premieres at the recent Dutch Film Festival, with films such as *Dolfje Weerwolfje*, *Patatje Oorlog* (Potato War), *Tony 10*, *Brammetje Baas* and *Mees Kees*, it is obvious that the pioneering work of BosBros has become commonplace. Dutch children's films often share recurrent characteristics: they are based on a familiar book or TV series; there is a voice-over (in which the main character introduces him/herself and invites the viewer into his/her thoughts); there are animation sequences (which are usually used to express fantasies); they are politically correct (there is always at least one black or coloured child in the class, and children who are 'different' are presented in a gentle, sympathetic way); the plot is dialogue-driven (the characters recount what is happening to them); the ending is happy (every problem can ultimately be resolved); and there is a grand finale (a contest or match, birthday or school show towards which the characters work). And of course there are the over-stylised sets with retro props and vehicles designed to appeal to parents' sense of nostalgia.

Nono the Zigzag Kid is an international co-production from the BosBros stable, and is a representative example of the broad array of children's films currently being made in the Netherlands. *Kauwboy*, with its sensory imagery and raw sense of reality, is the new odd one out.

"Trying to pinpoint what makes a good children's film is a rather frustrating exercise", says Redpath, "because the best films are often exceptions to any rule you might find. And we tend to select the exception rather than the rule."

KARIN WOLFS
Translated by Julian Ross

ESTHER SCHMIDT and SABINE VEENENDAAL, *The Dutch Touch. Vision and passion for children's films in the Netherlands,* Eye Film Institute, Amsterdam, 2012, 128 pp. Online: http://issuu.com/jannemieke/docs/thedutchtouch.

History

In Flanders Fields Museum Revisited

While Flanders prepares to devote the years 2014 to 2018 to large-scale commemoration of the First World War as part of a touristic-economic strategy designed to put a region and a brand (Flanders) on the map, the In Flanders Fields Museum has already set the ball rolling with a completely new scenography and a total area 50% larger than when it opened in 1998.[1]

The visitor is called on to "experience direct confrontation" with the First World War. For some years now there have been no surviving veterans of that conflict. Those who still have direct memories of the Great War – call them the last eye-witnesses – are now dying off. For instance, my mother, who was born in 1915, remembers the final Allied offensive in the autumn of 1918. She was then three years old, living near Kortrijk/Courtrai, and she remembers the German retreat and seeing British soldiers in kilts in the street. Now we shall never get closer than that. Very soon that war will slip away once and for all into the past and become as much a part of history as the Franco-Prussian conflict of 1870 or the Napoleonic wars.

The First World War began with a chain reaction of words and actions which everyone could see unfolding and nobody could get away from, and was greeted with euphoria on all fronts. Rarely has a war changed its features so rapidly: beginning with horses and chivalry, it ended with gas, tanks, utter degradation and horror. It was the first *Materialschlacht:* the machine-gun, together with artillery (responsible for two-thirds of all fatalities), changed the nature of warfare, in that from then on the advantage lay with the defender. This was the war in which for the first time fire was directed not at people but systematically and unremittingly at places, as the clear-sighted German writer Ernst Jünger commented. In the Great Mincing Machine individual acts of heroism no longer made any difference. In the slaughterhouses that were the field hospitals,

The burning Cloth Hall on November 21st 1914

constantly amputating and staunching the flow of blood, medicine advanced by leaps and bounds. And in 1918 Spanish 'flu, which would unleash a new genocide on Europe, was in the offing and the seeds of the next war were being sown.

At the end of the reorganised museum is a list of all the conflicts the world has known since the war which was to end all wars. The last item reads: "2011 – Révolution Syrienne" (sic).

The In Flanders Fields Museum, housed in Ypres' rebuilt Cloth Hall, tells the history of the First World War in terms of the West Flanders front: the invasion of Belgium and the early months of mobile warfare, the four years of static warfare in the Westhoek (from the beach in Nieuwpoort to the Leie in Armentières), the end of the war and its subsequent enduring commemoration. Over half a million Commonwealth troops died in the Ypres Salient: *a pars pro toto* of the Great War, which claimed approximately ten million victims.

To enhance the 'direct experience' element, on arrival every visitor receives their own poppy armband. A chip in the armband automatically

The Ypres Cloth Hall houses the In Flanders Fields Museum.

selects the appropriate language, enabling the visitor to discover four personal stories in the permanent exhibition. For instance, I was given among others the biographies of the curate Camille Delaere, who rendered exemplary service during Ypres' death-throes; a Canadian soldier killed near Ypres on his twenty-second birthday; a Belgian soldier killed just before the Armistice who was exhumed by his brother and transported on a barrow to his birthplace, the village of Oostvleteren, where the coffin had to stand for three days in the church porch because the pastor refused to reinter it.

At the end of the museum circuit Ypres seeks to promote itself as a town of peace. A message is sneaking into the museum. That doesn't bother me, but there is no need for it. Besides, learning *about* a war is not the same as learning *from* a war.

Compared with the original exhibition, there are more objects and less focus on war poetry. But the texts are well chosen: Stephan Zweig (who speaks critically of "Die great show Belgiens" that Ypres became after the war); John McCrae's inevitable poem 'In Flanders Fields'; and Ivor Gurney's heart-rending 'Memory, Let All Slip'. As for the images, paradoxically enough it is the non-'authentic' testimonies, those performed by actors, which make the greatest impression: a Flemish refugee telling his story;

four soldiers from four armies talking about the Christmas Truce; a curate from Dikkebus who fled to Reningelst and evokes life just behind the front in all its chaos and moral confusion; Fritz Haber, the chemist who perfected gas as a weapon of war and clinically demonstrates exactly what he planned and executed. But the testimony that most sticks in the mind is that of a doctor and two nurses. That was so, too, in the museum's original display. During my visit, this was the one thing that really impressed a chattering horde of fifteen-year-old English schoolgirls. Were they listening to the soundtrack composed especially for the museum (by Stuart Staples of the British group Tindersticks) which you hear (and don't hear) throughout your visit?

Now that the landscape has become the last surviving witness to the war, the museum is taking on the confrontation between the present day and the desolate, shell-torn countryside of the war years. Images of then and now jostle each other: today's modern piggeries, the green, well-tended meadows with idyllic round pools which are actually the flooded craters of old mines. It is astonishing to see how quickly a landscape recovers from total devastation (the agricultural areas were restored by about 1930; the urban areas took longer). The resilience of these landscapes and the shortness of human memory are preconditions for survival and continued exist-

An inside view of
the In Flanders
Fields Museum

ence. Fortunately Ypres has not remained the ruin ("holy ground") which Churchill had wanted to acquire for the British Commonwealth after 1918. And even the Menin Gate, described as a "sepulchre of crime" by Siegfried Sassoon on its dedication in 1927, has developed a patina which makes it an impressive commemorative monument. Not least because the 'Last Post' is sounded there every evening, a ritual that survives, and is stronger than ever, precisely because it has become meaningless, so that everyone – from firebrands to pacifists – can make it their own.

It was a good idea to incorporate the Cloth Hall's bell-tower into the museum circuit. This building, once the largest civil structure in Western Europe, came to symbolise British resistance in the Ypres Salient – especially after it had gone up in flames and been gradually reduced to rubble by the German artillery. Via a kind of Google Earth one can look at an aerial photo of the building as it is today and then gradually zoom back to the gaping ruin of 1917. These days, from the top of the rebuilt tower one can take in the landscape for miles around: from the Menin Gate to the ridge with Mesen church (once painted by Hitler) over the Flemish hills (Kemmelberg, Rode- and Zwarteberg, Catsberg and Casselberg, from which the French Marshal Foch observed Ypres), to Boezinge, the Ijzertoren, Langemark (where in 1914 the flower of German youth was cut to pieces by the British machineguns) and Passendale. ("I died in hell - / (They called it Passchendaele)", Sassoon).

"The In Flanders Fields Museum requires an attentive spectator and reader. It is a museum of peace that, dedicated to all wars, selects just one of them and puts it on the map: Ypres, so methodically laid waste, as the perfect *pars pro toto*. It is rooted in the region but is nowhere provincial, if only because you constantly hear and read four languages." That is what I wrote of the museum in 1998. And that judgment stands. More than that: In Flanders Fields has become the ideal starting point for a visit to the front line around Ypres. The Australian couple I met on the tower, who had come to Ypres straight from the American war cemeteries in Normandy, agreed with me on that.

LUC DEVOLDERE
Translated by Tanis Guest

www.inflandersfields.be.

NOTE

1. LUC DEVOLDERE, *Emotion at the Museum. In Flanders Fields*, in: *The Low Countries* 7, 1999, pp.273-275.

Versatile Uniformity
The Life of Jacob Revius (1586-1658)

The polymath or Renaissance man, so common in the sixteenth and seventeenth centuries, is a rarity today. The ideal expresses a culture of versatility which we have come to view with suspicion these days. A scientist who seeks to be politically active or a painter who wishes to write historical studies must surely be doomed to failure on one or both sides, according to current thinking.

The seventeenth century theologian Jacob Revius is an example of the early modern culture of versatility. In her excellent biography of Revius, titled *Eerst de waarheid, dan de vrede* (Truth before peace),[1] Enny de Bruijn presents a nuanced and persuasive portrait of a thinker whose work and ideas bring to life a fascinating period in seventeenth century cultural history.

Revius was not only a theologian and poet; he was also an author of historical studies on the papacy and Deventer, the city where he spent most of his life. Moreover Revius was closely involved in the large translation project which culminated in 1637 in the Statenbijbel, the Dutch Authorised Version of the Bible.

The connecting themes of Revius' activities were his faith and his belief that the basis of faith could be found in the word of God, as expressed uniformly and therefore unmistakably in the Bible. His poetry, sermons, historical work and countless theological disputes all serve to elaborate on that word.

Like most prominent theologians of the Dutch Republic in the seventeenth century, Revius belonged to the Dutch Reformed Church, and was therefore a Calvinist. His grandfather, the mayor of Deventer, belonged to the earliest generation of Protestants in the Netherlands. Revius himself is known as a representative of the orthodox Gomarist movement. In the past some have seen him as a strict hardliner, but De Bruijn's biography suggests we should moderate this view.

According to her, Revius was no Voetius, the most inflexible of the Gomarists, who emerged in Dutch cultural history as a fierce adversary of the philosophical and scientific modernism represented by Descartes around the middle of the seventeenth century.

Revius, too, was apprehensive about what he thought would be the disastrous consequences of the philosophy of Descartes, who wrote his most important works while in the Dutch Republic. In Revius' eyes Descartes' mechanistic worldview, combined with his defence of strict rationalism, must inevitably lead to denial of the importance of God, and in turn to the undermining of the worldview based on the creator's omnipotence. Revius saw the creation as God's second book, secrets of nature unmistakably reflecting the Bible. Anyone seeking to penetrate beyond visible reality must read the Bible, according to Revius: then the divine context of the universe would become clear. In the mid seventeenth century increasing numbers of scientists argued for an approach founded on empirical experimentation, not on the authority of tradition. Revius' worldview was threatened. After all, experiments contradicted tradition increasingly frequently and directly.

In the last decades of his life Revius fought day after day to maintain his theocentric worldview, a fight that we, as heirs of the Enlightenment, know he was doomed to lose. In 1642 he became head of the State College of Leiden University, where students of theology were educated, future clergymen who must keep the country on the path of true belief. The young men beneath him were often drawn to Descartes and even some of Revius' colleagues enthusiastically embraced the new philosophy.

De Bruijn's recent biography of Revius pays more attention to his life as a theologian than as a writer. He is not, however, the prototypical poet-pastor whose literary work is little more than theology in verse. Both Conrad Busken Huet and Martinus Nijhoff urged people to read Revius'

Jacob Revius © Wikimedia

poetry. His poetic voice reflects the core of his faith (the best known sonnet beginning with the line *"It was not the Jews, Lord Jesus, who crucified you"*, translation by Charles D. Tate). Here is an individual who professes his belief sensitively, but for whom the individual experience must be raised to a higher collective level. Revius expresses more than personal truth: it is a broadly applicable message that deserves to be disseminated for its universality.

JÜRGEN PIETERS
Translated by Anna Asbury

NOTE

1. ENNY DE BRUIJN, *Eerst de waarheid, dan de vrede, Jacob Revius* 1586-1658, Boekencentrum, Zoetermeer, 2012, 450 p. Available in Dutch only.

Gruuthuse Manuscript Back in Bruges

In February 2007, Flanders was startled by the news that the Gruuthuse Manuscript, which was compiled in Bruges around 1400 and contains, among other things, the oldest collection of Dutch songs with musical notation, had been sold to the National Library of the Netherlands in The Hague. The sale exposed a painful void in the policy on Flemish literary heritage, but it did mean that the manuscript, which had been in private hands, was now more accessible to researchers and the general public than it had ever been before. In collaboration with the Huygens Institute of the Royal Netherlands Academy of Arts and Sciences (KNAW), the National Library of the Netherlands created an excellent website that enables the reader to browse the manuscript in any direction, with a transcription of the texts and extensive expert commentary (see the information at the end of the article). Soon after, it was agreed with the city of Bruges that the National Library would collaborate in putting on a prestigious exhibition featuring this literary monument.

The exhibition has now been organised. It is called *Love and Devotion. The Gruuthuse Manuscript* and will be held till 23 June in the Gruuthuse Museum in Bruges. After a long absence, the manuscript will return to the palace of the wealthy nobleman, courtier, soldier and diplomat after whom it is named, Louis de Gruuthuse (c. 1427-1492). It must have been part of De Gruuthuse's valuable collection of books, the second largest in the Low Countries after that of the Dukes of Burgundy.

The Gruuthuse Manuscript is less ornate than the dozens of manuscripts owned by Louis de Gruuthuse, most of which are beautifully illuminated and date from several decades later. It is not known how the manuscript came to be part of Louis' collection. According to certain respected Bruges historians, it was never actually owned by him. They claim that the ownership mark on the recto side of the second folio - the Gruuthuse coat of arms surrounded by the chain of the prestigious Order of the Golden Fleece, to which Louis was admitted on 2 May 1461 - was forged in the eighteenth century in an attempt by the previous owners to give their family a noble lineage dating back to the Middle Ages. Researchers are currently using advanced techniques to analyse the ink in order to clarify the matter.

The manuscript owes its fame to the fact that it has given us several of the most beautiful Middle Dutch songs: the obscene *Het soude een scamel mersenier* (He was just a poor soldier of fortune), the moving elegy *Egidius, waer bestu bleven* (Egidius, where are you), the aggressive Kerelslied (Song of the churls), the airy *Aloeette voghel clein* (Aloette, my thrush, my sweet), the sombre and almost despairing *Vaer wech, Ghepeins* (Go away, thoughts). These songs are some of those most frequently included in anthologies of Dutch literature. The Gruuthuse Manuscript also contains the oldest - and largest - collection of profane lyric in Dutch with music notation from the Middle Ages: more than 150 songs in total.

Much less well known are the seven prayers that precede the collection of songs. Several of the prayers are very skilfully adorned with acrostics en virtuoso rhyme schemes. One of the prayers, a paraphrase of the *Salve Regina*, was composed with an acrostic by Jan van Hulst, who also immortalised his name in one of the sixteen poems that follow the songs and form the third part of the manuscript. This poet must have been a veritable jack-of-all-trades: he was not only a civic official but also a formidable cultural entrepreneur, attending royal visits, the Procession of the Holy Blood in Bruges, and performances of polyphonic song. He was also an acclaimed illustrator of manuscripts. Late in life he founded the Holy Spirit brotherhood, which later became the Chamber of Rhetoric of the same name in Bruges.

Although the sixteen poems make up by far the largest part of the manuscript, they are the least well known. They include love allegories in

The Gruuthuse Museum
in Bruges

the tradition of the French *Roman de la Rose* and the great allegories by French poets such as Guillaume de Machaut and Jean Froissart, as well as poems that are largely moralising or devotional in character. They are about suffering, the joys of Easter, and the vanities of this world. Notably, in one of the poems, spiritual love and profane love are weighed against each other.

One of the love allegories contains the acrostic Jan Moritoen. Klaas Heeroma, who published the songs in 1966, attributes all the amorous songs and poems to Moritoen and interprets them as an autobiographical account of a tumultuous and ultimately unsuccessful love life. We now know that Moritoen was a well-to-do furrier who even became alderman of Bruges. Heeroma's hypothesis therefore seems unlikely, and one can even wonder whether Jan Moritoen is mentioned not as the author of the poem but as the person who commissioned it. One poem certainly featured prominently in the highest circles of Bruges society: it was read aloud when the Feast of the Epiphany was celebrated by the *Witte Beer*, an elite jousting company whose members were predominantly burgomasters, aldermen, councillors, nobles and members of the urban patriciate. With its emphasis on fostering brotherly love in the city, the poem gives the impression that it was intended to calm the serious political strife that divided the elites of Bruges at the beginning of the fifteenth century.

Today, six centuries later, the Gruuthuse Manuscript provides fascinating insights into cultural, religious and political life in late-mediaeval Bruges. That is also the purpose of the exhibition: using the themes of love, devotion, *const* (skill, craft), music and kinship, it sets out to give visitors an impression of the lives of the urban elite at the beginning of the golden age of Bruges.

FRANK WILLAERT
Translated by Yvette Mead

www.kb.nl/bladerboeken/het-gruuthuse-handschrift

Love and Devotion. The Gruuthuse Manuscript,
till 23 June 2013 at the Gruuthuse Museum in Bruges
(www.museabrugge.be - www.liefdeendevotie.be).

Jan Frans Gratiaen
Michael Ondaatje's Ancestor from Flanders

The Canadian author Michael Ondaatje (1943) is best known for *The English Patient*. He was born in British Ceylon. In 1992 he founded the *Gratiaen Trust* for Sri Lankan-born authors writing in English. The Trust is named after his mother. She is descended from Jan Frans Gratiaen (1727-1788) from Bruges, founding father of a Dutch Burgher dynasty in Ceylon. Ondaatje briefly mentions the Flemish roots of his family tree in *Running in the Family* (1982). The June 2012 issue of Flanders' cultural heritage journal *De Biekorf* (The Beehive) searched the Bruges city archive for more. Consider this article as a birthday present for Ondaatje, 70 this year (2013).

Jan Frans was born and baptized in Bruges on the 1st of March 1727, a son of Michiel Gratiaen and Isabella de Cock. Michiel, like his father Pieter, was a weaver of *fustein* – a type of cloth made from hemp and cotton – and a member of the guild. When his business fell into debt he fled Bruges, leaving his family behind. Jan Frans grew up in an era of general hardship and crisis as a result of poor harvests and armed conflicts fought out in Flanders. He left Bruges in January 1746, aged eighteen, to board a ship of the *Verenigde Oostindische Compagnie* or VOC (Dutch East India Company).

In June he disembarked at the Cape on the southern tip of Africa. He stayed a couple of months (maybe his father lived there) before moving on to Ceylon, which was VOC trade territory. He arrived there in August 1747. He was listed as a musician, so it is likely he went for a job as such. As a member of a military band, he may have performed at social functions attended by his future wife, Anna Aletta Kokaart (or Cocquaart). She was fifteen when he married her in Colombo in December 1748. Five boys and two girls were born between 1750 and 1768. Ondaatje's mother, Doris Gratiaen, is descended from the youngest son Pieter Liebert (1766-1803),

Michael Ondaatje © Linda Spal

a Lutheran clergyman who studied in Germany.

Jan Frans did not pursue a military music career. In 1752 he was registered as an *ambtenaar*
(civil servant) of the VOC. In 1758 he was a clerk
in the consumer goods registration office in Cal-
petty, opposite the Dutch stronghold of Tutucorin, India. In 1759 and 1762 he was sworn in as
secretary (keeper of secrets) of the magistrate of
police. In 1770 he oversaw the arreek trade in Colombo, involving the buying, storing and selling of
areca palm tree nuts, used for the manufacture
of sirih, which people all over Asia like to chew.
Two years later he was a *fiscaal* (a magistrate
in the local courthouse), secretary and bookkeeper in Tutucorin. In 1776 he was registered
as an *onderkoopman*, a junior merchant serving
a VOC director of trade (*opperkoopman*). In 1783
he was a *fiscaal* and cashier in the southern Cey-
lonese province of Galle. Four years later he was
Galle's general overseer of trade, possessing a
coat of arms and a motto: *Depressa Resurgo* (I
rise from the depths). He had not, however, risen
to the highest ranks. When he died (1788), he had
eight grandchildren. In 1796 the British took over
Ceylon. The island's European establishment, including the Gratiaens, became anglicised.

In 1792 *Redeneeringen over nuttige muzikaale
onderwerpen* (Argumentations about Useful Musical Subjects), attributed to Jan Frans Gratiaen appeared posthumously as a large chapter
in Volume Six of the *Verhandelingen* (Journal or
Yearbook) of the *Bataviaasch Genootschap van
Kunsten en Wetenschappen* (Batavian Society of
Arts and Sciences). In her 2001 dissertation, *De
Taal der Hartstochten* (The Language of the Passions), Els Strategier states that Gratiaen literally copied the work from the original by Jacob
Lustig (1706-1796). Born in Hamburg, Germany,
Lustig was the long-time organist of the Protestant Martini church in Groningen in the Nether-
lands. He wrote in Dutch.

Lustig's *Twaalf Redeneringen over Nuttige
Muzikale Onderwerpen* (Twelve Argumentations
about Useful Musical Subjects) were published

in 1756 in twelve monthly instalments and afterwards compiled and sold as a book. A prime
mover of music criticism and inventor of the
music magazine, Lustig spotted the widening
gap between composers and audiences and he
tackled all relevant musical questions. Lustig
was the best possible Dutch language source for
Gratiaen to study through copying.

In his foreword Gratiaen mentioned that he
had attended opera performances at the Monnaie theatre (opened in 1700) in Brussels. In Paris he had met the famous violin teacher and virtuoso Jean-Marie Leclair. He complained about
the predicament i.e. virtual absence of western
concert music in Ceylon. Getting hold of Lustig's
work when he had already spent many years in
the East, the new ideas presented there must
have reminded Gratiaen how swiftly western
music was developing, while he himself could
not participate.

Did Gratiaen himself want his manuscript to
be published? Son-in-law Willem Sebastiaan
Boers, married to Gratiaen's youngest daughter,
Johanna Gerrardina, was a relative of Frederik
Willem Boers, a staff lawyer of Iman Wilhelm
Falck, the Governor of Ceylon. Willem S. Boers
was co-opted as a member of the Batavian Society of Arts and Sciences. When the Society's
editorial board was in desperate need of material for its 1792 issue, Boers may have suggested
publishing Gratiaen's manuscript. Printing copied manuscripts, often anonymously, was still
common practise for the sake of propagating
ideas and notions considered important. It would
have been too late for Boers to check the origins
of his father-in-law's manuscript. Or perhaps
Boers was instructed by the Gratiaen family in
Ceylon. In any case, Batavia's learned men were
unable to recognize an existing text. Just the
same, the Gratiaen name lives on to stimulate
creative writing.

LUTGARD MUTSAERS

285

Literature

© Jean Paul Yska

Green Pastures
Rutger Kopland (1934-2012)

The wave of secularisation that swept across Western Europe from the 1960s onwards had a liberating effect on many intellectuals. In the Northern Netherlands certainly, where Protestant churches had had a firm grip on the spiritual life of large groups of Christians, demythologisation was seen as a triumph. But God's departure left a formidable vacuum, since from now on one was left to one's own devices. If there is one Dutch poet whose work testifies to that laborious process, it is Rutger Kopland, the pseudonym of the psychiatrist and neuroscientist Rudi van den Hoofdakker (1934-2012). His first collection, *Onder het vee* (Among the Cattle), from 1966, opens with a psalm that in the meantime has become a classic, whose first stanza reads as follows:

> *The green pastures the still waters*
> *on the wallpaper in my room -*
> *as a frightened child I believed*
> *in wallpaper*
> (transl. James Brockway)

Kopland's early work has often been called ironic and melancholy, but what also strikes one on rereading it is a bitterness that issues from disappointment. The series *G* (1978) attempts in nine failed sonnets to confront and understand the painful absence of God. I wrote, says Kopland, a poem about G's face, about how 'it was so absent, I likened it / to water in which I could see the face / of a horse,' but when I looked up 'the far bank was deserted'. A typical feature of Kopland's poetry is the distance he creates by not so much presenting the simile itself, but rather the process of searching for a suitable image for what at the same time is and is not there. It is also Kopland's calm, reflective, conversational tone, without any striking rhythmical or musical effects, which creates the impression that the speaker has a somewhat detached view of the drama. He tries to cut big things down to size to make them manageable.

As he grew older, partly perhaps because he had a demanding job as a university professor that left him little time to explore his poetic world exhaustively, his poems became cooler, and more conceptual. The world had to speak for itself. That is not always successful, but it is in the series *Dankzij de dingen* (Thanks to the Things, 1989):

> *The morning when things reawaken,*
> *low light appears from the*
> *mahogany, table silver and china,*
>
> *the bread smells of bread again,*
> *the flowered teapot of tea*

Things reawaken and come to life, which has the irrevocable implication that they will at some point die again: 'The night in which things again become shadows / of themselves.'

Death is undoubtedly the principal theme of all poetry, and Kopland's work is no exception. If initially transience is still seen as a loss that saddens us, the poet gradually develops a mild kind of lucidity, which realises, indeed with a certain amused bewilderment, his total futility. True, the landscape of Northern Drenthe, where he lives, reminds him of the paradise that was held out to him as a prospect in his youth, but in the late work it is mainly an ancient location that takes no account of man's brief presence. The longer he looks at the farmland and the river, the stranger the surroundings become: 'all those years that I sat here looking, I've seen / the familiar change into / the unfamiliar, and return again' (2003).

The imperturbability of the landscape actually acquires a consoling quality. When the poet returns home after a period of illness, he observes that 'the garden is not altered / for it I've not been away' (2008). The garden does not remember him, it 'is there, just as I is there too.' Every metaphysical vista has collapsed in the previous half century. We are here; any spiritual connection is a mental construction and after a relatively short time we are reabsorbed into non-being. The analogy between the garden and the speaker suggests that the landscape is not granted eternity either.

In the Dutch-speaking world Kopland has always been a popular and fêted poet. Readers, particularly contemporaries, have sought solace in his casual wisdom. The street noise of our age scarcely penetrates this poetry, with the result that the poems evoke the atmosphere of a traditional agricultural Netherlands that was rapidly being swept away. It sometimes made this poetry rather too sedate, but does provide a space for spiritual reflection, albeit abandoned by God. I don't know how long people will continue to read Kopland, but it is crystal clear that his work has fulfilled an important function in the post-war Netherlands.

PIET GERBRANDY
Translated by Paul Vincent

JAMES BROCKWAY, *Memories of the Unknown*
(intro. J.M. Coetzee), Harvill, London, 2001
WILLEM GROENEWEGEN, *What Water Left Behind*,
Waxwing Poems, Dublin, 2005
RIA LEIGH-LOOHUIZEN, *An Empty Place to Stay*,
Twin Peaks Press, San Francisco, 1977

A Cutting Critic
Gerrit Komrij (1944–2012)

In 2012 Dutch literature lost Gerrit Komrij, poet, novelist, critic and anthologist; altogether a cultural institution.

Two days after Komrij's death my eye fell upon an obituary in a Spanish newspaper describing him as 'the national poet of the Netherlands'. That is correct, as Komrij held the title 'Poet of the Fatherland' for some time but it is also laughable, because the title is largely ironic, a sort of trophy for poets who compose in response to national current affairs. Komrij was an important poet, but not the greatest in the Netherlands, so what was it that gave him his unmistakably central place in Dutch literature?

Leaving a degree in Dutch literary theory at the University of Amsterdam unfinished, Komrij turned to literature in 1967 at the age of 23, first as a poet and editor at a publishing house, and later as a literary critic.
When Komrij started work as a critic he was still a young, unknown poet. After his poetic debut in 1968 with *Maagdenburgse halve bollen* (Magdeburg hemispheres) his criticism was a shock to the system, a noble stranger lashing out in elegantly written reviews, setting to work on established names with merciless sarcasm. Komrij's reviews were a punishment for some, a source of malicious pleasure for others. Komrij was notorious, claiming afterwards, 'at the time I had no idea of the effect of my articles, just as you realise only later that you looked just fine when you were young and unhappy.'

Komrij stopped reviewing at the end of the 1970s because he felt too much a part of that 'little world'. Nevertheless he remained active as an essayist and opinion former. He targeted TV – the neologism 'treurbuis', meaning 'sad box', was his – as well as architecture, modern art and politics. The range might seem broad, but there was an overarching theme: in all these domains Komrij sought to combat amateurism and slop-

Gerrit Komrij© Paul Levitton

piness. He was annoyed by praise for lack of literary technique, the fact that there were no entrance exams for representatives of the people, and so on. He hated people who hid their sloppy thinking behind jargon, and believed that writing a clear poem was much more difficult than writing an airtight poem. In keeping with this conviction, his poetry, although melancholy, was accessible and he did not shy away from humour. In addition to a great deal of non-fiction and poetry, Komrij published a handful of novels, the most important of which is *Verwoest Arcadië* (Arcadia Destroyed). In this semi-autobiographical work Komrij appears in the form of Jacob Witsen, a homosexual boy who lives mainly inside his own head. The outside world cannot compare to the fairytale he has made up for himself, but it gradually encroaches, as the boy grows up and must find his place in a continually disappointing reality. This book is effectively Komrij's declaration of his critical attitude to reality, the cabaret side to his personality and his predilection for playing with identity and masks.

The search for the lost Arcadia was to continue later. Komrij tried to emigrate to Greece when he was twenty, and moved to Portugal for good in 1984, together with Charles Hofman, the artist who had been his life partner since 1964.

Komrij has become a household name chiefly for his work as an anthologist. Being a cultural glutton and bibliophile, he had a broad general knowledge which helped him in compiling all kinds of anthologies. His best known work is *De Nederlandse poëzie van de 19de en 20ste eeuw in 1000 en enige gedichten* (Dutch poetry of the 19th and 20th centuries in 1001 poems), which really caused a stir among his peers. Each new edition of Komrij's weighty tome caused further ructions in the Republic of Letters. Poets gauged their importance by it: were they mentioned, and if so, how many poems were included? Those excluded could always claim to be proud of the fact. According to fellow writer and monument Jeroen Brouwers, Komrij's anthologies rescued more writers from obscurity than any museum of literary history.

Gerrit Komrij was born on 30th March 1944 in Winterswijk, in the province of Gelderland. He died, after a brief illness, in Amsterdam on 5th July 2012. Between those dates he became one of the best known faces of Dutch literature. He leaves behind his life partner, and a melancholy, hilarious, acerbic and extensive body of work.

MARK CLOOSTERMANS
Translated by Anna Asbury

Leonard Nolens
© Stad Brugge

Leonard Nolens
Winner of the Dutch Literature Prize

The Dutch Literature Prize, the most important literary award in the Dutch language area, was presented to the Antwerp poet Leonard Nolens (b. 1947) by Queen Beatrix of the Netherlands at the end of 2012. Since his debut with *Orpheushanden* (Orpheus hands, 1969), Nolens has published more than twenty poetry collections and five diaries. The anthologies *Manieren van leven. Gedichten 1975-2011* (Ways of living. Poems 1975-2011) and *Dagboek van een dichter* (A poet's diary)[1] each number more than a thousand pages.

The picture that emerges from Nolens' diaries is one of someone balancing between shunning and accepting publicity: a hermit writer who at the same time participates in the artistic life of Antwerp. Those who consider such things important are firmly put straight by Nolens: 'The diary isn't there to tell the story of your days, but to recount what they do with you'. Backing up this standpoint, the scarce anecdotal material serves to support his vision of poetry as something that is absolutely rooted in life, that flows through the finest blood vessels, and as something in which Nolens has invested himself totally. He is someone who has 'made a profession of his soul'.

Nolens' poems are both an analysis of that soul and a justification of his existence, his birth certificate. Without poetry, this poet does not exist. No surprise, then, that virtually all his collections begin with one or more 'birth poems'. Nolens then repeatedly confronts the identity that he has brought to life in his poetry with love (a second crucial theme in his work) and with a series of questions on how to live. He also not infrequently addresses other poets - linguistic compatriots and contemporaries, but also major dead poets such as Eugenio Montale, Osip Mandelstam, Paul Celan, Joseph Brodsky. These poems are homages, all of which also serve to define the place of Nolens himself.

Focused on communication as it is, this is a highly rhetorical and musical poetry. Nolens has given a strong impetus to a tradition which appeared outmoded. That is not simply a question of metre and rhyme: repetitions, shifts, contrasts, changes in tempo - his arsenal of musical techniques is inexhaustible; every single word contributes to an often stupefying array of sound variations.

For Nolens, music is a matter not just of form, but of an attitude to life. In his own words, he seeks to imbue his poetry with the 'musically controllable tone of honesty'; 'the notes of a musical grammatology' enable him to write 'a rounded text which gave me (...) a childhood of song and vibrancy, swaddled me in a warmth that was later lost in this adult universe which has lost the ability to resonate'. This is a reference to the major role played by music in his childhood. In the well-to-do bourgeois family in which Nolens grew up, in the little Limburg town of Bree, the grand piano was a constant companion. At the same time, as he writes in one of the many poems in which Bree figures, his family was 'a family of businessmen, teachers, priests, / Men who know the value of a word, the meaning of a number'.

As so often, this apparently prosaic observation is a subtle amalgamation of concepts, with the juxtaposition of 'meaning', which in the first instance is associated with 'word'', and 'value' which alludes to 'number' [in Dutch, the distinction is even finer, with *berekent* (= calculate) being switched with *betekent* (= mean)]. Nolens also repeatedly juxtaposes personal and possessive pronouns as a way of intimately linking personae, as in the final line of one of his 'birth poems': 'I cannot leave my room of yours'.

In recent collections, Nolens has increasingly become a commentator on his time and his generation. In *Bres* (2004), he presents a critique of the 1960s in poetic form. Where the slogan in 1968 was 'all power to the imagination', Nolens focuses attention on those who were striving for the same things at that time, but who wished to express themselves more subtly than through slogans: 'We were not some poetic theme of Mao. / We thought, we are making our own poetry. / We thought, we are making history here / On the quiet'.

And in his most recent collection, *Zeg aan de kinderen dat wij niet deugen* ('Tell the children we're no good', 2011), Nolens turns his attention to the legacy we will leave behind: 'Tell the children we're no good. / They'll have to pay for the dung pit, the cesspit / That we dug in our field of clouds, they'll have to / Clear out the celestial sewers, that dumping ground / Of shit and azure that the Ancients sang of'.

But even in this strongly ethical and socially critical poetry, music continues to dominate, the language dances. Nolens is like a dervish[2] who dances his truth to life.

AD ZUIDERENT
Translated by Julian Ross

NOTES

1. See *The Low Countries*, XIX, 2011, pp. 92-101.

2. *Derwisj* (Dervish) is also the title of a Leonard Nolens collection published in 2003.

Retranslating Couperus

It is a truism that good works of literature outlast their translations. A Dutch evergreen like *Max Havelaar* (1860) has been rendered three times into English, and in each case – as was brilliantly demonstrated by Ria Vanderauwera[1] – not merely updated but radically 'reframed'. Van Nouhuys (1868) presented the reader with a documentary exposé of colonial abuse, Siebenhaar (1927) with a biting satire that delighted D.H. Lawrence, and Edwards (1967) with a scrupulously annotated classic.

I myself have twice had first-hand experience of retranslation. On each occasion this involved novels by Louis Couperus, *Langs lijnen van geleidelijkheid* and *De stille kracht*, both published in 1900.[2] Both books had been previously translated by Alexander Teixeira de Mattos (1865-1921),[3] a Dutchman resident in England since childhood who became Couperus's regular translator. The first novel, in which a married woman flees to Italy, where she lives with a young Dutch artist before returning to her husband, might have been republished unchanged, but there were three principal objections to this: a) some scenes had been bowdlerised in response to the rather Puritan English publishing climate at the time; b) the book needed contextualising within Couperus's oeuvre, as a response to the contemporary debate on feminism, and as an example of the genre of boarding house fiction; c) the tendentious English title (*The Inevitable* in the US and, even worse, *The Law Inevitable* in the UK) begged the central question in the book: was Cornélie's submission to her husband the only possible outcome? In the retranslation a) presented no problems and b) was addressed in an afterword, but my alternative title suggestions regarding c) (*Little by Little* or *Slowly but Surely*) were overruled by the publisher, who opted for a modified version of the original American title. Dissenting from this choice, I suggested, not wholly tongue in cheek, that modern readers might wish to supply their own mental question mark.

The case of *The Hidden Force*, with its colonial East Indies setting, was more complex. In De Mattos' version the sex scenes had again been bowdlerised, but in 1985 an edition was published by the University of Massachusetts Press in the prestigious *Library of the Indies series*, in which the editor, E.M. Beekman, while retaining the bulk of De Mattos' text for reasons of 'congruence of tone with the original', restored suppressed passages, corrected a number of minor slips, and abandoned the titles 'sahib' and 'memsahib' as too closely associated with the

British Raj. In addition, there was an extensive apparatus of introduction and notes and a glossary of Malay terms.

So why retranslate? Beekman's strategy of inserting omitted passages into De Mattos' translation seemed an uneasy compromise, in which contemporary American slang rubbed shoulders with early-twentieth-century British English. The plethora of Malay words was a cumulative distraction, and two crucial terms were potentially misleading. I therefore retained a minimum number of Malay terms for local colour, explained them in the text on first occurrence, and replaced 'resident' (senior Dutch colonial official) and 'regent' (government-appointed native chief) with '(district) commissioner' and 'prince' respectively. Finally, the academic apparatus, aimed more at students and scholars than at the general reader, was replaced by an afterword in which Ian Buruma expertly positioned the book within the Dutch colonial experience.

The complicating factor in this case was that the University of Massachusetts translation was still in copyright, so that my primary task, besides producing an accurate, readable and atmospheric version, was to avoid any suggestion of plagiarism. This prolonged the translation process and required close scrutiny of both the Dutch source text and the 1985 composite translation.
The value of retranslation for successive generations depends of course in large measure on the quality of the extant versions. There seems, however, to be a tipping point after which the disadvantages (distance in time between source and target texts) are outweighed by the advantages (more accessible contemporary language, etc.). What in my view is *not* an option is a historicising or 'period' version. I was recently horrified to read in a literary journal that a translator preparing a new English version of *Madame Bovary* had acquired an 1850s French-English dictionary! Period flavour is all very well, but can easily slip into parody, which in my view does a disservice to the original.

My own plans after recent experiences? Though I prefer to work on first-time translations, where I have a freer hand, there is at least one Flemish classic I can think of that might benefit from less mid-Atlantic blur in vocabulary and syntax and more precision in rendering regionalisms. Whether a publisher will agree with me remains to be seen.

PAUL VINCENT

NOTES

1. 'Texts and Contexts of Translation. A Dutch Classic in English', *Dutch Crossing* 12 (December 1980), 34-54.

2. *Inevitable*, tr. Paul Vincent, London: Pushkin Press, 2005; *The Hidden Force*, tr. Paul Vincent, London: Pushkin Press, 2012.

3. *The Inevitable*, New York: Dodd, Mead & Co., 1920; *The Law Inevitable*, London: Butterworth Ltd, 1921. *The Hidden Force. A Story of Modern Java*, New York: Dodd, Mead & Co., 1921; London: Jonathan Cape, 1921

Music

An Alto under a Mop of Hair
The Success of Selah Sue

Her debut album has sold more than 200,000 copies already. She's had five gold records in Belgium, as well as gold in the Netherlands and platinum in France. In 2011 she received an EBBA, a prize which distinguishes her as one of the ten best European artists with cross-border success. Since then she has appeared at a great many summer festivals all over Europe, and the United States has also made her acquaintance. Selah Sue is her stage name and she boasts an imposing mop of hair piled up on top of her head. She was born Sanne Putseys in 1989 in the village of Leefdaal near Leuven. What is the secret of this young Flemish girl's success?

She's not yet 25, but has already been working with music for ten years. After a carefree childhood, Putseys' teenage years were emotionally turbulent, but in music she found a release. She started off strumming away at her guitar in her bedroom, venting her dark thoughts playing songs by - or influenced by - her idols, Erykah Badu, Lauryn Hill and Bob Marley. She then began to give sporadic performances in cafés and youth clubs in the Leuven area.

I saw Selah Sue give a concert in a café four years ago. She was nineteen then, and with a couple of her own numbers and a handful of covers of her favourite songs she had the rapt attention of the packed café. Along with the many other concertgoers, I heard and saw what Flemish singer-songwriter Milow (Jonathan Vandenbroeck) must have heard the year before when he "discovered" her at an open mic night in Leuven: "A girl, eighteen years old, a guitar and a voice. What a voice. I felt it immediately: this is huge."

It was lucky for Selah Sue that Milow crossed her path. He stood by her in word and deed. Not only was she his supporting act in Europe, he also advised her against signing with a big record company that was already waving a contract under her nose. It wanted to make her a pop princess: record a few prefabricated songs, take some glamorous photos while she was still young and try to make as much money out of her as possible in a short period of time. Say no and find your own way - that was Milow's advice.

Music manager Christoffel Cocquyt saw the young Selah Sue as Milow's supporting act. He

Selah Sue © Jean-Baptiste Mondino

immediately decided to take her under his wing and continues to advise her today. Concert organiser Werner Dewachter followed Cocquyt's lead. Together they form the business tandem which supports Selah Sue's musical talent.

In 2008-2009 the Ancienne Belgique (AB) in Brussels, one of the most important concert halls in Belgium, offered her the opportunity to be artist in residence, putting its knowledge at Selah Sue's disposal to jump-start her music career. She was supporting act at a couple of gigs, had a photo session and recorded several songs in a professional studio.

When she put the recordings on her MySpace page, she joined hundreds of thousands of others sharing their music with the world online. But Selah Sue stands out from the crowd with her alto voice and the rhythmic cadences that so impressed Milow and Cocquyt. Her numbers have masses of online hits and her name can be heard far outside professional music circles. She has transformed from the umpteenth teenager with a guitar into the next big thing in the Flemish pop world.

Still, it took until the spring of 2011 for her debut album, simply titled *Selah Sue*, to appear. Before producing the album she took the opportunity to grow further, writing songs and performing a great deal, in Belgium and abroad. There were other activities that will carry her name and fame further, too: a number of well-chosen TV appearances; collaboration with international artists (Moby and Cee Lo Green) and providing the supporting act for the international star Prince in front of an audience of almost 20,000. She also went in search of the right musicians and technicians to make her debut as professional and successful an album as possible. Her entourage picked Because Music, a French record company which has made Selah Sue an international top priority.

Her debut album came out simultaneously in the Benelux, France, Germany, Switzerland and Austria in March 2011, and later in the rest of Europe (except for the UK). You've already read the result in the first paragraph of this article: Europe has fallen for Selah Sue. The key factors are her voice, her songs (with their fluid mixing of black music genres such as soul and reggae) and her texts, in which she expresses her personal doubts and worries, always with an upbeat twist. Now Selah Sue is looking further afield, towards the United States. First a buzz was created around her name in the music world there. Perez Hilton's celebrity blog dropped her name a couple of times and then influential magazine *Rolling Stone* tipped her as one of the new faces of 2012. Selah Sue's debut album was officially launched in the States in 2012 by the renowned Columbia Records and received positive reviews. Her songs have been used in soundtracks for prominent TV series (including *Mad Men*) and in an advertisement for Yves Saint Laurent perfume, and she has appeared as the supporting act at a couple of concerts for other artists. But the US market is oversaturated and hard to penetrate, so it remains to be seen whether they will really be interested in a Belgian singer. Selah Sue and her entourage believe they can make it though, and are working hard. Her album is also set to go on sale in Japan, Australia and possibly in the UK.

Whatever her fate in the United States and further afield, Belgium and Europe are already eating out of young Sanne Putseys' hand. Perhaps the best indication of Selah Sue's success is this: a comedy sketch on Flemish TV recently parodied her characteristic voice, stuttering singing style and mop of hair. That kind of attention is generally reserved for politicians, media figures and members of the royal family.

PIETER COUPÉ
Translated by Anna Asbury

www.selahsue.com

Radiant with Soul and Inner Fervour
Alphons Diepenbrock (1862-1921)

After the death of Alphons Diepenbrock in 1921, it was soon discovered that the composer had lived exactly three hundred years after Jan Pieterszoon Sweelinck. This could not possibly be a coincidence. It was after all abundantly clear that Diepenbrock was the best composer the Northern Netherlands had produced since Sweelinck. And even now, when this point of view has been somewhat adjusted as a result of research in recent decades, Diepenbrock remains a composer who was unrivalled during his lifetime and is still considered the most prominent Dutch composer of the period from 1890 to 1925.

Alphons Diepenbrock was born into an important Catholic family in Amsterdam; his father was of high-minded Westphalian origin, his mother's family included both the Catholic leader Joseph Alberdingk Thijm and the Catholic architect Pierre Cuypers. The young Diepenbrock was introduced to the arts (music, architecture, literature) and the humanities at an early age. After his schooling at the gymnasium (± grammar school) he studied classical languages in Amsterdam, moving in circles that included poets, writers and thinkers (including the *Tachtigers*) and wrote his doctoral thesis on Seneca. At the same time it was clear to him that he was equally passionate about wanting to be a composer. But he did not study at a conservatory. This meant that, as a classicist, to many people he remained an amateur composer. He taught himself the craft, avoiding well-worn paths and rigid educational disciplines. Until 1895 he earned his living teaching classical languages at the gymnasium in 's-Hertogenbosch (in North Brabant) and after that by giving private lessons in Amsterdam.

With a career like this, he had to 'learn' to compose by actually doing it (score after score, and endless series of corrections), by listening (innu-

Alphons Diepenbrock (1862-1921)

merable concerts, fortunately sometimes of his own works) and by devouring one book of theory after another. He almost always had the feeling of falling short, was rarely content, complained of the toil that was his lot, and even more about the misfortune of having been born in the Netherlands. He detested the lack of culture in the Netherlands, hated the sombre and often cold weather, and frequently considered his own life a failure. His private life was also a struggle, both in his marriage to a strong protestant wife, Elisabeth de Jong van Beek en Donk, who gave him two daughters, and, on the other hand, his great love for the much younger pianist Johanna Jongkindt, who was his muse for more than ten years.

It was to Johanna that, in 1912, at the height of his fame, he wrote the following about his almost compulsive need to revise his compositions again and again: 'For me it's the only way to finally create things, even if only a few, that are utterly radiant with soul and inner fervour. What I have expressed in these works is my property and my life too.' Two years later, on 14th June 1914, he confirmed this in another letter to her: 'If I don't want to have worked for nothing all these years, and have the feeling of having failed completely, I have to raise those early works of mine that remain, and which I consider worthwhile, to the same technical standard as I am capable of now.'

In 1888 a new concert hall with its own orchestra was established in Amsterdam: the *Concertgebouw*. In 1895 the young Willem Mengelberg became the conductor of the orchestra, which soon became world famous. Diepenbrock became a friend of Mengelberg, was in certain respects able to guide him and, in his turn, had the opportunity to work with the orchestra himself after a few years. In this way his career as a composer ran largely in parallel with the successes of one of Europe's best orchestras, and he was able to make the acquaintance of such fellow composers as Mahler, Strauss and many other great masters, who like him were asked to come and conduct the orchestra.

Diepenbrock's oeuvre can be divided into music for the concert hall, for the theatre and for the church. What is more, almost everything he wrote is directly connected with language, with singing. His most remarkable composition, the *Missa in die festo* for tenor, male chorus and organ, consists of a mixture of Palestrina-style counterpoint and Wagnerian chromatics; it is exalted, intense in its faith, and has a unique sound. His best-known works are probably the compositions for the plays *Marsyas, of De betooverde bron* (Marsyas, or the Enchanted Spring, by the Dutchman Balthazar Verhagen, after Xenophon), *The Birds* (Aristophanes) and *Elektra* (Sophocles).

The majority of his oeuvre comprises songs accompanied by piano or orchestra. Each of his piano-accompanied songs, with words in French, German and Dutch, displays his exceptional sensitivity to language. He follows every turn and nuance of the language closely and provides it with a well-conceived interplay of lines and harmonic colour. The orchestral songs are at least as enchanting. The *Hymne an die Nacht* 'Gehoben ist der Stein' for soprano and orchestra (1899), the *Hymne an die Nacht 'Muss immer der Morgen wiederkommen'* for alto and orchestra (1899), *Im grossen Schweigen* for baritone and orchestra (1906) and *Die Nacht* for mezzo-soprano and orchestra (1911) are true symphonic poems with an *obbligato* vocal part and not just orchestrated piano songs. Even today, each and every one has the same eloquence and hymnic animation that they were praised for after their first performances.

In his major works, Alphons Diepenbrock tacked between his love of German culture (Brentano, Goethe, Nietzsche, Wagner, Mahler), French culture (Verlaine, Debussy) and Latin culture (Palestrina and the great Catholic thinkers). But ultimately what he left us is the always recognisable and unique music of Alphons Diepenbrock.

LEO SAMAMA
Translated by Gregory Ball

LEO SAMAMA, *Alphons Diepenbrock. Componist van het vocale* (Alphons Diepenbrock. Composer for the voice), Amsterdam University Press, 2012 (ISBN 978 90 8964 428 2).

2012 saw the issue of a new CD box: *Alphons Diepenbrock - Anniversary Edition*. It contains 8 CDs with almost 100 works, an extensive booklet and a bonus DVD with a live recording of the *Missa in die festo* at the *Concertgebouw* in Amsterdam (see www.etcetera-records.com).

Elections in the Netherlands
Blue And Red Join Forces

On the 12th of September 2012 Dutch voters went to the ballot box. For the fifth time in ten years the 150 members of the Second Chamber were elected. An election was necessary on account of the fall of the first Rutte cabinet. His party won the election. The liberals (VVD) had never done so well in the Netherlands before (41 seats). Just as two years previously, the social democrats (PvdA) were the party that came second (38 seats). So it looked as if little had changed, but that was just on the surface.

First let's go back to the previous elections. In 2010 it was also a battle between the VVD and the PvdA. Who would be Prime Minister, Mark Rutte or former mayor of Amsterdam Job Cohen? The latter lost the election by a narrow margin. Rutte became Prime Minister, but that only came about after an exasperatingly protracted formation period.

In the end the VVD was to take control together with the Christian democrats of the CDA. Both parties were far from having a majority, so they got support from the PVV, Geert Wilders' right-wing populist party. A new word made its entrance into Dutch politics: *gedoogsteun* (support on sufferance). The PVV didn't provide any ministers, yet did support the cabinet. Many of the rank and file of the CDA had enormous difficulty with this cabinet. They found it particularly difficult to stomach the co-operation with Wilders and his exceptionally harsh criticism of Muslims.

The Rutte I cabinet lasted two years. Eventually they could not agree over cuts. Wilders withdrew his support before the 2012 summer vacation, and on the 12th of September Holland had to go to the ballot box again.

The political landscape had changed somewhat in two years of 'Rutte'. At least, if you looked at the opinion poles. The traditional parties such as the CDA and PvdA were at around 15 (of the 150) seats and the liberals looked stable, but the SP, in particular, came out very high in the polls.

Mark Rutte

Diederik Samsom

The SP is the Socialist Party, which emerged in the early seventies from Maoists and Leninists. For years they were a party of agitators with a red tomato as their symbol.

The tomato has remained, but they are increasingly less 'anti'. The party has representatives in municipal councils and, more recently, at the provincial level too. The SP braced itself for participation in government in The Hague. The party leader, Emile Roemer, went into battle with Prime Minister Rutte.

For a long time it looked as if this would be the scenario for the elections. The leftist socialists and the liberals would fight for the top position. The old Christian and social democrats would be left behind and the greens wouldn't get a look in.

The election campaign proper started in Au-gust, with a new leader for the PvdA. Because the former Mayor of Amsterdam, Cohen, was languishing in the opposition, he was replaced by the energetic Diederik Samsom, a former Greenpeace spokesman and campaign leader. The campaign was carried out mainly on television. Debate after debate was to be seen on the box. Suddenly, from an impossible position, Samson came to the fore. The social-democrats shot up in the polls, following his win in the first debates.

The former Greenpeace man looked like a statesman, according to the analysis. He stood above the parties, didn't get involved in rows with anyone, maintained that co-operation was needed in a time of crisis, not polarisation. This message got through, at least in the polls. From a battle between Roemer and Rutte it turned into a battle between Samsom and Rutte. According to the viewers, Roemer, from the SP, wasn't doing as well in the debates, and his party dropped in the rankings. The further the Socialist Party dropped, the higher the star of the social democrats climbed.

In the final polls before the election VVD and PvdA stood at around 33 seats. But right up to the last minute more than forty percent of the Dutch population was still undecided as to how to vote. In the seventies it was clear who you were going to vote for, but in recent years Dutch voters seem to have lost all sense of direction. Populist parties became extremely popular. The party of Pim Fortuyn, who was shot dead in 2002, achieved a huge triumph in the election of that year (26 seats). When that party disappeared, Wilders, the Muslim hater, enjoyed enormous popularity (24 seats).

In the end, in 2012, the Dutch people voted for old established parties. Prime Minister Rutte's VVD grew even stronger and the PvdA followed close behind. The result was nothing at all like the polls from before the summer vacation. The electorate voted strategically, according to the analysis. Many voted for VVD to stop the PvdA from becoming too large, and vice versa. This did not give the SP the growth the party had hoped for (it stagnated at 15 seats), and the Greens were almost wiped out (down from 10 to 4 seats). Wilders' PVV fell right back (from 24 to 15) and the Christian democrats also had to lick their wounds (down from 21 to 13 seats). The only party of any size that seemed reasonably well able to resist the polarisation between VVD and PvdA was the leftist liberal D66 (from ten to twelve seats).

At the end of October 2012 the formation of a government with liberals and social democrats was completed. The Rutte II cabinet could get started. The VVD and the PvdA are parties full of contradictions, yet Rutte and Samsom were done and dusted in five weeks or so, unusually fast by Dutch standards. Savings of 16 billion euro had to be made. Mortgage interest relief (a tax concession for people paying off property loans) was scrapped, against the wishes of the liberals, and against the wishes of the social democrats the money for development co-operation was cut by one billion euro. Give and take. The latter didn't happen without a few skirmishes. In particular, Prime Minister Rutte had a lot of opposition from his own rank and file over the government's plans for levelling, whereby those with the broadest shoulders are to contribute more than the lowest paid. After some modification of the plans, the government could really get down to work. There is a problem in this in as much as although the government has a clear majority in the Second Chamber this is not the case in the Senate, the First Chamber. This means that there will have to be regular negotiations with the opposition to get legislation through parliament. So there'll have to be give and take there too.

Joris van de Kerkhof
Translated by Sheila M. Dale

The 2012 Local and Provincial Elections in Flanders

Just like all elections, the 14th October 2012 local and provincial elections in Flanders were described as important – but this time more so than ever. Before they actually took place they were proclaimed by the principal challenger, the N-VA and its Flemish nationalists, as a referendum on the federal government. Political opponents, who refused to recognize the national dimension to the local elections, could not prevent the local elections from also being seen as a sort of mid-term election between the federal elections of 2010 and the general election of 2014, which is already being hailed as "the mother of all elections". Because in 2014 the European, regional and federal parliaments will all be re-elected.

Seldom has there been more hype around elections than those of next year. In 2014, so certain analysts and quite a number of politicians dare to suggest (somewhat exaggeratedly), the Belgian model is at stake. That is why there was so much interest in the results of the October 2012 election: would N-VA be able to translate its electoral strength as the largest party in Belgium into local terms, or was it a question of the beginning of the decline of the party challenging the Belgian model? Would the traditional parties hold their ground, or would they fall further behind? The liberals of Open Vld were especially nervous, having seen a series of alarming opinion polls. The Christian Democrat CD&V wanted to maintain its position as the largest local party in Flanders. The Flemish socialists of sp.a were satisfied to remain stable, which would buck the

N-VA chairman Bart De Wever is the new mayor of Antwerp.
His party did well in the 2012 local and provincial elections in Belgium

trend of the continuing losses they had been suffering for years. In that respect it was also important how the other parties of the left, such as the Green party and the radical left PVDA+ would score locally. The far right Vlaams Belang wanted to avoid catastrophe. Following outright success in the local elections of 2006 the party started on a disastrous downward trend.

In addition, a handful of the major Flemish cities had the spotlight on them. During the campaign, which was given huge media attention, it seemed almost as if elections were only being organized in the ten major Flemish cities, there was relative silence over the remaining 307 municipalities. Above all, Antwerp, the principal city in Flanders, snatched an exceptional amount of attention, which meant the vote there was a kind of direct mayoral election between N-VA chairman Bart De Wever and the outgoing mayor, the socialist Patrick Janssens. In 2006 Janssens had defeated his great rival, Filip Dewinter, of Vlaams Belang, and in so doing had gathered a lot of "democratic forces" behind him. But with De Wever, and after six years in power, it was a different picture. People were watching for the N-VA score in a lot of other places, not just in Antwerp.

The 2012 local and provincial elections, as always, were about many varying questions, both local and national. In many cities and municipalities you could only explain the outcome by looking at the specific local context. This also explains why CD&V remained the largest local party. Yet these local elections also had a national dimension – local elections traditionally echo the national political trends. Without this it is difficult to explain why, frequently out of nowhere, N-VA suddenly broke through in so many cities. The party failed to reach the average figure that was predicted in national polls, but nonetheless took an enormous step forward and was the moral winner. Also because De Wever defeated Janssens convincingly in Antwerp, which meant that the Flemish socialists disappeared from the town hall of the biggest city in Flanders for the first time in ages.

Moreover, the provincial elections (second order elections in which voters show their naked preference, as it were, independently from what those elections are theoretically about) demonstrated that N-VA had lost none of its strength and is still on course for further growth in 2014. Although those same provincial elections also showed that CD&V are climbing out of the abyss. The battle for the centre is becoming unusually exciting in Flanders, which is so politically fragmented and volatile.

The predicted annihilation of Open Vld did not happen, so that they could be satisfied with a limited loss – although the score for the Flemish liberals remained below par. That was certainly the case for the Flemish socialists, the big loser in this election, together with Vlaams Belang. Vlaams Belang's defeat had already been announced beforehand and it was major too, which meant it attracted more attention than that of the sp.a. Compared with 2006, this party lost almost a quarter of its voters in the central Flemish cities that are so important to it. The gains in Ghent and Bruges were some consolation, but for sp.a this was the umpteenth defeat in a row. The Green party did relatively well, as indeed they did at the national level too, but they often had to form coalitions – sometimes of many hues – to get into power. It was not so easy under their own steam.

The surprise in these elections, which only came to light a few days later, was probably the strong score of the radical left PVDA+, in the small number of cities where the party had candidates. Although its success there was on a modest scale, symbolically it was significant: it cost sp.a in particular a lot of votes. PVDA+ was able to convince many voters in Antwerp with its active grassroots action – in those areas where the withdrawal of the socialists left the field open to politicians who were still prepared to appear on the street. Bart de Wever, for instance.

The local and provincial elections entailed no fundamental change compared with the federal outcome for 2010. In itself this tells us a lot: "the power of change" (the N-VA slogan) has so far failed to oust the power of the federal government parties. The shifts, compared with 2006, are considerable, but that was no surprise, since 2012 had been seen above all as a midterm election on the way to 2014. The federal government had shut up shop for it, as had also been the case to a large extent in 2006, and after the local elections it found itself confronted with a huge budgetary task in a climate that had been polarised by the local elections, because the N-VA beast seemed still to be untamed. So it was with some trepidation that the Flemish parties – certainly CD&V and Open VLD who have the most to fear from it – approached the delayed start to the federal political year 2012-2013, the last full year before the important confrontation in 2014.

The 14th October 2012 made itself felt for a while, but everyone is already looking towards June 2014.

CARL DEVOS
Translated by Sheila M. Dale

Science

Society on the Couch
Psychoanalyst Paul Verhaeghe's Cultural Criticism

Paul Verhaeghe, Professor of Clinical Psychotherapy at the University of Ghent, has been sparking debate in the Low Countries recently with his bleak cultural diagnosis. The target of his criticism is neoliberalism, which has elevated efficiency to the highest standard, and which equates success as a human being with productivity. This ideology has, Verhaeghe believes, penetrated every pore of our society, and even dominates our relationships with our bodies, partners and children.

Verhaeghe has for decades had a solid reputation within the scientific community as an expert on the work of Freud and Lacan. When *Does the woman exist?* (1987), the American version of his book *Tussen hysterie en vrouw*, was first published, it was praised by the high-profile Slovenian philosopher Slavoj Zizek as 'a must for anyone who wants to understand contemporary psychoanalysis'.

The psychoanalyst gained widespread fame at the end of the 1990s with his bestseller *Love in a Time of Loneliness* (1998), an in-depth and provocative analysis of the frictions that exist between men and women following the fragmentation of traditional power structures and the corresponding division of roles, which was translated into eight languages including English. But his public reputation really took off with the publication of *The End of Psychotherapy* (2009), in which he declares war on the currently widespread idea that all psychological problems are illnesses. These illnesses are attributed to faulty hereditary makeup or disorderly neurons inside the brain, and are best dealt with by pills.

In The End of Psychotherapy, Verhaeghe describes a new type of psychological complaint which he is seeing increasingly in his private psychotherapy practice, namely that of patients who have not been able to construct any kind of stable identity. They are empty and aggressive and, in

Paul Verhaeghe

the absence of an idea of who they are, latch onto their own bodies. Verhaeghe sees the disintegration of stable social groups as the main reason for the emergence of these new types of psychological disturbance. One develops an identity, the psychoanalyst claims, by emulating a group with which one, unsurprisingly, more or less identifies. But Verhaeghe fears that neoliberal society has attacked the connective tissue of social groups. 'The desire for short-term gains coupled with the diminishing importance of knowledge and experience is leading to the disappearance of those things that hold groups together: loyalty and solidarity,' he writes.

The Ghent philosopher further develops his ideas on the social origins of present-day psychological problems in his latest book *Identity* (2012). Here he argues that, from a very early age, as our personalities are being shaped, we are pulled back and forth between two poles: identification and separation, or, in Freudian terms, *'Eros*, which wants to merge together lovingly, and *Thanatos*, which wants to separate aggressively'. Stable personalities find a balance between these two primitive drives, but in neo-liberal times the focus lies heavily on separation and individualism. 'The result is competition, social isolation and loneliness,' argues Verhaeghe.

Another fatal threat to identity formation is the fact that nowadays, all traditional authority figures are under attack. 'There are no fathers anymore because the system does not permit any authority based on symbolism,' he writes. In the 1960s, rebelling against the traditional family and against power structures based largely on tradition was very liberating. But at the time, many people – including Verhaeghe himself – made a fundamental error in reasoning, and confused power with authority. And without authority figures, people who, because of characteristics such as age, knowledge or position, embody rules to which they too are subject, we will not make it.

The moral vacuum left behind by former authority figures has been filled by neoliberal ideology. The central article of faith of this religion is the conviction that all human beings have an innate drive to compete. If you allow them to exercise this drive freely, this will produce the best results and the most attractive goods. And this merciless competition is, morally speaking, responsible to boot. Because according to the meritocratic model, which Verhaeghe calls the fig leaf of neoliberalism, workers are paid according to their effort. Whether you are successful or fail to make the grade is dependent on your own efforts and abilities.

Anyone who does not manage to pull it off is considered either a failure or mentally disturbed. The role of psychotherapists nowadays is to get people back on the rails so that they can play their part in the system. Verhaeghe is convinced that the types of psychological disturbance they treat are closely bound up with neoliberal society, just as every form of society decides what constitutes ill and what constitutes normal.

Verhaeghe's main criticism of his colleagues is that they are trapped in a narrow world view and turn a blind eye to the interplay between psychological illnesses and the way society is organised. They have completely decontextualized the psyche and interpret psychological problems as glitches in the internal housekeeping that can be treated with pills. In a flash the patient is relieved of all responsibility: the fact that he has dropped out of the rat race is not down to his own lack of ability but to the genes he inherited or a chemical imbalance in his brain.

The Ghent psychotherapist is rowing hard against the dominant and prevailing current of thought which attributes all human behaviour to the genes and the brain. His ideas on the social origins of psychological wellbeing push the *nature–nurture* pendulum firmly back in the direction of *nurture*. Verhaeghe's sharp analysis of today's unhealthy social order is also very timely; not surprisingly he is a popular media guest and speaker throughout Belgium and the Netherlands. His social criticism hits a raw nerve in times when few people can shake off a permanent feeling of rootlessness and uncertainty. It is no coincidence that the most resonant cultural diagnosis around today has been made not by a philosopher or a sociologist but by a psychotherapist.

TOMAS VANHESTE
Translated by Rebekah Wilson

PAUL VERHAEGHE IN ENGLISH:

Love in a time of loneliness Three essays on drive and desire (original title: *Liefde in tijden van eenzaamheid. Over drift en verlangen*), The Other Press Rebus Press, New York London, 1999, 212 pages. Online: http://goo.gl/9d3m9.

Does the woman exist? From Freud's Hysteric to Lacan's Feminine (original title: *Tussen hysterie en vrouw. Van Freud tot Lacan: een weg door honderd jaar psychoanalyse*), New York London, The Other Press – Rebus Press, 1999 1996, 290 p – 269 pages.

Leo Kouwenhoven's Majorana Particles

If you ask Leo Kouwenhoven (1963), the overwhelming media attention for his discovery of the Majorana particle is just hype. He was invited to meet the Dutch Prime Minister Mark Rutte and almost seemed to have the Nobel Prize in Physics in the bag. A slight exaggeration, perhaps, but this nanophysicist has made a major breakthrough, and if the follow-up experiments go according to plan, he certainly has decent prospects for the prize.

Leo Kouwenhoven

It all started on 27th February 2012, at the annual meeting of the American Physical Society. Kouwenhoven presented his latest results to a packed Boston Convention Center, and became the hottest talk of the conference. The subject: strong indications of the existence of the Majorana particle, predicted by Italian theoretical physicist Ettore Majorana in 1937. The genius himself disappeared mysteriously off the face of the earth, but after a search lasting three quarters of a century his particle turned up in a physics laboratory at Delft University of Technology[1]. This was no coincidence. Kouwenhoven is a world leader in research on the electronic properties of nanostructures, particles with dimensions measurable in millionths of millimetres, which obey the laws of quantum mechanics. These laws may defy common sense (particles in two places at the same time), but they are indispensible for a fundamental understanding of the nanoworld.

Kouwenhoven was awarded a PhD *cum laude* from Delft University of Technology in 1992 and, having turned down an offer from Harvard, has been a professor at Delft since 1999. In 2007 he won the Spinoza Prize, the highest scientific award in the Netherlands. His research on quantum transport in semiconductor materials is constantly in top journals including *Nature* and *Science*. Kouwenhoven made his name constructing quantum dots, ultra tiny 'boxes' in which he managed to lock up a single electron, thereby making them potential qubits for a quantum computer. Qubits are not set to 0 or 1, like normal computer bits, they can be *0 and 1 at the same time*, exponentially increasing their computational power, so that a quantum computer can crack problems (decipher codes, search in a database) which are unthinkable for current supercomputers. There is a but: qubits must be stable and undisturbed by their environment - and there lies the rub. Even cooling them to just above absolute zero (-273 °C) seems not to help. Quantum computers exist only on paper.

This is where Majorana particles might help. As a professor in Naples in the thirties, Ettore Majorana played with the famous Dirac equation, the heart of quantum theory. He found an unusual solution: particles which are their own antiparticles, so their properties are effectively null. These particles with null properties initially received little attention, but in the seventies a search began to prove their existence. Since then cosmology has also shown an interest. A large proportion of the universe is missing. This 'dark matter' may consist of Majorana particles. At CERN in Geneva scientists are hard at work searching for Majorana particles, so far in vain. Kouwenhoven took a different tack. In addition to elementary particles (basic building blocks) there are also complex particles, which can be useful for calculations. The effect could be comparable to a Mexican wave in a stadium, a collective phenomenon conducted by a group of individuals. With the right combinations of materials and nanowires, ultra low temperatures and strong magnetic fields, you can create conditions in which synthetic Majorana particles, combinations of thousands of electrons, can occur. Kouwenhoven was familiar with such conditions from his previous research.

Kouwenhoven's Majorana particles appear at the ends of the nanowires. The 0.003 mm-long indium antimonide nanowire lies on a superconductive surface (no electrical resistance as long as it is cooled to just above absolute zero) and is exposed to a magnetic field. The current in the nanowire is measured with electrodes. The surges detected can only be explained by the presence of Majorana particles. But strong indications are not enough to satisfy peers in the physics world or the Nobel committee. Follow-up experiments in Delft have yet to provide hard proof. These are directed at measuring the special properties of the Majorana particles, which differ from what we know about the familiar elementary particles. To be specific, Kouwenhoven

would like to prove that Majorana particles conform to so-called non-Abelian statistics.

It is this property that makes Majorana particles suitable as qubits for a quantum computer. That is why Microsoft contacted Kouwenhoven in 2012, resulting in support from the US to the tune of a million dollars. Kouwenhoven now plans to build a real quantum computer based on Majorana particles, a project running into billions and requiring investors. Contact with Microsoft remains excellent. When *Science* published his Majorana article on 12th April 2012 Kouwenhoven was treated to Majorana cake at the head office in Redmond.

DIRK VAN DELFT
Translated by Anna Asbury

NOTES

1. See www.tudelft.nl/en. Delft is about halfway between Rotterdam and The Hague.

Society

Between Ghent, Geneva And Kenya
Marleen Temmerman

Marleen Temmerman

At the end of 2012, a Flemish gynaecologist was appointed Head of the Department of Reproductive Health and Research at the World Health Organization in Geneva: Marleen Temmerman (° 1953). Even before being appointed to this key post, Temmerman enjoyed international renown, and received a Lifetime Achievement Award from the prestigious *British Medical Journal* in 2010. This distinction is awarded to a doctor, politician, academic or researcher who has made a unique and essential contribution to improving healthcare. The competition for the award was stiff, with candidates from countries such as the United States, Canada and Great Britain, each with a long list of publications to their name.

Temmerman grew up in the kind of family which in the past was found everywhere in Flanders: Christian, hard-working and full of good intentions, but just a little unadventurous. At secondary school she was greatly interested in general social and political topics, and what were seen as her highly rebellious comments were not greatly appreciated. She was undeterred. Without batting an eyelid, she played truant one day to attend a lecture in Brus-

sels given by a Trotskyist economist, and she was also no stranger to lectures by socially critical professors of philosophy at Ghent University.

The fact that Temmerman chose to study medicine in Ghent rather than, say, sociology or economics, came as a surprise. Even more of a surprise was that she went to university at all. Studying was far from the norm in her family, and even less so for a girl, but her parents eventually gave up their resistance. It was written in the stars that she would be no ordinary student. She soon became a member of a socio-medical working group which discussed ways of improving medicine and the redistribution of property; she learned Turkish - there was already quite a large Turkish community in Ghent at that time - and worked as a volunteer in a health centre in a disadvantaged neighbourhood.

Whilst still studying, Temmerman embarked on a trip that was a harbinger of an important development in her life. She travelled to Rwanda, completely alone. She found the experience overwhelming. She had of course known that the gap between the rich West and Africa was wide, but she was staggered by the circumstances in which Rwandans lived and by the lack of staff and technical resources at the hospital in Butare.

It was to be some time before Temmerman returned to Africa. She specialised in gynaecology and obtained a post on the staff of Jean-Jacques Amy, professor at the *Vrije Universiteit Brussel*, the Dutch-speaking university in the Belgian capital. It was an interesting but strange time for Temmerman. In her work she was concerned mainly with infertility problems. She also performed abortions - in a period when abortion was still completely illegal in Belgium. She sometimes went straight from helping a woman who was unable to become pregnant to a woman in another room who was demanding an abortion.

In 1995 Temmerman's latent love for Africa received a powerful impetus. The University of Nairobi, which was a partner of the Institute of Tropical Medicine in Antwerp, was running a small study on the consequences of sexually transmitted diseases in pregnant prostitutes. Temmerman was awarded a grant to spend a month helping on the project. Two years later, there was a need for someone to develop the project further. The call of Africa had become very loud, and complete with husband and newborn child Temmerman left for Kenya to take up an appointment at the University of Nairobi. She was stationed in a public sector maternity clinic in a slum district or, more precisely, a valley in which 500,000 people lived together in the worst imaginable circumstances. Temmerman wrote a compelling description of her experiences in Kenya in her book *Mama Daktari: gynaecologe in Afrika* (Mama Daktari: Gynaecology in Africa), in which she talks at length about the appalling lack of infrastructure and resources, the almost unimaginable difference between rich and poor (including locally) and the striking cultural differences. The almost hopeless battle against AIDS is a constant background theme in the book. By way of illustration, when Temmerman began her assignment, roughly 2% of her patients were HIV-positive women; five years later, that figure had risen to 25%.

In 1992 the family decided to return to Belgium, but Africa would continue to play an important role in Temmerman's life. In 1994, she founded the International Centre for Reproductive Health (ICRH) together with several partners, including former colleagues in Kenya. The ICRH is a multidisciplinary centre operating within the Faculty of Medicine and Health Sciences at Ghent University. Besides research activities, ICRH implements projects in Europe, Latin America, Africa and Asia with a focus on developing training programmes and takes actions to defend sexual and reproductive rights. Its main objective is to improve sexual and reproductive health in its broadest sense. To this end, ICRH seeks to improve the acceptability, accessibility and quality of sexual and reproductive health services, and integrates a human rights based and gender sensitive approach in its analysis.

Until her appointment in Geneva, Temmerman was a professor of obstetrics/gynaecology at Ghent University and head of the Obstetrics Department at Ghent University Hospital. She combined these activities with a seat in the Belgian Senate, as a member of the social-democratic party sp.a. Despite her lack of real political experience, her work in the Senate attracted glowing praise from analysts. She also published books at regular intervals, on topics such as the violence sometimes perpetrated against women or about light-hearted (and less light-hearted) moments in her work as a gynaecologist.

Although Temmerman now lives in Switzerland, she will frequently be away from home. She will be found regularly in Kenya, the country to which she has returned repeatedly since her departure in 1992, thereby demonstrating that a cliché can also be true: once someone has been in Africa, they will always want to return.

HANS VANACKER
Translated by Julian Ross

www.marleentemmerman.be
www.who.int

Visual Arts

The completely renovated entrance hall.
Photo by Pedro Pegenaute

The Rijksmuseum Finally Opens Its Doors Again

In 1999 the Dutch government decided it was time for a complete renovation and remodelling of the Rijksmuseum, the national museum of the Netherlands in Amsterdam. A royal millennium gift of 100 million Dutch guilders (approximately 45 million euros) provided the initial impetus for an operation which would ultimately cost some 375 million euros. Ronald de Leeuw, the museum's General Director at the time, was very conscious of the escalating costs, but also knew that total restoration was the only way to breathe life and air back into a museum that had become clogged and torpid. The doors of the museum opened again on 13 April 2013, after a renovation lasting more than ten years. Both the building and its collection of the Dutch state's art treasures are now fit for the 21st century.

In 1885, the Dutch architect Pierre Cuypers (1827 - 1921) designed a stately, stylistically varied work of art, which on its completion was not only the largest building in the Netherlands but, strikingly enough, also a city gate: a public thoroughfare linking the heart of Amsterdam to the outlying districts runs straight through the middle of the museum. From its creation the museum has been a hybrid, an architectural icon and without doubt the most photographed building in the Netherlands. At the same time, for many the silhouette of the building stands as a symbol for the art treasures kept within.

During the 20th century, dozens of ambitious attempts at remodelling and renovation caused untold damage to the museum's original design. The biggest disruption to the building came in the 1960s, when two large inner courtyards were built over to meet the need for more space in the museum. The effect was to turn the building into a labyrinth, an unfathomable maze of rooms through which it was almost impossible for visitors to find their way. The biggest challenge facing the renovation architects was therefore to restore the building's open character.

The Spanish architectural duo Antonio Cruz and Antonio Ortiz came up with an obvious but skilfully implemented plan to restore the building to its former glory. The two inner courtyards were opened up again as if it was the most natural thing in the world. However, this required an architectural *tour de force*, in which all the earlier modifications had to be reversed and hundreds of thousands of kilos of concrete had to be removed from the building. As a result - so the story goes - the entire building became so much lighter that it rose several centimetres from the marshy Amsterdam soil on which it is built. Cruz and Ortiz went further, however, and lowered the floor level of both inner courtyards far enough to allow them to be connected via a passage that runs beneath the road running through the heart of the museum. The city gate and cycle path were left intact, but the two inner courtyards beneath are now linked together to form a single, central courtyard. The briefest of glances confirms that this new public space in Amsterdam can compare with the public spaces in and around other great national museums in Europe: the inner court of the *Louvre* in Paris, the entrance to the *Prado* in Madrid and the covered Courtyard of the British Museum in London have all been created in recent decades. Just as in those capital cities, the choice in Amsterdam was for light and space and timeless architecture. The architects opted to use sand-lime brick in contrast to the original, dark building materials, and created huge staircases, large enough to cope with large numbers of visitors, but plainly fashioned, so that from the moment they enter, visitors imagine themselves in another world. After passing through the imposing Atrium and going through the ticket checkpoint, visitors climb the original staircase leading to the completely renovated *Voorhal* (entrance hall), the *Eregalerij* (hall of fame) and the other rooms of the museum.

One of the most challenging tasks for the architects was to bring a late 19th-century building up to the requirements of the present day, but without damaging its status as a historic monument. The temperature regulation and security arrangements were brought up to date, partly through the use of a ring main running round the entire building and housing all the necessary technical apparatus. This enabled the rooms of the museum to retain their original proportions and allowed the unique sequence of rooms arranged around the central Atrium to be restored to their former glory. Under the leadership of restoration architect Gijsbert van Hoogevest, and using the knowledge and expertise of restoration specialist Anne van Grevenstein, the decorations hidden beneath the many layers of whitewash were studied. These have been selectively restored at key points throughout the building, enabling visitors to picture themselves back in the eclectic dream that Pierre Cuypers created in 1885.

For the first time in history, it was possible to review the entire museum concept of the Rijksmuseum. The former General Director Ronald de Leeuw developed a plan in 2004 for a chronological design, in which all parts of the collection would be staged in a mixed presentation. A transparent, easily navigable building would make it possible to lay out a clear circuit in which paintings, sculptures, crafts and historical objects would be displayed, arranged in chronological order. The new General Director, Wim Pijbes, continued this process when he took over in 2008, partly in response to the public debate that was going on in the Netherlands at that time about the ignorance of history and the arts among the younger generation. The French interior architect Jean-Michel Wilmotte built on this concept to create a restrained design for the building's monumental rooms. His intense grey, deep wall colours are in stark contrast to the bright, historical decorative scheme created by Cuypers. The display cabinets are now minimalist and with very restrained detailing, so that the works of art within are presented to visitors in an uncluttered way which enables all attention to be focused on the objects themselves.

The revamped Rijksmuseum aims to convey to art lovers a sense of beauty and an awareness of time. The inviting inner courtyards created by Cruz and Ortiz set visitor expectations high. Cuypers' rich decorations on the staircases and in the *Voorhal* and *Eregalerij* bring past times back to life, and the clean, restrained lines of Wilmotte's display cabinets show off the art treasures in the museum's collection at their very best.

After a decade of rebuilding work and an investment of hundreds of millions of euros, one work of art has finally been returned to its former place: Rembrandt's *The Nightwatch* has been rehung in precisely the same place as before, as if nothing had changed. And there the canvas hangs, awaiting new admirers - whose number is expected to exceed two million in the first year after the reopening.

TIM ZEEDIJK
Translated by Julian Ross

www.rijksmuseum.nl

Back on the Map
The Stedelijk Museum Amsterdam

The Museumplein in Amsterdam, host to the Stedelijk Museum, the Rijksmuseum, the Van Gogh Museum and the Concertgebouw © KLM - Carto

'The bathtub', it's called, the spectacular building which houses the recently reopened Stedelijk Museum Amsterdam. The colossal white hulk on the Museumplein[1] was already nicknamed during the design phase. Architect Mels Crouwel came up with the idea, designing the museum extension with his team at Benthem Crouwel. It's no surprise that the name caught on with the people of Amsterdam. The building's streamlined volume could hardly be expressed more aptly. The form of the construction, with diagonally sloping walls, over-hanging edge and legs immediately call to mind a gigantic bathtub. The association is confirmed by the rounded corners and the smooth white finish. The enormous, apparently floating bulk rests on a steel supporting structure. The outer walls are covered with a strong, ultra light synthetic fibre used in shipping and aviation. This high quality industrial composite produces smooth, seamlessly curved surfaces. The flamboyant modern entrance is a robust statement, which immediately dismisses the old nineteenth century museum building into the background.

The much talked about shape and white walls are reminiscent of the renowned interventions of Willem Sandberg (1897-1984), the legendary museum director who energetically went to work with whitewash on the somberly decorated brick interior in the fifties. Sandberg managed to put Amsterdam's Stedelijk on the map internationally. The modern art museum's rebellious white walls became as famous as the revolutionary works of art it served up to the public. It remains to be seen whether the Stedelijk will again achieve such a global position. The budget is probably too tight for that, but the bold architecture certainly has the allure and bravura.

In the nineties the Stedelijk Museum was much in need of renovation. The building was too small to house the illustrious and ever growing collection, let alone allow space for high-profile tempo-

rary exhibitions. Architects from the Netherlands and around the world let their imaginations run wild. Dutch architect Mels Crouwel, son of graphic designer Wim Crouwel, stood out head and shoulders above the rest. In 2004 the museum closed to construct his proposal. The architect offered an intelligent and original solution to the problem of space in the museum in its tight urban location. His idea was as simple as it was brilliant: for visitor services, such as tickets, cloakroom, shop and restaurant, he placed a lively plaza on the ground floor. The inner courtyard, sheltered by the bathtub structure, is only separated from the outside space by glass, making it a visual extension of the Museumplein. Underground another 1100 m[2] are allocated to a large open plan gallery. Crouwel placed further galleries above the entrance hall, in the closed bulk of the bathtub. Above these, as if floating on the bubbling bath foam, came space for the curators and museum staff. Crouwel's revolutionary design drastically reverses the orientation of the familiar museum building, moving the entrance to the back, on the Museumplein.

Photo by J. Lewis Marshall

The change required a sacrifice: the role of the glorious staircase, famous as a stage for artistic presentations and performances, was lost to the new plan. The illustrious history of the renowned staircase was remembered at the grand reopening of the museum by Queen Beatrix in September 2012. Dancers from the Dutch National Ballet performed a farewell dance choreographed by Hans van Manen on the thirty-seven steps.

The gain was immediately clear at the opening. The sloping top of the building creates a platform for the museum and its artists, a forecourt where the museum can communicate with its visitors, as in the Centre Pompidou in Paris. Performances and presentations take place under the roof. Films and images can be projected on the bathtub's smooth white walls. The entrance is transparent and inspiring. The bathtub and glass wall serve to diffuse the edges of the museum building. The plaza is like a continuous extension of the public space, creating the illusion that the Museumplein runs up to the historical wall of the original building. The exterior makes the most of the exciting contrast between A.W. Weisman's 19th century bricks and the 21st century extension with its industrial synthetics. The clash of styles is beautifully displayed in the entrance hall, the trendy bathtub visually separated from the richly decorated wall, lit by daylight, that has been restored to its former glory. Inside it vanishes with-

out a trace. All galleries are fitted out the same way, to the same measurements; walls, floors and light filters identically fitted and finished. The transition from old to new, so striking on the outside, is barely perceptible inside. For those really paying attention, a small, inconspicuous peephole allows the visitor the pleasure of standing on the bridge peeking down at the lively inner courtyard. To avoid disturbing the art lover's concentration, the route runs straight from the bathtub at the top down to the cellar, by-passing the noisy entrance hall. An extensive, much talked about escalator in a closed yellow tunnel, a contemporary nod to the old staircase, brings visitors underground in the blink of an eye.

But what about the collection? It is more beautiful than ever, arranged in surprising combinations evoking interesting associations in its serene white environment. The Stedelijk's permanent collection has an immediately uplifting effect. Once you have stood eye to eye with Luc Tuymans' beautiful, vulnerable portrait *H.M.*[2], Lawrence Weiner's intriguing piece of chalk on the table, Hans Arp's flowing bronze torso, Donald Judd's box sculpture and Karel Appel's frivolous wall paintings, there's no going back! This sparkling reception is followed by a historical voyage of discovery taking visitors past countless modern art icons. From Van Gogh's *Woman Rocking a Cradle* to Willem de Kooning's *Rosy Fingered Dawn*, from Ernst Ludwig Kirchner's

The Dancer to Alberto Giacometti's *Gazing Head*, from Marc Chagall's *The Fiddler* to Kazimir Malevich's *Yellow Plane in Dissolution*, sculptures and paintings follow one another in intriguing combinations. Piet Mondriaan's sparse compositions are adorned with the dynamic, fragile mobiles of Alexander Calder, while Dutch artist Herman Kruyder's *Distrust* forms a suggestive pair with Chaim Soutine's slaughtered ox. Edward Kienholz's *The Beanery* has been restored to its former glory; the surreal reflection of the drinkers with clocks instead of faces is a favourite with the public. A striking choice is the dedication of an entire wing of the museum to a permanent design exhibition. The highlight of this is Gerrit Rietveld's ultra modern 1926 piece *Harrestein Bedroom*. It is clear that director Ann Goldstein has serious plans for the *Stedelijk Museum*. The opening exhibition sets the tone for things to come. The retrospective of Mike Kelley, following the artist's sudden death, was a world first. It ran until 1st April 2013. The exhibition is to travel on to Paris, New York and Los Angeles.[3]

JULEKE VAN LINDERT
Translated by Anna Asbury

www.stedelijk.nl

NOTES

1. The large square which is also home to the Rijksmuseum, the Van Gogh Museum and the Concertgebouw.

2. Luc Tuymans' portrait of the Dutch Queen Beatrix.

3. The exhibition is on show in the MoMa in New York from 7th October 2013 until 5th January 2014 and in the Museum of Contemporary Art in Los Angeles from March to June 2014.

Pieter Bruegel the Elder in the Limelight Again

Pieter Bruegel the Elder (approx. 1525-1569) continues to fascinate new generations of art lovers. And certainly not only in Flanders - where, since the end of the 19th century his work has, consciously and unconsciously, been considered an historical representation of Flemish identity, even though it is by no means historically correct. There is tremendous interest all over the world for the master's oeuvre and for his intellectual and artistic legacy. In the last few years, numerous interesting publications have appeared, taking a wide variety of approaches and not only intended for the academic world, but also aiming to inform a much wider readership of the master's small but exceptionally rich and complex oeuvre. In this article I would like to turn the spotlight on the varied and abundant seam of current Bruegel research by making a small selection of what to me seem the most fascinating and stimulating recent contributions.

One publication that is undeniably monumental and important is *Pieter Bruegel* by Larry Silver, an American professor and specialist in 16th century Netherlandish art. Apart from the fantastic quality of the reproductions, the importance of this book lies in its synthetical and thematically classified study of the whole oeuvre - all the genres and all the subjects, in paintings, drawings and prints. Whereas in virtually every other study published over the last few decades, Bruegel has been studied from a specific angle, integrated approaches to this extremely complex oeuvre at this sort of level are exceedingly rare (there have of course been countless popular publications that aimed to do this, which were very inferior in academic underpinning and content). Silver's approach to Bruegel's iconography and place in cultural history - which has elicited numerous studies that were as 'scholarly' as they were entirely hypothetical - is balanced and subtle. Absolutely to be recommended for the expert and the enthusiast. This book is a worthy successor to Walter Gibson's more compact 1978 book on Bruegel, whose substance still stands up.

Pieter Bruegel the Elder, *The Wine of Saint Martin's Day*, painting discovered in 2010, Prado Museum, Madrid

Gibson has undeniably been the godfather of Bruegel research since the late 70s. His most recent addition to a long list of important publications is a study of the depiction of proverbs in Netherlandish art in the late 16th and early 17th centuries, a subject in which Bruegel played a crucial part. In addition to many publications on individual paintings of proverbs, this is the first study in which this topic has been covered systematically. Like many other books by Gibson, this one is a delight to read: balanced, well-written and with a down-to-earth look at the subject that is only possible if the author has an unrivalled knowledge of the iconography of Bruegel and his contemporaries.

As one might expect, in the last few years there have of course been talented young researchers in the United States and Europe who have devoted a dissertation to aspects of Bruegel the Elder's oeuvre. These are usually very much influenced by what in the trade is called 'new art history'. This is a slightly misleading label, as this is a research trend that has already been around for several decades and whose vague common denominator, to summarise it very concisely, is a highly postmodernist and theoretical approach. Although there is a lot of chaff amongst the corn, two recent dissertations definitely come to the fore – two studies that combine new angles with a keen eye, thorough art history knowledge and down-to-earth interpretation. The Dutch researcher Matthijs Ilsink compares Pieter Bruegel's oeuvre with that of Hieronymus Bosch (approx. 1450-1516); this comparison is often made, but it is usually limited to iconographic derivation. Ilsink shows convincingly that Bruegel emulated and was stimulated by the older master and his views as an artist, and entered into artistic dialogue and rivalry with him. It is also striking that Bruegel does this in a specific section of his work: everything associated with hell, the devil and evil. In an interesting aside, Ilsink also looks at the artistic rivalry between Bruegel and his successful contemporary Frans Floris.

Todd Richardson's ideas are based on the same premise, which is that in Pieter Bruegel's generation several artists became increasingly aware of 'art as art' and in their work also deliberately adopt positions on artistic and art theory choices, often in reaction to work by other artists; in short, a purposeful artistic dialogue. This young American researcher concentrates on Bruegel's late work and, carrying on from previous studies of his drawings and prints, demonstrates that it was with surprising frequency that the artist entered into dialogue with and was inspired by Italian art and art theory, as well as (indirectly?) by the legacy of classical antiquity.

Another approach is the research into materials and techniques, which, regarding Pieter Bruegel's oeuvre, only got going surprisingly late in the day. A book by Christina Currie and Dominique Allart is the most recent contribution in this field, and is a monumental publication that concentrates on research into the painting methods of Bruegel the Elder and his son Pieter Brueghel the Younger, whose oeuvre consists largely of copies of his father's work, which he continued making until well into the 17th century. The analysis of the way the young Brueghel copied his father's work (the originals of which he had often never seen) yields a treasure trove of information about the elder Bruegel's creative process and working methods, even more so than the research into the work of the father. This is the innovative strength of this study, which is intended more for the professional specialist.

One piece of striking news on the Bruegel front is the discovery of a couple of new works - an unprecedented rarity in this small oeuvre. I was fortunate enough to be closely involved in both instances: the discovery of what is called a *Tuechlein* in a private Spanish collection, an unusually large and ambitious painting in tempera on canvas that is now in the collection of the Prado in Madrid, and in 2012 the discovery of a landscape drawing by him. This last work - the last time an entirely unknown Bruegel drawing was found was in the 1970s - was part of an exhibition in which all the works by Bruegel in Antwerp collections were brought together, with special emphasis on his prints and research into the techniques and materials used in *Mad Meg*, the masterpiece in the Mayer Van den Bergh Museum in Antwerp. One curious fact which shows that interest in Bruegel is a worldwide phenomenon is the highly successful exhibition of all the prints after Bruegel held by the Royal Library in Brussels, which is now touring Japan. Yoko Mori, the Japanese professor and compiler of the exhibition, has spent decades studying Bruegel's work and is probably the first (and perhaps only) Japanese citizen to specialise in the drama of the chambers of rhetoric and sixteenth-century language and imagery in the Low Countries on which Bruegel often based his work. Even though he was blessed with a fertile imagination, Pieter Bruegel could probably never have imagined such a situation as this.

CHRISTINA CURRIE & DOMINIQUE ALLART, *The Brueg(H)el Phenomenon, Paintings by Pieter Bruegel the Elder and Pieter Brueghel the Younger with a Special Focus on Technique and Copying Practice,* three volumes, Koninklijk Instituut voor het Kunstpatrimonium, Brussels, 2012 (ISBN 978 2 930054 14 8).

WALTER GIBSON, *Figures of Speech, Picturing Proverbs in Renaissance Netherlands*, University of California Press, Berkeley, 2010 (ISBN 978 0 520 25954 6).

MATTHIJS ILSINK, *Bosch en Bruegel als Bosch, kunst over kunst bij Pieter Bruegel (c.1528-1569) en Jheronimus Bosch (c.1450-1516)* (Bosch and Bruegel as Bosch, art on art in the work of Pieter Bruegel (c. 1528-1569)), Stichting Nijmeegse Kunsthistorische Studies, Nijmegen, 2009 (ISBN 978 94 90128 173).

YOKO MORI et al., *The World of Pieter Bruegel in Black And White from the Collection of the Royal Library of Belgium, exhibition catalogue*, The Bunkamura Museum of Art, Tokyo, 2010.

TODD RICHARDSON, *Pieter Bruegel the Elder, Art Discourse in the Sixteenth-Century Netherlands,* Furnham / Burlington, Ashgate, 2011 (ISBN 978 0 7546 6816 9).

MANFRED SELLINK & PILAR SILVA MORETO, 'The Rediscovery of Pieter Bruegel the Elder's 'Wine of St Martin's Day', Acquired for the Museo Nacional del Prado, Madrid', in *The Burlington Magazine*, CLIII (December 2011), pp. 784-793.

MANFRED SELLINK & MAXIMILIAAN MARTENS, exhibition catalogue *Bruegel ongezien!, de verborgen Antwerpse collecties* (Unseen Bruegel! The hidden Antwerp collections), catalogue of the exhibition at the Museum Mayer Van den Bergh in Antwerp, Davidsfonds Uitgeverij, Louvain, 2012 (ISBN 978 90 5826 875 4).

LARRY SILVER, *Pieter Bruegel*, Abbeville Press, New York / London, 2011 (ISBN 978 0 7892 1104 0).

MANFRED SELLINK
Translated by Gregory Ball

Contributors

Dirk Van Assche
Deputy Editor *Ons Erfdeel vzw*
dirkvanassche@onserfdeel.be

Jan-Hendrik Bakker
Journalist
jhbakker@gmx.net

Abdelkader Benali
Writer
abenali@xs4all.nl

Derek Blyth
Journalist
derekblyth@lycos.com

Tom Christiaens
Journalist
Tom.Christiaens@howest.be

Marc Cloostermans
Critic
markcloostermans@gmail.com

Pieter Coupé
Secretary *Ons Erfdeel. Vlaams-Nederlands cultureel tijdschrift*
onserfdeel@onserfdeel.be

Dirk van Delft
Science journalist
dirkvandelft@museumboerhaave.nl

Luc Devoldere
Chief Editor *Ons Erfdeel vzw*
luc.devoldere@onserfdeel.be

Carl Devos
Professor of Political Sciences
Carl.Devos@UGent.be

Lieve Dierckx
Dance Critic
lievedierckx@skynet.be

Paul Geerts
Journalist
ge.pa@skynet.be

Piet Gerbrandy
Poet and Critic
psgerb@xs4all.nl

Marc Hooghe
Professor of Political Sciences
marc.hooghe@soc.kuleuven.be

Geert van Istendael
Writer
geert.van.istendael@telenet.be

Joris van de Kerkhof
Journalist
Joris.van.de.Kerkhof@nos.nl

Wessel Krul
Professor of Cultural History
w.e.krul@rug.nl

Jef Lambrecht
Critic
jef.lambrecht@gmail.com

Joep Leerssen
Professor of European Studies
J.T.Leerssen@uva.nl

Annemie Leysen
Critic
annemie.leysen@telenet.be

Juleke van Lindert
Critic
julekevanlindert@gmail.com

Matthijs Lok
Assistant Professor of Modern European History
M.M.Lok@uva.nl

Ludo Milis
Em. Professor of Medieval History
ludo.milis@gmail.com

Anne Marie Musschoot
Em. Professor of Dutch Literature
AnneMarie.Musschoot@UGent.be

Lutgard Mutsaers
Music Critic
lut@ision.nl

Merel van den Nieuwenhof
Art Historian
merelvdn@gmail.com

Jos Nijhof
Theatre Critic
nijhof@xs4all.nl

Cyrille Offermans
Writer and Critic
CyrilleOffermans@home.nl

Lodewijk Petram
Publicist on Economic History
info@lodewijkpetram.nl

Jürgen Pieters
Professor of Literature
Jurgen.Pieters@UGent.be

Herman Pleij
Professor of Medieval Dutch Literature
H.Pleij@uva.nl

Anneke Reitsma
Critic
info@annekereitsma.nl

Eric Rinckhout
Journalist/Art Critic
ericrinc@antwerpen.be

Leo Samama
Composer and Musicologist
leo@leosamama.nl

Manfred Sellink
Art Historian
manfred.sellink@brugge.be

Dirk Steenhaut
Journalist
dirk_steenhaut@hotmail.com

Bart Van der Straeten
Critic
BartL.VanderStraeten@UGent.be

Hans Vanacker
Secretary *Septentrion. Arts, lettres et culture de Flandre et des Pays-Bas*
septentrion@onserfdeel.be

Tomas Vanheste
Journalist
t.vanheste@kpnmail.nl

Paul Vincent
Translator
p-vincent@btconnect.com

Roel Vismans
Reader in Dutch
r.vismans@sheffield.ac.uk

Jeroen Vullings
Critic
jeroen.vullings@me.com

Frank Willaert
Professor of Medieval Dutch Literature
frank.willaert@ua.ac.be

Karin Wolfs
Film Critic
mail@karinwolfs.nl

Tim Zeedijk
Art Historian
T.Zeedijk@rijksmuseum.nl

Ad Zuiderent
Poet and Critic
ad.zuiderent@xs4all.nl

Translators

K.P.G. Aercke
Anna Asbury
Gregory Ball
Pleuke Boyce
Sheila M. Dale
Lindsay Edwards
Chris Emery
Donald Gardner
Tanis Guest
Susan E. Holdsworth
Michiel Horn
John Irons
Yvette Mead
Jonathan Reeder
Julian Ross
Helen Simpson
Paul Vincent
Rebekah Wilson

ADVISOR ON ENGLISH USAGE

Lindsay Edwards (Belgium)

Colophon

Association

This twenty-first yearbook is published by the Flemish-Netherlands Association 'Ons Erfdeel vzw', with the support of the Dutch Ministry of Education, Culture and Science (The Hague), the Flemish Authorities (Brussels) and the Provinces of West and East Flanders.
The Association 'Ons Erfdeel vzw' also publishes the Dutch-language periodical *Ons Erfdeel* and the French-language periodical *Septentrion. Arts, lettres et culture de Flandre et des Pays-Bas*, the bilingual yearbook *De Franse Nederlanden – Les Pays-Bas Français* and a series of books in several languages covering various aspects of the culture of the Low Countries.

Address of the Editorial Board and the Administration

'Ons Erfdeel vzw', Murissonstraat 260,
8930 Rekkem, Flanders, Belgium
T +32 56 41 12 01, F +32 56 41 47 07
www.onserfdeel.be, www.onserfdeel.nl
thelowcountriesblog.onserfdeel.be
VAT BE 0410.723.635

Kevin Vandenbussche *Head of Administration*
Adinda Houttekier *Administrative Secretary*

Aims

With *The Low Countries,* a yearbook founded by Jozef Deleu (Chief Editor from 1993 until 2002), the editors and publisher aim to present to the world the culture and society of the Dutch-speaking area which embraces both the Netherlands and also Flanders, the northern part of Belgium.

The articles in this yearbook survey the living, contemporary culture of the Low Countries as well as their cultural heritage. In its words and pictures *The Low Countries* provides information about literature and the arts, but also about broad social and historical developments in Flanders and the Netherlands.

The culture of Flanders and the Netherlands is not an isolated phenomenon; its development over the centuries has been one of continuous interaction with the outside world. In consequence the yearbook also pays due attention to the centuries-old continuing cultural interplay between the Low Countries and the world beyond their borders.

By drawing attention to the diversity, vitality and international dimension of the culture of Flanders and the Netherlands, *The Low Countries* hopes to contribute to a lively dialogue between different cultures.

ISSN 0779-5815
ISBN 978-90-79705-153
Statutory deposit no. D/2013/3006/3
NUR 612

Copyright © 2013 'Ons Erfdeel vzw' and SABAM Belgium 2013
Printed by Die Keure, Bruges, Flanders, Belgium
Design by Henk Linskens (Die Keure)

Prices for the yearbook 2013, no. 21

Belgium € 37, The Netherlands € 39, Europe € 39

Other Countries: € 45
All prices inclusive of shipping costs

You can order this book from our webshop at www.onserfdeel.be and pay by credit card

As well as the yearbook
The Low Countries,
the Flemish Netherlands
Association 'Ons Erfdeel vzw'
publishes a number of books
covering various aspects of
the culture of Flanders and
the Netherlands.

Wim Daniëls
Talking Dutch.
Illustrated; 80 pp.

J.A. Kossmann-Putto &
E.H. Kossmann
*The Low Countries.
History of the Northern
and Southern Netherlands.*
Illustrated; 64 pp.

Isabella Lanz &
Katie Verstockt,
*Contemporary Dance
in the Low Countries.*
Illustrated; 128 pp.

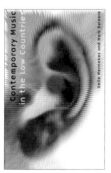

Mark Delaere &
Emile Wennekes,
*Contemporary Music in
the Low Countries.*
Illustrated; 128 pp.

*Standing Tall in Babel.
Languages in Europe.*
Sixteen European writers
about their mother tongues.
Hardcover; 144 pp.

Between 1993 and 2012
the first twenty issues
of the yearbook *The Low
Countries* were published.

EUROPE

NORTH
SEA

GRONINGEN
• Groningen
Leeuwarden
FRIESLAND

• Assen
DRENTHE

**NORTH
HOLLAND**

FLEVOLAND
Lelystad
Haarlem
• Zwolle
AMSTERDAM
OVERIJSSEL

The Hague
Utrecht
GELDERLAND
Arnhem
**SOUTH
HOLLAND**
UTRECHT

s-Hertogenbosch

ZEELAND
Middelburg
NORTH BRABANT

Antwerp
LIMBURG
Bruges
ANTWERP
**WEST
FLANDERS**
EAST
LIMBURG
Ghent
Hasselt
FLANDERS
FLEMISH BRABANT
Maastricht
BRUSSELS •
• Leuven
GERMANY
WALLOON BRABANT
Wavre
HAINAUT
• Liège
Mons
Namur
LIÈGE
FRANCE
NAMUR

LUXEMBOURG

Arlon
LUX.

0   km   50

© Carto

	Dutch language area
	French language area in Belgium
	Brussels bilingual area : Dutch and French
	German language area : in Belgium
	Bilingual area : Dutch and Frisian
⊙	Capital city
•	Provincial capital
—	National frontier
· · · · · ·	Provincial Boundary